THE

D I A R Y

OF A

COUNTRY PARSON.

VOL. II

PREVIOUSLY PUBLISHED

By R. Cobden-Sanderson

'The Godfather of Downing Street: Sir George Downing, 1623–1684.' An essay in biography by John Beresford.

'An extraordinary career, and in tracing it Mr. Beresford has given us an account of the epoch which could hardly be surpassed for lucidity, erudition, vivacity and charm.'

The Saturday Review.

'Gossip of the Seventeenth and Eighteenth Centuries.' By John Beresford. Second impression.

'Out of many a learned history of the period which Mr. Beresford so charmingly peoples, we have learnt far less than from these two hundred companionable pages.'

The Times Literary Supplement.

'Poems of Charles Cotton: 1630 – 1687.' Edited by John Beresford.

'This pious, scholarly, and admirably produced resurrection, from the original sole and single 1689 edition, of his collateral ancestor's poems.'

George Saintsbury in *The Nation.*

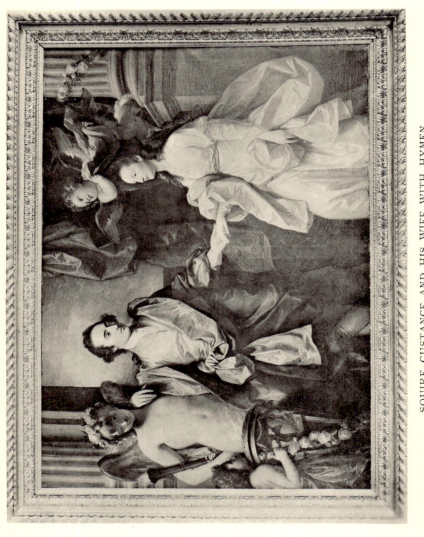

SQUIRE CUSTANCE AND HIS WIFE WITH HYMEN

From the picture by Benjamin West, P.R.A.

THE

D I A R Y

OF A

COUNTRY PARSON:

THE REVEREND

JAMES WOODFORDE.

VOL. II

1782 – 1787.

EDITED BY JOHN BERESFORD.

LONDON: HUMPHREY MILFORD,
OXFORD UNIVERSITY PRESS.
1926.

Printed in England
At the OXFORD UNIVERSITY PRESS
By John Johnson
Printer to the University

CONTENTS

ILLUSTRATIONS

v

INTRODUCTION

IF the Reverend James Woodforde has any ghostly
knowledge of earthly things, the welcome accorded to his
Diary, of which the first part was published last year,
must have caused him, as on another occasion one hundred
and fifty-five years ago, 'much secret pleasure and
satisfaction.'[1] Quite apart from the unanimity of the
public welcome, I have received numerous letters from
all sorts and conditions of men in divers parts of the
world—even from the ends of the earth, all aglow with
the pleasure Parson Woodforde's company had given
them.[2]

The present volume only covers a period of six years,
and it will therefore be seen that I have endeavoured
to meet the desire of many for a fuller publication
of Parson Woodforde's Diary than was possible on the
experimental plan of the first volume. As to the method
and principles adopted in editing the present volume, the
reader is referred to the ' Note on Editorial Method '.
Here it may be of use to set down with all convenient
brevity some general editorial observations.

The Diary of the Reverend James Woodforde is so full
of human interest, the story of the life of himself, his
relations, and his neighbours is told so simply and so
vividly that the reader may be tempted to forget that
he is in possession of a document of deep historical
significance.

[1] See vol. i, pp. 99–100.

[2] Among Parson Woodforde's appreciators (I may perhaps be allowed
to say) are Lord Rosebery, Mr. Saintsbury, and Mr. Stanley Weyman.

vii

The population of England and Wales in the
1780's was almost certainly not in excess of 7,500,000.
Even in 1801, the date of the first census, when the
Industrial Revolution was really beginning to affect the
figures, the population only numbered 8,873,000.[1] Of the
first quoted number—7,500,000—it would probably be
no exaggeration to say that three-fourths, certainly
two-thirds, were living in the country, mainly engaged in
agriculture. A diary, therefore, which illuminates that
country life which was the life of the majority of the
nation must clearly be of notable interest. The great
ones of the earth—the statesmen, the generals, the
practical men of genius—tend to monopolize, for obvious
reasons, the page of history. It is a mistake. However
eminent, important, and attractive such persons are, they
compose but a small part of the picture of life. It
requires the author of the *Elegy written in a Country
Church-yard* to set things in their proper philosophic
perspective ; it requires Parson Woodforde to describe
daily things as they actually were.

These years 1782 to 1787 see immense events : America
emerges, the wheels of the Industrial Revolution are
beginning to turn with increasing speed, the Ancien
Régime in France is tottering to its fall, a youth
destined to shake the world and to deluge Europe in
blood is studying mathematics and geography at the
military school at Brienne, Blake is beginning the Songs
of Innocence, the first step has been taken in the explora-
tion of the air. Inevitably spectacles so tremendous in

[1] See the figures quoted in Mr. A. H. Johnson's *The Disappearance of
the Small Landowner*, p. 112, published by the Clarendon Press, 1909.
The figure of 8,873,000 is the civilian population of England and Wales
in 1801 : in addition there were 470,598 soldiers and sailors recruited
from the United Kingdom (see Lecky, *England in the Eighteenth Century*,
vol. vii, p. 258, foot-note).

their influence upon posterity appear to occupy wholly the historic stage. But such spectacles do not engross the attention of contemporary men. If so famous a politician and person as Fox, while visiting the treasures of the Louvre, found his mind anxiously speculating as to the condition of his turnips at St. Anne's, it is obvious that less important persons will be concerned in such matters to an even greater extent.

It is therefore essential to perspective to bear in mind that at the same time that vast events were in the making, Parson Woodforde was coursing fine, large hares with his grey-hounds *Dutchess*, *Hector*, and *Reach 'em*; that he was sending pork, baskets of apples, and veal broth to his poor parishioners, giving alms to an old man playing on the dulcimer, bestowing pence upon all the village children on St. Valentine's day; that he was finding dinner in the company of a Bishop and a Baronet rather a strain, but on the other hand, rejoicing in the society of his farmers at the tithe-frolic, or in the more cultured society of the poet Cowper's cousins, the Bodhams and the Donnes; that despite the supposed immobility of the country gentry of the eighteenth century, Parson Woodforde thought nothing of journeying by coach all the way to Somerset—stopping in London on the way to see the sights, and fairly 'trimming it' down the Bath Road in the Balloon coach; that the American War had to be paid for in heavy taxes, and that nevertheless it was possible to maintain open house, keep two maidservants, two menservants,[1] and a boy, and three

---

[1] One of these was the skilled farm servant, Ben Leggatt, who ploughed, sowed, and mowed, disposed of the barley, wheat, and turnips in due season for the best price, bought the cow, fed the pigs, looked after the horses, and acted as Parson Woodforde's general factotum for £10 a year and his keep.

horses, and be very generous to one's niece and nephews on a little over £400 a year ; that woodpeckers could do dreadful damage to a thatched roof; that small-pox haunted even the dreams of the eighteenth century ; how sometimes it was necessary to send one's niece to ' Coventry ', and to be apprised by a neighbouring Parson in a secret churchyard meeting of the wiles of widows ; how villagers liked to have their children named after the daughters of Pharaoh, or of Job ; how stealing a sack meant three years in prison ; and how magnificently the pageant of Peace, and of the Patron Saint of Woolcombers—Bishop Blaise—paraded the streets of Norwich in 1783.

It is not to be expected that politics and political personages will find any but a small place in Parson Woodforde's diary. Nevertheless the casual meeting with the Prime Minister, the younger Pitt, held up at the Inn at Hindon in Wiltshire for lack of post horses, seems to bring that great man curiously close. Not that, apparently, he said anything to Parson Woodforde or to Nancy—he was indifferent to the fair—but that it is more interesting to realize the difficulties of the road, than the complexities of eighteenth-century politics. Again, an election when one of the candidates rode through the streets of the city at the head of between two and three thousand horsemen must have had a tonic effect on the spectators, and an even more startling effect on the voters.[1] And the reader will just catch a glimpse of one of the greatest benefactors of mankind—Mr. Coke of Holkam.[2]

[1] This was Sir John Wodehouse : needless to say he was successful, but mainly because he was a supporter of the younger Pitt : that is really the reason why he found three thousand horsemen to follow him.

[2] It is hardly possible to exaggerate the beneficence of Mr. Coke's career : for an excellent short account of it, see Mr. R. E. Prothero's

But the main interest of the Diary is its country interest. There is hardly a whisper of the Industrial Revolution now starting on its course through the discoveries and inventions of Kay, Hargreaves, Crompton, Cartwright, Cort, Arkwright, and Watt. If there is a whisper it is in the obscure visits of Alldridge, the pedlar, and Bagshaw, the Derbyshire man, to the Parsonage door, bringing with them cotton and thread and ribbons, or in the unemployment of a poor Weaver in Norwich, or in the establishment of the new Iron Foundry in that city.

And the fact that Parson Woodforde's Diary illuminates eighteenth-century landscape in no metaphoric sense has not only historical significance. Does not the Diary possess also its immediate significance to-day ? It seems to be forgotten, in the clamour of certain great industries, that Agriculture is still the greatest, because the pivotal industry of all. In numbers it approaches, if it does not at present surpass coal, the greatest of the individual, non-agricultural industries. In the way of skill, if the manipulation and manufacture of screws and machines and textiles and minerals requires skill, cannot the humblest agricultural labourer at 30s. a week manage ever mutable animals, drain the land, forecast the weather, lay the neatest hedges out of intractable thorns ? Moreover, he still speaks the language of the Bible, and of Shakespeare.

In the company of Parson Woodforde the reader will enter into that country peace ' that is forever England ' ; he will rejoice that Jack Warton wanted to be a plough-

(now Lord Ernle) *The Pioneers and Progress of English Farming*, chap. viii. Mr. G. M. Trevelyan says of Coke (*British History in the Nineteenth Century*, p. 145) : ' His life was a mixture of the patriarchal and progressive—old English of the best.'

boy, and not to worsen himself in the city ; he will mourn for Molly Dade, so pretty, so faithful, and so patient in her last illness ; he will dine at Christmas with old Thos. Cary, Thos. Dicker, Thos. Cushing, Ricd. Bates, Ricd. Buck, Thos. Carr, and Js. Smith my Clerk ; he will go afishing beside the river Wensum, the river that flows beneath Lenwade Bridge.

'Still glides the Stream, and shall for ever glide.'

JOHN BERESFORD.

ASHWELL END,
BALDOCK, HERTS.
October 21*st*, 1925.

In the preparation of this volume my thanks are due to my friend Dr. R. E. H. Woodforde, of Ashwell, Baldock, Herts, for so freely putting at my disposal the manuscript of the Reverend James Woodforde's Diary ; to my wife, but for whose help this book would not now be ready ; to Mr. Gerard Hopkins of the Oxford University Press, for smoothing the path of publication, and to the Printers for their excellent care ; to Mrs. K. A. Patmore for the Index ; to Mr. F. G. Cox and Mr. G. E. Manwaring, of the London Library, for help which made lighter my editorial task.

Finally, it is through the kindness of the late Colonel F. H. Custance, C.B., of Old Hall, Weston Longville,[1] that I have been able to include in this book the beautiful portraits of his great-grand parents, Squire Custance and Mrs. Custance, and the views of the river Wensum.

[1] In the Diary written Longeville, just as Lenwade is there Lenewade.

NOTE ON EDITORIAL METHOD

In the present volume of extracts from Parson Wood-forde's manuscript diary I have left out nothing of general interest, and, as far as I am able to judge, nothing of specialist interest. Nothing has been bowdlerized, omitted, or paraphrased *pudoris causa*. When the reader sees asterisks he can be confident either that Parson Woodforde is merely reciting his pleasant formula about dining, supping, and sleeping at home, or describing a dinner which has been eaten very often before, or giving the names of persons whom the reader by this time should know thoroughly well, or noting some daily event or fact recorded on other occasions. I do not claim that a verbatim edition of the complete diary would not contain information which might be of interest to some one, but I think I can claim that, so far as these years, 1782 to 1787 inclusive, are concerned, the main harvest is garnered in this volume, to be followed, if public appreciation continues, by another volume on the same plan.

It will be observed that the extracts in the present volume are so frequent that Parson Woodforde's life can be followed week by week, and often day by day. Hence there has been no need for the connecting link of description, a device which was essential in the first volume. If the reader desires to seek me he will find me in the foot-notes.

In writing these foot-notes I have adopted the following principles :

1. That in a work of this character an editor should deliberately err on the side of writing too few, rather than too many, foot-notes. Otherwise the peculiar atmosphere of the diary is dissipated, and the mind bored or confused : for foot-notes have a fiendish power at once of attraction and distraction.

2. That it is necessary to assume that the great majority of readers will be either relatively unfamiliar with contemporary eighteenth-century history, or will have forgotten what they may once have known well. Therefore, in order that Parson Woodforde's fairly rare references to public persons or events may convey the same sort of illumination to the modern mind that they bore to the 1780's mind, I have tried to give an occasional bird's-eye view of the wider world.

3. Wherever possible I have sought to illustrate Parson Woodforde's observations by comparing them with contemporary observations from very different pens, whether of Horace Walpole,[1] William Cowper, the Reverend George Crabbe, or other observers of men and manners, bearing in mind the brilliant dictum of Macaulay : ' This is the really precious part of history, the corn which some threshers carefully sever from the chaff, for the purpose of gathering the chaff into the garner, and flinging the corn into the fire.' [2]

J. B.

[1] For Horace Walpole's *Letters* I have used the noble Paget Toynbee edition in eighteen volumes, published by the Clarendon Press.

[2] Macaulay's *Essays*—the essay on Sir William Temple, p. 426, in the Oxford India paper edition.

craving peace,
The central feeling of all happiness,
Not as a refuge from distress or pain,
A breathing-time, vacation, or a truce,
But for its absolute self ; a life of peace,
Stability without regret or fear ;
That hath been, is, and shall be evermore !

WORDSWORTH, *The Excursion,* Book III.

PART II (*continued*)

WESTON LONGEVILLE, NORFOLK

The Diary

Anno Domini 1782

Jan. 1. I breakfasted, dined, supped, and slept again at home. Nancy and Betsy Davy breakfasted, dined &c. here again. To Mr. Pyle of Hockering who called on me this morning with his Bill—paid him the sum of 3. 2. 0. This being my Rotation Day [1], Mr. Howes and Mrs. Davy, Mr. du Quesne, Mr. Bodham and Mr. Smith dined &c. here. I gave my company for dinner a Leg of Mutton boiled and Capers, a Calfs Head boiled and a Piggs Face, a fat Turkey rosted, a Currant Pudding and Mince Pies. At Quadrille &c. this evening lost 0. 1. 6. All the Mony won at Cards this evening was by a general consent given to Betsy Davy—and which amounted to 0. 6. 6. My Company left me about 8 o'clock. It was very cold in the evening and some snow fell but it turned milder when they left us, and a gentle Rain fell.

Jan. 3. I breakfasted, supped and slept again at home— Nancy breakfasted, supped &c. here again. Betsy Davy breakfasted here and soon after she was sent for home to Hockering, where her Mother is— About 2 o'clock Mr. Du Quesne called here in his

[1] Parson Woodforde and certain of his neighbours were accustomed to entertain one another to dinner in regular rotation—hence the phrase 'Rotation Day'.

chaise by appointment and took Nancy with him in it to Mr. Custance's—I chused to walk thither—We all dined and spent the aft. and part of the Evening there with Mr. and Mrs. Custance, and spent our Time very agreeably and merrily there—after Tea and Coffee we went to Cards to Loo and were very merry at it—I lost at it o. 1. 6.

Nancy won at Loo o. 6. o.

To a Letter that Mr. Custance's Servant brought from the Post Office at Norwich yesterday—pd. o. o. 7. gave the servant that brought it the odd-pence—o. 5.

Mr. Du Quesne brought Nancy back in his Chaise abt. 9 o'clock—I returned as I went on foot. Mr. Du Quesne could not be prevailed on to sup here. We had a very elegant Dinner of two Courses and as elegant a Desert after Dinner. Mrs. Custance gave Nancy a gold Ring—Moco Stone and studded with garnetts—very kind indeed of her.

Jan. 4. . . . Busy all the morning in my garden, having enlarged my Pleasure Ground a Trifle by taking in part of the small Field near Goochs House. Nancy sent a Letter to her Father this Evening.

Jan. 7. I breakfasted, dined, supped, and slept again at home. Nancy breakfasted, dined &c. here again. To Mr. Cary for things from Norwich &c. pd. o. 11. 6. To my Servant Man Ben. Legatt paid this morning a Years Wages due to him the 6 Instant 10. o. o. To my Senior Maid Elizabeth Claxton paid also this morning a Years Wages due the 6 Instant 5. 15. 6. To My Servant Man Will: Coleman paid this morning a Years Wages due to him the 6 Instant 4. 4. o. To Ditto also for 20 Coomb of Grains pd. 1. o. o. To Ditto also for dressing my Wiggs a year

0. 10. 0. To my under Servant Maid Lizzy Greaves paid this morning also a Years Wages due 6th Instant 2. 0. 6. To my Boy, Jack Warton, gave this morning 0. 10. 6. Mr. Cary dined with our Folks to-day. My Taste very indifferent and so it was yesterday at Dinner. Everything tastes very disagreeable to me—I don't know what occasions it unless it is my having taken some Brimstone and Treakle—or having made use of some strong sage Tea every Day about 11. in the Morn' lately, I have also a small Cold, which might be the cause.

Jan. 12. I breakfasted, dined, supped and slept again at home. Nancy breakfasted, dined, &c. here again. Will went early to Norwich this morning to buy him some cloth for to make him 4 shirts—he returned home about 5 o'clock this afternoon—The Cloth cost him 1/9 p^r yrd.

Jan. 15. I breakfasted, dined, supped and slept again at home. Nancy breakfasted, dined &c. here again. Went to Church about noon and publickly presented a Child (by name Willm) into the Church, of Mr. Girlings Mr. Custances's Steward.—He lives in the Parish of Lyng but Mr. Baldwin sent his Compts. to me and desired me to do it—It had been privately named. From Western Church walked to Weston New Hall of Mr. Custances and there spent a full Hour with Mr. and Mrs. Custance, and returned home to dinner. They pressed me to dine there, but could not. . . .

Jan. 21. . . . By one and another, hurried all the day long—almost.

Jan. 22. I breakfasted, supped and slept again at home. Nancy breakfasted, supped &c. here again. Mr. Priest of Reepham called here this morning, and this being

Mr. Du Quesnes Rotation to-day, he went with us
to Du Quesnes about 1 o'clock—Mr. Du Quesne
sent his Chaise after Nancy and I went on horseback—
Mr. Priest went with Nancy in the Chaise from my
House. We dined, spent the afternoon and stayed
till near 10 o'clock this Evening at Du Quesnes.
Mr. and Mrs. Howes, Mrs. Davy and Mr. Smith of
Mattishall were our Company besides ourselves. We
had for Dinner a Leg of Mutton boiled and Capers,
some Brawn, a Turkey rosted and mince Pies. Mr.
and Mrs. Bodham could not be with us, being gone
to Swaffham to their Fathers. At four o'clock I was
obliged to leave the Company and went to Weston,
and buried one Thos. Mack of North-Tuddenham,
who fell from his Horse on Friday Night last and was
killed, being in Liquor—He was 61 Years of Age.
He was brought in a Hearse and a great many People
attended on the Occasion. I buried him about half
past four o'clock. I recd. for burying him a Silk hat
band and gloves and not living in my Parish, had my
Fee of 0. 10. 6. After I had buried the Corpse
I returned to Du Quesnes. We made it very late
before we got to bed. Neither myself or Nancy won
or lost at Cards to-night. Mrs. Custance called at
our House soon after we went.

Jan. 24. I breakfasted, and slept again at home. Nancy
breakfasted, and slept again here. To Jn. Pegg a
Qrs. Land Tax due Christmas for the Parsonage and
College Land, pd. this morn' 3. 0. 0. Mr. Custance
sent his Coach after us about 2 o'clock and Nancy
and myself went in it to his House and there dined,
spent the afternoon, supped and spent the evening
with him, Mrs. Custance, and a Mr. and Mrs. Price
from Norwich, very good kind of People. Mr. Price

is a young Man and a Clergyman, and a very sensible Man, and have seen much of good Company. We spent a very agreeable Day there and returned about 11 o'clock this evening home. We had for Dinner, a piece of boiled Beef, a fine Turkey rosted, Mutton Stakes, Sausages and a Pudding, Blamange, stewed Pears, Tarte, Trifle &c. After Tea we played at Loo at 3. per Dozen, very little lost, we lost nothing but Nancy won 0. 1. 0. For Supper, some of what we had for dinner.

Jan. 25. . . . My lower Maid Lizzy went to her Mothers this evening to sleep there, as she has my leave to go with her Mother to-morrow to Norwich to get a pair of Stays for herself.

Jan. 29. I breakfasted, supped and slept again at home. Nancy breakfasted, dined &c. here again. At 12 took a ride to Mr. Custances, stayed and chatted with them near an Hour. From Mr. Custances rode to Hockering to Mr. Howes's being his Rotation to-day and there dined, spent the afternoon and stayed till 9 at Night, with Mr. and Mrs. Howes, Mrs. Davy, the Widow Paine, relict of the late unfortunate Alexander Paine, Mr. Du Quesne, Mr. Bodham and Mr. Smith. We had for Dinner, some Salt Fish, a Piece of boiled Beef, a Turkey and Mince Pies. At Quadrille this evening lost 0. 1. 0. I did not get home till after 10 o'clock, and bitter cold riding home it was, being a hard Frost and Snow on the ground and windy. Nancy could not go being still indifferent, therefore she sent a Note early this morning to Mrs. Davy, to desire them not send the Chaise after her, as they promised. The four Breasts and Hands of my two Piggs, with one of the Loins I sent to my poor Neighbours, viz. to Gooch, to Clarke, to

Downing, to Norton, and to Nat Heavers. Nancy a good deal better this evening.

Jan. 30. ... Nancy very busy all the morning in making Cakes, Tarts, Custards and Jellies for to Morrow. Nancy brave to-day and pretty well exercised all day. Fair today but bitter cold indeed.

Jan. 31. I breakfasted, dined supped and slept again at home. Nancy breakfasted, dined &c. here again. Mr. and Mrs. Custance, and Mr. Press. Custance and Mr. Du Quesne dined, spent the afternoon, and stayed with us till after 8 o'clock this evening. I gave them for Dinner a Leg of Mutton boiled and Capers, a boiled Fowl and a Tongue, a batter Pudding, a fine Turkey rosted, Fryed Rabbit, Tarts, Custards and Jellies.—Almonds and Raisins, Oranges and Apples after. Port Wine, Mountain, Porter and Ale &c. After Tea we played at limited Loo. I lost at it 0. 2. 6.

Feb. 4. ... To a poor old Man that plays on the Dulcimer gave 0. 0. 6.

Feb. 8. ... This Day being appointed to be observed as a Fast on the present Troubles and Wars abroad,[1] I went to Weston Church this morning at 11 o'clock and there read Prayers proper on the occasion—but there was no Sermon after. I had a large Congregation—Mr. Custance was at Church—Mrs. Custance not, being so cold. After divine Service I walked with Mr. Custance to his New Hall, and there spent

[1] We were fighting at this time with our backs to the wall against the rebel Americans, the French, the Spaniards, and the Dutch, to say nothing of Hyder Ali in India : we had lost nearly all the American Colonies, a considerable portion of the West Indies, and Minorca. On the other hand we had captured various French settlements in India and in Africa, and Dutch settlements in India.

an Hour or better with them. We sent over after Church to Hockering to enquire after Mrs. Howes, and about 3 my Servant Boy returned and greatly surprized us by acquainting us that poor Mrs. Howes was no more—she died at one o'clock this morning—Pray God, she may be happy, and the Family comforted under so sore an affliction—She will be greatly missed by all the Rotation &c. Nancy and myself were greatly concern'd to hear of it and more so, as it was so unexpectedly. One Christopher Breeze from Lyng, a young man and lately a Driver of Mr. Custances, and who came after a copy of the Register, dined with our Folks in Kitchen. I gave him a Copy and would take nothing for it. Nancy sent a long Letter to her Aunt J^n Woodforde this Even'.

Feb. 12. I breakfasted, dined, supped and slept again at home. Nancy breakfasted, dined &c. here again. At 10 o'clock this morning took a walk to Hockering to attend poor Mrs. Howes's Funeral there to-day. The Snow was very deep in some Places as I went. My Man Will went with me—We got to Mrs. Howes's before 11 and there met Mr. Shelford senr., Mr. Du Quesne, Mr. Priest sen^r of Reepham, Mr. Potter of Scarning, Mr. Bodham, Mr. Smith, Dr. Thorne and Mr. Priest of Norwich. I found all the Clergy in gowns and some in Cassocks also—I did not carry my gown, as I did not know whether or not the Clergy appeared in them—I borrowed one however, of Mr. Howes and likewise a Band. Before we went to Church there was Chocolate and Toast and Cake with red Wine and white. At half past 11 o'clock we went to Church with the Corpse in the following Procession. The Corpse first in an Hearse and Pair

7

of Horses, then followed six Chaises, in the first
which was Du Quesnes went Du Quesne and
Dr. Thorne, in the second which was Mr. Shelfords
went Mr. Shelford and Mr. Smith, in the third which
was Mr. Priests, went Mr. Priest and myself, in the
fourth which was one from Dereham, went Mr. Potter
and Mr. Bodham, in the fifth which was from
Norwich went Mr. Priest of Norwich and a Mr
Forster the Undertaker, in the sixth which was
Mr. Howes's, went Mrs. Howes's two Servant Maids
in deep mourning. The Underbearers and Servants
all in Hatbands black closed the Procession and an
handsome appearance the whole Procession made—
we returned to Mr. Howes's in the same manner as
we went from it to Church—Mr. Du Quesne buried
her—The Pall-Bearers were Mr. Shelford, Mr. Priest,
Mr. Potter, Mr. Bodham, Mr. Smith and myself—
we had all black Hatbands and Gloves, but they were
white. Poor Mrs. Howes if she had lived till to
Morrow wch was her birth Day—she would have
been 69 Years. It was as decent, neat, handsome
Funeral as I ever saw and everything conducted
in the best manner—and by its being so I con-
clude that it was Mrs. Davy's good management.
Mr. Howes, Mrs. Davy &c. kept above stairs all the
Time—They desired me to walk up to them which
I did after the Funeral, but did not stay long with
them—found them low and left them so. After our
return from Church we had Cake and Wine and
Chocolate and dried Toast carried round. My
Servant and all Servants that attended and all the
drivers all had Hatbands and gloves given to them.
We walked back again and got home about half past
2 o'clock—and a bitter cold walk we had back, the

Wind in our Faces and it snowed most of the way, which was beat in our Faces. We walked over France Green and by Hockering Park House.

Feb. 14. . . . This being Valentine Day gave to 52 Children of this Parish, as usual 1 penny each o. 4. 4. Gave Nancy this morning 1. 1. o.

Feb. 19. . . . To a Man for a Door Matt pd. o. o. 6. To a poor old man and very deaf gave o. o. 1. The Barometer still keeps very high. Nancy and myself took some Brimstone and Treacle this evening going to bed. Nancy sent Mrs. Custance a new Silk Buffon of the spot-netting, this morning, as a present to her. She made it up also in the Buffon Fashion, she having borrowed Mrs. Custance's Machine.

Feb. 22. . . . Went out a coursing with my men this morning for four Hours and never could move or see a Hare, tho' we went over the most likely Places. Ben's Father joined us in our coursing to-day and he went home with us and dined with our Folks.

Feb. 23. . . . Nancy breakfasted here and soon after breakfast Mr. Custance's Coach came for her in which she went to Mr. Custances and there dined, supped and slept. She is to go to the Play this evening at Norwich with Mr. and Mrs. Custance. It is very kind in them.

Feb. 24. I breakfasted, dined, supped and slept again at home. I read Prayers and Preached this morning at Weston. Neither Mr. or Mrs. Custance at Church this morning. And I had but a small Congregation as it was wet. It was very damp and cold at Church— About 1 o'clock my Niece returned home in Mrs. Custance's coach and she dined &c. at home. She was thoroughly fatigued by going to the Play last Night—they did not get home from the Play till

9

near 12 o'clock—Nancy was highly diverted with the
Excursion—And Mrs. Custance was very kind indeed
to her, gave her a full dress'd Cap which becomes her
well.—They drank Tea at the King's Head before the
Play with Sr. Edmund Bacon and Lady and they all
went together to the Play. The Play was the School
for Scandal and which Nancy wished for—The entertainment was Tom Thumb—and both performed
very well. Mrs. Custance and Nancy made the best
appearance in the Theatre amongst the Ladies last
night, it was said.

Feb. 28. . . . Was rather uneasy to-day on Account of
being afraid that I have got the Piles coming or
something else—unless it is owing to my eating a good
deal of Peas Pudding two or three days ago with a
Leg of Pork.

Mar. 2. . . . Had a very disagreeable Night of it, could
not sleep but very little, being so exceedingly low
spirited and which continued on me almost the whole
Day. A good deal of blood came from me to-day.
I got up at 6 o'clock this morning. Nancy complained very much of her bad Knee to-day and was
still worse at going to bed. Great Debates in the
House of Commons this week. The Ministry had
nineteen Majority against them. Colonel Barré put
the prime Minister Ld North quite in a Passion.
Ld North called to Order from the Chair in his reply
to Colonel Barré.[1]

[1] On February 22, 1782, there was a debate in the Commons on General
Conway's motion for putting an end to the American War.

Colonel Barré in supporting the motion referred to ' the deceit and the
inconsistency of Ministers ' throughout the war, but it was after the
motion had been put, and lost by only one vote, that the scene occurred
between Colonel Barré and Lord North. Colonel Barré proceeded to
complain ' of the indecent conduct of the noble lord in the blue ribbon

Mar. 4. . . . Nancy complained very much in her Knee,
is rather low on it, for fear it should prove to be a
return of her Complaint which she had about
4 Years ago. But I hope to God that it will go away
again. Thank God! that I continue better and in
better Spirits—A fine large Hare being found sitting
this morning between 11 and 12 o'clock by one of
my Servants—I went out and saw her coursed, but
she got away, tho' she was closely followed by
Dutchess for a very long way. We tryed afterwards
for another, but could meet with never another, tho'

in giving notice of so important a matter as the opening of the budget,
in a thin House of a Friday,' and used very offensive language. ' He
called the noble lord the scourge of his country, said he had drained its
resources, spent its cash, and reduced it almost to beggary ; he had
ruined Great Britain as a state, emptied the pockets of the subjects, and
his conduct to that House was insulting and intolerable,' and more of the
same kind. Lord North—though the most urbane of men—was stung
by Barré's abuse, and prefaced his reply by referring to ' language . . .
so extremely uncivil, so brutal, and so insolent '. Uproar ensued, and the
Prime Minister was called to order. Finally he made a handsome
apology, though to the modern reader it would seem that Lord North's
language was mild compared with the ferocious bombast of Colonel
Barré. General Conway repeated his motion against the American War
on February 27, and carried it against the Government by nineteen votes.
See *The Parliamentary History*, vol. 22, 1028–85.

It should be added that Colonel Barré (1726–1802) who began his
career as a soldier—he was by the side of the dying Wolfe at Quebec—
had subsequently entered Parliament under the patronage of Lord Shelburne. There he speedily made his mark as an Orator. When his patron
became Prime Minister in July, 1782, Barré was given the lucrative office
of Paymaster General. Not long afterwards Barré lost his sight. Lord
Fitzmaurice in his admirable and definitive life of Shelburne refers to
a story that Lord North, who was also visited with the same calamity,
meeting Barré at Tunbridge, said : ' Ah, Colonel, whatever may have
been our former animosities, I am persuaded there are no two men who
would now be more glad to *see* one another than you and I '. (Fitzmaurice's
Shelburne, ii. 287.)

we stayed out till 4 this afternoon. When I returned from coursing found Du Quesne at my House who had been there two Hours, and came to dine with me—I ordered Dinner at 3 but did not get home till 4—The Dinner over done—Du Quesne dined and smoked a Pipe and returned home—We had only for Dinner a Breast of Veal rosted—Mr. Hardy dined with our Folks as he was out with us.

Mar. 6. . . . Mrs. Custance with her 3 little Boys and their Nurse made us a long visit this morning—and walked about my garden—Mrs. Custance seems mightily taken with my garden and the Bason in the middle. Mr. Symonds of Reepham came to my House this morn' and cleaned my lower Clock and my Jack—he dined with our Folks in the Kitchen—I p^d him for a brass Case to my large burning glass or reading glass 0. 1. 0. Cleaning my Clock—also paid him 0. 2. 6. Cleaning my Jack—also paid him 0. 1. 0. To Nancy at Cribbage this evening—lost 0. 0. 6.

Mar. 8. . . . Mrs. Custance with her eldest Son made us a visit this morning—She came to enquire for Nancy —very kind in her. Mrs. Custance also gave her a pair of small gold Ear-rings. Nancy I think is a small matter better. Very cold North Westerly Winds all Day.

Mar. 11. . . . Went down with my nets this morning to Lenewade Bridge to catch a few Fish for Mr. Custance—but the Water was so high and wind so rough that we could do nothing at all—we tried two or 3 Times, but could catch nothing worth catching. Therefore at Noon we returned home with our Nets—Harry Dunnell went with us and therefore dined here. To the Miller for putting down his Hatches gave 0. 1. 0. Good News from America arrived, how that St. Kitts was retaken by our Troups and 6000 French Troups taken.[1]

Mar. 12. . . . Had but little sleep last Night, the wind being exceeding high all the Night—And this morning continues as high if not higher—NWW—About Noon the Wind rose higher and blew quite a Hurricane till Sun-setting and then it rather abated, and about 10 was quite mild, but very cold. The Wind being so very high frightened greatly myself and Nancy, but I thank God we received no Damage. The Tiles from my Cellar and the old Part of my House were some of them blown down, with some Thatch from the NW Corner of the new Part of the House. We both sat up to night till after 12 o'clock —I was quite tired out having but little rest all last night. I never knew the wind continue so long and so high. All last Night and all this whole Day near the same. It made me quite ill and took away my appetite. A great deal of Damage I apprehend must have been done to the Shipping and likewise Houses &c. on Land. Pray God! have mercy on all the poor Sufferers—and accept O Lord! my sincere thanks for what we have escaped.

Mar. 13. . . . Thank God I had a very good Nights rest last Night. John Norton came last night to me to pay me for some Turnips that I spared him, to the Value of ten Shillings and to have a few more— I would not take the mony for them being a Neighbour and that I would give a few more to him—and

---

[1] Horace Walpole, on the same day, also refers to this 'News' which was unfortunately not substantiated. St. Kitt's was taken by the French on February 13 of this year, and was not recovered till peace was made in 1783. See Horace Walpole's *Letters*, vol. xii, 190 and 210 ; and Lecky's *England in the Eighteenth century*, vol. v, 123 and 185.

likewise to John Gooch. I took a ride to Hockering this Afternoon and drank Tea with Mr. Howes, Mrs. Davy and the Widow Payne. Mrs. Davy acts as Mistress of Mr. Howes's House. Returned home to Weston by 7 this evening.

Mar. 14. . . . Nancy complained much of her knee this afternoon and was very low upon it, being afraid that it is getting bad again—but pray God ! prevent that. I was very low also this evening on her account &c.

Mar. 17. . . . A great deal of Snow fell in the Night, and many heavy Storms of Snow, Hail &c. most of this Day. I read Prayers and Preached this afternoon at Weston. Had a small congregation, owing to the Weather. None of Mr. Custances Family at Church. Having heard that Thos. Thurston's Wife (who is and has been ill a long while) longed for some rost Veal from my House, having therefore a Loin rosted for Dinner, I sent her a good Plate of it.

Mar. 20. . . . I got up rather early this morning being disturbed by a noise in my Study, in cleaning of it, at which I was rather angry and scolded a little.

Mar. 21. . . . The poor Woman whom I sent some Veal to Sunday died yesterday morning—She eat nothing afterwards till she died, But she eat hearty of the Veal I sent her.

Mar. 22. . . . I buried Eliz: Thurston Wife of Thos. Thurston this afternoon at Weston, aged 45 Yrs. It snowed all the whole Day with very cold high Wind.

Mar. 26. . . . Mr. Custance sent us a note this morning to invite us to Dinner on Thursday next—which we accepted—Edmund their Servant Boy a very clever Lad came on one of the Coach-Horses with the

Note, and as he was going to Du Quesnes and the Coach H: being too much for him—I lent him one of my Horses to go there.

Mar. 27. . . . Mr. Smith was so kind to offer (without being asked) to serve my Church for me when I go into the West, as long as I shall chuse to be absent from Weston. Mr. Du Quesne was rather down in the mouth to-day, as the present Ministry are all for certain going out.[1]

Mar. 28. . . . It being very wet and windy all the morning long, I sent a Note to Mr. and Mrs. Custance to excuse our waiting on them on the Weather's account, as it would be bad for the Coach &c. to be out in it—but Mrs. Custance sent me back a very polite Note and would not accept of any such excuse —and therefore about half past 2 o'clock Mr. Custance came after us in the Coach and we returned with him in it to Weston House and there dined and spent the afternoon with him, Mrs. Custance, and a Mr. Prideaux a gentleman of large Estate in Cornwall—and grandson of Dean Prideaux of Norwich.[2] We had for Dinner Cod Fish and Oyster Sauce, a Chine of Mutton rosted, a Couple of boiled Chickens and Tongue &c. first Course—a rost Pig, Macaroni, small Puddings plain and Currant, Tartlets and a very pretty Pyramid of Jelly in the Centre, a Landscape appearing thro' the Jelly, a new Device and brought from London—After Tea and Coffee we played at limited Loo at 6^d a Dozen—and limited to 30 Fish—at w^h I won 0. 3. 6. Nancy lost at it 2*s*/0*d*— but I returned it to her afterwards. We stayed at Mr. Custances till 9 o'clock and then returned back

---

[1] See footnote on pp. 10–11.
[2] See p. 288 and footnote thereto, vol. i.

as we went, in Mr. Custances Coach—We spent a very agreeable Day there indeed.

Mar. 30. . . . An entire change of the Ministry it is said took Place on Monday last—I hope for the best.[1]

Mar. 31. . . . I read Prayers and administred the H. Sacrament this morning at Weston—being Easter Day. Mr. Custance and Mr. Prideaux at Church this Morn'. And both received the H. Sacrament from my Hands. J^s Smith my Clerk, and the Widow Gaff, and Jacks Brother Tom Warton dined with our Folks. Mrs. Custance was not at Church—her youngest Son being dangerously ill in the white-Throat.

Apl. 1. . . . Mr. Custance sent after Nancy this morning to spend the Day with Mrs. Custance and to have her Hair dressed by one Brown, the best Ladies-Frisseur in Norwich. About Noon the Weather turned out very wet and the Wind very high and so continued till 9 at Night. The Barometer sunk from this morning at 10 o'clock to 10 at Night 13 Degrees from No. 28–17 to 28–4. Nancy returned home about ½ past 9 o'clock this Even', with her head finely dressed of but very becoming her. Mrs. Custance would not let Nancy pay the Barber, but she paid for her and it cost no less than half a guinea. Mrs. Custance gave the Barber for dressing her Hair and Nancys the enormous sum of one guinea—He came on purpose from Norwich to dress them.

---

[1] On March 20, 1782, Lord North announced his resignation, assuring the House of Commons that 'the present administration was no more'. It had been tottering for some time (see footnote on pp. 10–11). The Marquis of Rockingham now became Prime Minister, with Lord Shelburne and Mr. Fox as Secretaries of State; the new Ministry was announced in the House on March 28. (See *Annual Register*, 1782.)

MRS. CUSTANCE

from the portrait probably by Henry Walton, F.S.A.

Mrs. Custance (God bless her) is the best Lady I ever knew.

Apl. 6. . . . Mr. Custance and Mr. Prideaux made us a Morning Visit—They caught us on the Hop—I was in the Garden—busy in seeing my people laying Turf down—Nancy upstairs—Neither of us saw them coming till they were at the Door—They came walking. To Spraggs, Gardner, for Work pd. o. 7. 6.

Apl. 11. . . . It being a very fine morning I took a ride by myself to Mr. Custance's—but neither of them at home—Then went to Witchingham and saw Bathurst's [1] Parsonage House, the Roof of which is very bad towards the North and some of it down and more falling—I found Harrison the Tenant very luckily there, as he does not now live in the House—as it is so bad—but he lives at a Brother in Laws (Wright) at Attlebridge. I returned home to Dinner by 3 o'clock.

Apl. 13. . . . Mrs. Custance called on us about 2 o'clock, but stayed a very short Time with us, as she was afraid that she kept us from Dinner—She brought Nancy a Hair Comb and Cushion, both entire new fashions—but very dear—Nancy p^d for the Cushion and I paid for the Comb to Mrs. Custance. They both cost and which we p^d to Mrs. Custance o. 7. o. Each of them was 3*s*/6*d*. Fashions very dear following them.

Apl. 16. . . . One Mr. Aldridge who carries about Cottons, Linens, Muslins, Lace, Holland, &c. in a Cart and comes round regularly this way once in ten Weeks, called at my House this morning, and

---

[1] Dr. Henry Bathurst, the non-resident Rector of Witchingham : he was later (1805) to become Bishop of Norwich (see short account of him in vol. i, p. 295). There is a fine statue of him in Norwich Cathedral.

I bought of him a Piece of Holland (alias Irish Cloth) for Shirts, 25 Yards at 3s/–d per Yard—for which I pd. him 3. 15. 0. For half a Yard of Cambrich for Chitterlons 0. 5. 0. For 7 Yards of Lace Edging for Nancy p^d 0. 5. 0. For 4 Yards of Ribband for my 2 Maids p^d 0. 2. 0. Nancy also bought of him 4 Yards of Pink Ribband 0. 2. 0. Also she bought 1 Yrd and ¼ of Lace for Mrs Davy 0. 3. 0. It rained incessantly all the Day long, and in the Afternoon very heavy Rains fell, the Wind also very high, and so continued till we went to bed—Wind ENE— I intended to have rode to Norwich to Day, if no Rain.

Apl. 21. . . . Saw the first swallow this morning for this year. My Neighbour John Clarke dined with our Folks to-day. I read Prayers and Preached this Afternoon at Weston. Mr. Custance at Church but not Mrs. Custance.

Apl. 23. . . . About 5 o'clock this Evening took a ride to Norwich and my Servant Will went with me—we got there half past 6 and supped and slept at the Kings Head. Sent a Letter to Dr. Bathurst this Evening and in that Letter some Norwich Bills to the Value of 20. 0. 0. I put the Letter into the Post Office myself this Evening. From thence went to my Taylors to know if he made Ladies Riding Habits, which he does for many Ladies. From thence went to one Porters in Cockey Lane and bespoke a large Hair-Portmanteau and am to give 0. 15. 6. and then returned to the Kings Head to sup and sleep.

Apl. 24. I breakfasted, dined and spent the afternoon at Norwich—I dined at the Shilling Ordinary with 7 or 8 Strangers. At Lewis's Shop this morning for

4 Y^{rds} of long Lawn at 3s/6d per Yrd for Nancy to make her riding Habit Shirts and ½ Yrd of corded Muslin for Ruffles &c. at 9s/–d p. Yrd for both paid Lewis— Lawn 14s/od—Muslin 4s/6d—o. 18. 6. For a riding Hat for Nancy of one Oxley in the Market Place with real Ostrich Feathers and Ribband pd. 1. 13. 6. It is to be sent home by Cary on Saturday next. To a Pr. of Habit-Gloves for Nancy of Ashly p^d o. 1. 6. To a Tail Comb and another Comb for Nancy of Baker p^d o. o. 10. Bespoke of my Upholsterer, Horth, two Pairs of Blankets 1 P^r of 16s/–d—the other of 12s/od—I bespoke also of him a Matress for my Bed. Called on old Mr. Francis and took up the Bond to Acourt Dodd for 100 Pound—it being p^d by me in December last—rec^d back some Interest of o. 10. o. To a p^d of Soachong Tea at the India House p^d o. 8. o. It is kept by one Roper a neat old Quaker. Paid and gave at the King's Head o. 13. 11. To a little Box of Dutch Toys for Children of Baker p^d o. o. 6. We got home to Weston about 7 o'clock this Evening and supped and slept at the Parsonage. Nancy glad to see me returned. Very wet and very windy after we came home. I was quite tired walking about so much today.

Apl. 25. . . . Vast deal of Rain with high Wind all the last Night and all this whole Day long and like to continue. It was Howes's Rotation to day but we could not go. I sent a Note over to him this morning. Poor Neighbour John Horner very bad in the Fever and ague, was taken about a week ago. I had some Veal Broth made for him and sent it up to him—but poor Fellow was dead before it came.

Apl. 26. . . . Nancy breakfasted at home and then went to Mr. Howes's at Hockering, he having sent his

Chaise after her before I was up—tho' very wet—
She is gone to spend a Day or two with Mrs. Davy—
I did not much approve of it as none but Servant
Man and Boy came after her—I ordered Will to
attend her on Horseback to Hockering. It rained
again all last Night and like to continue all Day.

Apl. 29. . . . I buried my poor Neighbour John Horner
this Evening aged 57 Years—poor Fellow, I am very
sorry for him.

Apl. 30. . . . At Noon took a ride to Mattishall and
there dined at Mr. Smiths with him, Mr. Howes
and Mrs. Davy, Mr. Du Quesne, Mr. and Mrs.
Donne of Broome, Mr. and Mrs. Bodham, and
Miss Bodham. The first Opening to day of Mr. Smiths
House and we spent a very merry and agreeable Day
there. We had for Dinner a Pike boiled with some
Perch, a Piece of rost Beef, a couple of Fowls rosted
and Tongues, Puddings, Tarts, Custards, and cold
Lobster. At Quadrille this Evening—won 0. 1. 6.
I did not get home till after half past 9 o'clock.
Mr. Smiths House is small, but Furniture handsome.

May 1. . . . Mr. Custance, then Mr. Du Quesne, then
Mrs. Custance made us a morning Visit—and they
all met together here—Mr. Custance went away
first, and then Mr. Du Quesne, Mrs. Custance stayed
with us till half past 2 o'clock. Mrs. Custance was
mightily pleased with the new Hat that I bought
for Nancy to wear with her riding Dress. I sent by
her for her little Boys a small Dutch Box of Toys.
Rec^d a Letter this Evening from Dr. Bathurst, by
Mr. Custance Servant—Sr Edmund Bacons Servant
brought it to Mr. Custances.

May 4. . . . Mr. Priest of Reepham and Mr. Du Quesne
dropped in upon us about Dinner Time and they

both dined and spent the Afternoon with us. I gave them for Dinner a Leg of Mutton boiled and Capers some beef-Stakes and a rosted Rabbit. Nancy had her riding Habit brought home this Evening a broad Cloth of 1 guinea a yard—Colour Pompadour Waist-coat, white ribbed Dimnity—both lappelled.

May 7. . . . About 12 o'clock to night I was called up by Ben, my Man Will: being taken very bad in the Cholic, I went to him immediately, and got him some gin, after drinking that, he soon became better and I returned to bed again.

May 9. I breakfasted, supped and slept again at home— Nancy breakfasted, supped and slept again at home. At 11 o'clock this morning went to Church and publickly baptised Mrs. Custance's 3ʳᵈ Son, William. The Revᵈ Mr. Collier and Wife two of the Sponsors and I believe Mr. and Mrs. Custance stood proxy for the others. After the Ceremony Mr. Custance made me a present of five guineas wrapped up in clean white Paper—5. 5. 0. I went from Church with Mr. and Mrs. Collier and Mrs. Custance in Mr. Cus-tances Coach to Weston House and after putting down Mr. Collier there, The Ladies and myself took a ride to my House, and they got out, went into my House for a few Minutes took a walk in my garden and then they returned to Weston House again. Nancy could not make her appearance as she was in the midst of dressing herself to go to Mr. Custances— Mr. Du Quesne came to my House about 2 o'clock, and he went with us in Mr. Custances Coach about half an Hour after to Weston House where we dined and spent the afternoon with Mr. and Mrs. Custance and Mr. and Mrs. Collier—and did not return home till after 9 o'clock this Evening to the Parsonage.

Mr. Du Quesne returned with us in Mr. Custances Coach and he very soon after rode home to Berries. We spent a very agreeable and merry Day there. We had for Dinner 1ˢᵗ Course—Stewed Tench, Ham and Fowls, Harrico of Mutton, Peas Soup, and a Rump of Beef boiled on the side Table with Roots &c. 2ⁿᵈ Course—Pigeons and Asparagus, Orange Pudding, Maccaroni, Custards, Tarts, and Jelly prettily set of with Blamange coloured like what it represented. Desert—9 Dishes—Oranges, Almonds and Raisins, blanced Almonds covered with sweet coloured seeds, Apples, Cherries preserved, Olives, Cakes. Plates and Dishes for the Desert quite new and very beautiful—Madeira, Port and Mountain Wines—Parmesan Cheese also at Dinner. After Tea and Coffee we all played at Loo—at which I neither won or lost anything—Nancy lost 6 pence. Mr. and Mrs. Collier seem to be good kind of People especially Mr. Collier—He has a very large Fortune—Gave to Nancy this Evening after Supper o. 10. 6. Nancy made her appearance in her new riding Habit at Mr. Custances and the first Time of wearing it. Mr. Du Quesne paid me to day what I lent him Tuesday being o. 6. 6.

May 10. . . . Mr. Smith of Mattishall made us a Visit this morning to acquaint me that he has lost a Brother, and therefore could not serve my Church in my Absence so fully as he wished to have done, as he shall not be at Mattishall for the two first Sundays, being going from Home on Sunday on the above melancholy Occasion and cannot return for 3 or 4 Weeks—and also to desire me to officiate for him at Mattishall in the afternoon on Whitsunday which I promised him—He shall be able to assist me all the

Time in my absence but the two first Sundays.
I desired him to stay and dine with us but he could
not. Mr. Howes called on us about 6 o'clock,
smoked a Pipe, drank a Dish of Tea and then went
home. . . .

May 11. . . . It is reported that 11,000 Dutch are
landed in Yorkshire.[1]

May 13. . . . Mr. and Mrs. Custance sent us a Note
this morning, that if we were disengaged, they would
drink a dish of Tea with us in the Afternoon in a
friendly way—I sent a note back that we should be
very glad to see them, and about 5 o'clock they came
and stayed with us till after 8. Mr. Cary dined with
our Folks in Kitchen.

May 14. . . . I bled my 3 Horses this morning. It
being my Rotation Day, Mr. and Mrs. Bodham,
Mrs. Davy, Mr. Howes and Mr. Du Quesne dined
and spent the Afternoon with us—Mrs. Davy supped
and slept here as she is to spend a Day or two with
Nancy. I gave my Company for Dinner, 4 Spring
Chickens boiled and a Ham, part of a Rump of Beef
boiled, a Leg of Mutton rosted with sweet Sauce and
a boiled Plumb Pudding. At Quadrille this Evening
lost 0. 1. 0.

May 16. . . . Mrs. Davy breakfasted, dined and spent
part of the afternoon here. To Jn. Pegg a Q^{rs} Land
Tax for Rectory &c. at 4, 3. 0. 0. To Do. ½ Yrs.
Window Tax 23, 1. 2. 7. To Do. ½ Yrs. House
Tax at 6^d in the P^d 0. 1. 9. Mr. Howes dined and
spent part of the Afternoon with us. About 5 o'clock
this Afternoon Mr. Howes and Mrs. Davy went to
Mr. Carters at Ringland to Tea and then for

---

[1] Needless to say this was an idle rumour : see for a similar rumour
vol. i, p. 260.

Hockering. To Spraggs, Gardner for work p^d 0. 5. 3. To Ditto. for a Peck of Potatoes p^d 0. 0. 8.

May 17. . . . We dined and spent the Afternoon at Mr. Custance's with him, Mrs. Custance, Sr Edm^d Bacon and Lady. We had for Dinner for the 1st Course Fish, boiled Beef at the Side Table, Stewed Mutton, Veal Cutlets, Neck of Pork rosted and baked Puddings—2nd Course—Spring Chicken. and Asparagus, Ham sliced, Pickled Salmon and an Apple Tart—Parmesan Cheese afterwards. Sr Edmund Bacon and Lady were obliged to set of for home about 5 o'clock this Evening. 15 Miles beyond Norwich. They went in a Phaeton and Pair—with a Head to it. It rained when they set of and likely to continue. We returned home about 8 o'clock as we went in Mr. Custance's Coach—it rained as we returned. Sent a letter to my Sister Pounsett this Evening by Cary to let her know that we are obliged to put of our Journey for one Week longer as I cannot get a Supply for Trin: Sunday.

May 19. . . . I read Prayers and administered the H: Sacrament this morning at Weston Church—Mr. and Mrs. Custance both there. After Dinner I rode to Mattishall and there read Prayers and Preached, published Banns, churched a Woman, and gave Notice of a Sacrament on Sunday next, for Mr. Smith who is gone to Bedford on the Death of a Brother. I had a very cold ride there and back. A smart Frost this Night and very cold. J^s Smith my Clerk dined here to day in the Kitchen being Whitsunday and Sacrament Day. The Widow, Patience Allen, dined with our Folks today.

May 21. . . . Mr. Custance made us a morning Visit and stayed with us an Hour—he walked here from

Weston House. He told us some good News, ' that Admiral Rodney has had an engagement in the West Indies with the French and came of Victorious. He took the French Admiral Count De Grasse with his Ship of 110 Guns. took 3 or 4 more men of War and sunk another.'[1] Looked over my Shirts, Stocks, &c. this morning.

[1] Rodney's victory of April 12, 1782, off Dominica, in the West Indies, over the French fleet commanded by De Grasse, was one of the most decisive in the history of war. It shattered the principal French fleet—the fleet in the West Indies, prevented the planned junction of that fleet with the Spanish fleet for the conquest of Jamaica, re-asserted England's prestige which had been reduced to vanishing point by recent American, West Indian, and Mediterranean disasters, and, as a consequence, enabled the Rockingham and Shelburne ministries to negotiate peace on far more favourable terms at Paris. Admiral Rodney writing to my Lords of the Admiralty from the *Formidable*, at sea, on April 14—the ' expressive Letter ' which so rightly delighted Parson Woodforde on May 22—thus reported his victory : ' It has pleased God, out of his Divine Providence, to grant to his Majesty's arms a most complete victory over the fleet of his enemy, commanded by Count de Grasse, who is himself captured, with the Ville de Paris, and four other ships of his fleet, besides one sunk in the action. This important victory was obtained on the 12th instant, after a battle which lasted with unremitting fury, from seven in the morning till half past six in the evening, when the setting sun put an end to the contest. . . . The enemy's whole army, consisting of 5,500 men, were on board their ships of War. The destruction among them must be prodigious, as, for the greatest part of the action, every gun told ; and their Lordships may judge what havoc must have been made, when the Formidable fired near eighty broadsides. . . . That the British flag may ever flourish in every quarter of the globe, is the most ardent wish of him, who has the honour of being, with great regard, etc. etc., etc.'

The Admiral's regard would have been a good deal less had he known that the Whig Government of Lord Rockingham, as yet unaware of his victory, were on the point of recalling him (the letter of recall is dated May 1). As soon as the news of the victory reached England the Ministry did their best to retrace their steps. Rodney was thanked by both

May 22. . . . The good news that we heard Yesterday is all true. I saw Admiral Rodney's Letter in the Gazette at Du Quesne's and a most excellent, good and expressive Letter it was.[1]

May 23. . . . Took a Catalogue this morning of my old Coins. Poor old Kemp died this morning—and it is said that he was starved—His wife behaved shocking bad to him and she is a sad Creature indeed. She and his Children have wished him dead a long while as is reported. Tho' he was but indifferent himself—hope [h]is change is for the better.

May 25. . . . Took a ride to Norwich this morning and Will with me. We got there about 12 o'clock and stayed till 7 in the Evening. It being Market Day the City was all alive and in a Hurry. Went and bespoke 4 Places, 3 inside and 1 outside, in the London Post Coach for Wednesday Evening next. At Bakers for Things, trifles p^d o. 1. o. I dined at a pastry shop on 3 Cheese Cakes—for that and other things there paid o. o. 6. . . .

May 29. . . . Very busy all the Morning, packing up our things for to go into the Country, as we set out in the Evening. Mr. Du Quesne, who goes to London with us dined and spent the Afternoon with us—and

Houses of Parliament, was made a Baron, and was given a pension—later attached to the title in perpetuity—of £2,000 a year. It is one of the ironies of politics that Rodney had owed his re-appointment to the crucial theatre of naval warfare in the West Indies specially to King George III, Lord Sandwich, and the North ministry. Had the Rockingham ministry come in earlier Rodney would never have been appointed, as the Whigs were furious with him for his alleged misdeeds in the Dutch island of St. Eustatius—taken by Rodney in the spring of 1781. (For Rodney's letter see Mundy's *Life of Rodney*, vol. ii, 255-8 ; for the victory generally see Lecky's *History*, &c., vol. v, 171-4 ; see also Horace Walpole's *Letters*, vol. xii, 250-1.)   [1] See preceding footnote.

about 5 o'clock this Evening Nancy and myself went in Lenewade Bridge Chaise, and Mr. Du Quesne in his own Chaise, for Norwich and there we drank Tea at the Angel where the London Coach puts up and in which we are to go in to Night. To the Driver of the Lenewade Chaise gave o. 1. 6. Paid and gave at the Angel for eating &c. o. 2. 6. My Servant Will Coleman went with us and is to go into the Country with us. We met Mr. Priest of Reepham and his Son S^t. John at Norwich—The latter is going to Bury in the outside of the London Coach. No inside Place vacant. For 2 inside Places in the London Coach p^d at Norwich 1. 16. o. For 1 outside Place in Do. p^d at Do. o. 10. 6. To extraordinary weight of Luggage at 1½ per P^d p^d o. 8. 6. At 9 o'clock this Evening we all set of for London.

May 30. We travelled all night long and I thank God safe and well. We breakfasted at Sudbury—and I paid there o. 2. 6. Our Coach was quite full having six in it—4 gentlemen and 2 young Ladies. We got to London about 2 o'clock in the Afternoon all safe and well, thank God for it. To Coachmen from Norwich gave o. 4. o. We did not like the Inn where the Coach put up (which was the Swan and 2 Necks in Lad-Lane.) therefore we got into a Hackney Coach and drove to the Bell Savage on Ludgate Hill and there dined, supped, and slept. Mr. Du Quesne went with us there and dined and spent the Afternoon with us—In the Evening he went to the Arch-Bishops at Lambeth where he supped and slept.[1]

[1] The Archbishop of Canterbury at this time was Dr. Frederick Cornwallis : he was brother-in-law of Mr. Charles Townshend of Honingham, hence Mr. Du Quesne's acquaintance with him (see footnotes to pp. 211 and 318, vol. i).

Nancy bore her Journey very well as did Will and myself. We were all very glad to get to bed to night, being tired.

May 31. We breakfasted, dined and spent the Afternoon at our Inn. Before we breakfasted, I hired a Coach and we went in it to St. James Park. Will also went with us. From the Horse Guards we all walked up the Park to St. James's Palace and saw the Guards relieved at 9 o'clock—a very pretty sight. We also saw most of the State Rooms in the Palace. Gave to People at St. James's Palace o. 3. 6. From thence we walked up the Park to the Queens Palace but did not go into that—the Royal Family being there. After that we walked down the Park back to the Horse-Guards and there took a Hackney Coach and returned to our Inn to breakfast. Mr. Du Quesne came to us at breakfast—and after breakfast, Nancy, myself and Will took a Coach and went to the Tower and saw the Horse Armory, the small Armory, the Artillery, the Regalia, and the wild Beasts.[1] Mr. Du Quesne went with us in the Coach as far as the Royal Exchange and there he took his Leave of us. At the Tower gave in the whole o. 9. o. From Breakfast to Dinner we were taken up in seeing the Tower, and did not dine till 5 o'clock at our Inn. For Coach hire to Day p^d o. 5. 6. After Dinner we walked to a Milleners Shop and I bought 3 dressed Caps for Nancy, for my Sister Pounsett and her little girl, with about 10 Yards of Ribband besides—p^d there

[1] Zoological gardens were as yet non-existent, and one went to the Tower to see the wild beasts, specially the Lions. ' The lions of the Tower are the origin of that application of the term " lion " to any conspicuous spectacle or personage, which has long since become universal.' Lecky, *England in the Eighteenth century*, vol. ii, p. 216.

1. 10. 6. To a small Paper Caravan for the above p^d 0. 1. 6. I went by myself and gave a Peep into St. Pauls Church this aft: To a Barber this Afternoon for shaving &c. gave 0. 1. 0. For 2 inside Places in the Salisbury Coach p^d 2. 2. 0. For 1 outside Place Do. p^d 0. 10. 6. Paid and gave at the Bell Savage for all of us abt. 1. 15. 0. They were very civil People at the Bell Savage Inn by name Barton and a very good House it is. About 10 o'clock at Night we set of in the Salisbury Coach from the same Inn for Salisbury, and the Coach guarded. I was bit terribly by the Buggs last Night, but did not wake me.

June 1. We travelled again all night long and I thank God got safe and well to Salisbury between 2 and 3 o'clock in the Afternoon—The Coach was full also. Gave the Coachmen that drove us 0. 4. 0. We breakfasted at Whitchurch for which I pd. 0. 2. 6. Paid at Salisbury for extraordinary Luggage 0. 6. 6. At Salisbury we made a running Dinner and between 3 and 4 in the Afternoon we got into a Post Chaise for Hindon—and Will went on an hired Horse thither. Pd. and gave at Salisbury for Chaise, Horse &c. abt. 1. 1. 0. We got to Hindon abt. 6 o'clock— then took a fresh Chaise and set of for Stourton and Will on a fresh Horse. Pd. and gave at Hindon for Chaise &c. abt. 0. 12. 6. We got to Stourton abt. 8 o'clock, then we took a fresh Chaise and set of for Cole—and Will on a fresh Horse. Paid and gave at Stourton for Chaise &c. abt. 0. 12. 6. We got to Cole about 10 o'clock and I thank God safe and well and found my good Friends there all well—blessed be God for all things—and accept my most sincere and unfeigned thanks for thy great goodness to us in preserving us from all the Dangers of so long a

Journey that we have taken. My good Friends were very happy to see us and waiting impatiently for our arrival. Sister White and her Daughter were at Cole expecting us and they supped and slept at Cole. Nancy, myself and Will all supped and slept at Cole. I was terribly swelled in the face and hands by the Buggs. Mr. Pounsett with my Sister and little Maid very glad to see us.

June 5. We breakfasted, supped and slept again at Cole. Mr. Thomas, Curate of Cary, spent the morning with us afishing and about 1 o'clock he walked with Mr. Pounsett and myself to Mr. White Sen^{rs} at Ansford where we dined and spent the Afternoon with Mr. and Mrs. White Senr and Mr. and Mrs. White Junr. Brother Heighes spent the Afternoon with us—In the Afternoon we went and saw My Brother Heighes's House—alias Castle—built by J^s Clarke and in which Brother and his Daughter Juliana lives—It is a pretty place and well laid out. From thence we walked and Brother Heighes with us to my Brother Johns and Sister Clarkes and Mr. Robert White Juniors—then back to Mrs. Whites and then to Cole. Neither my Sister or Nancy went with us to Ansford. Juliana Woodforde spent the Aft: with her Sister at Cole.

June 8. . . . Mr. Robert White Junr dined and spent the afternoon with us. Mr. Pounsett, myself and Robert White went up the river towards Pitcomb this morning afishing with Nets and we caught several good Trout with Roberts Net. Brother John spent the Afternoon with us at Cole.

June 11. . . . Mr. and Mrs. Pounsett, Nancy and myself went to Ansford about 1 o'clock to my Brother Johns and there we all dined and spent the Afternoon

with Brother John and his Wife, Mr. Richd Clarke
and Wife, Mr. J^s Clarke. Brother Heighes and
Sister Clarke and Sam spent the Afternoon there.
We had for Dinner some Fish, 3 Chickens boiled and
a Piggs Face, a Leg of Mutton rosted and a baked
plumb Pudding. Mr. Richd Clarke came after Nancy
in his Chair this morn' but we had hired a Chaise
for her and my Sister from Cary in which they went
by themselves—Mr. Pounsett went in Mr. Richards
Chair and I walked to Ansford. My Sister Pounsett
returned home from Ansford on horseback and
Mr. Pounsett and myself walked back home to Cole.
We left Nancy at my Brother Johns, as she is to spend
a few Days there with her good Aunt Woodforde.
To an old Servant of mine (by name Luke Barnard)
whom I saw at Ansford to day gave o. 2. 6.

June 14. . . . Mr. Leir of Ditcheat made us a morning
Visit. He was an old School-Fellow of mine at
Winchester—and is now Rector of Ditcheat, lately
vacant by the Death of his Father. Mr. and Mrs.
Pounsett and self took a walk to Ansford and there
dined and spent the afternoon at Mr. Robert White
Junr with him, his Wife, Mr. and Mrs. White Senr
and their Daughter Anne, My Brother John Wood-
forde and Wife and Nancy, and Mr. J^s Clarke. We
had for Dinner a fine Joal [1] of Salmon, a boiled Tongue
with mashed Potatoes, a Leg of Mutton rosted, a
Currant Pudding and a Gooseberry Pye. I gave
Nancy for Pocket Money this Afternoon 1. 1. 0.
I gave old Alice Stacy, Will^s Grandmother 0. 1. 0.
Gave Robert White's Maid coming away 0. 1. 0.
We spent a very agreeable Day at Ansford and we
returned to Cole on foot about 9 o'clock.

[1] Joal = Jowl, i. e. the head and shoulders of a salmon.

31

June 15. . . . Very poorly indeed to day owing I believe
to eating Salmon yesterday and drinking Cyder soon
after it. Dr Penny of Castle-Cary spent the Afternoon
with us, he looks hearty and well—I was very glad to
see him. He still lives with the Duke of Beaufort at
Badmington. Mrs. Pounsett Senr dined and spent
the afternoon with us.

June 16. . . . Was very ill all last night and continued
so all day long, and was with it very low indeed—
could eat little or nothing all day—going to bed took
a good dose of Rhubarb, which I hope will be of great
service, and may it please God to grant its desired
Effect. Mrs Pounsett Senr dined and spent the
Afternoon with us. I designed to have went to
Pitcomb Church this morning had I been well enough.

June 17. . . . Had a much better night, than last night,
and I thank God am much better than yesterday. . . .

June 18. I breakfasted, supped and slept again at Cole.
Very violent Storm of Thunder and Lightning with
heavy Rains about 10 o'clock this morning—but
I thank God no Damage was done by it at Cole, and
I hope no where else, either by Land or Water.
The Thunder was the most rumbling I ever heard.
About 1 o'clock Mr. and Mrs. Pounsett and self
went to Ansford and dined and spent the Afternoon
at James Clarkes, with him Mrs Richd Clarke, my
Brother John his Wife and Nancy, Sister White,
Brother Heighes and Mr Thomas. We had for
Dinner, 3 Fowls boiled, a bit of Pork boiled, a Leg of
Mutton boiled and Capers, a green Goose rosted and
asparagus and a baked plumb Pudding. We spent a very
merry day there—Brother Heighes's D^r [daughter]
Juliana spent the Afternoon there with us. After
Dinner Brother Heighes talked very angry to Nancy.

We got home to Cole between 9 and 10 at Night and as we went—Jenny on Horseback and we on foot. We heard at Ansford that there were 3 Men struck down in Pilton Church by the Lightning this morning.[1] One of them killed instantly—but the others like to recover. The Man that was Struck dead was tolling a Bell for a Person lately dead, the other two were near him. Pray God have mercy on the poor Man.

June 20. . . . I took a Walk by Myself about Noon to Ansford and there dined and spent part of the Afternoon at my Brother John's, with him, his Wife, Nancy and Mr Thomas. Mr Pounsett came to us in the Afternoon and then my Brother John, Mr Pounsett, Mr Thomas and self took a walk to Cary and drank Tea and smoked a Pipe at Mr. Thomas's. We had for Dinner to day at my Brothers' a Leg of Lamb boiled and Spinnage, a couple of Fowls rosted and Asparagus and a nice Batter Pudding with Currant Jelly. Sister Pounsett and her little Maid went to Ansford in one of the Bruton Chaises (which I hired to bring back Nancy to Cole) this Afternoon and drank Tea at Mrs Whites. M^{rs} Jⁿ Woodforde and Nancy met them at Mr Whites. We all returned to Cole about 9 o'clock at Night. Mr Pounsett and myself walked back again to Cole. Had a very long Letter whilst I was at my Brother Johns, from M^r Du Quesne dated the 18 Instant from Lambeth Palace—wherein he acquaints me that in Norfolk the 31 of May there happened at Weston and adjacent Villages a most terrible Tempest of Thunder, Lightning and Hail there which did great Damage to Mr Custances new House and likewise

---

[1] Benjamin Franklin had invented the lightning-conductor in 1752, but evidently this church was not yet fitted with one.

broke many of my Windows—The Corn in Weston
Field almost all destroyed by the Hail which were as
big as Bulletts and were 12 Inches deep in Weston
Field—Thank God! no lives are said to be lost.
Nancy supped and slept at Cole. My Letter from
Du Quesne was franked by Mr. Townshend. Very
sickly in London in the Influenza. Very few escape—
Mr. Du Quesne has been confined to his Room in it—
Mrs. Townshend was very dangerously ill in it.
Called on old Mrs Penny, Mr Francis Senr, Dr Viggarr,
old Mr Maby, John Burges, but he was not at home,
and Sam Burge this Even'. We met Mrs Melliar
and Sally Francis in a Chair as we were walking back
to Cole and we had some Chat together—Mrs Melliar
asked me to her House very genteely. J^s Clarke was
with them—we met them at Mr Thorntons at Hony-
wicke. We did not go into Mr Thorntons being late.

June 23. . . . Mr Pounsett and my Sister, Nancy and
self took a Walk after Dinner to Pitcomb Church
and there heard Mr Richd Goldsborough read Prayers
and Preached but rather affected. As we came back
from Church we stopped by a very fine Spring in
Pitcomb Street in which I threw in a Shilling for the
Boys there to scramble for o. 1. o. We also called
in at Taylor Wilmots and drank some of his Ale—
I gave his comical Maid Nan o. 1. o.

June 24. . . . Sister White and her Daughter and
honest Joseph Perham of Butly spent the morning,
dined and spent the Aft: with us. Poor Joseph came
over on purpose to see me.

June 28. . . . Gave my Sister Pounsett and Nancy to
each of them 2 Hatbands—1 white Silk and 1 black
Silk for Calashes.

July 3. I breakfasted, supped and slept again at Cole.

About 12 took a ride to Cary and Ansford, called on Rich. Clarke and J^s Clarke, Mrs White, Brother John and Sister Clarke and Brother Heighes—I dined and spent part of the Afternoon with my Brother John, his Wife and Brother Heighes at my Brother Johns. In the Afternoon my Brother John and self took a ride to Counsellor Melliars at Gallhampton, smoked a Pipe with him and his eldest son the Doctor and then we returned together to Dr. Clarkes where we drank a glass of Cyder on horseback and then we went to our respective homes.

July 5. . . . Charles Clarkes Wife and Son supped here, and slept at old Mrs Pounsetts—She has most consummate assurance. We had for Dinner some Trout, Ham and 3 Fowls, a Leg of Mutton rosted, Custards and Gooseberry Pye.

July 8. . . . After breakfast my Sister Pouncett and self took a ride to Westcomb to make Mrs Donne a visit and her Sister Davison. We found them very low and very indifferent—they both looked very dejected —Mrs. Donne having very lately lost her Husband, Dr Donne, a very worthy good kind of a man—I knew him very well and am sincerely sorry for him—He was ill but a few Days. We saw at their House a Mr Norris who serves the Curacy of Batcomb— a Mrs Salmon of Wells and a Mr Salmon her Brother of Bristol there—We stayed with them about an Hour and then my Sister went back to Cole behind her Servant Ellis and I went on to Shepton Mallett and dined and spent the Afternoon there at Mrs Figges's who has also had great losses lately— losing both her Husband and her Mother Mrs Paine —I found her in tolerable spirits much better than I expected—She had just dined upon some cold

Shoulder of Mutton—I had some Bacon and Eggs—
boiled Mutton &c. for Dinner—About 4 o'clock
went and called on my Sister Pounsetts little Maid at
Mrs Barnes's School—She looked very well and seemed
very happy with her School-Mates. Mrs Barnes has
a tolerable School and a good House. From thence
I walked to Lawyer Whites and there drank Tea
with him, his Wife, Mr Robt. White Junr and Wife,
of Ansford and Miss Holly Dawe of Ditcheat who
came with them—About 7 o'clock Bob and his
Wife, Miss Dawe and self set of for our respective
Homes—we went home to Ditcheat with Miss Dawe
and then I went with Bob and Wife to Ansford and
afterwards I went on to Cole—it was near 10 o'clock
before I got home this Evening. Miss Dawe is a
very handsome, genteel young Lady. I was almost
tired by the Time I got home. To Turnpikes &c.
to day gave and pd. o. o. 6. P^d Mr Pounsett this
morning for Chaise Hire o. 5. o.

July 9. . . . Brother John spent part of the Afternoon
and Evening with us and before he went begun to be
rather noisy.

July 15. . . . Mr Pounsett rode to South Cadbury in
the Afternoon to attend the Funeral of old Mr Slade
there this Evening—He did not return till near 10.
My Man went with Mr Pounsett. My Sister, Nancy and
self took a Walk this Afternoon to Mrs Hunts at Pitcomb
and there drank Tea with Miss Hunt, her two Brothers
Dodington and John and a Mr Brown of Dorsetshire—
Old Mrs Hunt did not make her appearance—being
above stairs. We returned to Cole about 9 o'clock.

July 17. . . . Nancy's Brother Sam[1][1] called on us in the

---

[1] This is Samuel Woodforde, R.A. (1763–1817), for brief account of
whom see foot-note to p. 208, vol. i.

Afternoon and he stayed and supped and slept at Cole. He is very much grown and greatly improved—He is still at Mr Hoares of Stourhead and kindly patronised by him in his Painting—He sticks close to Painting and Mr. Hoare has got him into the Royal Academy and pays all his Expenses—and he has many Presents also of him. Sam is grown a very fine handsome young Man. We should not have known him, had not Mr Pounsett told us who he was as he passed by the Window. Sam slept at old Mrs Pounsetts—He is smartly dressed. Nancy sent a Letter this Afternoon to Mrs Bodham.

July 20. . . . Mr. Thomas spent the Morning with us Yesterday, he came to ask me to preach for him on Sunday but I could not, as I brought no Sermon with me—The last Time I was in the Country I had some Sermons with me and was never asked to preach therefore I thought it of no Use to bring any now. Sister Pounsett rode to Ansford behind Ellis this morning and there stayed and dined and spent the Afternoon at Mr Whites.—Mr Pounsett rode in the Evening to Ansford after her.—They did not return home till near 10 at night—I went out in the Evening afishing by myself and caught 1 Trout and 1 Eel.

July 21. I breakfasted, supped and slept again at Cole. Took a ride about noon to Ansford and dined and spent the Afternoon at my Brother Johns, with him, his Wife, Mrs Richard Clarke, my Sister Pounsett, Nancy and her Brother Sam, Mr Robert White Junr and Wife—Sister Clarke and Son Sam, Brother Heighes, Sister White and Daughter and Juliana Woodforde spent the Afternoon with us there as they returned from Ansford Church this Aft: Sister

Pounsett went to Ansford early this morning, soon enough to go to Cary Church this morning there. I did not go to Church to day, but hope what I did in my Closet, was acceptable to the Divine Goodness. We had for Dinner some Peas and Pork, a piece of boiled Beef, a Couple of Ducks rosted and a Batter Pudding. We returned to Cole between 9 and 10 o'clock.

July 27. . . . Had a long Letter from M^r Du Quesne to day. All at Weston Parsonage well, and not so much damage done by the late Storm as was expected. Brother John spent part of the Afternoon, supped and spent the Evening with us.—Am afraid it is but poor Times with him—am very sorry for it—He is very generous and too much Company hurts him greatly. I gave him change for four Crown Pieces.[1]

August 2. I breakfasted, dined, supped and slept again at Cole. Nancy breakfasted, dined &c. &c. again at Cole. Nancy's Brother Ralph, who is very like Sam, walked by here this Morning and we called him and he stayed with us an Hour.—I gave him o. 1. o. He is 15 Years of Age and a very fine Lad he is. At Quadrille this Afternoon lost o. 1. o. Gave Nancy this Evening sixpence to play one Rubber of Cribbage with me for half a Crown and I won it very soon indeed—but I gave her the whole stakes o. 5. o.

The entries for nearly two months are now missing, from August 6th to October 2nd, 1782. It seems probable that the Diarist made the entries during this

---

[1] Readers of the first volume of this Diary will remember Brother John very well—in the earlier Somerset days of the Diarist's life : for a summary account of him see p. 177, vol. i.

period in some temporary booklet, as there is no gap in the neat, numbered volumes—the present volume ending on August 6th, and the next one beginning on October 2nd. Sometime in the interval he returned to Weston, where we rejoin him.

Oct. 17. . . . A very pleasant and agreeable Day today. It being my Rotation to day, Mr. Howes, and Mrs. Davy; Mr. and Mrs. Bodham, Mr. Du Quesne and Mr. Smith, dined and spent the Afternoon and stayed till after 8 o'clock in the Evening with us. We had for Dinner a Ham and a Couple of Fowls boiled, a Couple of Rabbitts smothered with Onions, a Surloin of Beef rosted and some grape Tarts. At Quadrille this Evening won o. 4. o. Lent Du Quesne this Evening o. 3. o.

Oct. 18. . . . As Nancy and myself was walking in the road near the bottom of the Garden—Mr. Press Custance's Man Breeze met us, and was coming to my House with a Letter that he rec^d at the Post Office for me—it was from my Sister Pounsett— I paid and gave for it o. 1. o. Soon afterwards on the same road we meet the Hon: Charles Townshend and had some Chat with him. We were but shabbily dressed—It was in the morning between 11. and 12. o'clock. To Cason for a Sack of Non-parells pd. o. 10. 6. To Clark Hewitt this Evening for a Tub of Gin wch he brought in a Basket, smuggled Gin pd. 1. 5. o.[1] Gave him for his trouble of coming over o. 1. o.

Oct. 19. . . . Busy in readg Evelina a Novel, lent Nancy by Mrs. Custance—there are 3. Volumes of it

---

[1] For some remarks on smuggling, see vol. i, p. 197.

—wrote by a Miss Burney—they are very cleaver and sensible.[1]

Oct. 23. . . . Mr. Symonds came here this Afternoon and cleared my Jack and took away the Compass Wheel, as it required so large a Weight to it and was always breaking the Line—I hope now it will go better and with a less Weight, and above one Quarter of the Weight.

Oct. 24. . . . Nancy came home about 12 o'clock and Mrs. Davy and another Lady (a Mrs. Church) with her. Mrs. Davy and the other Lady did not stay long—Nancy stayed and dined, supped and slept here. Mr. Hall, just returned from Andover in Hants, came here about Noon and he dined, supped and sat up all Night at my House, having no bed but mine which I offered to him, but he would not accept of it, therefore obliged me to sit up with him all Night.[2] We had for Dinner a Piece of boiled Beef, some Herrings which Mrs. Davy brought here and a Couple of Ducks. Mr. Pyle dined with our Folks—his men at work here.

Oct. 25. I breakfasted, dined, supped and slept again at home. Hall went away about 10 o'clock. I was quite ill all day by setting up last night and will not do it again for any Hall in the Kingdom—He might have as well went to Lenewade and slept as he used

[1] Miss Burney's (1752–1840) *Evelina* had appeared in January 1778, and her *Cecilia* in the summer of 1782. Horace Walpole was naturally at this moment criticizing *Cecilia*: it is equally natural that Parson Woodforde in the country should only now be reading *Evelina*. (See Macaulay's essay on Madame D'Arblay, and Walpole's *Letters*, vol. xii, p. 339.)

[2] The reader will find frequent references to Mr. Hall of Winborough in vol. i (see index). Parson Woodforde began by liking him, and in 1779 had made an expedition to the Norfolk coast with him (vol. i, p. 251).

to do—but he minds nothing but self and his Money. I slept about noon for 2 Hours and tolerably well. Nancy breakfasted, dined, &c. &c. again at home. Nancy sent a Letter this Evening to her Aunt Woodforde.

Oct. 26. . . . Had the Cramp baddish in the Night in both legs, however had a tolerable good night on the whole, and am greatly refreshed by it and am brave to day.

Oct. 31. . . . Mr. Custance made us a long morning Visit. Rec^d a Letter last Night by Mr. Custance's Servant from the Post Office at Norwich, from Dr. Oglander, Warden of New College to petition me to pay my Subscription towards the new painted Window in New College Chapel—which was lately put up there, my Subscription was ten Pounds and which I shall send, soon after my Frolic, to New College.[1] Gave Nancy this morning an old brown silk gown very good never the less, and was my late Aunt Parrs. It being very windy to Night neither myself or Nancy went to bed till after 12 o'clock—(tace).

Nov. 2. . . . Mr. Townshend sent his gamekeeper to me this morning to desire me to confine my Grey-hounds as they were seen hunting very near his House to day. Nancy was very entertaining this Afternoon.

Nov. 5. . . . Between 11 and 12 o'clock to day I rode down to Lenewade Bridge and Will went with me, and there met most of Bathurst's Parishioners who paid me their respective Compositions for Tithe &c. I dined and spent the afternoon till 5 o'clock with them and then paid the Bill and returned home.

[1] See vol. i, pp. 264–5, for the Diarist's charming account of this window after the design by Sir Joshua Reynolds : the Diarist saw it first on 12 September 1779, when it had just been put up.

Mr. Wilson sent me a note by his Servant which I answered and by his Servant sent him 12. 10. 0. being his Quarterage for the Curacies to Michaelmas. At Cribbage this Evening with Nancy lost 0. 2. 0.

Nov. 9. . . . Mr. Smith of Mattishall made us a morning visit, but could not dine with us, his Rotation next Thursday, he very kindly invited Nancy. I offered to pay Mr. Smith this morning for his serving Weston for me in my late long absence but I could not prevail on him to accept of anything.

Nov. 11. . . . Heard this morning that poor Mr. Kerr died Yesterday. I hope it will prove a happy Change for him. To Mr. Cary for things from Norwich, &c. p^d 0. 6. 2½. To my maid Betty for things, &c. p^d 0. 17. 2. My Butcher took my young Greyhound by name Reach'em to keep for me for some time. My head maid Betty Claxton went yesterday to see her Mother at Melton, she being very ill—returned at Night. Sent Ben early this morning to lower Earlham [1] near Norwich where was an Auction of Cattle &c. I sent him to get a Cow and Calf if he could, but he could not.

Nov. 13. . . . Ben's Father spent the morning and dined with our Folks—He brought 2 Ferretts with him to kill some Rats for me in my Barn. We had 4 killed if not more. About 2 o'clock Mr. Howes and Mrs. Davy came here and they dined and spent the Afternoon here—In the Evening they returned home and took Nancy with them who is [to] sleep there to night and to morrow she is to go with them to Mr. Smith's being his Rotation. From Mr. Smith's she is to go and spend a few Days with Mrs. Bodham by particular desire. We had for Dinner to day some

[1] See vol. i, p. 233, foot-note.

Tripe, some Mutton Stakes, a small Piece of boiled Beef, a fine Turkey rosted and some Grape-Tarts. Gave Jack some Rhubarb this Evening, he not being well.

Nov. 15. . . . Very dull for me in the Evenings now Nancy is from home.

Nov. 16. . . . Had a Letter this Evening from my Sister Pounsett—all well. Another Letter came also for Nancy, and I believe from her B^r Sam. Cobb of Mattishall a Rat-Catcher and whom I formerly employed came to my House this morning by Order, and I engaged with him for to kill all my Rats at one Guinea Per Annum and likewise to kill all my Mice. And the first Guinea is to be paid the first of Decem^br 1783—I gave him for Entrance Mony 11. 0. He is to come as often as there is Occasion for him—And is to be kept in Victuals and drink.

Nov. 20. . . . Mr. Custance made me a Morning Visit, and desired that we would dine with him Monday next. Mrs. Custance soon after Mr. Custance was gone made me a Visit and stayed with me till near 2 o'clock. Very soon after Mrs. Custance was gone Mr. Howes with Mrs. Davy and Nancy came here and they stayed and dined and spent the afternoon with me—and Mr. Howes with Mrs. Davy prevailed on me after many Entreaties and at last with great reluctance on my Part, to let Nancy return with them to Hockering as they are going to Norwich to-Morrow, which I did, tho' much against me. Poor Mr. Howes and Mrs. Davy had set their hearts so much on it, that they were made very uneasy at my refusing them at first, and they almost cried and said that they would never be friendly with me if I did not admit of it. Mr. Howes said he would never enter my Doors more. The chief and principal Reason I gave, was, I did not approve or ever could that my Niece should make so free at Mr. Priest's— Mrs. Davy having sent a note this morning before they came here, that she with Nancy intended dining with them to Morrow at Norwich. It made me rather uneasy after they were gone back as I cannot by any means approve of it on any Account neither should I at last, unless to make old Mr. Howes easy. Mr. Custance told me this morning that he had a few Days ago about 80 Turkies, geese, Ducks, and Fowls stolen from [him] in one night—many of them that were fatting. This is the time of the year that many idle Fellows from Norwich go about the Country stealing Poultry to send them to London to make a Penny of them. I never had any stolen yet, but daily expect it. Burrows of Morton had but a few Days ago also taken from him Poultry to the Amount of 3 or 4 P^{ds} value. We had for Dinner to day one Fowl boiled and Piggs face, a Couple of Rabbitts smothered with Onions, a Piece of rost Beef and some Grape Tarts.

Nov. 25. . . . Mrs. Custance sent me this morning as a Present a genteel Mohogany Fire-Screen—very kind of her. To Mr. Cary for things from Norwich, &c. p^d 1. 1. 6. To my Maid Betty for things p^d 0. 9. 0. Between 2 and 3 o'clock Mr. Du Quesne called here in his Chaise and took Nancy in it to Mr. Custance's and I went with them there on Horseback and took my Servant Man Will with me thither and there we dined and spent the Afternoon and part of the Evening till 9 o'clock with Mr. and Mrs. Custance and Mr. Press Custance—we returned as we went. We had for Dinner boiled Turkey and Oyster Sauce, a very fine Ham, Piggs Fry, and Peas Soup—2nd Course, Rabbit Fricasséed, a fine Hare rosted, Rice Pudding, Patties of Lobster, Tartlets and Rasberry Jam Tarts. After Tea we played at Loo at 1/- per Dozen and confined to 2/6—at which I lost the sum of 0. 18. 0. Recd. a Letter from Dr. Bathurst at Mr. Custances p^d 0. 1. 0. We got home a little before 10. Mr. Du Quesne would not get out of his Chaise—rather too dark to night. This being the first Time of Will's dining at Mr. Custance's House, the Servants made him too welcome by making him rather merry which made him very Saucy after he got home or rather crazy.

Nov. 26. . . . I talked with Will this morning but very quietly. Clerk Hewitt of Mattishall Burgh brought me a Tub of smuggled Gin about 4 gallons, just as we were at Dinner to day—for which I paid him 1. 5. 0. Gave him besides for bringing it to me 0. 1. 0. He stayed and dined with our Folks in the Kitchen.[1]

Nov. 28. . . . Mrs. Custance made us a morning Visit and stayed with us about an Hour. She told us that her Tenant Mr. Girland as he was coming from Reepham one Evening last Week—two Men stopped him on the road on foot, one of them took hold of his Bridle and said to him, your Mony Sir !—but he knowing the Voice of one of them, he then said, I did not know you Sir, I did not design to affront you. The two men are well known and bear very

---

[1] If Clerk Hewitt was parish clerk of Mattishall Burgh, he bears an uncanny resemblance to his contemporary, the Smuggler Mr. Trumbull, so wonderfully described by Scott in chaps. xiii–xiv of *Redgauntlet*. Doubtless Clerk Hewitt's subterranean accommodation also resembled Mr. Trumbull's.

good Characters, one of them is my Neighbour John
Gooch, the other was Tom Thurston who keeps the
Hart—I apprehend they were both very much in
Liquor—but it looks bad.

Nov. 30. . . . Nancy had a brown Silk gown trimmed
with Furr brought home this Evening by Cary from
her Mantua Maker Miss Bell. It was a very good rich
silk that I gave her which formerly belonged to my
poor Aunt Parr, whose Effects came to me.

Dec. 3. . . . This being the Day for my Tithe Auditt,
the following Farmers paid me their Tithes, Girling,
Peachman, Howlett, Rising, Forster, Herring, Dade,
Mann, Js. Pegg, Page, Andrews, Wm. Bidewell,
Case, Ringgar, Js. Pegg, Norton, Buck, Rush, Silvie,
Cary, Burroughs, Baker, Thos. Leggatt, Wm. Leg-
gatt, Rose Bean for the Widow Pratt, rec^d in all to
day 265. 3. 0. They all dined here, but J^n_o Pegg
and Mr. Mann and stayed till near 11 at night.
Forster behaved so insolent towards me that I dont
intend to have him ever again at my Frolick. Poor
J^n_o Buck broke one of my Decanters. I gave them for
Dinner, some Salt Fish, a Leg of Mutton boiled and
Capers, a Knuckle of Veal, a Piggs Face, a fine Surloin
of Beef rosted, and plenty of plumb Puddings.
J^s Smith, my Clerk, dined with our Folks in Kitchen.
I dined with the Farmers in the great Parlour, Nancy
dined by herself in the Study. Wine drank 6 Bottles.
Rum drank 5 Bottles besides Quantities of strong
Beer and Ale.

Dec. 6. . . . I lent this morning to Wm. Bidewell, he
being rather distressed on his note of Hand—the sum
of 10. 0. 0. About 11 this morning took a ride to
Norwich to pay some Bills, got there about 1 o'clock,
put up my Horse at the King's Head and there dined,

supped and slept. My man Will went with me part of the Way and returned home to Dinner by Nancy's desire. As soon as I got to Norwich I called first on Mr. Forster the Attorney and paid him a Year's Rent for the Miss Le Neve's, he being their Guardian the Sum of 16. 0. 0. From thence went to Mr. Priests my Wine Merchant and paid him a Bill for Wine &c. 15. 13. 6. From thence went to Mr. Locke's Coal-Merchant and paid his Clerk (himself not being at home) a Bill of 17. 10. 0. From thence went to Mrs. Brewsters and paid her a Bill for Tea and other matters 11. 9. 0. From thence went to Mr. Manning's Brazier and paid him a Bill for things had of him 5. 0. 6. From thence went home to my Inn and dined about 4 o'clock and after sitting my usual Time I walked out and went to Mr. Smith's my Mercer and pd. him 14. 5. 0. From thence went to Mrs. Garlands my Taylor and paid her a Bill of 2. 0. 0. From thence went to Mr. Scotts and paid him a Bill for Breeches for my Servants of 1. 7. 0. From thence went to Mr Horths my Upholsterer and paid him a Bill of 2. 17. 0. From thence went to Mr. Buckles my Ironmonger and paid him a Bill of 0. 11. 6. Then went home to Supper &c. at my Inn. For a Snuff Box at Bakers—leaving mine at home pd 0. 4. For ½ an oz. of Snuff also pd 0. 0. 1¼. Gave Forster my Taylors' Man 0. 1. 0.

Dec. 7. I breakfasted at my Inn, and after breakfast went to Mr. Lewis's, Linen Drapers, and bought a gown for my Niece of a very pretty new-fashioned Calicoe 5 Yards and ½—and a Body Lining pd. for both 1. 4. 3. From thence went to Mr. Frost's, Master Builder, but he was not at home, therefore could not pay him. From thence went to Mr. Jack-

sons the Brewer and paid him for a Barrill of Porter
1. 13. 0. From thence went to Mr. Francis's
Attorney and paid him for Pension to Coll., Procurations &c. 3. 2. 7½. Gave Mr. Francis also to send to
New Coll: with my Compts. to that Society, towards
painting the Chapel West Window and to which
I subscribed the sum of 10. 0. 0.[1] From Mr. Francis's
went to my Inn, paid my Bill there which amounted
with Servants Vails 0. 11. 9. Called also this
morning on Miss Bell, my niece's Mantua-Maker in
St. Stephens and paid her 1. 4. 0. My Servant Man
Will: came to Town about 12 o'clock. Coming out of
Town called on Mr. Whistler the Painter in St. Giles
and paid him for painting my Chancel 2. 13. 6.
Took Horse at his House about 2 o'clock this Aft.
and set of for my own House at Weston and Will
with me, got home, I thank God safe and well about
4 o'clock and found my Neice &c. all well and then
supped and slept in my own bed, comfortably.
Nancy breakfasted, dined, &c. &c. again at home.
She was well pleased with her new gown. Mr. Howes
was at my House Yesterday and Du Quesne today.

Dec. 12. ... Between 11 and 12 took a ride to Mr. Custance's and made them a morning visit, both at home,
after being there some little Time, Lady Jernegan
and a Mrs. Nicholls an old elderly Lady came there
and I left them there after staying about an Hour,
and from thence went to Du Quesnes, it being his
Rotation got there before 2 o'clock, and there dined
and spent the Aft. with him, Mr. Howes and
Mrs. Davy, Mr. and Mrs. Bodham, Mr. Smith,
Mr. Priest of Norwich, Mr. Priest and his Daughter
Rebecca of Reepham. We had for Dinner some

[1] See foot-note on p. 41, preceding.

Fish, 3 Fowls boiled and a Piece of Ham, a Saddle of Mutton rosted, a Plumb Pudding and some Apple Tarts. I returned home about 9 o'clock to Weston, at quadrille &c. lost at Du Quesnes o. 2. o. Lady Jernegan, whom I never saw before, is a fine woman, tho' large, and extremely sensible, but very much given to Satire. She is a rigid Roman Catholic and breeds her Children up that way.[1] It was rather late before we got to bed to Night.

Dec. 13. . . . Mrs. Custance made us a long morning Visit to day, she spoke to me concerning a Servant Maid and I recommended Lizey's Sister Sukey to her and she seemed to approve of her by my recommendation, she lived last at Du Quesne's but Betty, tho' her own Aunt, and Master and Mistress of Du Quesne's House did not like her, tho' a very good girl I believe—she is to go to Morrow in the Morn' to Mrs. Custance's on my recommendation. Mr. Custance's Servant brought Nancy a long wished for Letter from her Brother Willm. now stationed at New York in North America, very happy and very well, has gone thro' a good deal and weathered it all. It was dated from Sandy Hook, New York Aug: 19. He has taken many Prizes and is in no want of Cash. Shoes he says are at 13/6 Per Pair and a Coarse Shirt

[1] Sir William Jerningham or Jernigan, Bart., of Cossey, Norfolk, was born on 7 March 1736, and succeeded to the baronetcy (created 1621) 21 January 1774. He married 16 June 1767, Nancy (born 17 October 1747), daughter of Henry, 11th Viscount Dillon, by Charlotte, daughter of George Henry (Lee), 2nd Earl of Litchfield. Sir William died 14 August 1809, and his wife 2 March 1825. (Cokayne's *Complete Baronetage*, vol. i, pp. 171–2.) It is, perhaps, not uninteresting to observe that Lady Jerningham, through her Lee descent, was a great-great-granddaughter of King Charles II, and Barbara Villiers, Duchess of Cleveland : see my *Godfather of Downing Street*, chap. vii.

he is obliged to give for 1. 6. 0. He is on Board the Astrea Frigate with his old Capt. Squire, whom I hope will prove a good Friend to him. He met with also a Capt. Foukes of the Lion of 64 guns who is very kind to him, a Somerset Man and a Near Relation of Mr. Robt. White Senr.[1] I sent a Letter to Mrs. Pounsett as did Nancy to her Brother Sam.

Dec. 16. ... Mr. Priest of Norwich sent a Man on foot this morning to my House with a Note and a Present to us of a fine fore Q^r of London Lamb and 2 Seville Oranges. I gave the Man that brought it, as much Victuals and drink as he would have and 0. 2. 6. To Mr. Cary for things from Norwich &c. p^d 0. 2. 11.

Dec. 17. ... We brewed some Table Beer to day. Nancy and self were very merry this Evening.

Dec. 20. ... Sent Will very early this morning to Norwich to get some Fish for Dinner as Mr. and Mrs. Custance dine here to-day, he returned and brought home some fresh Cod and Oysters by 12 at Noon. I gave him to go to Market, last Night 0. 10. 0. About 3 o'clock Mr. and Mrs. Custance came here in their Coach and four, and they dined, spent the Afternoon and stayed till after 8 at night. I gave

---

[1] The reader will, of course, remember William Woodforde (nephew Bill), who figures so frequently in vol. i. The salient facts in his life were that he was the eldest son of Brother Heighes, and was born 4 May 1758. He entered the Navy late in December 1778, saw service on the Barbary coast, in American waters, and in search of the desperate buccaneer Paul Jones. When peace was made he seems to have left the Navy. In 1788 he eloped with Miss Anne Dukes, aged 17, whom he married. He built himself a house at Gallhampton, Somerset, and lived also for a time at Lulworth Cove. In 1804 he raised the first corps of Somerset Volunteer Infantry, and was the Lieutenant-Colonel Commandant when it became the East Somerset Regiment of local Militia. He died at Ansford on 23 July 1844, aged 86. For his attractive portrait, see vol. i.

them for Dinner a fine Cod's Head boiled and Oyster Sauce, a Leg of Mutton boiled and Capers, a fine Turkey rosted, a Batter Pudding and Currant Jelly, Tarts and Custards. After Tea we played a Rubber of Whist Mrs. Custance and self against Mr. Custance and Nancy and we beat them out of the sum of o. 1. 6. Will brought me a letter from my Brother Heighes this morning from the Post Office in which he informs us that J⁵ Clarke is going to marry Holly Dawe and that Robt. White Junr. had recd. a Letter from Nancy's Brother Bill at New York in America the Contents of which near the same as he sent us. Sent Mr. Priest of Norwich by Cary this Evening a fine Hare caught this Afternoon near my House. Nancy also sent by him a very, very long Letter to her Brother Bill at New York in N. America in Answer to one from him to her lately recd.

Dec. 21. . . . To poor People of Weston today being St. Thomas Day for some thing against Christmas as usual on this Day, and which I hope always to do —gave o. 16. o. About Noon went out with my People a coursing—stayed till after 3 o'clock—had but little Sport tho' we brought home a fine young Hare. Cobb the Rat-Catcher was here to day and he dined with our Folks in Kitchen. He came whilst I was out, found him at home on my return after being here near 4 Hours. I was not pleased and informed him when I wanted him again that I would send to him.

Dec. 24. . . . To Widow Horner for Hulver [Holly] agains[t] Xmas Day gave 1. o. The same as I used to give to her late Husband. Paid Will for things from Norwich &c. o. 8. 7.

Dec. 25. . . . This being Christmas Day I went to

Church this Morn' and then read Prayers and administred the Holy Sacrament. Mr. and Mrs. Custance both at Church and both received the Sacrament from my Hands. The following poor old Men dined at my House to day, as usual, Js. Smith, Clerk, Richd Bates, Richd Buck ; Thos. Cary ; Thos. Dicker ; Thos. Cushing ; Thos. Carr—to each besides gave 1/0—in all 0. 7. 0. I gave them for Dinner a Surloin of Beef rosted and plenty of plumb-Pudding. We had mince Pies for the first Time to-day.

Dec. 26. . . . To Weston Ringers gave this morning 0. 2. 6. To my Butchers Boy, Billy Stouton gave 0. 1. 0. To my Blacksmiths Boy, Charles Spaule gave 0. 1. 0. To my Malsters Man, J^s Barrett gave 0. 1. 0.

Dec. 27. . . . About 12 went out a coursing, ran two good Courses and killed one of the Hares which Jack found sitting and for which I gave him as usual 0. 1. 0. My young Greyhound Hector performed incomparably.

Dec. 30. . . . Sent Mr. Smith this morning early a fine young Hare and a Note with it—Had one in return with thanks. About 1 o'clock Mr. Howes, with Mrs. Davy and her 2 Children Betsy and Nunn came to our House and they dined and spent part of the Afternoon with us. About 4 this Afternoon they returned to Hockering all but Betsy Davy, who is to spend a few Days with Nancy. We had nothing for Dinner but a small bit of boiled Beef, a Breast of Veal rosted and some mince Pies. Betsy Davy supped and slept with Nancy to night.

Jan. 1. . . . Just as we had finished Dinner Nunn Davy, Betsy's Brother called here, eat a Mince Pye, drank a glass of Wine and returned to Hockering. He brought some Salve for Betsy's Chilblains, Mr. Howes Servant Man came with him. To Betsy Davy this Evening gave a New Years Gift which was a pretty Half Crown of George 2nd 2. 6. Made Nancy also a Present of a new Years Gift this Evening of five Guineas 5. 5. 0. bitter cold all Day with Snow and hard Frost after.

Jan. 2. . . . Nunn Davy called here just as we had dined to see his Sister, he brought some Salve for Betsy's Feet. He eat a mince Pye, drank one Glass of Wine and was of.

Jan. 4. . . . To poor old Joe Adcocks Wife who very lately fell down and broke her Thigh—sent her by Will 0. 1. 0.

Jan. 7. I breakfasted, and spent most of the Morn' at home. Nancy breakfasted, and spent part of the Morn' at home. Betsy Davy breakfasted, and spent part of the Morn' here. Mrs. Davy breakfasted with us this morning. As soon as the Ladies had breakfasted, they set of for Norwich and Nancy with them. I stayed till near 12 before I set forth for Norwich and my Servant Will: went with me—We all went by appointment to Mr. Priests and there dined, supped and spent the Evening. Mrs. Davy and Nancy slept at Mr. Priests. I slept at my old Inn the Kings Head. Mr. Du Quesne dined, supped and slept at Mr. Priests. We had for Dinner some fresh Salmon and Oyster Sauce, a boiled Turkey and Oyster Sauce, a fore Qr. of London Lamb, mince Pyes, &c. Mrs. Cooper, Miss Blomfield, Mr. and

Mrs. Fearman, Mr. Reeves, Mr. Starkey, and Mr. Mully drank Tea this Afternoon with us at Mr. Priests and all stayed to Supper but Mrs. Cooper and Miss Blomfield. After Tea we had a vocal and instrumental Concert—Nancy sung. Mr. Du Quesne, Mr. Reeves, Mr. Starkey and Mr. John Priest played on their violins. Mr. Fearman on the Base-Viol and Mr. Mulley on the Organ—a very good Concert. We did not sup till near 10 at night—and then we had a very handsome supper—A Couple of boiled Fowls and Oyster Sauce, a rosted Hare wch I sent them— one Duck rosted, a hot Tongue, Tarts, Italian Flummery—Blamanche black Caps and sweet-Meats. I did not get to bed till after 12 to-night. Gave Mr. Priests Maid coming away 0. 1. 0. Sent Dr. Bathurst a Letter to day and in it Bills to the amount of forty Pounds.

Jan. 8. . . . After breakfast I went to Mr. Priests, and then I went with Mr. Priest, Mr. Du Quesne, Mrs. Davy and Betsy, and Nancy to see a wonderful Phœnomena in Nature a Heifer 3 years old with two distinct Heads and quite perfect Horns, Eyes, Mouths, &c. It chewed the Cud in both Mouths and eat with both at the same Time. We treated the Ladies which cost us apiece 0. 1. 0. After that we walked back to Mr. Priests and there we parted. I went by myself about the City, a shopping—For 2 Decanters p^d 0. 6. 0. To 6 small Tumblers p^d 0. 2. 0. To 2 very small Tumblers p^d 0. 0. 6. To a little Basket to carry them home p^d 0. 0. 6. At Chases for a Play called the Foundling p^d 0. 0. 6. At Allums Sadler p^d a Bill of 0. 12. 6. To Mileham Barbor p^d for a Wig 1. 1. 0. Called at Mr. Francis's and paid him some Quit Rents that I had recd. for him of 3. 7. 0.

My Servant Lad, Jack went with the Chaise yesterday to Norwich and dined and slept at the Kings Head. He went to be measured for some new Cloaths, &c. We had for Dinner to day at Priests, a boiled Pike, a Turkey rosted, Tarts, &c. &c. We had for Supper some cold Turkey, Ham, &c. &c. Mr. Priest and self went this Evening with Mrs. Davy, Betsy and Nancy to a Play which was a Comedy, Womans a Riddle—The Farce was the Anatomist—both very droll. Very little Company indeed at the Play. I treated Mrs. Davy and Nancy—Betsy had the Mayors Silver Ticket—I p^d for 3—0. 9. 0. I paid also for a Coach for the Ladies 0. 3. 0. From the Play I returned with the Ladies to Mr. Priests and supped there—stayed there till near 11 o'clock and then went away. Gave this Evening to a poor Person 0. 0. 6.

Jan. 11. . . . But very poorly all day—no Appetite at all. Expected much a Letter from my Sister Pounsett this Even' but had none—It was a great disappointment to me.

Jan. 13. . . . This Evening paid all my Servants their Years Wages [1]—due January 6, 1783.

To my Head Maid, Betty Claxton p^d .	5.	15.	6
„ „ Lower „ Lizzy Greaves p^d .	2.	0.	6
„ „ Man Will: Coleman p^d . .	4.	4.	0
To Ditto for Grains p^d . . .		17.	0
To Ditto for dressing my Wiggs p^d .		10.	0
To Ditto what he owed me I gave .	1.	1.	0
To my Farming Man Ben Leggatt p^d .	10.	0.	0
To my Boy, Jack Warton . . .		10.	6
Gave to him besides as a free gift .		2.	6

[1] The reader will find some observations on wages, prices, and the cost of living at this period in vol. i, pp. 71–3.

Jan. 14. . . . This being Mr. Howes's Rotation Day, he sent his Chaise after Nancy about 2 o'clock, and Betsy Davy came in it after her—I went with them on Horseback and there we dined and spent the Afternoon with Mr Howes, Mrs. Davy, Mr. and Mrs. Bottom, Mr. Smith, Betsy and Nunn Davy. We had for Dinner a Cods Head, a Leg of Mutton boiled, a Turkey rosted and mince Pies. At Quadrille this Evening won 0. 1. 0. which I gave to Nunn Davy. Mr. Du Quesne could not be there as Mr. Townshends Audit was this Day, and he at Honingham. Nancy returned home in Mr. Howes's Chaise by herself. Mrs. Davy never came to the Chaise Door with her when she came away, but stayed in the Parlour. We got home safe and well (thank God) by 9 o'clock. Paid Nancy for Cambrick &c. brought for me at Norwich 0. 7. 6.

Jan. 18. . . . My Study Grate pleases me much, no smoking. To Mr. Hardy for 2 Days Work and Man p^d 0. 5. 6. To Do. for Allowance for Beer and Man 2 Days 0. 1. 0. Doubleday, who is putting up some new Barns Doors for me, dined with our Folks today. Advanced this Evening to Js. Smith, himself and Son being hedging and ditching for me 0. 10. 6.

Jan. 19. . . . I read Prayers and Preached this Morning at Weston. Mr. and Mrs. Custance with Lady Bacon at Church. Mr. Hardy dined with our Folks to day. I gave my Head Maid, Betty, leave to go and see her Brother at Sr Wm Jernegans[1] this Afternoon, she is to stay 2 or 3 Days there—My Man Ben carried her. Sent to old Mary Adcock who very lately broke her thigh, a hot rosted Fowl, a fourpenny Loaf and a Bottle of Beer.

[1] See foot-note, p. 49, preceding.

1783

Jan. 24. . . . Nancy was low at Dinner owing to me—
Was sorry for it.

Jan. 25. . . . This Evening the Ipswich News brought
us the joyful News of Peace being signed at Ver-
sailles the 20 of this month and recd. at London
the 25. No mention of the same in either of the
Norwich Papers. The above Peace is with America,
France and Spain, but not with the Dutch—Tho'
daily expected by them.[1]

Jan. 26. . . . Thos. Carr dined with our Folks to day.
I read Prayers and Preached this Afternoon at
Weston. Mr. Custance and a Mrs. Collier, an
elderly Lady, at Church. Sent old Mary Adcock at
Noon—a hot rosted Fowl, a fourpenny Loaf and a
Bottle of Beer.

---

[1] The provisional articles of peace between England, France, and Spain
were signed on 20 January 1783, the similar articles with the United
States having been signed on 30 November 1782. The preliminary
treaty of peace between Great Britain and Holland was not signed till
2 September 1783, but long before this a truce had put an end to hostilities
between English and Dutch. Thanks to Lord Rodney's victory (see
foot-note, p. 25, preceding), to differences between the Americans
and the French, to the skilful diplomacy of the Prime Minister, Lord
Shelburne, in London, and of his representative in Paris—Mr. Alleyne
FitzHerbert (afterwards Lord St. Helens)—the peace was better than it
might have been. We lost America and Minorca ; we gave up Florida ;
we restored various conquests in Africa to France, and in India to France
and the Dutch. On the other hand, we recovered six West Indian islands,
and we retained Canada and Gibraltar—both, at one time during the
negotiations, in jeopardy. Horace Walpole in his letters at this time,
said with his usual sense : ' When I do learn all the articles, I intend to
like all, for I must be so fair as to say that they will be better than I expected we should ever obtain.' Again : ' I am content with peace in
the lump.' See for full details, Lecky, *England in the Eighteenth Century*,
vol. v, pp. 184–205 ; Lord Fitzmaurice's *Shelburne*, vol. ii, chaps. iv, v,
and vi ; Walpole's *Letters*, vol. xii, pp. 390–8.

1783

Feb. 5. . . . To a poor old Man with a Dulcimer gave
0. 0. 6.

Feb. 7. . . . Sent a very long Letter to my Sister
Pounsett. Very wet Season indeed, every Day
Rain, my Garden almost covered with Water—every
Ditch brim full.

Feb. 10. . . . To Ben this Evening for a Horse which
he bought this morning for me of John Norton, a
short dark Punchy Horse with a Hog main and
dock'd Tail aged 10 Years next Midsummer, and one
that bears a very good Character in the draft Way
and one that is very hardy and always kept so p^d
Ben 4. 4. 0.

Feb. 11. . . . Mrs. Custance with her 3 little Boys and
Hetty Yollop their Nurse made us an early morning
visit and stayed with us till after 12 o'clock.

Feb. 12. . . . Nancy alarmed me in the Night about
1 o'clock by sending Betty to wake me and to tell me
that she heard People coming into the House at the
back Door, upon which I got immediately up, and
Will, Ben, and myself went down Stairs to the back
door opened and went out, but saw nor heard anything. I soon went to bed again as did all the rest.
The Dogs without nor within made the lest noise.
My Head Maid Betty went up to Mr. Custances this
Afternoon being invited there to a Frolic given on
Account of Mr. Custance's Eldest Sons Birth Day,
and there she stayed and supped and spent the
Evening till after 11 o'clock. I sent Jack after her
at night.

Feb. 14. I breakfasted, dined, supped and slept again
at home. Nancy breakfasted and spent the morning
at home and [at] 2 o'clock Mr. Custance's Coach
came after her to go and spend a few Days with

Mrs. Custance during Mr. Custance's absence— I was invited to dinner but I desired Nancy to apologise for my not going. To 68 Valentines to Day gave o. 5. 8. Nancy dined, supped and slept at Mr. Custances.

Feb. 17. . . . I walked out after breakfast with my Folks a coursing and was out from ½ past 10 in the morning till ½ past 4 in the Afternoon and we saw but 1 hare all the Time and that just at last—She got up so far before the Greyhounds, that they had no chance with her. Mr. Hardy joined us and he dined here. Mrs. Custance and Nancy called at my House whilst I was out this morning. Nancy came after her Habit, &c.

Feb. 20. . . . Nancy breakfasted, dined and spent part of the Afternoon at Weston House and in the Evening she was brought home in Mr. Custance's Coach and supped and slept once more at the Parsonage. Mr. Custance came home to Dinner to day. Mr. Custance sent by Nancy to me this Evening a very handsome Register for the Parish, the old one being almost out—It is a small Folio of 59 Leaves of Parchment interleaved with blank Paper bound in red Morocco Leather, handsomely gilt and lettered and in a handsome Russia Leather Case, tyed with garter blue Ribband. It is a very handsome Present to the Parish of Weston. Foster came to me this morning about a Piece of Charity Land belonging to Ringland, tho' in this Parish and adjoining to Foster's Land mine—that if I had a mind for it, he would not oppose me. I told him that he might do as he pleases that I shd. bid for it—but wd have no favour from him, after his late Behaviour, I also told him that his Tithes after this year be taken in hand.

1783

Feb. 23. ... I read Prayers and Preached this Afternoon at Weston. Neither Mr. or Mrs. Custance at Church —After Sermon I desired the principal Parishioners to wait a few minutes, and shewed them what an handsome present Mr Custance had made them in giving them a new Register. They were highly pleased and desired me to return thanks.

Feb. 24. . . . Washing Week and but indifferent Weather. I sent Ben to Ringland about 2 o'clock to bid for some Charity Land adjoining to me about 15 Acres which was put up to be let to the best bidder—I told Ben to bid no more than 13. 10. 0— which with 3/0 an acre for tithe would make it 1. 1. 0. Pr Acre—We could not get it—One Hardy of Honingham, Mason, hired it for 16. 5. 0. Pr Annum and for 14 Years—One Dobbs of Ringland and Burroughs of Morton bid also for it.

Feb. 26. ... Mr Howes and Mrs Davy came here about 2 o'clock, and they dined and spent the afternoon with us. Mr Howes went home about 5 o'clock and Mrs. Davy was left here to spend a day or two with Nancy. We had for Dinner a piece of boiled Neck of Pork and greens and a Shoulder of Mutton rosted. Mrs. Davy supt and slept with Nancy. It was a very severe Frost all Day, much the coldest Day this Year or the last—It snowed thick in the Morning. I could not have thought that either Mr Howes or Mrs Davy would have ventured out such Weather. I buried a little girl of Neighbour Goochs this Evening at Weston—her name was Judith and but 4 Years old. She was taken in a violent Fever all at once on the 18 Instant and continued worse and worse till Monday Morn and then poor Soul expired—She complained all the Time of nothing else but a violent Pain in her Thigh.

1783

March 2. . . . I read Prayers and Preached this morning
at Weston. Mr Custance at Church, tho' he has a
bad Cold. After Service at Weston I walked home,
drank a small glass of warm white wine and eat a bit
of baked bread, and then walked to Mattishall with
my Servant Man Will: Coleman with me, and there
read Prayers, Preached and christened a Child by
name Hannah, for Mr Smith. It was terrible bad
walking and very cold but very fair over-head—Frost
and Snow on the Ground, wch on the Suns thawing
it, made it bad travelling. I was at Mr Smiths but
did not stay long there, and neither eat or drank, or
was any offered to me. I did not get home till near
6 in the Evening. We did not dine till near 6 o'clock
this Evening. The cold air got into my stomach and
made me very ill all day long—My Boots also made
one of my Heels very sore, and almost lamed me.
I was very glad when I returned home, but could eat
very little for Dinner, as I found myself very fainting,
but I thank God, did not faint and tolerable before
Bedtime. I carried a little Geneva with me in a
little Flask—but as soon as I sat down at Mr Smiths,
I broke my flask-Bottle and lost all my Geneva.
March 5. . . . Much colder than yesterday—Wind
much higher and Frost more severe—The coldest
Day for some years. I was very low and indifferent
all day long. The Barometer very low, and the
Wind being very rough when I went up to my
Chamber to go to bed, being not the lest sleepy,
I lighted my Fire, and sat down and read the Life of
Lewis 14 of France till after 2 o'clock in the morning
and then went to bed, the Wind still high. I heard
some Noise between one and two but it did [not] last.
March 6. . . . The first thing I was informed of when

I came down stairs, was, that my Stable had been broken up, in the Night and that there was stolen out of it, a Hatchet, a Hook, a Bridle, and a pair of hedging Gloves of Bens. There was seen Yesterday a Couple of idle Fellows passing and repassing my House, I saw them once go by, one of them was in a long blue Coat, the other in a brown one. They came in at the back Window of the Stable, which they cut away, to wrench it open with a large stick wch was found just by, they left behind them a P^r of Sheep Sheers broke directly in the middle—They also took Bens Cart Whip, which they left on the Muck-heap. I think myself well of, in having so few things stolen as there were so many in the Stable and in the Corn Room. I sent for Harry Dunnell to mend the Window and to John Spaule to make some new iron work for the same, all which were done by the Evening and all right again. Harry Dunnell dined with our Folks and for his work to day I gave him 0. 1. 0. There were several Stables in the Parish broke into besides mine last night, Peachmans, Bucks, Widow Pratts, Manns and Forsters—and several things stolen. Nancy was very much alarmed on hearing the above. I did not go to bed to Night till after 12 o'clock.

Mar: 7. . . . Memorandum—The Barometer yesterday (which I forgot to mention in Yesterday's Notes) was lower than ever I remember it to be, it being below every Mark on it by about two divisional Lines— that is—27–18—Now no Barometer is marked at all below 28. I was remarkably low all the whole day yesterday. N:B: the Barometer continued to be as low as above described, from the Time I got up Yesterday till 10 at Night. To Sam: Wright who

The first thing that I was informed of when I came down
Stairs, was, that my Stable had been broken up, in the Night
and that there was stolen out of it, a Hatchet, a Hook,
a Bridle, and a pair of hedging Gloves of Ben's ———
There was seen yesterday a Couple of idle fellows passing
and repassing my House, I saw them once go by, one of them
was in a long blue Coat, the other in a brown one ——
They came in at the back Window of the Stable, which
they cut away, to wrench it open with a large stick w^{ch}
was found just by, they left behind them a p^r of Sheep
Shears broke directly in the middle — They also took
Ben's Cart Whip, which they left on the Muck-heap —
I think myself well off in having so few things stolen
as there were so many in the Stable & in the Corn Room
I sent for Harry Dunnell to mend the Windward to
John Spencer to make some new Iron work for the same
all which were done by the Evening & all tight again ——
Harry Dunnell dined with our Folks and for his
work to day I gave him ——   0:1:0
There were several Stables in the Parish broke into
besides mine last night, Peachmans, Buchs, Widow
Pratts, Maxes, and Loosters — and several things stolen —
Nancy was very much alarmed on hearing the above ——
I did not go to bed to night till after 12. o'clock ——

Mar: 7 — I breakfasted, dined, supped & slept again at home —
Nancy breakfasted, dined &c. &c. — again at home —
Memorandum — The Barometer yesterday (which I forgot
to mention in yesterday's Notes) was lower than ever I
remember it to be, it being below every Mark on it by
about two divisional lines — that is 27 — 18 — now no
Barometer is marked at all below 28 ——
I was remarkably low all the whole day yesterday —
N:B: the Barometer continued to be as low as above
described, from the Time I got up yesterday till 10 at Night —
Jo Sam: tonight who brought me my Hook that was stolen
and which he found in his Yard — I gave —0:1:0
the Hook being marked, the Rogues did not chuse to carry
away far, for fear of their being discovered ——
Mr Custance's Servant brought me 2 Letters to day from
Honor &c. — 1. from my Sister Bassett who mentions
that Mr Clarke, was married to Miss Daws of Ditcheat,
and Mr Tom Barge to the Widow Whitehead &c. &c. ?
the other from Dev^d Metz concerning an old Servt
one George Hutchins that lived with me at the Lower
House in the Year — 1760 — how long he lived wth me &c.

Mar: 8 — I breakfasted, dined, supped & slept again at home —
Nancy breakfasted, dined &c. &c. — again at home —
My Hatchet was also found this morning in my Ditch
in the Yard in the Yard — found by my Boy Jack —
Mrs Custance made us a morning Visit to day ——

brought me my Hook that was stolen and which he
found in his yard,—I gave o. 1. o. The Hook being
marked, the Rogues did not chuse to carry away far,
for fear of their being discovered. Mr Custance's
Servant brought me 2 Letters to Day from Norwich—
1 from my Sister Pounsett who mentions that
J^s Clarke was married to Miss Dawe of Ditcheat, and
Mr Tom Burge to the Widow Whitehead &c. The
other from David Maby concerning an old Servt one
George Hutchins that lived with me at the Lower
House in the year—1768—how long he lived wth
me &c.

Mar: 8. . . . To a poor Boy by Name Allison of Lyng,
turned out of doors by his Parents as he says—gave
this Even' o. o. 6. A change of the Ministry will soon
take place as mentioned on the Papers—Ld North
and Charles Fox have shook hands—O North, how
low art thou fallen.[1]

---

[1] This is the only heartfelt political ejaculation which Parson Woodforde has hitherto permitted himself in his Diary : it is noteworthy that
it should be reserved for the coalition of Charles James Fox and Lord
North in 1783, for it suggests that hatred of peace-time coalitions is
a fundamental part of the English character. The coalition was, indeed,
very shameless. Fox had denounced North throughout his administration in terms of almost incredible ferocity : ' from the moment ', he had
said, ' when I shall make any terms with one of them [the North adminis-
tration], I will rest satisfied to be called the most infamous of mankind.'
A year had passed, and behold Fox (who hated Lord Shelburne beyond
measure) combining with North to defeat the Government over the just
concluded peace ! They neither could, nor would upset the peace, but
they determined to condemn it. The coalition of North's Tories and
Fox's Whigs became effectual in the House of Commons in February 1783,
and on 24 February Lord Shelburne was compelled to resign. Still,
George III turned with disgust from the coalition of two men, one of
whom (Fox) he hated almost on principle, and the other (North), he now
hated because he held he had deserted him a year ago. From 24 February

1783

Mar: 11. . . . To one Chapman of great Witchingham, who lost all that he had almost by a Fire last Week gave 0. 5. 0. I gave him also for Dr. Bathurst 0. 10. 6. I gave him also for Nancy 0. 2. 6. Nancy was very ill to day, vomited very much in the Evening just before she went to bed. Was better after.

Mar: 20. . . . Nancy and myself dined, spent the afternoon and part of the Evening till 8 o'clock at Weston House, with M^r and Mrs Custance and Mr Press Custance—Mr Custance sent his Coach after us, and we returned in the same—We had for Dinner a rosted Pike, Rump of Beef boiled, a Beef Stake Pye, Mutton Stakes and rosted Bullock's Heart. 2nd Course—Frill'd Oysters, a rost Fowl, Pudding, Rammakins. After Tea we played at Loo at which I lost 0. 6. 6.

Mar: 23. . . . I read Prayers and Preached this Afternoon at Weston. I buried this Evening at Weston poor old Thos Reeves commonly called Dr Reeves— aged 71 years. Mrs. Davy came here about 7 in the Evening in Mr Howes's Chaise and she supped and slept here as did the Driver and the Horses—She came here by appointment this Evening to carry Nancy with her to Norwich early in the Morning to see the Grand Procession of Bishop Blaize &c.[1] It was very kind of her indeed. No Person besides ever gave her the most distant offer. And if Mrs Davy

to 2 April 1783, England was without a ministry, while the king vainly turned here and there for an alternative government. He failed, and on 2 April Fox and North became Secretaries of State, with the Duke of Portland as nominal Prime Minister. For full detail of these transactions, see Lecky, *England in the Eighteenth Century*, vol. v, pp. 205–20, and Fitzmaurice's *Shelburne*, vol. ii, chap. vii.

[1] See foot-note to next entry.

had not been so kind, she could not have gone, as I could not by myself have made it agreeable to Nancy without some Lady being with her.

Mar: 24. . . . About 6 o'clock this Morning we all got up to go to Norwich and after breakfast we set forth at 8 o'clock, Mrs Davy and Nancy in the Chaise, myself on Horseback, Will, Ben and Lizzy on horseback, Jack went behind the Chaise as I was willing that all sh^d go that could. Betty, my Upper Maid stayed at home being Washing Week. We all got to Norwich about 10 o'clock—The Road we went was filled with People on Horseback and foot, going to see the fine Sight—Ben carried Lizzy behind him on Phyllis and the first Time she ever carried any one, double, and she carried her very well and safe, to Norwich and back again. I put up my Horses at the Kings Head—Mrs Davy and Nancy were at Mr Priests. The grand Procession began about 11 o'clock this morning—I saw them first beyond Black Friars Bridge near St. Saviours Church and a very pretty and grand Sight it was. The Order of the Procession was as follows.

Four Trumpeters
Marshal-Man
Peace
Orator
Banner of Brittania
Plenty
Drums and Fifes
20 Argonauts
Hercules

Lynceus ⎧   The Golden Fleece   ⎫ Tiphy[s]
Zetes   ⎨ borne on a grand Palanquin ⎬ Calais
       ⎩   by four Men   ⎭

Castor { Jason drawn in a Phaeton
by four Horses } Pollux

Standard of the Argonauts

20 Argonauts

Militia Band

Standard of the City

Two Vergers

Orator

{ Bishop's Chaplain
in a Phaeton and Pair }

{ Bishop Blaize
in a Phaeton drawn by 6 Horses }

Standard of the City.

The book-keepers, Shepherds and Shepherdesses belonging to the different Societies of Combers 12 Companies—Seven Companies on foot—Five Companies on Horseback.

Mr. and Mrs. Custance, Sr Edmund Bacon and Lady at the Kings Head, I called on them about 11 o'clock, and gave them an Account of the grand Sight and eft with them a Paper of the Procession. I never saw so great a Multitude of People in my Life collected together, the Market-Place was as full as it could be, both in the area, at the Windows and on the Tops of the Houses—and every Street besides full of People from all Parts of the County. The Procession proceeded thro' every principal Street of the City and it lasted till 4 in the Afternoon. We eat some cold Ham and Veal at Mr Priests about 2. A Mrs Goddard an old Maid, Du Quesne's Maid Betty and a Miss High with her in Du Quesne's Chaise were at Mr. Priests, as was Miss Priest of Reepham. About ½ past 4 we all set forth for Weston and got home about 7 o'clock, rather fatigued. Mem: Just without the Gates Mr Howes's Chaise broke down, one of the Axle-Trees being broke, which my Servant Boy Jack, behind the Chaise, found out—but luckily for it we were near Mr Howes's Coach Maker, a Mr Baldwin, who lent them a carriage leaving the old Shatterdan behind to be mended. Paid and gave to day at Norwich abt. 2. 6. We were all highly delighted indeed with this Days Sight—it far exceeded every Idea I c^d have of it. Hercules, Jason, and Bishop Blaize, were exceedingly well kept up and very superbly dressed. All the Combers were in white ruffled Shirts with Cross-Belts of Wool of divers Colours—with Mitred Caps on their heads— The Shepherds and Shepherdesses were little Boys and Girls on horseback, very handsomely and [with] great Propriety dressed. Orations spoke in most of the principal Streets. I never saw a Procession so grand and well conducted.[1]

---

[1] This grand procession was a combined celebration of the conclusion of peace, and of the patron saint of the Norwich woollen trade—Bishop Blaise. The legend of Bishop Blaise is this. He was Bishop of Sebaste in Armenia, and perished sometime between A. D. 289 and 316 in one of the persecutions of the Christians. He had fled to a cave. There he was fed by the birds whom he healed of any illness, and was adored by all the wild beasts, lions and tigers, who always waited quietly till the saint had finished his devotions before asking his benediction. Soon he was dragged from his cave by the persecutors. On his way to his trial he performed two miracles. He extracted a fishbone from the throat of a child who was choking to death, and he caused a wolf to restore a poor woman's only pig. He perished after frightful tortures, among them his flesh being torn with iron combs, ' such as are used to card wool '. He became one of the ' Fourteen Holy Helpers ' invoked by the faithful—his feast day was 3 February—and enjoyed a remarkable popularity in the Middle Ages in England, France, Germany, and Italy. He was the patron saint of woolcombers, whether at Norwich, at Paris, or

1783

Mar: 31. . . . Bottled of my Gin this morning, 2 Q^{rt} Bottles of true Measure deficient, a Tub ought to run 20 Bottles—this only 18. Very indifferent all Day I have been and very comical.

Apl: 3. . . . Very fine Day quite hot at Noon—As the Weather is so fine, must give away, I believe, 3 Acres of Turnips—they being now worth little or nothing any where else. I refused 5 Pound for them in December of Mr Girling which as Times turned out contrary to what was expected I had better had then closed with him—But then Turnips were worth 40 shillings Per Acre—And Mr Howes gave 3 P^d per Acre for them.

April 8. . . . We dined and spent the Afternoon and part of the Evening till 9 o'clock at Mr Custances with him, Mrs Custance, and Mrs Goodall widow of Dr Goodall, Mr Prideaux and his Brother Charles Prideaux, both Cornish Gentlemen of great Fortune and both very agreeable Men—Mrs. Goodall a squinting old Lady, sensible but very bold and rather satirical. We had for Dinner—first course— Fish, a Piece of rosted Beef, Mutton Stakes, Pork Stakes, Peas Soup, Potatoes baked, and a Yorkshire

---

at Rome, and he was invoked for all ailments of the throat. (See the detailed and charming account of Bishop Blaise by Miss Ella B. Edes in the *Dublin Review*, 1889, vol. xxii, pp. 340-6.)

The other characters in the grand procession—Jason, Hercules, Castor and Pollux, Lynceus, Zetes, Tiphys, Calais—are there because they went in search of the Golden Fleece together with the other Argonauts. Time was when Norwich streets had been gay on various festivals with the procession of twenty companies of different crafts with patron saints, banners and beauty. Bishop Blaise of the woolcombers, who so delighted Parson Woodforde, alone enjoyed this resurrection of medieval glory, sharing it with the wistful return of Peace. (Blomefield, *History of Norfolk*, vol. iii, p. 206, contains a list of the twenty city companies.)

Pudding—2nd Course—Fricasied Fowl, a rosted Pigg,
Jellies, Tartlets, Lobster, Pickled Salmon, and Cheesecakes. After Tea and Coffee, I played a Pool of
Quadrille, with Mrs Goodall, Charles Prideaux and
Nancy—at 3^d p^r Fish. At which I lost all that was
lost being o. 2. o. Mr Custance sent his Coach after
us and we returned home in it.

April 10. . . . Mr Howes was this Day married to his
4th Wife, a Mrs Brown.

April 11. . . . Mrs. Davy sent us some bride-Cake this
morning from Hockering and with a Note to Nancy.

April 14. . . . Mrs. Davy drank Tea this Afternoon with
us, and about 7 o'clock in the Evening returned to
Hockering and Nancy went with her to spend a day
or 2 there.

April 15. I breakfasted, supped and slept again at
home. To Mr Alldridge (who travels the Country
with a Cart of Goods) for 6 y^ds of dark Cotton p^d
o. 12. o. Nancy still at Mr Howes's at Hockering.
At 1 o'clock took a ride to Hockering to Mr Howes's
and there dined and spent the Afternoon with
Mr Howes, his new Wife an agreeable Woman enough,
Mrs Davy, Nancy, M^r and Mrs Bodham and Mr Smith.
Miss Bodham also dined &c. there. We had for
Dinner a Piece of boiled Beef, a Fillet of Veal rosted
and some Bacon, some Mutton Chops, a baked
Pudding, Pye and Custards. After Tea we played
Quadrille at which I won o. 4. o. I got home to
Weston about ½ past 9 this Evening.

April 17. . . . Mrs Custance and Mrs Goodall with her
made us a morning Visit—stayed with us about half
an Hour. As soon almost as they were gone Mr Custance called on us, and stayed with us near about the
same time. Nancy took a Vomit this Evening just

before she went to bed by order of Dr Thorne who sent it. Mr Pyle (whose men are at work for me) dined with our Folks.

April 22. . . . This being my Rotation Day I sent Will early this Morning to Norwich after some Fish and he returned about 11 o'clock with a Cod's Head and Shoulders and Oysters. To old Goody Doughty for some Oranges and Lemons pd. o. 1. 6. Very wet, very cold and wind excessive high almost the whole Day throughout—very tempestuous sometimes. The Weather being so very bad, I had but few at my Rotation, only M^r and Mrs Howes, Mrs Davy and M^r Du Quesne. None of the Matishall Folks came or could be well expected of them—which I am sorry for. I gave the Company that did come for Dinner, Cod and Oyster Sauce, a Piece of rost Beef, a currant Pudding, a Couple of Fowls and Asparagus, Custards and Jellies. At Quadrille this Evening after Tea— won o. 2. o. Abt. 8 o'clock my Company left us and the Evening was rather more calm than the rest of the Day. Du Quesne looked very hearty and well after his Journey—He has got at last a Prebendarick Stall in the Church of Ely worth £300 Pr Annum.[1]

April 26. . . . This Evening on the Norwich Paper an Account of the Death of our Bishop Dr Philip Younge, who died Wednesday last at his House in London, of the Stone and Gravel, and who was many

---

[1] Mr. Du Quesne almost certainly owed this plum of preferment to the Archbishop of Canterbury—Dr. Cornwallis—who was the brother-in-law of Mr. Charles Townshend, Mr. Du Quesne's Squire at Honingham (see foot-note, vol. i, p. 318). I find from *Alumni Cantabrigienses*, by J. and J. A. Venn, that Mr. Du Quesne—Thos. Roger—was educated at Eton and King's College, Cambridge, of which college he was a Scholar and Fellow (1741). From 1756 to his death in 1793 he was a country parson in Norfolk.

years afflicted in that Disorder.—He was a Man much beloved by his Clergy. Pray God ! grant Relief to all who labour under so dreadful a Disorder—And happiness to those who die of it.[1]

April 30. . . . About 1 o'clock took a ride to Mr Smiths at Mattishall and there dined and spent the Afternoon, it being his Rotation Day, with him, Mr. and Mrs Bodham, Miss Bodham, a Miss Kitty Johnson, Niece of Mrs Bodham's, Mr. and Mrs. Howes, and M^r Du Quesne.—Mrs. Davy not there but at Dereham, on account of a little Miff between her and Mr Smith—but what, we know not. We had for Dinner a Leg of Lam[b] boiled, a Piece of rosted Beef, a baked plumb Pudding, some Crabbs, Tarts, Rasberry Creams, and hung Beef, grated. I called on Dr Thorne before Dinner, saw his Wife, Garden and House—all very neat indeed but small. At Quadrille this Evening won o. 4. o. I played the finest Sans Prendre Vole to Night, that I ever had— Not a loosing Card in hand—It was Mattadores,

---

[1] Dr. Philip Yonge (1710–83) does not appear to have been a very distinguished bishop, if the absence of a notice of him in the *D. N. B.* is any indication. He was a Fellow of Trinity College, Cambridge, was made Master of Jesus College in 1752, was at various dates Public Orator and Vice Chancellor, and in 1758 was promoted to the Bishopric of Bristol, from whence in November 1761, he went to Norwich. He owed his promotion to the episcopal bench to that great creator of bishops, the Duke of Newcastle, who made a great deal of use of him in connexion with academic patronage, promotions, and appointments in the University of Cambridge, of which the duke was Chancellor. In personal appearance the bishop bears an uncanny resemblance to Queen Victoria— see his portrait in Mr. Winstanley's *The University of Cambridge in the Eighteenth Century.* From that work and from Le Neve's *Fasti* the above brief particulars of the bishop are gleaned. ' He was a man much beloved by his Clergy '—Parson Woodforde's tribute perhaps makes up for the absence of a *D. N. B.* notice.

9 black Trumps in Spades and the King of Hearts—
I was the last Player ; after the first Card was played,
I declared the Vole. I did not get home to Weston
till 10 at Night.

May 1. ... The 2 Fellows who were suspected breaking
open my Stable and many others, were tried this
Day at the Sessions at Norwich and convicted of the
Robbery of stealing a Sack from Mr Howlett and are
to remain in Prison for three years—which I hope
will do good.

May 5. ... Nancy quite ill this morning by the Wind
in her stomach—It is unlucky as she is going out.
Dr Thorne called here this Morning about 12 o'clock
but did not see Nancy as she was dressing to go out.
Dr Thorne bled my Servant Willm, this morning as
he often complains of a giddiness in his head.—He
had also some Powders to take for a Day or two. ...

May 6. ... To a Man who comes from Windham and
carries about stuffs for Gowns &c. for 27 yards and
half at 9^d per yard p^d 1. 0. 6. Gave both my Maids a
Gown apiece of it and of the same Colour, something
of the Pea Green. Gave Nancy also, to make a Skirt
for her of a light blue 6 y^ds. Nancy much better to
day tho' not quite well yet. Cobb the Rat-Catcher
dined with our Folks to day. We caught and killed
about 3 Dozen of Rats in the Barn before Dinner
to day—3 old female Rats with their young ones—
2 old dog Rats and some half grown.

May 13. ... I was very much alarmed this morning
about 11 o'clock, in feeling a kind of numbness in
my left Hand, and likewise that part of my Tongue
affected, it continued some time till near 1 o'clock.
I took some Hartshorn Drops in Water directly
almost. It made me very low on the occasion all the

Day long. About 1 o'clock myself and Nancy took a ride to Mr Bodhams at Mattishall and there dined and spent the Afternoon and part of the Evening till 8 o'clock and then we rode back to Weston again as we went that is, Nancy went behind Ben on Phyllis, I rode my Mare and Will had the little Mare. I sent Will to Dr Thornes when at Mattishall for him to come to Mr Bodhams to me, but he was from home. M^r and Mrs Howes, Mrs Davy, Miss Bodham, Miss Johnson, Mr Smith and us dined with M^r and Mrs Bodham this being Mr Bodhams Rotation—Du Quesne not there, being gone a long Tour in the North &c. We had for Dinner some Maccarell, a Piece of boiled Beef, a fore Q^r of Lamb rosted and a plumb Pudding. At Quadrille this Evening won 0. 0. 6. Nancy very stiff and tender on her return home from Mattishall. Nancy won at Quadrille this Even' 0. 1. 6. I took a good dose of Rhubarb going to bed to Night.

May 14. . . . Was a great deal better this morning— thank God. Dr Thorne came here about Noon— but did not think proper to bleed me for my Complaint—He will send me a Vomit to take this Evening &c. In the Afternoon sent Will to Mattishall after the above. About ½ past 9 this Evening I took the Emetic Powder in a tea-cup of warm water—it did not take any Effect till very near half an Hour after, and then it operated by very little after the first straining. I took a little warm red Wine and Water after it and went to bed.

May 15. . . . At half past 6 this morning took a black Dose of Physic in bed, then laid down till half past 7 then got up and came down to breakfast. I had a very disagreeable Night of rest, sweated a vast deal and started much in my Sleep, being in the Horrors. Mrs Custance made us a long morning Visit till after one o'clock—during the Time that Mrs Custance was here Mrs Davy from Hockering came here, having been sent for by me to spend a few Days with Nancy, and she dined supped and slept here with Nancy. Soon after Mrs Custance left us, Dr Thorne came here and stay'd ab^t an Hour. In the Afternoon M^r and Mrs Custance with their eldest Son Hamilton, came here, and drank Tea and stayed till 8 in the Evening with us—We dine with them Saturday. I was brave (thank God) this Evening—my Physic having operated very well—Altho' hurried so much to day. I began taking going to bed some Camphire and Nitre Powders.

May 16. . . . I was very much hurried again last Night in my Dreams. In the Evening I took a ride to Honingham and buried a little Girl of ab^t 2 Years of John Shorts the Clerk there. I found myself much better the best part of the Day, but going to bed was very hot wch hindered me from sleeping soon. I took my Camphire &c. Powders, three Times to day. I believe they do me much good—eat very hearty for dinner to day. No Malt Liquor, cheese, or salt Meats or Beef or any thing seasoned am forbid making use of for some time. Mrs Davy and Nancy on foot, met me on my return from Honingham this Evening ab^t the White Horse and I walked back with them, sending my Horse home by Jack.

May 19. . . . Mrs Davy breakfasted and spent the morning at Weston. Mr Page called on me this morning and paid me the remaining mony due to me for Tithe 1782—3. o. o. He paid me also a Quit Rent wch I had p^d for him o. 5. 5. This being

Mr Howes's Rotation Day—Mr H. sent his Chaise after Mrs Davy and Nancy ab^t 1 o'clock, in which they went to Hockering, and I went with them on Horseback and there we dined and spent the Aft. with M^r and Mrs Howes and only Mr Smith besides. M^r and Mrs Bodham could not come on Account of the bad Weather which was very much so to day. We had for Dinner a Piece of boiled Beef, a Q^r of Lamb rosted, some Pickled Salmon and a baked Pudding. Whilst we were at Tea this Afternoon Betsy Davy came to Hockering in a returned Chaise from Dereham. We were very glad to see her especially her Mother. She is grown a very smart healthy young Lady. At Quadrille this Evening won o. o. 6. My Man Ben came to Hockering in the Evening on Phyllis to carry home Nancy behind him —we got home about 9 o'clock, Nancy very little fatigued. To Mr Cary for things from Norwich &c. this Morn p^d 4. 6½. Of Ditto—for Butter—2 Pints rec^d 1. 2. I thank God I daily get better and stronger.

May 21. . . . There were 17 Teams carrying Gravel on the new Road by my House this morning they begun at 6 o'clock and continued till 3 in the Afternoon— My little Team with them all the Time and carried 6 Load—Mr Howlett one of the Surveyors attending on the Road all the Time—He breakfasted and dined with us. I gave Howlett for the Men when they had done o. 5. o. Mr Custance called on me this morning ab^t 11 o'clock by appointment, and I took a ride with him to see some Road in the Parish of Hockering which is very bad, and we rode after to Hockering and called on the surveyors there, Shaddelow and Howard, whom we met together in the Street at

Hockering and we talked with them ab^t the above road, and which they promised tho' but faintly, to have mended—We saw Mrs Davy and Daughter walking in the Street, and spoke to them. We then returned back to Weston, stopp'd at Hungate Lodge and went over the House &c. which is repairing. We came together after as far as my House and there parted. Thank God am brave and well to day. The Teams brought to-day upon my Road, full 100 Load.

May 24. . . . A Mr Love (Journeyman to Mr Whistler Painter at Norwich) dined with our Folks in Kitchen to day—He calling by my desire as I wanted to speak to him about putting Mr Custance's Name in the new Register Book which he lately made a Present of to the Parish. Had a long Letter from my Sister Pounsett this Evening wherein she mentions that poor Mrs Figgus is dead.

May 26. . . . I buried poor Joe Adcocks Wife this Evening aged 43. Pray God comfort the poor Man in his distress, he having buried, his Father and Mother and Wife within 6 Weeks.

June 1. . . . Three of Mr Custances Servant Maids drank Tea with our Maids this Afternoon.

June 5. [He had gone to Norwich the day before.] I breakfasted at the Kings Head—and after being shaved I walked to Mr Francis's—then to Priests to taste some Port Wine and there bespoke a Q^r of a Pipe. Called at Beales in the Fish Markett and bought 3 Pairs of fine Soals—2 Crabbs—and a Lobster—P^d him for the above and for some Fish I had before of him 0. 8. 4. About 11 o'clock sent Will home with the Fish to have for Dinner as I have Company to dine with me to-day. At Mr Bakers for a P^r of large Scissars to trim Horses p^d 1. 6. At Dittos—for 2 P^d of Pinns for Nancy and Mrs Davy p^d 4. 8. Called at Buckles and bespoke a large Lock for my Back-Door. At Quantrells Gardens for a Glass of Gin and Water p^d o. 3. Paid and gave at the Kings Head o. 8. 9. Called on my Sadler Allum and bespoke a Pillion for Nancy. Called on my Upholsterer Horth and bespoke a Bolster Tick and some Paper to paper one of my Garretts. Gave my Barber—Milsham—this morning o. 1. o. About 1 o'clock I mounted my Mare and set of for Weston and did not get home till near 4 o'clock on Account of my poor Mare, she having filled herself so much on dry Meat last Night—I was afraid that she would have dropped on the road as she puffed and blowed so terribly—I walked her most part of the way—and I got of and walked many Times—It vexed and fretted me much on Account of having Company to Dinner.—It was also very hot and was obliged to wear my great Coat, the Pockets of which also were loaded with 2 Pounds of Pins &c., however I did get home at last as did my Mare—And I found Mr Smith and Mr Baldwin with my Ladies at home. I was pretty much fatigued with the Heat and fretting. Mr Smith and Mr Baldwin dined and spent the Afternoon and part of the Evening with us till 9 at Night. Nancy and Mrs Davy dined, breakfasted, supped &c. again here. We had for Dinner 3 P^r of fine Soals—a Leg of Mutton rosted, and some Gooseberry Tarts. After Tea we got to Cards, at Loo, at which I won 4. o. I dined, supped and slept at home.

June 12. . . . Clerk Hewitt of Mattishall brought me this Afternoon a Tub of Gin—And as my last was deficient 2 or 3 Bottles of Measure—was allowed

3/0^d—therefore I only paid for the above 1. 2. 0. Gave Clerk Hewitt for his trouble of bringing it 0. 1. 0.

June 13. ... Mr. Custance's 3 little Boys with 2 'Nurse' Maids came here this Afternoon and stayed here till 8 at night. I gave the little Boys for their Supper some Strawberries and milk with which they were highly delighted. They came here on foot but went back in the Coach. Mrs. Alldis the Housekeeper called here in the Afternoon and she drank Tea with the Nurse Maids and ours in Kitchen.

June 14. ... Mr. and Mrs. Custance called on us this morning and very genteelly thanked us for our Civilities to the young gentlemen yesterday. They were very much pleased with it. Nancy took an airing with Mrs. Custance afterwards. I went to Mr. Forsters this morning being sent for—his Wife being very dangerously ill in the Fever. She wanted to receive the H. Sacrament—but I postponed it till Monday. Her Mother was with her. I did not see Forster himself. To Mary Norton for weeding 5 Days and ½ at 6^d pd. 2. 9. To Ditto for allowance for Beer at 1½^d pd. 0. 9. To Eliz: Mace for weeding 5 Days and ½ at 6^d pd. 2. 9. To Ditto for Allowance for Beer—1½^d—pd. 0. 9. To Thos Cushing for 17 Rod of ditching only at 10—14. 6.

June 16. ... I walked to Forsters this morning between 11 and 12 and read Prayers and administered the H. Sacrament to Mrs. Forster who is something better to day—Her Mother was with her and received the Sacrament also with her. After I came down Stairs from Mrs. Forster I saw Forster and Herring of Ringland—Mr. Forster was very sorry for what he had said and if I would forgive him, he w^d beg my

Pardon—which I did and he promised never to affront me more—so that all matters are made up.[1]
To Mr. Cary for things from Norwich &c. pd. o. 6. 8.
Of Ditto—for 7 Pints of Butter at 7^d rec^d o. 4. 1.
To Goody Doughty for 3 Lemons p^d o. o. 6. I privately baptised a Child of Billy Bidewells this morning at my House—by name William. Mr. Custance sent us some beans and a Colliflower this Even'.

June 23. ... This being my Rotation Day the following Company dined and spent the Afternoon here— Mr. and Mrs. Priest and their son John from Norwich, Mr. and Mrs. Howes, Mr. and Mrs. Bodham, Mr. Ashull, Mrs. Davy and Mr. Smith. I gave the Company for Dinner, a leg of Lamb boiled, Carrotts and Turnips, a Rump of Beef rosted and Cucumbers, a fine Ham, Peas and Beans, four Chicken rosted, Gooseberry Tarts and Custards—Desert—Some very fine Oranges, Almonds and Raisins and plenty of Strawberries and Cream—all which looked very well. Plumb Cake and Bread and Butter at Tea. We smoked a Pipe under the old Tree in the Garden. To Goody Doughty for Oranges and Lemons p^d o. 1. 6. I sent Will this morning to Norwich after Fish but there were none to be got—He brought back some Lamb, &c.

June 25. ... Very uncommon Lazy and hot Weather. The Sun very red at setting. To a poor old crazy Woman this morn' gave o. o. 6. Nancy and myself dined and spent part of the afternoon at Weston House with Mr. and Mrs. Custance—Mr. Rawlins dined also with us—whilst we were at Dinner Mrs. Custance was obliged to go from Table about

---

[1] It will be remembered that Forster had been excessively insolent to the diarist at the latter's frolic on 3 December 1782.

4 o'clock labour Pains coming on fast upon her. We went home soon after dinner on the Occasion—as we came in the Coach. We had for Dinner some Beans and Bacon, a Chine of Mutton rosted, Giblett Pye, Hashed Goose, a Rabbit rosted and some young Peas,—Tarts, Pudding and Jellies. We got home between 5 and 6 o'clock. After Supper we sent up to Mr. Custances to enquire after Mrs. Custance who was brought to bed of a fine girl about 7 o'clock and as well as could be expected.

June 26. . . . I walked up to Mr. Custance's this morning soon after breakfast and named the little Girl by name Frances Ann, and a very pretty Infant She is. After I had named it Mr. Custance and self walked down to Lenewade Bridge to an Auction of Beeston's there. We stayed there about ½ an Hour and then walked back again to Weston House and then I walked back to my own House. Very uncommon hot, misty Days—with cold Nights.

June 27. . . . After breakfast Nancy and self dressed ourselves and walked to Hungate Lodge to make the first visit to Mr. and Mrs. Micklewaite who were both at home and appear to be tolerable agreeable People—He is very young. She is much older and appears rather high. We stayed about half an Hour with them and then returned.

June 29. . . . I read Prayers, Preached and churched 3 Women this morning at Church. Mr. Custance, Mr. and Mrs. Micklewaite, and my Niece at Church this morning. Recd. for churching the 3 Women 0. 1. 6. Gave Chapman's Wife one of the above 0. 0. 6. One of the Women gave me a bad sixpence— The Women churched, were Chapmans Wife, Billy Bidewell's Wife, and Brands Wife of E. Tuddenham.

I rode to Honingham in the Afternoon and there read Prayers and Preached for Du Quesne. A strange Man was seen lurking about the Craft this Aft.

June 30. . . . I privately named a Child this morning of Dinah Bushell's by name Keziah One of Job's Daughters Names.[1] To Mr. Cary for things from Norwich &c. pd. o. 11. 1. Of Ditto for 6 Pints of Butter recd. o. 3. 6. To Betty for things pd. o. 1. o. I privately named a Child of Brands of East Tuddenham, by name—John—this Afternoon—Mr. Love the Painter dined with our Folks in Kitchen. He brought me the new Register from Mr. Whistlers wch. I sent by him to have Mr. Custances Name in gold letters.

July 4. . . . About 1 o'clock I took a ride to Mr. Baldwins at Ling, and there dined and spent the afternoon with Mr. and Mrs. Baldwin, a Mrs. Brookes, Mr. Bodham and Mr. Smith and a Mr. Burney a young Clergyman and an Oxonian he was of St. Mary Hall and under Dr. Nowell and Rawbone. Also he is first Cousin to the ingenious Miss Burney, Authoress of Evelina and Cecilia.[2] Miss Nancy Baldwin and two other young Misses of Mrs. Brookes drank Tea with us in the Afternoon. They went to Norwich in the morning, and there dined. We had for Dinner to day, some fried Eels, Beans and Bacon, a Leg of Mutton boiled and Capers, a Couple of rost Chicken,

---

[1] ' So the Lord blessed the latter end of Job more than the beginning : for he had fourteen thousand sheep, and six thousand camels, and a thousand yoke of oxen, and a thousand she asses. He had also seven sons and three daughters. And he called the name of the first, Jemima ; and the name of the second, Kezia ; and the name of the third, Keren-happuch. And in all the land were no women found so fair as the daughters of Job : and their father gave them inheritance among their brethren ' (Job, chap. 42, vv. 12–15).

[2] See foot-note, p. 40, preceding.

a very fine Lobster, Tarts and Syllabubs. After Dinner we had a fine Melon and some Cherries. I returned home to Weston before 9 this Evening. To Mr. Baldwin's Servant Man gave o. 1. o. To some poor ragged Children at the fall gate at Ling o. o. 6. To 2 naked Children on Colin Green at the fall gate o. o. 6. Almost all my Hay stacked this Evening and in fine Order. The best Hay-Stack we ever had at Weston.

July 6. . . . I rode to Honingham this morning and there read Prayers and Preached for Du Quesne. I read Prayers and Preached this Afternoon at Weston. Neither Mr. or Mrs. Custance at Church. Mr. Micklewaite and Wife were there and dressed smartly. I think they have not behaved very civil or genteel to us in not returning our Visit to them.

July 9. . . . Mr. and Mrs. Micklewaite called on me this morning in their Chariot and made a morning Visit, stayed about half an Hour and then returned home. They enquired after Nancy and left Compts. for her. I should have been glad that she had been at home.

July 13. . . . I read Prayers and Preached this morning at Weston. Mr. Custance was at Church but no one else in his Seat. It being excessive hot this morning, one poor Woman by name Hester Dunham fainted away in the Church. She soon recovered by smelling to my Bottle of Salts which I sent to her by my Clerk. I rode to Honingham in the Afternoon and there read Prayers and Preached for Du Quesne. The Weather still very uncommonly hazy and Sun red.

July 15. . . . Nancy got up very Early this morning and rode behind Ben to Mr. Bodhams at South Green, she got there before they were down Stairs. She went away before breakfast, and before I was up. At one o'clock I took a ride to Mattishall to Mr. Smiths it being his Rotation Day and there dined and spent the Afternoon with him, Mr. and Mrs. Bodham, Mr. Ashull, Mrs. Davy and Nancy. Mr. and Mrs. Howes not there which I think very rude, as they promised, and their going this day to Shipdam but I apprehend they intend dropping the Rotations which for my Part I am not sorry for, as Mrs. Davy is soon going to board at Mattishall in the Parsonage House. We had for Dinner 3 boiled Chicken, a Tongue, some Peas, a piece of rost Beef, Cherry Pudding and Cheese Cake. At Quadrille this Evening lost o. o. 6. Between 8 and 9 this Evening Nancy and self sat of on Horseback for home and got there I thank God safe and well before 10 o'clock—Nancy but little tired.

July 18. . . . We had an agreeable sprinkling of Rain this Afternoon without either Thunder or Lightning, praised be God for it. Nancy slept up in the Garrett over me to night and by herself for the first Time. She likes the Garrett so well that she intends often sleeping there—It is also to be papered &c.

July 19. . . . Rec^d a Letter this Evening from the Bishops Office concerning a Confirmation being at Aylesham Sep. 15.

July 25. . . . Mr. and Mrs. Bodham and Mr. Smith dined and spent the Afternoon with us, it being my Rotation. We invited Mr. and Mrs. Howes and Miss Howes, but they would not come themselves nor let Miss Howes. I have therefore done with them entirely. We had for Dinner 3 Fowls boiled and a Piggs Face, a Scuffling[1] of Lamb rosted, a Couple of Ducks and some Peas and Currant Tarts. At Quadrille this Evening lost o. 2. o.

[1] Whatever this was it is not in the *N. E. D.*

July 28. . . . .This has been the hottest day this year, and I believe the hottest that ever I felt, many say the same. We fully expected a Tempest to day, but thank God had none.

July 29. I breakfasted, supped and slept again at home. Nancy got up very early this morning and went behind Ben to Mattishall to Mr. Bodhams being his Club Day and there she breakfasted and spent the Afternoon and in the Evening returned as she went, to Weston, where she supped and slept again at home. Mr. Custance sent us a Note this morning to invite us to Dinner on Tuesday next to meet Mr. and Mrs. Micklewaite. About 1 o'clock I took a ride to Mattishall to Mr. Bodhams and there dined and spent the Afternoon with him, Mrs. Bodham, Mr. and Mrs. Ball of Catfield, Sister to Mrs. Bodham, Mrs. Davy, Mr. Smith, Mr. and Mrs. Howes, Mr. Ashull and Nancy.—We had for Dinner a Piece of boiled Beef, some Beans and Bacon, a couple of Ducks rosted, a Veal Pye and some Apricot Dumplins. At Quadrille this Evening won 0. 2. 0. As we were coming away Mrs. Howes came to me and asked me to their House it being their Rotation next, but I entirely refused to go, as they had not only kept away from mine very lately, but would not let Miss Howes come who was very desirous of coming to Weston. I gave it to her, and most of the Company seemed pleased with my behaviour. We did not get home till after 9 in the Evening. Nancy was obliged to change Horses, the flies teazing Phyllis very much which made her kick a little.

Aug. 4. . . . In the evening Nancy and self took a walk to Mr. Micklethwaites at Hungate Lodge and there drank Tea by appointment with Mr. and Mrs

Micklethwaite. They behaved very obliging—we returned home by 8.

Aug. 5. . . . Nancy and self dined and spent the afternoon at Weston House with Mr. and Mrs. Custance, Sʳ Thomas Beauchamp and Lady,[1] and Mr. and Mrs. Micklethwaite. They sent their Coach after us and we returned home in it. We had for Dinner some fresh Water Fish, Perch and Trout, a Saddle of Mutton rosted, Beans and Bacon, a Couple of Fowls boiled, Patties and some white Soup—2nd Course—Pigeons rosted, a Duck rosted, Piggs Pettytoes —Sweetbreads—Rasberry Cream, Tarts and Pudding and Pippins. After Tea, Lady Beauchamp and self played a Rubber of Whist against Mr. Custance and Mrs. Micklethwaite and we came of Conquerors and Winners—each won 0. 4. 0. We spent a very agreeable Day and got home by abt. 9 o'clock. Mrs. Micklethwaite was very stately and reserved. Mrs. C. does not much admire her I believe.

Aug. 8. . . . My Servant Boy Jack Warton taken very ill in the Fever that is going about—I gave him some Rhubarb.

Aug. 9. . . . My Boy still very bad tho' not so bad as yesterday. My Under Maid Lizzy Greaves taken very ill also in the Fever. I sent this morning early for Dr. Thorne and he came here about 11 o'clock and he examined them and in the Evening they are to have some things from him to take. I took a ride

---

[1] Sir Thomas Beauchamp-Proctor (1736-1827) was Mrs. Custance's brother (see vol. i, p. 227), and succeeded his father in the baronetcy September 13, 1773. He lived at Langley Park, near Norwich, and was sheriff of the county in 1780-1. He married on May 5, 1778, Mary, second daughter of Robert Palmer, of Sonning, Berks (see Cokayne's *Complete Baronetage*, vol. v, p. 88).

back with Mr. Thorne to Mattishall called at the
House where Mrs. Davy is going to board but she
was not there. I called then on Mr. Smith who
pressed me to dine with him, but I could not promise
as I was going to Mr. Bodhams—I called then at
Mr. Bodhams and there dined and spent part of the
Afternoon with him and Mrs. Bodham. We had
a Harvest Dinner a Rump of Beef rosted and a plumb
Pudding. Mr. B: finished carrying his Wheat this
day. From Mr. Bodhams I went about 4 o'clock to
Du Quesnes House and there met Nancy by appointment. I had not been there long before I rode to
Honingham Church and there buried Miss Harriot
Townshend about a year and a Qr. old, the youngest
Daughter of Charles Townshend, Esq.—She was
brought in a mourning Coach and four Horses—with
3 Servant Maids dressed in black Hoods &c. &c.
There were 4 Pall-bearers all old Men and his Tenants
who had white Gloves and white silk Scarfs. I had
also the same and nothing else. She was buried in
the Chancel. It was a very handsome Coffin. I rode
back from Honingham Church to Du Quesnes and
there drank Tea with Nancy, and after that Nancy
and self returned home to Weston abt. 8. o'clock.
To Turnpike and given to Children p^d o. o. 3. We
found both of our sick Servants gone to bed and very
ill. I had them both up and to each gave a Vomit
abt. 10 o'clock and then sent them back to bed after
it had done working. They were both very feverish
and very ill.

Aug. 10. . . . Both my ill Servants very bad all day
especially the Maid. They both took Physick this
morning. I hope they will do well.

Aug. 11. . . . To Goody Doughty for 6 Lemons p^d

o. 1. o. Both my Servants rather better but still very indifferent.

Aug. 12. . . . Both my ill Servants a good deal better today in the Morn, but both very indifferent again in the Afternoon. Dr. Thorne called here this Morn to see them again. Mr. Micklethwaite sent us a Note to desire that we w^d dine with them Friday next, but we are then engaged.

Aug. 14. . . . I sent Will: early this morning to Hockering, after Mrs. Davy who returned here to breakfast, and she dined, supped and slept here with Nancy. My Maid Lizzy very ill today, worse than ever, and kept her Bed most part of the Day. Dr. Thorne came here whilst we were at Dinner, and he dined with us but obliged to leave us immediately after Dinner, having a great many Patients to visit. He ordered that Lizzy should begin to take the Bark[1] immediately as the fever was abated, and which I sent for to his House this Evening. She begun taking the Bark at 10. this Night and is to take it every two Hours till she has taken a Dozen Papers. If it purges her she is to have 4 Drops of Laudanum in her Bark when she takes it then 3 Drops—then 2. then 1 Drop which will take of the purging. Betty is to set up till 4. in the morning to give her the Bark and then Will: as he brews to Morrow, will give it her. We had for Dinner to day a boiled Leg of Mutton and Capers, a Duck rosted and one of Nancy's Pudding with Jelly.

---

[1] The use of Peruvian bark (i. e. quinine) in medicine was greatly extended by that eminent physician, botanist, collector of manuscripts and *objets d'art*, and godfather of London streets, Sir Hans Sloane (1660–1753). See Lecky, *England in the Eighteenth Century*, vol. ii, p. 223, and for an account of his remarkable life the *D. N. B.* Sir Hans Sloane succeeded Sir Isaac Newton as President of the Royal Society in 1727.

Aug. 16. . . . Lizzy not quite so well to day, the Fever returning but not so bad as Thursday. Dr. Thorne called here this morning and saw her, ordered to leave of Bark till her Fever is quite of—and then take it every 2 Hours again.

Aug. 17. . . . Betty gave Lizzy a Powder of Bark abt. 4. o'clock this Morn' and another about 6 but she being much worse afterwards I would [not] let her take any more. In the Evening sent to Dr. Thorne and he sent her some Camphire Powders, and not take any more bark at all. I rode to Honingham this morning and there read Prayers and Preached for Du Quesne he being not yet returned. Mr. and Mrs. Townshend and a Mrs. Cornwallis Widow of the late Arch-Bishop of Canterbury at Honingham Church. Mr. Townshend sent to me to dine with him to day but could not as I am to serve my own Church in the Aft: I read Prayers and Preached this afternoon at Weston. Mr. Custance and a Mrs. Collier an elderly Lady at Church. Lizzy still very weak and a pain in her Head still.

Aug. 19. . . . Lizzy a good deal better to day but very weak still. My Boy Jack complained again to day a good deal with a Pain in his Head and one foot exceeding tender. Very sultry with Thunder at a great distance this After: A large Ball of Fire for miles round was seen last Night between 9. and 10. o'clock by many People. Mrs. Wrights House of Ringland shook a good deal at that Time, it was rumoured about, and frightned the Folks much. I apprehend it was a slight shock of an Earthquake. We thought we heard a heavy rumbling about.

Aug. 20. . . . My two ill Servants much better to day than yesterday. Dr. Thorne called to see my Servants again this Morn'. People are daily falling down in the reigning illness.

Aug. 25. . . . We had a violent Tempest of Thunder, Lightning, and heavy Rain with it from Noon till 2 in the Afternoon, but I thank God it did no injury to us. The Lightning was excessive strong indeed and the Thunder very loud. Mrs. Custance sent Nancy a Note this Morning to desire us to drink Tea with them this Afternoon, and we sent word back that we would, but the Tempest happening after we sent a note to let them know that we could not, as it still continued raining, but desired their Company to Morrow Aft: at Parsonage. To Mr. Cary for things from Norwich &c. pd. 0. 6. 8½. Of Ditto for 1. Pint of Butter rec^d 0. 0. 10.

Aug. 26. . . . Lizzy and Jack very bad today especially the latter. Mrs. Townshend with her two Daughters made us a morning Visit, and invited us to Dinner on Thursday next, and that Mr. Custance would take us with him and Mrs. Custance in their Coach to Honingham Hall. Mr. and Mrs. Custance drank Coffee and Tea with us this Afternoon. Mr. Custance acted yesterday for the first Time as a Justice at Lenewade Bridge. Lizzy's Mother came here Sunday Evening and slept here with her Daughter, and is to stay here during our washing, she breakfasted, dined, supped and slept here yesterday, and did the same to day.

Aug. 28. I breakfasted, supped and slept again at home. Nancy breakfasted, supped and slept again at home. Lizzy's Mother breakfasted, dined and spent the Afternoon here and in the Evening returned to her home. My sick Servants but indifferent again to day. About 2. o'clock Mr. and Mrs. Custance called here by appointment and took Nancy and self with them in their Coach to Mr. Townshends at Honingham where we dined and spent the Afternoon with Mr. and Mrs. Townshend, Mrs. Cornwallis,[1] Widow of the late Arch-Bishop of Canterbury's and who is also Sister to Mr. Townshend, Mr. and Mrs. Custance, and Mr. Du Quesne—The latter of whom we were glad to see, as it was so long since we saw him. Mr. and Mrs. Townshend behaved very genteel to us. The drawing Room in which we drank Tea &c. was hung with Silk. The Chairs of the same kind of Silk and all the wood-work of them gilded, as were the Settee's. The looking glass which was the finest and largest I ever saw, cost at secondhand 150. 0. 0. The Height of the Plate was seven feet and half, and the breadth of it was five feet and half, one single Plate of glass only. The frame and Ornaments to it, was carved and gilded and very handsome. There was two Courses at Dinner besides the Desert. Each course nine Dishes, but most of the things spoiled by being so frenchified in dressing. I dined on some fryed Soals, some stewed Beef with Caper Sauce and some Hare rosted, but very insipid. After Coffee and Tea we got to Cards to Loo at which I had the good Luck to win abt. 0. 1. 0. Mrs. Cornwallis and Nancy did not play Cards with us but with the Children, Miss Caroline and Miss Amelia Townshend, about 3. or 4. years old. Nancy

[1] I find the following amusing reference to Mrs. Cornwallis in a letter of Horace Walpole's to the Countess of Upper Ossory, dated December 18, 1781: 'I was diverted last night at Lady Lucan's. The moment I entered, she set me down to whist with Lady Bute—and who do you think were the other partners ? The Archbishopess of Canterbury and Mr. Gibbon '. (Walpole's *Letters*, vol. xii, p. 120.)

sung one Song then Mr. and Mrs. Custance, Nancy
and self came away about half past seven o'clock, we
got home about 8 o'clock. To Page's Harvest Men
gave a Largess of o. 1. o.

Aug. 31. . . . My Man Will went to bed this Evening
bad. Lizzy very poorly—Jack still continues mending.

Sep. 2. . . . After breakfast Nancy and myself took a ride
to Du Quesnes and from thence to Mr. Bodhams
at Mattishall where we dined and spent the Afternoon with him, Mrs. Bodham and Miss Bodham.
We had for Dinner a Leg of Mutton boiled and
a Couple of Ducks rosted and Apple Tarts. We
returned home by 8. in the Evening. Will: very
bad all the time he was out to day. Ben also complained this Evening—Jack also bad to-day. Almost
all the House ill in the present Disorder and which
is called the Whirligigousticon[1] by the faculty. It is
almost in every House in every Village. Mr. and
Mrs. Bodham have had it and not well yet. The
popping of guns about to Day frightned my Mare.
To Turnpike to day p^d o. o. 2. Gave to Children
besides o. o. 3. Mr. Smith was at Mr. Bodhams before
dinner, but could not stay and dine with us.

Sep. 4. I breakfasted, supped and slept again at home.
Nancy breakfasted, dined, &c. &c. again at home. To
Largesses to day gave o. 2. o. About 1. o'clock
Mr. and Mrs. Custance called here in their Coach
and took me with them to Norwich to dine with the
Bishop. I was dressed in a Gown and Cassock and
Scarf. We got there to the Palace abt. 3. o'clock,

---

[1] The 'Disorder' in fact appears to have been a bad local outburst
of malaria; see the entry for March 13, 1784, where it is referred to as
the ague, and where a detailed account of Dr. Thorne's method of treat-
ment is given.

and there dined and spent the Afternoon with his
Lordship Dr. Bagot, and his Lady Mrs. Bagot, whose
Name before Marriage was Miss Hay, the two
Miss Hay's her Sisters, two Mr. Hay's her Brothers,
a Mr. Gooch the Bishop's Chaplain, Dr. Brook of
Yarmouth, Mr. Buxton of Easton, and his Nephew
the Revd. Mr. Buxton, Mr. Du Quesne, Mr. Priest
of Reepham, and 5 strange Clergymen. There were
20 of us at the Table and a very elegant Dinner the
Bishop gave us. We had 2 Courses of 20 Dishes
each Course, and a Desert after of 20 Dishes. Madeira,
red and white Wines. The first Course amongst
many other things were 2 Dishes of prodigious fine
stewed Carp and Tench, and a fine Haunch of
Venison. Amongst the second Course a fine Turkey
Poult, Partridges, Pidgeons and Sweatmeats. Desert
—amongst other things, Mulberries, Melon, Currants,
Peaches, Nectarines and Grapes. A most beautiful
Artificial Garden in the Center of the Table remained
at Dinner and afterwards, it was one of the prettiest
things I ever saw, about a Yard long, and about
18 Inches wide, in the middle of which was a high
round Temple supported on round Pillars, the Pillars
were wreathed round with artificial Flowers—on one
side was a Shepherdess on the other a Shepherd,
several handsome Urns decorated with artificial
Flowers also &c. &c. The Bishop behaved with
great affability towards me as I remembered him at
Christ Church in Oxford. He was also very affable
and polite to all the Clergy present. Mr. and Mrs.
Custance were exceedingly pleased, with both Bishop
and Mrs. Bagot, as seemed everybody else.[1] About

[1] Dr. Lewis Bagot (1741–1802) was the seventh son of Sir Walter
Bagot, and was educated at Westminster and Christ Church, Oxford, of

half past 6. o'clock we all withdrew from the dining
Room to the Library or Drawing Room, where we
had Tea and Coffee brought round to each of us.
There was a strange Lady that came to Tea with
us. Abt. half past 7 Mr. and Mrs. Custance and self
took our Leave as did the rest of the Company, we
got home between 9 and 10. It lightned a good
deal as we came home. Mr. Custance would carry
me quite to the Parsonage as we returned home, tho'
I desired him to put me down at the Church. I was
exceedingly pleased with this Days excursion. Nancy
rec^d a long Letter from her Brother William dated the
29 June from Staten Island in North America brought
by Mr. Custance's Servant from Norwich this Evening. The Letter came to o. 2. 4. He is very well and
has escaped many Dangers in America. He sent
inclosed in his Letter some Continental Money Paper
valued there at 10 Shillings and which he desired to
be given to me.

Sep. 5. ... Lizzy, Jack, Ben and Will: something better
in the Day time but in the Evening Ben and Will
were taken very bad again. About 3 o'clock I walked
up to Mr. Micklethwaites at Hungate Lodge, and
there dined and spent the Afternoon with him, his
Wife, old Mrs. Brainthwaite Mother to Mrs. Micklethwaite, a Mr. and Mrs. Blofield from London and
Miss Spencer, Sister to Mrs. Blofield. Mrs. Blofield
is a merry, sensible, pretty young Lady. After Tea

which he became successively Canon and Dean. He was made Bishop
of Bristol on February 23, 1782, and translated to Norwich in 1783. In
1790 he was again translated to St. Asaph. His wife was a niece of the
Earl of Kinnoul, and sister of Dr. Hay of Christ Church. 'Amiable,
gentle, benevolent, humble and laborious'—such are the pleasing epithets
applied to Bishop Bagot in the *D. N. B.* His portrait by Hoppner is in
the Hall of Christ Church.

we got to Whist at which I lost 0. 4. 0 Mrs. Blofield and self against Mrs. Micklethwaite and Miss Spencer. We lost 2 Rubbers quickly having such bad Cards. I returned home about 9. o'clock in the Evening. We had for Dinner, hashed Calfs Head, a Goose rosted, A Turky, Partridges, Mushrooms, baked Apple Pudding and Lemon Cream. Desert, a Pine Apple, Peaches, Nectarines and Pears. To a Largess today gave 0. 1. 0.

Sep. 10. . . . Will and Ben still very indifferent, this their worst Day. Stormy and cold in Morning and Afternoon. I walked to Church this morning between 11 and 12 and publickly baptised Mr. Custance's little Maid by name Francis Anne—Lady Bacon and Lady Beauchamp stood Godmothers, and Mr. Custance stood Proxy. After I had performed the ceremony Mr. Custance came to me and made me a Present of 5. 5. 0. wrapt up in a clean piece of Paper and desired that Nancy and self would dine with them to day and that he would send his Coach after us at 2 o'clock. We therefore dined and spent the Afternoon at Weston House with Mr. and Mrs. Custance, Lady Bacon, Lady Beauchamp and Mr. Press Custance. After Tea we got to Loo at which I lost 0. 9. 0. We returned home as we went in the Coach about 9 o'clock. We stayed up to night till after 11 o'clock on Account of its being a fine Evening and a total Eclipse of the Moon, which begun a Qr before 10 o'clock.

Sep. 13. . . . My Servant Will: Coleman very bad all day, worse than he has been at all. My other Servants tolerable. Pray God poor Will may do well again.

Sep. 17. . . . Ben, Lizzy and Will: much worse to day especially Ben and Lizzy. Ben complained much of a pain in his Bowels. I gave him some Rhubarb on going to bed to night.

Sep. 18. . . . Ben very bad to day, Will: also bad and Lizzy worse.

Sep. 27. . . . Will and Lizzy still very poorly my other Servants brave. We heard this Morning by my Butchers Lad that the Revd. Mr. Baldwin of Lyng was dead—am very sorry for him.

Sep. 28. . . . Jacks Brother Tom dined with our Folks to day. All my Folks brave but Will—He is still very bad. I sent to enquire for Mrs. Baldwin and Miss this Morning; and they are as well as can be expected in their Distress. I read Prayers and Preached this Afternoon at Weston. None of Weston House Folks at Church this Afternoon.

Oct. 3. . . . I had a very indifferent Night indeed last Night, much oppressed with low Spirits and much hurried with startings &c. in my sleep. About 12. o'clock I took a Walk to Weston House and saw Mr. Custance's Children, all whom I found much better and lively. Mr. and Mrs. Custance not at home being gone to Sr. Edmund Bacons for a few Days, they come home on Sunday next. Mr. and Mrs. Bodham and with them a Miss Mary Donne abt. 15 Years of Age Daughter of Mr. Donne, Surgeon at Norwich came here about 2 o'clock, and they dined, spent the Aft. supped and slept at my House. Their Servant John did the same. Their two Horses also stayed here all Night. Miss Donne slept with Nancy in the Tent bed in the Attic Story. Mr. and Mrs. Bodham slept in the Room opposite me. We had for Dinner, a boiled Leg of Mutton and Capers, a fine fat Goose rosted and Apple Sause, a Pudding and Currant Tarts. For supper a Couple of Chicken rosted and Mushroom Sauce. After Tea we got to Quadrille at which I won o. 4. 6. Nancy won also this evening o. 2. 6. Mr. Bodhams Servant Man slept with our Will: who is something better to day and waited at Table. I did not get to bed till 12. at Night. I was brave I thank God all Day and drank plenty of Port. Nancy sent a Letter this Evening to her Brother Sam[1]. Nancy was very ill this Evening and vomited a good deal. She was however much better after some Rum and Water.

Oct. 5. ... All my Folks, thank God, better than they have been. I read Prayers and administered the H: Sacrament this Morn' at Weston. Mr. and Mrs. Custance not there being from home. Neither Mr. or Mrs. Micklethwaite at Church—tho' they sent me a Note that they would drink Tea here in the Afternoon if we were disengaged—I sent an Answer back that we were not engaged and likewise let them know that it was Sacrament Sunday, and therefore thought that they would attend. Nat Heavers and his Wife and Js. Smith my Clerk, dined in Kitchen. Between 6 and 7 this Evening Mr. and Mrs. Micklethwaite came here and drank Tea and returned home abt 8. Mr. and Mrs. Custance returned home from Sr. Edm[d] Bacons this Afternoon, as I sent to enquire after them.

Oct. 6. ... My Folks continue better, thank God for it. I rode down to Mr. Howletts this morning and christned a Child of his, born last Night, by name William—and it being the first Child that I have christned since the Act[1] took place concerning the

---

[1] This Act was passed by the Coalition Government of 1783, and entitled, 'An Act for granting to His Majesty a Stamp-duty on the Registry of Burials, Marriages, Births, and Christenings'. A sum of 3*d*.

Duty to be raised on Christnings Burials and Marriages, and therefore recd. the Duty of 0. 0. 3. I called
at Weston House on my Return and spent an Hour
with Mrs. Custance—Mr. Custance was not at home.

Oct. 9. . . . We breakfasted at 8. this morning and
directly after Will and myself took a ride to Norwich
stayed there till after 2. o'clock and then returned
home by 4. o'clock to dinner, rather fatigued than
not. Soon as I got to Norwich I went to Alderman
Gays in St. Giles's and took out a Licence for enter-
ing Baptisms, Burials, &c. without Stamps p^d for it
0. 6. 0. which the Parish is to return to me for the
same. Alderman Gay is the only Person for granting
such Licences throughout the whole County of
Norfolk. From thence went to Mr. Priests but did
not stay at all. Thence to Miss Browns Millener
and paid her a Bill for Nancy for things of 2. 10. 8.
Thence to Mrs. Francis's in St. Stephens, and there
saw Mr. and Mrs. Francis, a Mrs. Laton and old
Mr. Francis, with the latter I walked to the Swan
and there wetted with him that is, drank a glass of
Wine together p^d for it 0. 0. 6. Thence went to
Adcock Staymaker in Red Lion Lane, St. Stephens
and p^d his Wife for a pr. of Stays for Nancy 1. 11. 6.
For a very fine Lemon at a Grocers Shop pd. 0. 0. 2.
At Bakers for a Comb for craping Hair pd. 0. 1. 0.
At Do. for a Machine for Paste pd. 0. 1. 0. At Do.
for a Dozen of French Basket Buttons pd. 0. 0. 4.

had to be paid in respect of each entry in the register, the Parson being
authorized to demand and receive the said sum. It was one of the new
taxes to meet the burden of the American War. It was repealed by Pitt
in 1794, as it ' was acknowledged to have an injurious operation as regards
the morals of the people ' (see Stephen Dowell's *History of Taxation and
Taxes in England*, vol. ii, pp. 180–2 and 210, and the Act itself, 23 Geo. III,
c. 67).

At Chase's for a Box of Wafers pd. o. o. 3. At Do. for a Paper of steel Sand pd. o. o. 5. At Do. for Westminster Magazine for Sep^{tr} pd. o. o. 7. At Do. for the Bishop's Sermon for the Hospital pd. o. 1. o. For Rum and Water at the Kings Head &c. pd. and gave o. o. 6. A great deal of Company of the first Rank in Town the Sessions Ball being last Night and the first Families at it. Mrs. Custance not well enough to be at the Ball a very great disappointment to her as she set her heart on it, and greater will it be to her when she hears that almost every Person of Note was at it. 262 People in the Room. Nancy was well pleased that I went and what I did for her. To 2 Pr. of Gloves for myself at Norwich pd. o. 3. 8.

Oct. 11. . . . Mr. Custance made us a morning Visit and invited us to dine with some Company at Weston House on Monday. Recd. a disagreeable Letter this Evening from my Brother Heighes concerning his being distressed for Cash.

Oct. 12. . . . Had another disagreeable Letter this morning from the Bishop's Register to preach at the Cathedral of Norwich on the Sunday Morn' Feb: 8 next. I read Prayers and Preached this Aft: at Weston Church. Neither Mr. or Mrs. Custance at Church.

Oct. 13. . . . I privately baptized at my House this morning a Spurious Daughter of Anne Heavers by one Wm. Large of this Parish—by name Hannah. To Goody Doughty for 3 Lemons pd. o. o. 6. To Mr. Cary for things from Norwich &c. pd. o. 17. o. We dined and spent the Afternoon at Mr. Custances at Weston House, with him, Mrs. Custance, Mr. and Mrs. Fenn of Dereham, Captain Laton and his Wife, Mr. Carter, and Mr. Du Quesne. After Coffee and

Tea I played a Rubber of Whist with Capt. and
Mrs. Laton and Mr. Du Quesne. Mrs. Laton and
myself against Mr. Laton and Mr. Du Quesne. We
beat them a full Rubber for which I won o. 5. o. and
which sum of 5ˢ Mr. Du Quesne owes me. We
returned home about 8. o'clock as we went in Mr.
Custances Coach who was so kind to send it after us.
Captain Laton and his Wife, very agreeable Folks.
We had for Dinner a Pike, Ham and Fowls, Leg of
Mutton rosted &c. Partridges, a Hare, Tarts,
Jelly, &c. Grapes, a Pine-Apple, Apples, Pears and
Sweatmeats, Walnutts &c. for a Desert.

Oct. 15. . . . I sent Ben early this morning to Norwich
after some fish and he returned home before 12.
o'clock with some Whitings, Oysters, and a fine
Lobster. Very dry and warm Weather for the Season.
This being my Rotation Day Mr. Du Quesne, Mr.
Bodham and Mr. Smith dined and spent the After-
noon with us. We had for Dinner some fine boiled
Whitings, some fresh Herrings fryed, a Couple of
Fowls boiled and a Piggs Face, a piece of rost Beef
and Kidney Beans, a Currant Pudding and some Tarts.
At Quadrille this Evening lost o. 1. 6. Mr. Du
Quesne paid me for serving Honingham in his late
Absence for 14 Sundays 7. 7. o. N.B. Mr. Du Quesne
did not pay me at all for serving his Church 3. Sundays
before Easter last, which he promised. Mr. Du
Quesne paid me what I won of him at Mr. Custance's
on Monday last—being o. 5. o. They stayed with us
till after 9 o'clock.

Oct. 17. . . . This being St. Faiths Fair Day, I took
a ride there this morning about 11. o'clock, stayed
there about 2. Hours and returned home to Dinner
by 4 in the Afternoon. Will: went with me—We

went thro' Ringland, Taverham, and Drayton, I cannot think it above 7 miles there. My upper Maid and Ben by leave went to the Fair. For Cakes, Oysters &c. at the Fair—pd. o. 1. o. Lord Buckinghamshire's[1] Coach and six there—Mr. Custance's Coach and four—Sr. Willm. Jerninghams &c. &c. there. It was a most pleasant Day for the Fair and People. A good many Scotch Beasts and Scotch Men with them there.

Oct. 24. [He had gone to Norwich the previous evening.] I breakfasted, supped and slept again at the Kings Head. After breakfast I dressed myself in my best Coat and Waistcoat and then walked down in my Boots to the Bishops Palace and had a long Conversation with the Bishop abt. many things—but what I went to his Lordship chiefly on, was my being appointed on the Combination List to preach at the Cathedral the 8. of February next, when my Name had been inserted but a few Years back. To which his Lordship replied, that as I did not then preach in propria Persona was one Reason, and the Second was that he was willing that the Pulpit at the Cathedral should be filled properly by able and beneficed Clergy, and that it was rather a Compliment conferred by him on those that he so appointed. From the Palace walked to Mr. Morpheus and stayed with him near an Hour—from thence went to Mrs. Brewsters and bought some Needles for Nancy pd. o. 1. o. Gave my Barber this morning for shaving me o. 1. o. About 2 o'clock went to Mr. Priests and there dined

[1] Lord Buckinghamshire was John Hobart (1723–93), 2nd Earl of Buckinghamshire. His seat was Blickling Hall, Norfolk. He was at one time Member for Norwich, and from 1777–80 he was Lord Lieutenant of Ireland : see *D. N B.*

and spent the Afternoon with him, his Wife and Son
J$^{n}_{o}$. We had for Dinner a boiled Neck of Mutton
and a brace of Partridges and some Tarts. After
Dinner a Mrs. Barker a beautiful Woman whose
Maiden name was Quarles made a Visit to Mrs. Priest.
There is one more Sister of hers unmarried and also
very handsome. Pd. Mr. Priest this Afternoon for
2 oz: Rhubarb o. 5. o. To Do. for a Q^{r} of a Pd. of
Magnesia pd. o. 1. 4. To Do. for a Q^{r} of a Pd. of
Cream of Tartar pd. o. o. 3. Abt. 4 this Afternoon
left Mr. Priests and went to one Studwell China Man
in the Market Place and bought 2 China Pint Basons,
and half a Doz. half Pint Tumblers, half a doz.
upright Beer Glasses and a black Tea Pot pd. o. 13. 6.
To my Fishmonger, Beale, for Fish sometime back
pd. o. 4. 6. To divers other things this Evening
o. 1. o.

Oct. 26. . . . I got up this Morn' exceedingly out of
Humour and continued so till Dinner. I was very
sorry for it. I read Prayers and Preached this Afternoon at Weston. Mr. and Mrs. Custance, Mrs. Davy
and Nancy at Church. We did not dine till after
4 o'clock this Afternoon.

Oct. 30. . . . Ben busy in plowing for Wheat as it is
to be set.

Nov. 1. . . . Mrs. Davy breakfasted, dined and spent
part of the Afternoon here till 4 o'clock and then
my Man Will: carried her behind him to Mr. Bodhams where she is to spend a few Days by appointment. Mrs. Davy, Nancy and myself took a little
Walk this Morning before Dinner—we called at the
Widow Horners where we saw some fine Children
of the Widows Daughters—I gave to them o. o. 6.
Had 20 People, Men, Women and Children setting

Wheat for me in Cary's Close to day. They set near two Acres in the Day. To Spraggs, Gardner for work, &c. pd. o. 10. o. We were rather dull after Mrs. Davy left us. Had a long Letter from my Sister Pounsett this Even.

Nov. 4. . . . It being very fine Weather to day Nancy went with me to Mr. Bodhams Rotation. Will carried her behind him, on my little Mare—we got there abt. 2. o'clock after having a very pleasant ride and it being quite a Summers Day, and there we dined and spent the Afternoon with Mr. and Mrs. Bodham, Mrs. Davy, Mr. Du Quesne and Mr. Smith. We had for Dinner a Piece of boiled Beef, a Couple of Swaffham Rabbitts boiled and Onions—a Couple of Fowls rosted and a plumb Pudding. At Quadrille this Evening lost o. 1. o. I got home to Weston this Evening about 9 o'clock. I left Nancy behind to spend a few Days at Mattishall.

Nov. 5. . . . Recd. for a Certificate of a Persons being buried in Woolen at Hockering according to the Act o. 1. o.[1] Finished setting three Acres and half of Wheat this Even'. The Quantity of seed Wheat to set the whole was six Bushells and one Peck, that is, as near as can be seven Peck and half to an Acre. Expence of setting it 8 Shillings per Acre, Allowance &c. included—I had 4 Diblers and sixteen Setters and they finished the whole in two Days.

Nov. 7. . . . Mr. Custance made me a long morning Visit and offered to send his Coach after me to dine with him to day by appointment, but I told him

[1] Burial in sheep's wool was compulsory by two statutes of Charles II's reign (1666 and 1678), the object being the encouragement of the wool industry. See Cunningham's *Growth of English Industry and Commerce*, vol. ii, p. 393, foot-note.

that Mr. Du Quesne who dines also at Weston House to day would take me with him in his Chaise thither as he promised and therefore abt 2 o'clock Du Quesne did call on me, stayed with me abt. half an Hour and then we both went to Weston House in our Gowns and Cassocks (as we are to meet the Bishop of Norwich there to day) and there we dined and spent the Afternoon with Mr. and Mrs. Custance, The Bishop and his Lady Mrs. Bagot, his Lordships Chaplain Mr. Gooch, and Sr. William and Lady Jernegan. Mr. and Mrs. Branthwaite were also invited but did not come, the former having sent word in the Morning that he had the Gout. The Bishop was not dressed in his Gown and Cassock, but in a purple Coat and a short silk Cassock under it. The Company all broke up about half past seven o'clock. I got home by 8. Could not prevail with Du Quesne to Stay and sup with me on his return. We had for Dinner some stewed Carp, Ham and Fowls, a fine Cygnet rosted &c. &c.—the first Course —a brace of Pheasants rosted, a fine Hare rosted, Blamange, Green Peas, Jelly &c. &c. the second Course. Many Dishes of Desert afterwards but nothing extra. The Bishop took Du Quesne very genteelly in to preach a Charity Sermon the ensuing Year at Norwich towards the Support of the Charity Schools there. Sr. Willm. Jernegan is a very fine Man, very easy, affable and good natured. Lady Jernegan is a fine Woman but high and mighty.[1] They are both of the Romish Persuasion. It being Friday and a Fast Day of Course to them, they however eat Fowl, Pheasant and Swan and Sr. William

[1] After all she was a great-great-granddaughter of Charles II and Barbara Villiers : see foot-note, p. 49, preceding.

eat some Ham. Upon the whole we spent an agreeable Day, but must confess that being with our equals is much more agreeable.

Nov. 8. . . . Went out a Coursing to day with my Folks, coursed two Hares, killed one and one Rabbit— so that we had tolerable sport—we coursed several Rabbitts. I was out with my People four Hours— they were out six.

Nov. 11. . . . Dr. Bathursts Tithe Frolick—stayed and dined and did not get home till 7 in the Evening and very dark. Almost all the Farmers attended and we were very harmonious. I called at Mr. Custances as I went down and stayed there half an Hour. Mr. and Mrs. Custance were gone about an Hour before to Sr. Thos. Beauchamps, and I believe they design staying there a few Days.

Nov. 12. . . . Mr. Thorne called on me this morning— His left arm was in a Sling, having lately been thrown out with his Wife of a one Horse Chaise. She received but little Injury. Mr. Thorne's Arm was the worse. About 1 o'clock took a ride to Mattishall and there dined and spent the Afternoon at Mr. Smiths it being his Rotation, with him, Mr. and Mrs. Bodham, Mrs. Davy, Nancy, Mr. Ashill, Mr. Du Quesne and Mr. Priest of Reepham. We had for Dinner some stuffed boiled Beef, 3 Chickens, 2 rosted, 1 boiled, a Piggs Face, a Currant Pudding, Syllabubs, Tartletts, Tarts, &c. &c. At Quadrille this Evening lost 0. 3. 0. I did not get home this evening till 10 o'clock and a bitter cold ride we had home. In Hockering Street we me[t] a Man very drunk as we came home having got from his horse and could not get up again. He did however by help get up at last, and we went home with him being a Mr. Smith a Farmer and who lives on Hockering Heath. I thank God he got home safe.

Nov. 13. . . . Mr. Pyle called on me this morning and desired me to lend him five guineas which I did 5. 5. 0. Sent Will and Jack this morning after Nancy at Mattishall who returned to Weston about 2 o'clock, rather tired by riding from thence, and is come home with a cold but otherwise very well—and she dined, supped and slept at home—after being at Mr. Bodhams from Nov^br 4.

Nov. 19. . . . About 1 o'clock I took a ride to Norwich on Dr. Bathursts Accounts, got there abt. 3 o'clock, went Directly to the Bank and had a Draught of 170 Pd for Cash and Notes advanced for the same— I then went to the Kings Head inclosed the above Draught of 170. Pound in a Letter to Dr. Bathurst, sealed it up and immediately walked down to the Post Office and put the same into the Box. Ben went with me to Norwich and returned in the Evening. I sent Ben when we got to Norwich to Mr. Priests with a fine Hare which we caught Yesterday. I supped and slept at the Kings Head. To extraordinaries this Evening pd. 0. 1. 0.

Nov. 20. I breakfasted and slept again at the Kings Head. Was greatly disturbed all last Night by a very noisy Club (called the Thumb Club) being directly under me and making a very great Noise all the Night long and did not leave the House till 8 in the Morn'. They hallowed and hooped all Night, broke above 12 Shillings worth of Bowls and Glasses. Pd. Studwell, China Man for things sent me 1. 0. 0. Pd. Baker for things this morning 0. 7. 4. Whilst I was at Bakers met by chance there, one Mr. Campbell a Clergyman in these Parts, and has the Living

of Weasingham, an old Acquaintance of mine of
Oriel College and afterwards of Worster Coll: He
asked me kindly to come and see him, I did the same
to him, and we exchanged our Addresses. With him
was a Mr. Parr a Clergyman and who lives at Norwich
and was formerly of Magdalen Coll: Oxon. At
Chases for 2 Ladies Pocket Books pd. o. 2. o. At
Ditto—for a Magazine for October pd. o. o. 6.
I dined, spent the Afternoon, supped and spent the
Evening at Mr. Priests with him, his Wife, their
Son John, Mr. Priest and Miss of Reepham, Mr. Du
Quesne, Mrs. Cooper, and Mr. Southerton, Mr.
Priests Journeyman. After Tea we had a Concert
of Musick 7 Hands—viz. Mr. Du Quesne, John
Priest, Mr. Reeves, a Mr. Stileman, a Mr. Harding-
ham, young Mr. Marsh, and a Mr. Smith, a Miss
Blomfield drank Tea, was at the Concert, and supped
and spent part of the Evening with us. It was a very
pretty Concert. Hardingham who played the Base
seems to be a most agreeable young Man and a
Gentleman of Fortune as is Mr. Stileman—both
Capital Performers especially Hardingham. Miss
Blomfield stayed to Supper but none of the rest.
I escorted Miss Blomfield home after Supper. After
the Concert and most of the Performers gone away
we had a Country Dance till Supper about half an
Hour. I danced with Miss Priest, Mr. Du Quesne
with Miss Blomfield. Mr. Priest of Reepham with
Mrs. Priest of Norwich, and Mr. Priest of Norwich
with Mrs. Cooper. I did not get to my Inn till
12 o'clock this Evening. We had for Dinner to day
a boiled Turkey and Oyster Sauce a fore Quarter of
London Lamb rosted, a Couple of Partridges rosted,
a boiled Tongue and a baked Pudding. For Supper

a Couple of Fowls boiled and Oyster Sauce, a fine Hare rosted, &c. &c.

Nov. 21. I breakfasted and spent the morning at Norwich. My Servant Ben came with my Horses after me this Morn'. I thank God, had a very good Night of rest—no Noise. Mr. Priest of Norwich made me this morning a Present of a fine String of the real Portugal Onions 20 in No. The largest of them weighed sixteen Ounces and half and measured 14 Inches in Circumference. Ben carried them home for me about noon. For some Eels and Oysters to carry home pd. o. 2. o. To a Glass of Rum and Water at the Swan pd. o. o. 6. Gave Mr. Priests Servant Maid this Morn' o. 1. o. To a Pound of Battell Gunpowder pd. o. 2. o. At my Inn paid this morning o. 4. 3. Gave to Servants there &c. o. 3. 6. Set of for Weston about 2 o'clock and Du Quesne went with me as far as Easton Dog and there we parted—got home about 4 o'clock to Dinner I thank God safe and well and found Nancy &c. the same. I dined, supped and slept at home as did Nancy. I expected to have found Mrs. Davy with Nancy as she promised to be at my House as Yesterday, but her being ill prevented her coming. Gave Nancy one of the Ladies Pocket Books for 1784. Gave her also a pretty pocket Leather Inkhorn.

Nov. 23. . . . Charlotte Dunnell is reported to be with Child by old Page. She lately lived with him as Housekeeper.

Dec. 2. . . . This being my Tithe Audit Day, the following People attended, and paid me every thing that was due. Howlett, Girling, Baker, Bush, Forster, Peachman, Michael Andrews for his Brother Stephen who is ill, Mann, Silvy, Js. Pegg, Jn. Pegg, Dade,

Page, Buck, Ringgar, Norton, Bidewell, Burroughs, Herring, Thos. Leggatt, Willm. Leggatt, Case, Bean for Mrs. Pratt, Rising, and Tom Cary—They all dined, spent the Afternoon and Evening till 10. o'clock, and then they all went to their respective homes, it being my desire that they would not stay after 10 o'clock. I gave them for Dinner a Leg of Mutton boiled, and Capers, some Salt Fish, plenty of plumb Puddings and a Couple of boiled Rabbitts, with a fine large Surloin of Beef rosted. Plenty of Wine, Punch and strong Beer after Dinner till 10 o'clock. We had this Year a very agreeable meeting here, and were very agreeable—no grumbling whatever. Total recd. this Day for Tithe 286. 15. 0. Paid out of the above to Steph: Andrews 0. 15. 0. Ditto to Mr. Dade 6. 17. 0. Ditto to Mr. Mann 4. 14. 0. Ditto to Mr. Bidewell 0. 13. 0. After the Company was all gone and we thought everything were agreeable and happy in my House, we were of a sudden alarmed by a great Noise in the kitchen, and on my immediately going out there found my Servant Man Will: Coleman beating about the Maids in a terrible manner and appeared quite frantic and mad. I seized him by the Collar and as soon as he was loose, he ran out into the Yard and jumped into the Pond there in a moment but he was soon taken up by Ben, which frightened us so much that we were obliged to sit up all night. We got him to bed however about 1 o'clock and after some time he was somewhat quiet—but it frightned us so much that Nancy and self did not go to bed till 6. in the morning. Ben and Jack did not go to bed at all. The reason of his being so, was on Lizzy's Account, as he wants to marry her and she will not, and he is very jealous.

Am afraid however that it proceeds from a family complaint, his Father having been crazy some time. It is therefore now high time for him to leave me which I shall endeavour to do the first opportunity. It made me very ill almost instantly and made my niece very·unhappy as well as ill also.

Dec. 3. . . . We did not get up till near 11. o'clock this morning and both far from being well being so much disturbed. Will something more sedate this morning but still looks very wild. I talked with him this morning for sometime and advised him to go into the West. I was very ill in the Afternoon—cannot eat. The Widow Horner paid me for Tithe 0. 4. 6. I gave her out of it 0. 1. 0. To Norton yesterday—gave 0. 5. 0. My Dogs having injured a Sow of his sometime back. We got to bed to night in tolerable good time.

Dec. 4. . . . Dr. Thorne called here this morning, I told him abt. Will: but he only advised him to live low he is much better to-day—but still looks wild.

Dec. 5. . . . To Mr. Palmer my Malster, this morning pd. a Bill of 29. 16. 6. Mr. Palmer paid me out of it for 10 Coomb Barley 6. 12. 6. To Mr. Ames, Cooper, paid a Bill of 0. 13. 0. To Mr. Cantrell of Lenewade Bridge pd. a Bill of 11. 0. 0. At 12 o'clock walked to Weston Church and buried one Susannah Thurston of Morton aged 27 Years. She lived with Michael Andrews as do her 2 Sisters. Michael Andrews pd me my Fee for burying her 0. 10. 6. About 2 o'clock Mr. and Mrs. Custance called on us and took us into their Coach, and we all went to Du Quesne's where we dined and spent the Afternoon and stayed till 8. in the Evening and then returned as we went. Mr. Smith of Mattishall

dined &c. with us there. At Loo this Evening I won
0. 3. 0. We had for Dinner some Skaite, a Leg of
Mutton boiled and Capers, a rost Turkey, some Peas
Soup, a brace of Partridges, frilled Oysters, &c. and
the Charter Custard. We got home by 9 o'clock
and to bed about 11. I was very low and indifferent
this Evening—took some Rhubarb, going to bed to
night wch. I hope will do good.

Dec. 10. [He rides to Norwich, pays various Bills,
among them a Bill for £12 19s. 6d. to Mr. Priest his
Wine Merchant.]

. . . Mr. Du Quesne came to Priests about 4 o'clock
and we supped and spent the Evening together at
Priests with him, his Wife, their Son John and one
Wilkins a young Man. Myself, Du Quesne, Mr. Priest
and Son went about 7 o'clock to hear a Lecture from
one Cary on Mimickery and we were very merrily
entertained by him for one Hour and half, a good
deal of good Company there. We each paid at going
in 0. 2. 0. In the Afternoon also went to Brown-
smiths and bought 6 yrds. of Pink Silk, Lutestring for
a Coat for Nancy and for which paid at 5/9 Pr. yard—
1. 14. 6. I slept at the Kings Head. Du Quesne at
Priests.

Dec. 12. . . . Mrs. Davy breakfasted and spent the
morning at Weston and about 12 my Man Will
carried her behind him to Mattishall to her new
boarding Place. Between 2 and 3 Mr. Custance sent
his Coach after Nancy and self to go and dine with
them which we did and stayed till 8 at Night and
then returned as we went. I offered to pay Mr. Custance for 7000 Bricks had of him last Summer but he
would not take anything which was extremely kind of
him. We had for Dinner some Fish, Peas Soup,

boiled Beef, rosted Hare, Macaroni, Tarts and baked
Pears. We had quite a snugg Party of us, only
Mr. and Mrs. Custances and ourselves. After Tea
we played Quadrille for nothing.

Dec. 16. ... Mr. Pyle called here this morning, I spoke
to him rather warmly about his Bill, thought it too
high, desired him to look over his Book again, and
wait on me to Morrow. He seemed rather uneasy
at it.

Dec. 22. ... To 46. poor People of Weston against
Xmas gave 1. 3. 0.

Dec. 23. ... Great Debates in both Houses of Parliament about the East India Bill being rejected by the
Lords, having passed the Commons.[1]

[1] If the reader desires to have some understanding of the political
situation in England between December 1783 and April 1784, he must
endure the following very brief historical disquisition, otherwise this
entry, that for March 27, 1784, and those for the first half of April will
not have the significance they deserve. The East India Bill was the
rock on which the coalition government of Fox's Whigs and North's
Tories (see note on pp. 63–4, preceding) was wrecked. The measure was
mainly Fox's, and its object was finally to transfer the supreme power
in matters political, administrative, financial, and commercial in India
from the Company to seven Commissioners appointed by Parliament.
Much in this direction of government control had already been accom-
plished by Lord North's Act of 1773, establishing a proper Judiciary
and a Governor General, but the continuance of oppression and mis-
government made a further reform essential in the interests of the natives.
The measure passed the House of Commons, but was thrown out by the
Lords at the instigation of George III on December 17, 1783. Fox and
North were forced to resign on December 19, and on the same day
William Pitt became Prime Minister at the age of 24. The objection
to the Bill by the King, the Lords, Pitt—and as it turned out, the country
at large—was, in effect, profound distrust of Fox and coalition. The
Bill involved the concentration of an immense patronage in the hands
of the Ministers of the day, and the country was sick of massive political
jobbery. However, the King's personal interference was unconstitutional,

1783

Dec. 25. . . . I dined today being Christmas Day at
1 o'clock and the following poor old [People] dined
here also, viz. Thos. Cary, Thos. Dicker, Thos.
Cushing, Ricd. Bates, Ricd. Buck, Thos. Carr, and
Js. Smith my Clerk. After they had dined I gave to
each one Shilling 0. 7. 0. Pray God! ever continue
to me the Power of doing good. I read Prayers and
Preached this Afternoon at Weston. Mr. and Mrs.
Custance both at Church.

Dec. 27. . . . Gave Nancy this morning to make up
for the 10 Pound I promised her at Xmas 5. 15. 6.
She having had the other before in things and Cash.
Nancy has recd. from me this Year in Cash and
things bought for her by me the Sum of 17. 18. 10.
Mr. Cary not going to Norwich to day as usual on
Account of the Snow—I sent Ben on foot about
11 o'clock, he being not unwilling to go, after Letters
and News from Norwich and he returned about
7 in the Evening with the news only, there were

and the proper step was now a dissolution of Parliament. This Fox
was determined to resist at all costs, as he thought he had only to
defeat Pitt's minority government over and over again in the House
of Commons to return quickly to power himself. The political battle
was ceaseless in the House of Commons till, on March 24, 1784, the King,
on Pitt's advice, dissolved Parliament. Pitt knew the country was now
overwhelmingly in his favour, and Fox was in the hopeless position of
having palpably tried to prevent an appeal to the people. Parson Woodforde's graphic account of the Norwich and county elections in April
1784, throws a vivid light on the political passion roused by the election,
and on the popularity of the younger Pitt, who was returned triumphantly
to power with an immense majority. Finally it should be added that
in this same year Pitt carried his own Indian measure of a Board of
Control which effected the same objects as Fox's measure, but left the
Company less trammelled, and still in possession of Indian patronage.
The Pitt system survived till 1858. (See Lecky, *England in the Eighteenth
Century*, vol. v, pp. 229–60.)

3 Letters for me at the Post Office, but Ben not being there soon enough, Mr. Custance's Servant had them.

Dec. 28. . . . I read Prayers, Preached by desire of Mr. Custance and administered the H: Sacrament this morning at Weston. Mr. Custance at Church and at the H: Sacrament. Considering the Quantity of Snow falling this morning there was a respectable Congregation at Church and at the H: Sacrament. Amongst the rest was my Thatcher Harrison and recd. the H. Sacrament from my hands. He is reputed to be a rank Methodist. My Clerk Js. Smith and poor old Widow Pulley dined here. Rec'd this Morning from Mr. Custance's Servant three double Letters from Dr. Bathurst at Oxford which I expected. My Servant Ben paid the Servant for them o. 3. 6. Mr. Custance desired me to preach to day on account of his qualifying himself for his late new Office.[1] Very cold with much Snow and a severe Frost.

Dec. 30. . . . Mr. Custance's Servants, George, Harry, Haylett the Gardner with the Cook Maid, Betty and Sukey Chamber-Maids all supped and spent the Evening with our Folks in Kitchen. They stayed till 10. o'clock and then walked home. I gave them a Couple of rost Fowls and some good Punch. Won of Nancy at Cribbage this Evening o. 2. o.

Dec. 31. . . . Dr. Thorne and a Mr. Pinching a young Clergyman, of Cambridge called here this Morn' and stayed an Hour. Harry, Mr. Custance's Servant brought me a Couple of wild Ducks and a Leash of Snipes this morning. Excessive hard Frost with high Winds—I think I never knew it colder than this morning.

[1] i. e. presumably of Justice of the Peace.

Anno Domini 1784.

Jan. 1. I breakfasted, dined, supped and slept again at home. Nancy breakfasted, dined &c. &c. again at home. About 12. o'clock walked to Church and publickly presented a Child of Harry Dunnells in the Church, Mary by name. At Cribbage this Evening with Nancy won 0. 1. 6.

Jan. 5. . . . Paid my Servants their Wages due this Day as follows :

To Betty 1 Yrs. Wages due this Day and for Tea also pd.	5. 15. 6
To Lizzy Do. Do. Do. pd.	2. 12. 6
To Will Coleman—for a Years Wages	5. 5. 0
To Do. dressing Wiggs—10ˢ 0ᵈ— Grains 13ˢ 0ᵈ	1. 3. 0
To Do. for 2. Pairs of Shoes	0. 12. 0
To Ben Leggatt 1. Yrs. Wages due this Day	10. 0. 0
To Jack Warton a Years Wages ,, ,, ,,	1. 1. 0
To Mr. Mony by his Servant Sam: Hardingham paid a Bill for Lime today of	2. 10. 0

Jan. 8. [Betsy Davy had come to stay with Nancy on January 6th.]

. . . About 12. o'clock Betsy Davy and myself took a Walk to Weston House it being a hard Frost, and we stayed there till half past 2. and then we walked back again to dinner by ½ past three o'clock. We saw both Mr. and Mrs. Custance and all the Children. I had a Pigg killed this morning which weighed 10 Stone and 7 Pound, a very pretty Pigg.

Jan. 14. . . . Will, Ben, and my upper Maid Betty, supped and spent the Evening last Night with Mr. Custance's Servants and stayed till after 11.

o'clock. Betty stayed and slept at Weston House. Hamilton's Birth-Day was kept last Night at the Squires. Betty was home pretty early this morning. Nunn Davy came to see his Sister this morning and I made him stay and dine with us. Himself and me had good Sport after Rabbitts in the Cover with our Dogs, and killed a brace up there. I made Nunn carry one of them home with him, to Mattishall. At 4. o'clock I sent him home—Ben went with him to Hockering to put him in the right road. At Cribbage this Evening with Nancy lost o. o. 6.

Jan. 21. . . . Bitter cold, very hard Frost, and much Snow in the Night. I went out with my Man this morning tracing Hares, we found one fine one which the Dogs killed. At Cribbage this Evening with Nancy won o. 2. ò. She was very sulky and sullen on loosing it, tho' not paid. She did not scarce open her Mouth all the Even' after. Mr. and Mrs. Hardy supped and spent the Even' with our Folks.

Jan. 22. . . . Very cold with more Snow and freezes very sharply also. Left of playing Cards with Nancy, she owes me o. 4. 6. She was very sulky all Day to Day and Evening. No stirring out this Weather.

Jan. 24. . . . It being a deep Snow and very hard Frost Mr. Cary did not go as usual to Norwich, therefore I sent Ben early in the Morn' on foot thither for News &c. &c. Ben returned about 4 o'clock with the things. Nancy had a Letter from her Brother Willm. who is now at Spithead, lately come from W. America.

Jan. 26. . . . Nunn Davy, Betsy's Brother, came here this morning on horseback and he stayed and dined, supped and slept here. He slept by choice with my Servt Willm. Gave Nunn this Evening to carry to

School 0. 1. 0. At Cribbage this Evening with Nancy won 0. 1. 0. I rejoiced much this morning on shooting an old Wood-pecker, which had teized me a long Time in pulling out the Reed from my House. He had been often shot at by me and others, but never could be a match for him till this Morn'. For this last 3. Years in very cold Weather did he use to come here and destroy my Thatch. Many holes he has made this Year in the Roof, and as many before. To Goody Doughty for 7 Lemons pd. 0. 0. 6.

Jan. 28. . . . Very fair but bitter, bitter cold and very hard Frost all day. At 12 o'clock I took a walk to Weston House, Mr. Custance was gone to Norwich, and Mrs. Custance so ill about her little girl being very bad that I could not see her. I stayed and played with the Young Gentlemen about half an Hour and then walked to Weston Church and buried a little girl of Wm. Larges—aged 3 Months. I then walked home to Dinner about 3 o'clock.

Feb. 6. . . . I sent after Mrs. Davy this morning about 9 o'clock by Will and she came to my House about 2 o'clock. To J$^{n}_{o}$. Pegg a Qrs. Land Tax for Rectory &c. 3. 0. 0. Mrs. Davy dined, supped and slept here. At Cribbage this Evening with Nancy won 0. 1. 6.

Feb. 7. I breakfasted and spent part of the Morn' at home. Nancy, Mrs. Davy and Betsy did the same. Snow very deep indeed and bitter cold Weather. About 11 o'clock this morning myself, Mrs. Davy, Betsy and Nancy got into Lenewade Bridge [Chaise] to go to Norwich as I am to preach to Morrow at the Cathedral. We were obliged to have four Horses the Snow being so very deep. We got to Norwich I thank God safe about 2 o'clock. We were obliged to go round by Mr. Du Quesnes to get to the Turnpike

road as soon as we could on Account of the Snow
wch. was very deep indeed especially over France
Green and no Tract of Wheels to be seen. We were
very fearful going over that Green as it was very
dangerous. It was very hard work even for the four
Horses to get over that Green. It was much better
on the Turnpike. The Snow in some Places was
almost up to the Horses Shoulders. Towards Lynn
the Snow is much deeper and the Road to it almost
impassable. Will went on horseback with us to
Norwich. We all dined, spent the Aft: supped &c.
at the Kings Head. To the Drivers of Lenewade
Chaise gave 0. 3. 0. To 4 Box Tickets to go to the
Play this Even' pd. 0. 12. 0. Norwich Streets and
Market Place nothing but Ice, very dangerous walking
about, very bad also for Carriages. At 6 o'clock we
all went to the Theatre which was unusually crowded
on Account of the Money recd. to night being to
be given in Charity to the poor of Norwich. The
Play was, As You Like It, and Rosina the Entertainment. I never saw the Boxes so full before. There
was taken this Evening at the Theatre 71 Pounds.
To a Coach to the Theatre and back again for 4 pd.
0. 4. 0. I walked down to Bunns Garden before
Dinner and saw his Air Balloon[1]—but it was not
floating.

Feb. 8. We breakfasted and slept again at the Kings
Head. At 10. o'clock this morning we all went in

[1] Balloons had been invented by the brothers Montgolfier, and first
ascended in France in June 1783. 'Do not wonder', wrote Horace
Walpole to Sir H. Mann on December 2, 1783, ' that we do not entirely
attend to things of earth : fashion has ascended to a higher element.
All our views are directed to the air. *Balloons* occupy senators, philo-
sophers, ladies, everybody. France gave us the *ton.* . . .' (Walpole's
Letters, vol. xiii, p. 96).

a Coach to the Cathedral. I went full dressed and being Preacher sat next to the Sub-Dean Dr. Hammond. Whilst the Anthem was singing I was conducted by the Virger to the Pulpit and there Preached a Sermon from these Words ' Let your light so shine before Men that they may see your good Works and glorify your Father wch. is in Heaven.' After Sermon was over I walked back to the Vestry, had my Hood taken of, and then a Person came to me and gave me for Preaching 1. 1. 0. I gave the Virger for the Use of the Hood 0. 1. 0. Neither Bishop, Dean or Mayor at the Cathedral. The Cathedral was not crowded owing to the cold. Lady Bacon was at the Cathedral and immediately after I had conveyed the Ladies back to the Inn and I had undressed myself, I waited on Lady Bacon and sat with her some Time at her Lodgings at one Hirsts. We all then went to Mr. Priests where we dined, spent part of the Afternoon, supped and spent the Evening with him, his Wife, and their Son John. In the Afternoon we took Coach and went to Alderman Starling Days where we drank Tea with him, his Wife, his Mother, and Sister in Law, his Son and a Capt. Poole, a very good kind of a young Man. Mr. Day behaved with great Politeness and everything very genteel. As we returned in the Coach from Mr. Days we were very near being overturned before we got to Priests. To Coaches this Day for us pd. 0. 8. 0.

Feb. 9. We breakfasted at the Kings Head and stayed in Town till near 2. this Afternoon and then we had a Chaise and four from the Kings Head and set of for Weston to get there by Dinner. I walked down to Mr. Frosts this morning and pd. him a Bill for things had of him in 1780, 2. 16. 0. To my Barber this morning gave 0. 2. 0. At Chases for Books pd. 0. 3. 1. At Scotts for a Pr. of Gloves pd. 0. 2. 2. At Bakers for things pd. 0. 4. 0. Paid and gave at the Kings Head abt. 3. 0. 0. Called at Mr. Francis's, Priests, Buckles, Smiths my Mercer and Garland my Taylors. We got I thank God safe home to Weston about 4. this Afternoon—the Snow as deep as we went and harder work for 4 Horses than going to Norwich. Gave the Drivers as they brought us home safe 0. 3. 0., some strong Beer and some Victuals. We did not dine till near 5 this Afternoon. Lent to Mrs. Davy this morning at the Kings Head 2. 2. 0. Mrs. Davy, Betsy, and Nancy dined, supped and slept at Weston.

Feb. 16. I breakfasted, dined, &c. &c. again at home. Nancy breakfasted, dined, &c. &c. again here. Mrs. Davy, and Betsy breakfasted, dined, &c. &c. here again. Mr. Mann and Mr. Buck Overseers of the Poor called on me this Morn' to desire me to subscribe something to the Poor during this very severe Weather and gave them for myself and Nancy 2. 2. 0. Mr. Custance subscribed towards the Poor 5. 5. 0. To Mr. Cary for things from Norwich &c. pd. 0. 13. 0. To Will for Expenses at Norwich &c. pd. 0. 13. 10. To Betty for things pd. 0. 4. 3. Paid Mrs. Davy what I owed her being 0. 2. 0. Mr. Matthews Exciseman of Mattishall, with whom Mrs. Davy boards, called here about Noon on Mrs. Davy and he dined on some cold Meat and then returned back. Did not get to bed till after 1. o'clock Mrs. Davy not being very well.

Feb. 19. . . . I went with our Folks a tracing in the Snow this morning after a Hare, started 3 and killed one. To Will: finding a Hare sitting gave 0. 1. 0.

At Cribbage this Evening with Mrs. Davy won
0. 1. 0.

Feb. 27. . . . We were all very low, dull and cross to-
day owing to it being a very wet, dull, and windy
Day. At Cribbage this Evening we lost 0. 1. 0.
Mrs. Davy and Betsy were to have gone home to day
but the Weather turning out so bad, deferred it.

Feb. 28. . . . Mrs. Custance made us a long morning
Visit, She had not been out before for 6 Weeks
having been confined so much by the Weather. At
Cribbage this Evening we lost 0. 1. 0. Had a Letter
this Evening from my Sister Pounsett in which she
informed us that poor Richard Clarke died Feb. 17.
at Cary—I hope he is happy. He has left his Wife
(Patty Clarke) £100 to be paid immediately and £10
Per Annum added to her Settlement and the use of
all the Furniture, To Frank Woodforde's Wife £50.
To Sophy White £50. To Sam Clarke £50. To my
Brother John and Wife £10 each. To Painter Clarkes
Children £10 each and To Charles Clarkes Boy 10
Pounds &c. &c.

Mar. 1. . . . Mrs. Davy and Betsy breakfasted, dined
and spent the Aft. here, but Mr. Matthews coming
after them in a one Horse Chaise before Dinner, they
all went together for Mattishall about 5 o'clock.
My Servant Will: went with them and returned by
7 o'clock. Mr. Matthews dined with us in the Parlour.
Gave Betsy Davy this Morn' a pretty half Crown
Piece. I sold about 4 Acres of Turnips this Morn'
to Mr. Howlett at 30s Per Acre to be fed of with
Sheep only, not one to be pulled, and to be fed of by
old Lady Day or thereabout.

Mar. 4. . . . To Goody Doughty to reconit [?] being
distressed gave 0. 1. 0.

Mar. 7. . . . I read Prayers and Preached and Churched Mrs. Alldis this morning at Weston. Mr. and Mrs. Custance at Church. Nancy very ill all day with Cholic Pains.—I gave her some Rhubarb going to bed, which I hope will do good. Her Complaint I believe is something of the Fever that has been so frequent of late. All my Servants have had it. Nancy and self have escaped it hitherto but now I think we shall both have our Share of it.

Mar. 9. . . . Nancy very ill again this morning, kept her bed almost the whole Day. I sent for Dr. Thorne early, he came about 12 o'clock—says it is the Fever Nancy has which has been so long about these Parts. Mr. Thorne left a Vomit for to be taking to night and a Rhubarb Powder to take to Morrow. Nancy however eat some Rabbit for Dinner. To Goody Doughty for 4 Lemons pd. o. o. 6. To a Boy (named Willmot) from Dereham with Muffins for 14 of them I paid him o. o. 6.

Mar. 11. . . . Nancy taken very ill this morning about 3 o'clock worse than ever. Mr. Thorne came here about 11. and brought some bark for her to take to begin at 12. o'clock and then every 3 hours till bed Time. Nancy did not get out of bed till 6. this Afternoon. She was then something better.

Mar. 12. . . . Nancy a good deal better this morning, she takes the bark to day every two Hours till bed time. She complained of a great Lightness in her head and rather giddy—was below Stairs all Day.

Mar. 13. . . . Nancy brave to day (tho' this Day is the Day for the intermitting Fever to visit her) but the Bark has prevented its return—continued brave all day. Dr. Thorne and Betsy Davy with him on a little Hobby called on us this morning and stayed with us about half an Hour, but could not prevail on them to dine. Sent Ben early this morning to sell a Cow and Calf for me which he did and returned home to dinner. Ben sold the Cow and Calf, and which I recd. of him 6. o. o. Dr. Thorne's Method of treating the Ague and Fever or intermitting Fever is thus—To take a Vomit in the Evening not to drink more than 3 half Pints of Warm Water after it as it operates. The Morn' following a Rhubarb Draught —and then as soon as the Fever has left the Patient about an Hour or more, begin with the Bark taking it every two Hours till you have taken 12 Papers which contains one Ounce. The next oz. &c. you take it 6. Powders the ensuing Day, 5 Powders the Day after, 4 Ditto the Day after, then 3 Powders the Day after that till the 3$^{rd.}$ oz. is all taken, then 2 Powders the Day till the 4$^{th.}$ oz: is all taken and then leave of. If at the beginning of taking the Bark it should happen to purge, put ten Dropps of Laudanum into the Bark you take next, if that dont stop it put 10. drops more of Do. in the next Bark you take—then 5 Drops in the next, then 4, then 3, then 2, then 1 and so leave of by degrees. Nancy continued brave but seemed Light in her head. The Bark at first taking it, rather purged her and she took 10 Drops of Laudanum which stopped it.

Mar. 14. . . . Nancy breakfasted, dined, &c. &c. again at home. She was brave today and eat very hearty. I read Prayers and Preached this Afternoon at Weston. None of Weston House Gentry at Church this Afternoon. Bitter cold Wind. Frost all Day, very cold indeed. We did not dine till after Church this Afternoon. Thos. Cushing and Nathaniel Heavers dined with our Folks in Kitchen. They have [been] hedging and Ditching for me all the last Week.

Mar. 18. . . . Nancy brave again now by taking the Bark.

Mar. 23. . . . About 11. this morning took a ride and Will: with me to Mr. Du Quesne's, stayed there about half an Hour, then went to Mattishall called on Mrs. Davy and Betsy both at home, but Mrs. Davy was very ill and in bed—stayed there half an Hour, then walked to Mr. Smiths found him at home and disengaged, therefore promised to take a Family Dinner—then walked to Mr. Bodham's saw Mr. and Mrs. Bodham, and Miss Bodham—they wanted me to dine there but was preengaged to Mr. Smith. Stayed there almost an Hour. Saw at Mr. Bodhams a Mr. Wright of Downham a Surgeon, and Billy Hewett. Returned to Mr. Smith by 2 o'clock and there dined with him only—We had for Dinner some minced Veal, some cold slices of Pork and a plum Pudding. Mr. Bodham came and smoked a Pipe with us after Dinner. About 5 walked down by myself to Mrs. Davys and there drank [tea] with her and her Daughter Betsy, stayed there till 6 then mounted my Mare and returned home. Got home about 7 o'clock—spent a very pleasant Day.

Mar. 27. . . . A poor Woman brought a Child this morning to me from Witchingham to desire me to privately baptize it, being very bad ever since it was born—which I did directly by name Benjamin—It was born last Sunday and scarce a moment free from crying ever since. The poor Infant cried all the time it was here, very black in the face, and seemed to be in much pain. Pray God release him from his great misery. It is a child of Willm. and Eliz. Southgate.

Nancy had a long Letter from her Sister—in which she mentioned that old Mr. Pew is dead, died in Ilchester Jail—poor Fellow said a little before he died, that he had been like a hunted Hare for many Years before. His eldest Son Willm. is since conveyed to the same Jail—and I believe he deserves it. Hope the poor Father is now happy. His Family gave him certainly much uneasiness. . . . By the Papers, Parliament was dissolved on Thursday last and a new Parliament to meet the 6 of April next. Hurly, Burly Times at present.[1] Pray God defend Old England, from all Enemies at home as well as from foreign ones.

Mar. 31. . . . Of one Bagshaw a Derbyshire Man and who carries a Pack with divers things in it to sell, bought a whole Piece of black Ribbon 18 Yards of it at $3\frac{1}{2}^d$ per Yard worth 5^d pd. o. 5. 3. Nancy bought some coloured Ribbon at 5^d worth 8^d. To a Qr. of a Pound of 9^d Thread worth 10^d I pd. o. 2. 10. To a Qr. of a Pound of 4^d Thread very good pd. o. 1. 4. To 2 oz: of 4^d Thread and 2 oz: of 3^d Thread pd. o. 1. o. Gave the Maids 2 oz: each besides of 4^d thread o. 1. 4. Very hard Frost this Evening. Snow all Day before.

April 2. . . . Wrote a long Letter to my Sister Pounsett to day which is to be sent to Norwich to Morrow. The Weather seems to be inclined to alter, as it is much milder today than it has been of late. Many

---

[1] See foot-note, pp. 111–2, preceding. Parson Woodforde's epithet of ' Hurly Burly ' was peculiarly apposite to the political witches' cauldron of that time. The reader will remember *Macbeth's* opening :

> ' I *Witch*. When shall we three meet again,
> In thunder, lightning, or in rain ?
> 2 *Witch*. When the hurlyburly 's done,
> When the battle 's lost and won.'

Farmers are now greatly distressed for their Stock and some obliged to slay them half fat, on Account of the Scarcity of Provision for them. The Turnips rot very fast of late. I never knew so severe nor so long a Winter as this has turned out—It snowed all the Afternoon this Day. The Land has not been free from Snow since the 23 of December last.

April 3. . . . Hurly, Burly Times at Norwich, an Election coming on, on Monday next for that City.[1] Mr. Townshend and Sr. Jn̄o. Wodehouse rejected at Yarmouth and obliged to retire peaceably. Sr. Harbord Harbord, Mr. Hobart, and Mr. Windham stand for the City of Norwich.[2] Sent Ben early this morning to Norwich to sell some Barley for me and to be sent next Week. He returned to Dinner, and sold what Barley I have to dispose of to one Clover at 15s. 3d. Pr. Comb. for as much as I could send next Week.

April 5. . . . After breakfast I took a ride to Norwich and Ben went with me. The Election for Members of Parliament for that City coming on to day. We

[1] See foot-note, pp. 111–2, preceding.

[2] Taking the candidates here named in order—the reader will find an account of Mr. Townshend in vol. i, p. 211 ; Sir John Wodehouse, 6th Baronet of Kimberley, Norfolk, was born in 1741 and died in 1834. He was M.P. for Norfolk from 1784–97, in the latter year being created Baron Wodehouse of Kimberley ; Sir Harbord Harbord, 2nd Baronet of Gunton, Norfolk, was born in 1734 and died 1810. He was M.P. for Norwich (six Parliaments) from December 1756 to 1786, in the latter year being created Baron Suffield of Suffield, Norfolk ; Mr. Hobart was presumably Henry, fourth son of the 1st Earl of Buckinghamshire, and brother of the 2nd and 3rd Earls. Though unsuccessful now, he secured election later on—in 1786 ; Mr. Windham was the eminent statesman for some account of whom see vol. i, p. 219. He was one of the few successful Whig coalition candidates in the 1784 general election. (The above particulars are gleaned from Cokayne's *Complete Baronetage*, Cokayne's *Complete Peerage*, Burke's *Peerage*, and the *D. N. B.*)

got there about Noon—saw a great deal of Hurly, Burly. 3 Candidates Sr. Harbord Harbord ; Mr. Hobart, and Mr. Windham. Sr. Harbord's Son rode for him. It was a pretty sight to see them all Chaired and carried many Times round the Market Place. Sr. Harbord and Mr. Windham seemed to be most successful. The Poll begun closing up ab^t six in the Evening. I stayed till 8 o'clock and it being then not finished I set of for home. It was said that Windham had 70 majority over Hobart. Sr. Harbord was sure from the beginning. Went without any Dinner whatever—drank Tea in the Afternoon at Mr. Priests with several Ladies. Mr. Priest's Brother of Reepham and Beccy Priest there. Had a cold ride home and was much fatigued having walked too much to day about Norwich—got home abt 10. thoroughly tired and after Supper was very ill, thought I should have fainted—The Fatigue of this Day was too much. To My Fishmonger Beal for fish sometime ago pd. o. 3. 4. For trifling expenses besides at Norwich pd. also o. 1. 6.

April 7. . . . We dined, spent the Afternoon, supped and spent the Evening at Weston House, with Mr. and Mrs. Custance, Mr. Prideaux and his Brother Charles. Mr. Custance sat of for Norwich almost immediately after Dinner to attend a Committee there concerning Sr. John Wodehouse, being a Candidate for the County and to Morrow being the Day fixed for the Nomination Mr. Custance stayed at Norwich all Night. We stayed at Weston House till 10. at Night. After Tea and Coffee we got to Cards at Vinct' one. Nancy lost at it 1s. 6d.— and I lost at it o. 1. o. We went to Weston House in their Coach and returned in the same.

April 8. . . . I got up this morning a little after 6 eat
some cold Meat and drank half a Pint of small Beer—
then mounted my Mare and went of for Norwich
and Will. with me. We got there about 9 o'clock—
put up my Horses at the Wool-Pack in St. Giles's
then walked to Mr. Priests where I met Mr. Priest
of Reepham. About 11 o'clock Mr. Priest and
Brother and self walked down to St. Andrews Hall
where was a most prodigious Crowd of People
assembled together to hear the Nomination for the
County Election which is to be Wednesday—14
Instant. A very little after 11. the High Sheriff
Sr. Thos. Durant came and then the Doors were
opened and we all went into the Hall. The High
Sheriff then mentioned the occasion of their meeting
&c. but the Noise was so great the whole Time that
I could not hear a single word. Sr. Edward Astley,
Sr. John Wodehouse, and Mr. Coke are the Candidates.[1] The two former met with great applause
but the latter very little. There was a board intro-
duced with Astley and Coke wrote upon it in large
Capitals, but it was no sooner exposed than it was
pulled down and broke all to Shivers. And then all

[1] Taking these candidates in order—Sir Edward Astley, 4th Baronet of
Melton Constable, Norfolk, was born in 1729 and died in 1802. He was
M.P. for Norfolk from 1768–90 ; Sir John Wodehouse (see preceding
foot-note) ; Mr. Coke was the famous Mr. Coke of Norfolk, i. e. Thomas
William Coke, 1752–1842, who by his agricultural experiments trans-
formed the cultivation of West Norfolk from rye growing to wheat
growing, specialized in breeds of sheep, cattle, and pigs, and generally
benefited his country, his county, his neighbours, and himself. He was
made Earl of Leicester in 1837. He was M.P. for Norfolk from 1776–84,
and again practically continuously from 1790–1833. He was a devoted
supporter of Fox, hence his temporary unpopularity in 1784. (For
Astley, see Cokayne's *Complete Baronetage*, for Coke the *D. N. B.*)

for Wodehouse. About 1 o'clock the Meeting ended —from the Hall I went about the Town with Mr. Prideaux and his Brother (whom I met in the Hall) till near 2. then walked to Mr. Priests and there dined with him, his Wife and Son John, Mr. and Miss Bekky Priest of Reepham. We had for Dinner rost Beef and a Yorkshire Pudding. About 3 took leave of Mr. Priest and walked down to Bunns Gardens almost and designed to go in, but the Air Balloon which was to be exhibited was launched of just as I got there.[1] I saw it however as it rose—it was a small one—and soon went out of my Sight gradually, I saw it also on its coming down which was very soon indeed. It went about two Miles by what I could judge. From thence walked to the Wool-Pack, Mounted my Mare and set of for Weston —got home abt. 6. To my Fishman, Beales, went to see for Fish, but none. To trifles at Norwich pd. abt. o. 1. o. It was Tombland Fair to day at Norwich. Recd. a Letter to Day from Dr. Oglander Warden of New College that he with some Friends were to be at Lenewade Bridge Wednesday and to desire me to attend—Unlucky Day being the Election Day.

April 13. I breakfasted, dined, &c. &c. again at home. Nancy breakfasted, made a running dinner upon a Mutton-Stake about 1. o'clock, and then sat of in Lenewade Bridge Chaise with my Upper Maid with her, as likewise my Servant Lad, for Norwich, to be at the County Election for Members of Parliament, which begins to Morrow at the Shire-Hall on Castle Hill. It was talked that there would be a severe Contest between Sr. John Wodehouse, Sr. Edwd. Astley and Mr. Coke, but Yesterday it

[1] See foot-note, p. 117, preceding.

was the common report that Coke had declined the Poll. I am (as is Mr. Custance) for Sr. John Wodehouse only, Sr. Edwd. Astley having made an unlucky Junction with Mr. Coke—whose parliamentary Conduct has been quite opposite of late Sr. Edwd. Astley having voted for the popular Mr. Pitt and Mr. Coke for Fox, and Lord North.[1] My Maid and Boy returned from Norwich abt. 5 o'clock. They brought me word that Nancy got very well there and is at Mr. Priest's, being invited thither by them. Very soon after Nancy went I took a ride to Weston House but both Mr. and Mrs. Custance were gone to Norwich. I stayed about an Hour with the little Folks and returned home to Dinner by 3 o'clock.

April 14. I breakfasted upon some Mutton Broth about 6. o'clock and very soon after breakfast I mounted my Mare and went of [to] Norwich and Will: went with me for to be at the County Election for Members of Parliament. We got to Norwich a little after 8. o'clock—put up my Horses at the Wool-pack, and then walked to Mr. Priests and there made a second breakfast on Tea and Toast. Nancy was not down Stairs. About 10 o'clock the Market Place and Streets in Norwich were lined with People and almost all with Wodehouse's Cockades in their Hats. After breakfast I went to Mrs. Brewsters and got 6 Cockades all for Wodehouse—3 of them of blue and Pink with Wodehouse wrote in Silver on the blue, the other 3 plain blue and Pink for my Servants at home. About 11 o'clock Sr. John Wodehouse preceded with a great many Flaggs and a band of Musick, made his public Entry on horseback, attended with between

---

[1] For the political situation at this time, see foot-note, pp. 111–12, preceding.

two and three Thousand Men on Horseback, They
came thro' St. Giles's, then thro' the Market Place,
then marched on to the Shire House on the Castle
Hill and there Sr. John Wodehouse with Sr. Edward
Astley were unanimously chosen Members for the
County. After that they had dressed themselves
handsomely and were chaired first round the Castle-
Hill and then three times round the Market Place
amidst an innumerable Number of Spectators and
the loudest acclamations of Wodehouse for ever.
Sr. Edwd. Astley met with little Applause, having
joined Coke before. I never saw such universal Joy
all over the City as was shown in behalf of Sr. John
Wodehouse. I dined at Mr. Priests with him, his
Wife, Son John, Mr. Priest of Reepham and Daughter
Bekky and 2 strange Ladies. We had for Dinner some
Whitings and a Fillett of Veal. Pd. at Studwells
China Shop a small Bill of o. 3. o. I intended to have
went out of Town to night but our Warden of New
College with Peckham the Steward, and Jeffries and
Jeanes the Outriders came to Norwich this Afternoon
they being on their Progress and went to the Swan
Inn—therefore soon after Tea I went to them and
there supped and spent the Evening with them, they
were very glad indeed to see me and so was I them.
They had been to Witchingham and there heard that
I was at Norwich at the Election there. It happened
very unluckily that I could not see them at my House,
as of all Days but this, I could have contrived to be
at home. They all looked pretty well but the Warden
who looks thin and has a very bad cold and a Cough.
I sent Will home this Evening and to come again to
Morrow. I slept if I can call it so, at Mr. Priests
and very uncomfortably indeed—did not go to bed

till near 2 in the morning. Miss Priest, her Father, Mr. Priest of Norwich and Son being at the Assembly. To little trifling expenses at one Place and another pd. 0. 2. 6.

April 15. I breakfasted at Mr. Priests and then went to the Swan and saw the New College Gentlemen. And after they had breakfasted, I walked with them to the Castle-Hill—To the Cathedral—to the Bishops Palace—To Sr. Andrews Hall—to the new Bridge— To the new Presbyterian Chapel—To the Play- House &c. I walked with them from 10 in the Morning to near 2 o'clock in the Afternoon—Was quite tired. Then went to Mr. Priests, dressed myself and walked to Mr. Francis's and there dined being invited, with him, Mrs. Francis, Mr. and Mrs. Parrott of Saham, Our Warden, Peckham, Jeffries, and Jeanes and Mr. Francis's Brother of Edgefield. We had for Dinner a nice Dish of Fish— Rump of Beef boiled, Veal Cutlets with forced Balls —a Turkey rosted and some Lemon Cream. I could not stay to drink Tea with them, being engaged to go to the Play with my Niece &c.—therefore I walked to Mr. Priests drank a Dish of Tea and then Mr. Priest, his Brother and Daughter of Reepham, Nancy and myself went to the Theatre about 6. o'clock— got into the Boxes. The Theatre was never more crowded, The Play being by desire of Sr. John and Lady Wodehouse—It was the School for Scandal. The Entertainment—the poor Soldier. Soon as ever Sr. John and Lady Wodehouse made their appear- ance—an universal Clap with Wodehouse for ever resounded from all Parts of the Theatre and the same on their leaving the Theatre. We walked to the Theatre and back again. I gave Miss Priest a Ticket and my Niece one I paid for 3 Box Tickets o. 9. o. Nancy went home with the Priests and there supped and slept again. I went to my old Inn the Kings Head and there I supped and slept, tho' very sadly, my Sheets not being Clean. To trifling expenses to day pd. o. 2. 6.

April 19. . . . To Mr. Mann's Nephew Rose, paid a Poors Rate this morning for Land in hand at 11*d*. pd. 1. 7. 8¾. To Mr. Cary for things from Norwich &c. pd. o. 2. 6¾. To People, stubbing up Furze in the Cover—gave—o. 1. o. Haylett, Mr. Custance's Gardner, a good sober Fellow supped with our Folks in Kitchen. My under Maid Lizzy very bad in the Fever again, and very luckily for her Dr. Thorne called here in the Afternoon, drank a Glass or two of Wine with us—saw my Maid and happened to have in his Pocket a Vomit and a Rhubarb Powder which he left for her.

April 21. . . . At 3 o'clock took a walk to Mr. Micklethwaites and there dined and spent the Afternoon and great part of the Evening with him, Mrs. Micklethwaite, Mr. and Mrs. Branthwaite of Taverham, Captain Laton and his Lady, and two young Ladies by name Howe. We did not dine till very near 5 o'clock—drank Tea at 8—and then got to Cards, at Vinct' une, at 3*d*. per Fish—and played till 10 and then I came home, tho' very much pressed to stay and supp with them. All the other Company stayed to Supper. I won at Cards this Evening o. 5. o. We had a very genteel Dinner and Desert after. The first Course at Dinner was Fish, a piece of rost Beef, Pork Stakes, Soup, hashed Calfs Head, a boiled Fowl and Piggs Face.—2nd Course was stewed Sweetbreads, a fore Qr. of Lamb rosted, Jellies, Custards,

Lemon Cream, Syllabub and Blamange. Desert—
Oranges, Pistachio Nutts—blanched Almonds and
Raisins, and preserved Cherries. Miles Branthwaite
asked me to meet the present Company at Dinner to
Morrow at Taverham but cd. not promise as my
Niece was not very well.

April 24. . . . Ben got up very early this morning to
go to Norwich with 5 Coomb of Barley for to sell
for me there and to bring back a Qr. of a Pipe of
Port Wine from Mr. Priests for me, it having been
bespoke before. Lizzy still continues poorly in the
Ague and Fever. Ben returned between 4. and 5.
this Afternoon having sold my Barley, and brought
home safe the Wine from Mr. Priest. Recd. for the
Barley 3. 16. 3. I gave Lizzie a Camphire Powder
to take at Night.

April 30. . . . To Clerk Hewitt for a Tub of Gin this Aft.
pd. 1. 6. 0. My Maid Lizzie (than[k] God) is much
better. The red Bark agrees with her and she continues taking it.

May 6. . . . To John Pegg a Qrs. Land Tax pd. 3. 0. 0.
To Ditto ½ yrs. Window Tax pd. 1. 2. 7. To Ditto
½ yrs. House Tax pd. 0. 1. 9.[1] Mr. Donnes Servant
Man Charles of Broome came here this morning with
a Note from Mrs. Bodham of Mattishall to Nancy,
to acquaint her that Mr. B. is exceeding ill at Thorn-
ham not able to write.

May 7. . . . About 12 o'clock took a ride to Weston
House and stayed there till half past 2 o'clock. Mr.
and Mrs. Custance both at home—I took a walk with
Mr. Custance down to the Garden, and there
Mr. Custance made the Gardner (Michael Hylett)

---

[1] For some historical account of these taxes, see vol. i, pp.
57–8.

cut a Cucumber for me to carry home to the Parsonage.

May 11. Mem: Mr. and Mrs. Custances Children, Hambleton, George, Willm. and Miss Fanny were all inoculated[1] on Saturday last at Norwich by Dr. Donne. They are to stay at Norwich till well.

May 13. . . . About 1 o'clock Mr. and Mrs. Custance called here and took Nancy and self into their Coach and we went to Mattishall to Mr. Smiths with them, where we dined and spent the Afternoon with Mr. Smith only. We had for Dinner some Maccarel, a Leg of Mutton boiled and Capers, a Couple of Fowls rosted and Pigs Face. Plovers Eggs. Cheesecakes, Tarts, Rasberry Cream and Custards. After Coffee and Tea we got to Cards to Loo, at which I won four Shillings—Nancy won 2 Shillings 0. 4. 0. About 8 we sat of from Mattishall, got home about 9. Mr. and Mrs. Custance put us down on their return at the Parsonage and then took their leave of us. Mrs. Custance very anxious about her Children, they being at Norwich and under Inoculation.

May 17. . . . Ben hard at work today in plowing up the Cover, very slow work, owing to the Furze Roots being left. He begun upon it this morning to go thro' with it.

May 18. . . . This being Mr. Smiths Rotation I rode to Mattishall about 1 o'clock and there dined and spent the Aft: with Mr. Smith, Mr. Du Quesne and a Mr. Codman with him, Mr. and Mrs. Bodham, Miss Bodham and a Miss Betsy Donne of London, a fine showy Girl. After Coffee and Tea we got to Quadrille at wch. I won 0. 0. 6. We had for Dinner some Cods Sounds and Tongues with Egg Sauce,

[1] For inoculation against small-pox, see vol. i, pp. 40–1.

a Couple of Fowls rosted, a Piece of rost Beef, Tarts, Trifle, Plovers Eggs &c. It was also Mattishall Gaunt to day, and a great many People were there being a fine Day.

May 19. ... Mr. Custance drank his Coffee here this Afternoon and stayed with us till near 9 o'clock. Mrs. C: is at Sr. Edmd. Bacons—the little folks all as well as can be expected in their Condition.

May 24. ... Nancy got up very early this morning and went of for Mattishall to Mr. Bodhams in Mr. Bucks Market Cart. Ben went with her to drive. She was gone before I was down Stairs, tho' she had very little or no rest all Night as it thundered, and Lightned a good deal after we got up Stairs. I had a very disagreeable Night of it also on the above Account—I only laid down with my Cloaths on till near 6 in the Morn' then got into bed.

May 26. ... At 11 o'clock took a ride to Church to attend at a Vestry there held for examining things belonging to the Church. Mr. Howlett, Mr. Mann, Stephen Andrews, and John Buck only attended— From Church rode to Mr. Custance's but both Mr. and Mrs. Custance were gone to Norwich to see their Children now under Inoculation. I took a ride afterwards to Du Quesne's and there dined and spent the Afternoon with him, Mr. and Mrs. Priest of Norwich and Mr. Mrs. and Miss Priest of Reepham. We had for Dinner some Pike and Maccarel, a fore Qr. of Lamb rosted, Pidgeon Pye—Charter &c. &c. I carried Mr. Du Quesne a Cucumber in my Pocket. After Tea Mr. Du Quesne, Mr. Priest of Reepham and myself played a Game of Bowls on his Green. I lost o. o. 6. To some Children opening the Gate gave o. o. 6. I returned home to Weston

1784

about 9 this Evening. We had a most gracious Rain this Evening and it lasted.

May 27. . . . After Dinner I went to Norwich and Will: with me. We got to Norwich about 5 o'clock. Will returned home with the Horses in the Evening. I supped and slept at the Kings Head. As soon as I got to Norwich I went and saw Mr. Custances Children at Thorne's Cabinet Maker in St. Stephens Church-Yard. I found them all brave. Hambleton and George have the small Pox pretty full. Willm. and Miss show very little of it. To necessary things this Evening—paid o. 1. 6.

May 28. I breakfasted at the Kings Head. After breakfast I dressed myself in my Gown and Cassock and went to the Cathedral to attend the Bishop's primary Visitation there. More than 40 Clergy attended. Dr. Grimwood Preached. After the Sermon the Clergy were all called over—and after that the Bishop gave us a long but very good Charge. After the Charge we all adjourned to the Maids Head, and there we all dined—and the Bishop dined with us. We had an excellent Dinner and very good Wine afterwards. We each paid for our Dinner o. 2. 6. There were 40 Clergy sat down to Dinner besides his Lordship—The Bishop treated his Clergy with Wine. We did not dine till near 4 o'clock. The Bishop left us about 6 o'clock. I soon followed him. For Exhibiting my Letters of Orders and Institution to Mr. Baker the Official pd. o. 6. o. For Procurations to the Bishop pd. o. 2. 7. To a pair of new Gloves at Scotts pd. o. 2. o. My Man Will: came to Norwich about Noon with my Horses. He waited on me at Table at the Maid's Head. I returned to my Inn soon after 6 o'clock this Evening undressed, put up

136

my things, and then put on my Boots paid my Bill &c. at the Kings Head which was 0. 6. 0. went afterwards and saw Mr. Custances Children and then mounted my Mare and went for Weston. Got home rather fatigued about 9 o'clock. I had a good deal of Chat with the Bishop to day. I sat pretty near him at Dinner. I supped and slept again at home. I called at Priests just as I left Town. There were few Clergy that I knew at the Visitation only Dr. Sandby, Mr. Collier, Mr. Gooch, Mr. Priest, Mr. Thomas, Mr. Humphrey, Mr. Willins &c. To my Barber Mileham gave 0. 1. 0.

May 31. ... A smock Race at the Heart this Afternoon, I let all my Folks go to it but Lizzy, and all came home in good Time but Will who being merry kept me up till 11 o'clock and then went to bed without waiting any longer for him, and just as I was going to sleep he came and made a Noise under my Window and then marched of and I went to sleep.

June 1. ... I gave Will notice this morning to leave me, but Nancy hearing of it prevailed on me to try him a little longer with us—but am afraid it won't do. I married at Weston Church this Morning by Banns Willm. Hill and Hester Dunham both old People. Recd. only for marrying them having recd. 2s. 6d. before—0. 2. 6. Goody Doughty called here this morning and paid me some Mony I lent her a while ago—being 0. 10. 6. Du Quesne called here between 2 and 3 o'clock, he is going with us to dine at Mr. Custances whose Carriage came after us whilst Du Quesne was here. We went in the Coach and Mr. Du Quesne rode on horseback. Mr. Custance and Mr. Collier came after us in the Coach but they did not get out. Mr. and Mrs. Collier, Mr. Du

Quesne and us were all the Party that dined at Weston House. We had for Dinner Spring Chicken and Ham, Harrico of Mutton—Goose Gibletts—Patties and rost Beef on the side B. 2nd Course a Green Goose, Pidgeons, Trifle &c. &c. After Tea we got to Cards, at Loo, at which I lost o. 4. 6. We did not return home this Evening till near 10 o'clock.

June 5. . . . Nancy rec^d a Letter from her Brother Sam this Evening which gave her great Spirits, he having lately been introduced to the Queen and presented her a Picture of his Painting being her Son Prince Frederick. Sam talks of great things, of being soon knighted. Am very glad that his Lot fell in so fortunate a Soil—And his Merit is deserving the same. Sam's News too great to be true, am afraid.[1]

June 10. . . . About 3 o'clock this Afternoon Mr. and Mrs. Custance called on us, took us into their Coach and carried us to Mr. Micklethwaites where we dined and spent the remaining part of the Afternoon and part of the Evening with Mr. and Mrs. Micklethwaite, Mrs. Branthwaite Senr of Norwich, Miles Branthwaite and Wife, a Miss Howes, and Mr. and Mrs. Custance—we returned as we went in Mr. Custance's Coach between 8 and 9 o'clock. We had a very genteel Dinner, Soals and Lobster Sauce, Spring Chicken boiled and a Tongue, a Piece of rost Beef, Soup, a Fillet of Veal rosted with Morells and Trufles, and Pigeon Pye for the first Course—Sweetbreads, a green Goose and Peas, Apricot Pye, Cheese-

---

[1] For a note on Samuel Woodforde, R.A., see vol. i, p. 208. His hopes of knighthood were not realized. Prince Frederick is the Duke of York (1763–1827), who now surveys London from his column on the Steps. He was unfortunate as a commander in the field, but as an administrator and army reformer he was most efficient.

cakes, Stewed Mushrooms and Trifle. The Ladies
and Gentlemen very genteely dressed. Mr. Micklethwaite had in his Shoes a Pair of Silver Buckles
which cost between 7 and 8 Pounds. Miles Branthwaite had a pair that cost 5 guineas.

June 17. ... Prodigous fine growing Weather indeed.
Very busy all the Morning in writing.

June 21. ... At 8 o'clock this Morning mounted my
Mare and rode to Du Quesnes by myself, he had not
begun breakfast, I therefore made a very good second
breakfast with him. From Mr. Du Quesnes I rode
on to Mattishall, called at Mr. Bodhams, neither of
them at home being gone to Swaffham, as old
Mr. Bodham is given over. From thence went to
Mr. Smiths, stayed with him ½ an Hour and then
went down to Mrs. Davy's and Mr. Smith with me I
stayed full an Hour at Mrs Davys and returned home to
Weston to Dinner—Mr. Smith pressed me much to
dine with him. Nunn Davy's Eyes are still very bad
and he looks very bad.

June 25. [The Davys had come over on the preceding
day] ... Nancy, Mrs. Davy and Betsy, got up very
early, long before I was awake, and they breakfasted
about 6 o'clock and at 7. they all set of in Lenewade
Bridge Chaise for Norwich—they were gone before
I was down Stairs. They return in the Evening to
Mrs. Davy's at Mattishall where Nancy is to stay
a few Days with Mrs. Davy. Betsy Davy is to be
left at Norwich to go in the Diligence as far as
Titteshall this Evening in her road to Pulham.—
Titteshall Ram is about a Mile from Mrs. Roupes at
Pulham.

June 28. ... Between 1. and 2 o'clock I took a ride
to Mr. Thornes of Mattishall by appointment, and

there dined, supped, spent the Evening and stayed till after 3. in the Morning with Mr. and Mrs. Thorne, Mrs. Davy, Miss Betsy Donne, Mr. and Miss Pinching, Miss Woodforde and Mr. Smith. We had singing all the Night long by Miss Donne &c. We had for Dinner, a boiled Leg of Mutton without Capers, a rost Piece of Beef, rost Fowls and a face, a rost Goose without the lest seasoning or Gravy and Peas. Gave the Servant Maid on coming away— o. 1. o. Got home about 5 o'clock in the Morn' and went to bed directly.

June 30. . . . Mr. Cantrell sent me word this morning early that his C.[haise] was pre-engaged to Miss Lombe unknown to him—therefore was obliged to send Will to Mattishall to acquaint them of being disappointed and could not send for them—Ben also being gone to Norwich for Fish. The Rotation therefore is to be put of, and only the Priests Families and Du Quesne to dine here to day. To Mr. Cary for things from Norwich &c. p^d o. 5. 6. Sent by Will to Mrs. Davy a Couple of nice Spring Chicken, half of a plumb Cake, and Tongue and some Potatoes. Thus far at 2 o'clock—when lo! a Market Cart arrived at my House from Mattishall with Three Ladies in it, Mrs. Davy, Miss Betsy Donne and Nancy who all stayed and dined, supped and slept here. Mr. and Mrs. Priest and Son Rich^d of Norwich, Mr. Du Quesne and Mr. Smith dined and spent the Afternoon here. We had for Dinner some fryed Soals—4 boiled Chicken with some Bacon—a Goose rosted—Neck of Mutton boiled and Capers— Peas—and Pudding and Tarts. Mrs. Davy brought back the Chicken I sent to her which we had for Supper—with other things. About 8 in the Evening

most of the Company left us. Mrs. Davy and Miss
Betsy Donne slept in Nancy's Room and Nancy in
the Garrett over me. Miss Donne is a most agreeable young Lady, full of vivacity, very pretty with
an excellent Voice.

July 2. [The Ladies had returned to Mattishall on the
previous day.] . . . About 1 o'clock I took a ride to
Mattishall and there dined, supped and spent the
whole Night at Mr. Smith's, with him, Mr. and
Mrs. Thorne, Mr. and Miss Pinching, Mrs. Davy,
Miss Betsy Donne and our Nancy. We had for
Dinner at Mr. Smith's, boiled Beef, rost and boiled
Chicken, part of a fine ham, a Couple of Ducks
rosted and Peas—Pudding, Tarts and Cheesecakes.
For Supper a cold Collation, with Lamb-Stakes and
Gooseberry Cream and green Peas &c. We were
very merry the whole Day and all Night, singing all
Night long by Miss Donne. She is an excellent lively
girl indeed and about 17 Years Old. We broke up
at 4 in the Morning. I immediately sat of for Weston
—got home about 5 o'clock—and went to bed
directly—Saw the Sun rise coming home. To Mr.
Smith's Boy—Robin gave 0. 1. 0. I went to
Mr. Hewitts in the Afternoon to desire that Miss
Donne might sleep at Mr. Thornes to Night.

July 3. . . . I got up about 9 o'clock and soon after
breakfast I took a ride to Mattishall to see Mr. and
Mrs. Bodham and there dined and spent the Afternoon with them, Betsy Donne and Nancy Woode-
forde. I called at Mrs. Davy's and Mrs. Thornes.
Mrs. Davy gone this morning for Pulham. My Man
Ben came after Nancy about noon in a Market Cart—
After Tea I returned to Weston as did Nancy, but
she was at home before me : I was very flat and dull

on leaving my dear Miss Betsy Donne. Nancy supped and slept again at home. We are both glad that this Week is over. Nancy rec^d this Week from her Brother Sam from London a neat genteel and pretty Baloon hat. Mr. and Mrs. Custance are gone to Sr Thomas Beauchamps to spend a few Days with them at Langley Park.

July 5. . . . After Dinner I paid Lizzy half a Years Wages due this Day, and then dismissed her from my Service, as she is going on my recommendation to Weston House. I gave her extraordinary o. 2. 6. I paid her for Wages 1. 6. 6. In the Evening sent Ben with a Market Cart for my New Maid who lives at Mattishall and she came here about 8 at Night and she supped and slept here. Her Name is Molly Dade about 17 years of age—a very smart Girl and pretty I think. Her Friends bear great Characters of Industry &c.

July 15. . . . We were to have had Betsy Davy and Mary Roupe over from Mattishall to have spent this Day with us but Mrs. Davy's going to Pulham yesterday on a Love Affair with a Mr. Rand who went with her and came back with her, but Matters however could not be settled then. Mr. Rand is a Man of very good Fortune, keeps a Carriage and is an Apothecary and has great business—A very sensible Man, a Batchelor about 50 years of Age. And lives at Snettisham near Burnham. To a Man this morning that brought a very pretty kind of a Monkey to shew gave 1. o^d. He called it the Mongooz from Madagascar.

July 16. . . . About 10 o'clock this morning Mr. Matthews with a Cart full of young Folks came to my House—viz, Betsy Davy, Hannah Thorne, Mary

Roupe and Nunn Davy—they all spent the Day with us, and a pretty Day it was. Nothing but Noise the whole Day long—Between 7 and 8 sent them back to Mattishall as they came. Mr. Matthews went home before Dinner. Ben went back with them in the Cart.

July 17. . . . Mr. Love finished painting my Parlours this Day at Noon. Hylett, Mr. Custance's Gardener was this morning turned out of his Place and payed of—being found out by Mr. Custance in sending Fruit &c. to Norwich by the Elsing Carrier—Mr. Custance went after the Carrier himself this morning and took from him 4 Quarts of very fine Strawberries and some Cucumbers packed up by Hylett for to be sold. Mr. Custance in a very great Passion.

July 19. . . . Nancy went this morning before 7 o'clock behind my Man Will to Mrs. Davy's at Mattishall where she is to spend a few Days with her. . . .

July 20. . . . At 4 this Afternoon I mounted my Mare and rode to Mattishall where I drank Tea and stayed till 9 in the Evening at Mrs. Davy's with her, Mr. and Mrs. Bodham, Miss Donne, Mr. Du Quesne and Nancy Woodforde—Mr. Smith was to have been there also—but went for London this morning very suddenly and much discomposed. The Cause of it is this, Mrs. Davy had a Letter this morning from Mr. Rand who is distracted after her, the Contents of which were communicated to Mr. Smith, which made him almost frantic, he immediately made Mrs. Davy an Offer to marry her after his Mothers Decease, what answer was returned I know not, but he marched from Mattishall directly. Mrs. Davy was extremely low and uneasy about it. After one Pool of Quadrille we had a Syllabub and some Rasberries with Cream and Sugar—and Wine. We all broke up about 9 o'clock rather after. At Quadrille this Evening won 0. 1. 0. To Mrs. Davy's Maid gave coming away 0. 1. 0.

July 22. . . . At 11 o'clock went to Church to attend at a Vestry ab^t moving of the Singing Seat—Mr. Peachman, Dade, Page, Forster, J^n_o Pegg, Stephen Andrews, Howlett and J^n_o Buck attended also— Mr. Peachman, with some others were for letting of it remain where it is—but they all said that they would agree to have it placed wherever I pleased— Accordingly I fixed to be a proper Place for it behind the Font and so inclose the Belfry—wch was concluded on and so the Vestry was dissolved. They all behaved extremely obliging to their Rector. Between 2 and 3 I rode up to Weston House and there dined and spent the Afternoon with Mr. and Mrs. Custance, and Mr. and Mrs. Collier of Quebec near Dereham. Mr. Charles Collier and Wife very agreeable People. Soon after Tea they went of for Quebec—I stayed till after 9 looking with Mr. Custance over a new Set of Copper Plate Prints respecting Captain Cooks Voyage[1] to Kamskatsca—very fine they are, cost 10 Guineas.

[1] 'Captain Cook's *Voyage* I have neither read nor intend to read. I have seen the prints—a parcel of ugly faces, with blubber lips and flat noses, dressed as unbecomingly as if both sexes were ladies of the first fashion ; and rows of savages, with backgrounds of palm-trees. Indeed, I shall not give five guineas and a half—nay, they sell already for nine, for such uncouth lubbers ; nor do I desire to know how unpolished the north or south poles have remained ever since Adam and Eve were just such mortals. My brother's death has made me poor, and I cannot now afford to buy everything I see. It is late, to be sure, to learn economy. . . .' Doubtless the real reason was the last—the need for economy—which made Horace Walpole so acid on this subject in his letter to the Countess of Upper Ossory on June 19, 1784. The *Voyage* in question was the

SQUIRE CUSTANCE

from the portrait probably by Henry Walton, F.S.A.

1784

July 28. ... Very fine pleasant Day—In the Afternoon
sent my Servant Will to Mattishall after my Niece,
who came home safe and well about 7 o'clock. Jack
went also with Will to open the Gates. Nancy
supped and slept once more at home.

July 29. ... About 11 this morning walked to Weston
Church and there read Prayers, this Day being
appointed a Day of general Thanksgiving to Almighty
God for restoring Peace once more to these Nations.
Mr. Custance at Church as was also Mrs. Micklethwaite. I had a large Congregation at Church to
Day. Nancy intended to have went but the Rain
prevented her.[1] My Maid Molly's Father and Mother
came over here about our Dinner Time with Nunn
Davy and they all dined, and spent the Afternoon
here.

Aug. 4. ... About 10 o'clock this Night a Clergyman
by name Cam[p]bell (Vicar of Weasingham in this
County and formerly of Oriel Coll: Oxford and after-

great Captain James Cook's third voyage, 1776-9, when he was in search
of the north-east passage, discovered the Sandwich Islands—so named
by him after the then First Lord of the Admiralty, and was killed by the
natives through a tragic combination of circumstances on February 14,
1779. He did not himself actually explore Kamskatka, but his com-
panions did so later in that spring. The authorized account of the
voyage with 86 plates, provided at the cost of the Government, was
brought out by Dr. Douglas in the summer of 1784. The price was
£4 14s. 6d., but after three days every copy was sold out—hence the rise
in price. (See *The Life and Voyages of Captain James Cook*, published in
1836 by the Rev. George Young, p. 447 ; *Captain James Cook* by Arthur
Kitson (1907) ; Walpole's *Letters*, vol. xiii, pp. 160-1.)

[1] The peace had been concluded for some eighteen months (see note
on p. 57, preceding), but the formal winding up of wars between several
belligerents takes time (as we know), and it was not till June of this year
that the definitive treaty was *ratified* between Holland and England.
(See *Annual Register*, 1784-5, p. 194.)

L

wards Fellow of Worcester Coll: in the same University) came to my House and he supped and slept here—himself and horse. I remember him at Oriel Coll: but not so intimate as to expect that he would have taken such freedom especially as he never made me a Visit before. He slept however in the Attic Story and I treated him as one that would be too free if treated too kindly. It kept me up till after 12 o'clock.

Aug. 5. . . . Mr. Campbell breakfasted here on Milk only and after breakfast I took a ride with him to Norwich being Assize Week and there spent the Day —but returned in the Evening to Weston by myself, leaving Mr. Campbell behind—and whom I saw nothing of all the Day after I left him on coming into Norwich. He went to a private House, a Mr. Parr in St Giles's. At 11 o'clock (as we got to Norwich about 10 this Morn') I walked by myself down to the Cathedral and heard the Assize Sermon preached by Mr. Parr the gentleman above mentioned—but could not hear distinctly on Account of the Church being so full. It was near half an Hour long—but seemed good. Only one Judge at Norwich this Assize, and his Name was Lord Loughborough, Lord Chief Justice of the Court of Common Pleas— late Solicitor General—Alex: Wedderbourne.[1] The

[1] Alexander Wedderburn (1733–1805), created Baron Loughborough in 1780 as Lord Chief Justice, and Earl of Rosslyn in 1801, was both a very able politician and lawyer. In politics he was eminent for apostasy, starting his career as a Tory satellite of the Earl of Bute, turning Whig during the Wilkes controversy, then reverting to Toryism when offered the Solicitor-Generalship by Lord North in 1771 ; Whig again when the Regency trouble of 1788 came on, but Tory in 1793, when made Lord Chancellor by Pitt in succession to Lord Thurlow. He is perhaps best remembered as Solicitor-General, for his incomparably vitriolic but witty

Bishop and Dean both at Church. Met with Mr. Custance, Sr Edm^d Bacon, Taswell, Mr. Francis &c. at Norwich. I dined at the Kings Head on a flying Dinner. I put up my Horse at the Woolpack in St. Giles's. Paid and gave at the Kings Head o. 2. o. Paid and gave at the Woolpack o. 1. o. I sat out from Norwich to return home about 7 o'clock and got home about 9 o'clock.

Aug. 7. . . . Mrs. Davy and Nunn came here about 9 this Morn' and they breakfasted, dined and spent the Aft: here. Mr. Matthews brought Mrs. Davy behind him and he breakfasted with us in Parlour but returned home soon after—He came after her in the Evening. Mr. Smith came here about 2 o'clock and he dined and spent the Afternoon with us, and he and Nunn with Mrs. Davy left us ab^t 8 this Even'.

Aug. 8. . . . I read Prayers and Preached this morning at Weston. Mr. Custance at Church, as was my Niece. The Singing Seat being moved one Day this last Week down towards the Belfry, made the Church appear much more to advantage—Mr. Custance approved of it much as did myself and Nancy. My head Maid Eliz: Claxton this afternoon immediately after Tea [gave notice] that she should go at Michaelmas in these abrupt and ungracious Words ' Sir, I shall leave your Service at Michaelmas next '. I told her that I thought the notice short. She gave no reason whatever for leaving it. It rather disconcerted and flurried my Niece.

onslaught on Franklin early in 1774, when the latter was involved in the dark business of the Hutchinson letters, the publication of which did so much to exacerbate feeling between England and the American colonists. (Lecky, *England in the Eighteenth Century*, vol. iii, pp. 365–6, vol. iv, pp. 150–1, vol. v, p. 415, and vol. vii, p. 20 ; see also *D. N. B.*)

1784

Aug. 9. . . . Nancy and self were both hurried this Morn' as soon as we came down Stairs, she having rec^d a Note from Mrs. Bodham to acquaint us that she with Mr. Bodham would come to us to Morrow Evening from the Rotation at Du Quesne's and that they w^d spend a few Days with us if agreeable—I had also a Note from Mr. Du Quesne about the Clubb to Morrow. It is also our Washing Week and dont know what to do—Mr. Bodhams Man John went down to Lenewade Bridge to bespeak the Chaise for to Morrow. But the Chaise was engaged for 2 or 3 Days.

Aug. 10. . . . About 1 o'clock took a ride to Du Quesne's being his Rotation, and there dined and spent the Afternoon with him, Mr. Smith, and Mr. Bodham— And both the Priests from Norwich and Reepham were there also. We had no Ladies at all there to day being so wet. We had for Dinner some Eels, a boiled Leg of Mutton and Capers, a rost Goose, the Charter and Tarts. At Quadrille this Evening won o. o. 6. I got home to Weston about 9 this Evening. I was very near meeting with a very bad Accident as I went to Du Quesne's, in the narrow Lane just by his House, meeting with a one horse Chaise, which to avoid as far as I could and getting by the Chaise my Mare slipt upon all Fours just before the Wheels and grazed my Leg a little but very luckily she got up again without any further damage. O Lord! accept now my sincere thanks for thy great goodness to me in preserving me from such great Danger as I was then in, and ever make me mindful of thy goodness. Towards a Subscription for old Goody Doughty to set her up once more and proposed by Mr. Smith, Mr. Du Quesne, myself and

Mr. Bodham, gave to Mr. Smith for her—we each subscribed 1ˢ 0ᵈ.

Aug. 17. . . . Mr. and Mrs. Bodham and Mrs. Davy, supped, spent the Evening and slept here—As they intend to spend a few Days with my Niece and me. Mr. and Mrs. Bodham slept in the Parlour Chamber. Mrs. Davy and Nancy in the Garrett over me.

Aug. 18. . . . Mr. and Mrs. Bodham and Mrs. Davy, breakfasted, dined supped and slept again at Weston Parsonage. About 11 o'clock we all went down to the River on a fishing Scheme—I had Lenewade Chaise for the Ladies—Mr. Bodham and self went on horseback. The Day was rather unfavourable being sometimes stormy—but we did not return home to dinner from Fishing till 5 o'clock this Aft: we were all pretty well fatigued by that Time. Nunn Davy came to us about 2 o'clock. Daniel Breeze, Mr. Bodham's Man John, Ben, Will and Jack were my Fishermen—We had very fine sport indeed to Day—as we caught six brace of Pike of very good size, two brace of very pretty Trout, two brace and half of very fine Perch, besides at least a Coomb of flat Fish. I sent Mr. Custance a brace of the best Trout. The Ladies went into Mr. Forsters House to see Mrs. Forster. Mr. Forster not at home. Mrs. Forster behaved very civil to us, as did Mr. Wade Partner with Mr. Forster—We sent Mrs. Forster a brace of Pike—Gave Cantrell also a Pike. We carried with us some cold Meat &c. Breeze and Newman the Chaise driver dined with the Folks in Kitchen. Nunn Davy dined with us, and soon after Dinner he returned to Mattishall. To Newman the Driver when he went home gave 0. 1. 6. We had 4 Shillings worth of Beer at Cantrells and a Pint of White Wine.

We carried also with us a Bottle of Gin which did not last very long. We had for Dinner a Leg of Mutton boiled and the large Pike Mr. Custance sent us Yesterday, we had rosted with Pudding in his Belly—We did not dine till after 5. After Tea we got to Cards at which lost o. o. 6.

Mem: Mrs. Custance brought to bed of a fine Girl yesterday in the Afternoon ab^t 2 o'clock.

Aug. 20. . . . Mr. and Mrs. Bodham and Mrs. Davy breakfasted, dined and spent the Afternoon with us till 7 in the Evening and then they went in Lenewade Bridge Chaise for Mattishall directly after Tea. We had for Dinner to day some Beef Stakes, a large Piece of boiled Beef, a Couple of rost Chicken, Tarts &c. It rained incessantly all the Day long and very heavy. Mr. Bodham and self got to Back-Gammon this Morn' about 11 o'clock and played till Dinner Time. I lost at Back-Gammon to Mr. Bodham o. o. 6. I sent a Letter to Mr. Francis this Evening by Cary respecting the Servants Tax.[1]

Aug. 23. . . . This Morning one Sally Barber (Servant Maid at present to Mr. Hewitt of Mattishall) came here to offer as a Servant in Betty's Place who is going to be married at Michaelmas—After some Conversation and being so well recommended by Mrs. Hewitt, I agreed to take her and give her five Guineas Per Annum but no Tea at all—She demurred a little about the smallness of the Wages, but at last agreed, and took the Earnest Money of me, being usual here, of o. 1. o. Mr. Custance sent me a Note and begged that I would dine with him on Friday next on a fine Haunch of Venison—which I promised —It is very kind in him.

[1] See foot-note, vol. i, p. 234.

Aug. 27. . . . Nunn Davy came here about 1 o'clock
with a Note from his Mother to my Niece—Nunn
stayed and dined with Nancy on beef stakes and
a rost Fowl.   Between 2 and 3 o'clock I walked by
myself up to Weston House and there dined and
spent the Afternoon with Mr. Custance, Lady Bacon,
a Miss Hickman an old Maid but immensely rich,
a little Boy, a Nephew of hers by name Baker—
Mr. Du Quesne, Mr. Priest of Reepham, and a
Mr. Eaton a young Man and is Rector of Elsing—
A neat and agreeable Man.   We had for dinner
some Pike, a Couple of Fowls boiled and Piggs Face,
green Peas Soup and a prodigious fine and fat Haunch
of Venison given by Sr John Wodehouse to Mr. Custance—The second Course was a Fricasse, a Couple
of Ducks rosted, green Peas, plumb Pudding, Maccaroni &c.   We broke up about eight in the Evening.
I was at home by nine—I walked home as I went
by myself.

Sep. 1.   . . . Mr. Hardy and Boy fastened up 3 Windows
with Brick for me, and having finished by Noon
I sent them both into my Wheat Field to sheer
Wheat with my three Men.—And they dined, &c.
here.   A very fine Day, than[k] God, for the Harvest.
Mr. Custance sent us a brace of Partridges which
was very kind of him as it is the Day of Shooting.

Sep. 4.   . . . I sent Mr. Custance about 3 doz: more of
Apricots, and he sent me back another large Piece of
fine Parmesan Cheese—It was very kind in him.
Nancy had a Letter from her Brother Sam, nothing
in it.   I finished carrying Wheat this morning.

Sep. 15.   . . . Went out with my Greyhounds this morning about an Hour in Weston great Field—found
a Hare coursed her and killed her—during the time

that I was out, Mrs. Custance with Mrs. Collier Senr called on my Niece and stayed with her near an Hour. To Largesses to day gave 0. 4. 0.

Sep. 18. . . . Nancy walked with me to the Church after Breakfast where we stayed near 3 Hours in seeing a Path made for Nancy from the great Door to the Chancel Door. All my three Men made it whilst we were there. To Largesses to day gave 0. 1. 0.

Sep. 19. . . . I read Prayers and Preached this Morn' at Weston. Mr. and Mrs. Custance with Mrs. Collier Senr at Church as were Mrs. Micklethwaite, her Brother in Law, and my Niece. Mr. Custance acquainted me at Church that his very worthy Friend Mr. Prideaux very lately departed this Life.

Sep. 20. . . . After breakfast I walked to Ben's Father's and there read Prayers to his Daughter Eliz: Leggatt who is (I am afraid) in a deep Consumption, she looked poor Girl, very bad and keeps her Bed—I sent her last Night by her Brother some Tar water and a Bottle of Tent. Since my Maid Molly Dade has taken Tar Water she is greatly altered for the better, as well again. To Largesses to day gave 0. 7. 0.

Sep. 21. . . . Mr. Du Quesne with two Friends of his, Clergymen, by Name Cotman and Vaugh[a]n, made us a morning Visit—walked over my Garden and then went. Mr. Micklethwaite also called this morning to desire me to come to his House to Morrow and christen his little Boy. Soon afterwards Dr. Thorne called on us and stayed with us about an Hour. To Largesses to day gave 0. 2. 0. About 2 o'clock I took a ride to Du Quesne's and there dined and spent the Afternoon with him and his two Friends, Mr. Vaugh[a]n and Mr. Cotman—stayed till 8 in the

Evening and then returned home to Weston Parsonage, after an unpleasant ride it being very dark
and disagreeable. At Quadrille this Evening after
Tea lost o. 1. 6. A Box was brought to my House
this morning for Mrs. Davy—which I sent to her in
the Afternoon.

Sep. 22. . . . About 12 o'clock took a ride to Weston
House, spent half an Hour with Mr. and Mrs. Custance, Mrs. Collier Senr and Mr. George Beauchamp,
and came back. At 2 o'clock took a Walk to Mr.
Micklethwaite's and there dined, spent the Afternoon, supped and spent the Evening with him, his
Wife, his Father and Mother, old Mrs. Branthwaite,
Captain Micklethwaite and Wife, Mr. Jonathan
Micklethwaite and my Niece.—About 5 o'clock we
dined. Before Dinner I publickly baptized their
little Boy at home, which I did not much like, but
could not tell how to refuse—He was privately named
before at Norwich I believe—His Name is Nathaniel.
Old Mrs. Branthwaite and old Mrs. Micklethwaite
were the Godmothers—and old Mr. Micklethwaite
and his Son Captain John Micklethwaite were God-
fathers. We had a very genteel Dinner and Supper.
Old Mr. and Mrs. Micklethwaite and his Son the
Captain, the strangest kind of People I almost ever
saw. Old Mrs. Branthwaite almost as strange and
vulgar. Nancy was sent for in their Carriage and we
returned home in it about 12 at night—very windy,
very wet, and very dark ; I thank God we got home
however safe. I gave the Driver and the Man behind
it each 1. o.–o. 2. o. After Tea and Coffee We got to
Whist at which I won o. 1. o. Coming away this
Evening Mr. Micklethwaite made me a present, for
christening his Child, of 1. 1. o. Upon the whole

spent an odd disagreeable kind of a Day—as did also Nancy—we laughed much after we got home.

Sep. 24. . . . Poor Betty Leggatt, Bens Sister, departed this Life very early this morning, and I hope is gone to a better. . . .

Sep. 28. . . . My Maid Betty has not been able to do any thing for this last Week owing to a bad Thumb and is still bad. Poor Molly Dade my other Maid very bad in a Cough and am afraid it is rather consumptive—She has increased it to day by easing the other Maid in helping her and she is so foolish to tell Molly that she is in a Consumption—which makes the poor Girl very unhappy.

Sep. 29. . . . I sent for Widow Greaves this morning to come to my House for a few Days to assist our Maids, they being not able to do much at present—She came just at breakfast, and she breakfasted, and dined here and went home in the Evening, as she could not sleep here this Night, being wanted at her own home.

Oct. 4. . . . This Day being appointed for holding the Generals at Aylsham, about 10 o'clock I mounted my Mare and took a ride thither, and there dined and spent part of the Afternoon with the Clergy &c. I got to Aylsham by 12 went to Church and met the Clergy just coming out of Church—The Arch-Deacon, Mr. Younge not there—Mr. Baker the Official acted for him—We dined at the black Boys. The Company at Dinner was as follows.—Mr. Baker Official, Mr. Bryant Preacher, Mr. Taswell Reader, Mr. Whitmill, Mr. Priest, Mr. Carr, Mr. Bell, Mr. Leath, Mr. Addison, Mr. Sandeford, Mr. Jewell, Mr. Paul, Mr. Morphew's Son, and his Clerk Mr. Stouton and myself.—We had for Dinner, Ham and

Fowls, a Couple of Ducks rosted, a Fillet of Veal rosted, a Rice and a Potatoe Pudding. To young Morphew for Procurations &c. p^d 0. 9. 7½. To Ordinary and extraordinary pd. 0. 3. 0. About 4 in the Afternoon set of for Weston, got home just at six—It is full 10 Miles thither. My Man Will: went with me.

Oct. 6. . . . My Maid Molly, I think, is a good deal better. Widow Greaves here again all Day and Night.

Oct. 7. . . . Jack told me this morning that he is advised to get another Place being too old for a Skip-Jack any longer. He wants to be a Plow Boy to some Farmer to learn the farming Business as he likes that best—I told him that he was very right to try to better himself, and at Lady Day next he is to leave my House for that purpose. He has been a very good Lad ever since he has been here. Widow Greaves here again all Day and Night.

Oct. 9. . . . To one Bagshaw for 2 pair of coursing Stockings made of the Wool from the Sheeps back without ever being dressed at all, and knit p^d 0. 5. 0. Sent Ben with a Sample of Wheat to shew at Norwich to the Millers that come to the Market after Wheat, and he returned in the Evening and told me that he had sold it to a Mr. Bloom of Trowse Mills near Norwich for 26^s 6^d per Coomb to be carried to Norwich and which I think a very good Price for it— It was very good Wheat and weighed 18 Stone and half per Coomb.

Oct. 10. . . . My New Maid (in Betty's Place) Sally Dunnell came here this Evening, which was sooner than we expected her by a Day—but we contrived for her to sleep here &c. tho' my other Maid nor

Mrs. Greaves were as yet gone. They all slept here to night. I published Bettys Banns for the last time this Aft: at Church—I suppose she will marry very soon. My new Maid seems to be a mighty strapping Wench.

Oct. 11. . . . After breakfast paid my Maid Eliz: Claxton who leaves me to day, three Q^{rs} Wages— being 4. 7. 0. She breakfasted here and left us about 11 this Morn'. Paid Mrs. Greaves also for the Time she has been with us this Morning at 6^d Pr Day 0. 5. 0. She had both Victuals and Lodging here also. She left us about the same Time. Mrs. Custance with her eldest Son made us a long Morning Visit from 12 till 2 o'clock. Gave poor old Mary Dicker this Morn' 0. 1. 0. She came to pay Rent for her House belonging to the poor Widows of this Parish.

Oct. 12. . . . At 11 this Morning walked to Church and married my old Maid Eliz: Claxton to Charles Cary of this Parish by Banns—rec^d for marrying them—0. 5. 0. and which I gave to the Bride after. She was dressed in a Linnen Gown that my Niece gave her some time back. After I came from Church I went out a coursing with my Men—was out 4 Hours —had no sport whatever—could not get sight of a single Hare. To one Aldridge this Morn' for a Piece of Cotton for a Morning Gown for me— 6 yards at 2/4 0. 14. 0. To Ditto. for 5 yards of Orange and Purple or rather blue Ribband for a Purse for myself p^d 0. 2. 6. Nunn Davy came here whilst I was out a coursing but could not find me— he dined here and went home.

Oct. 13. . . . Ben went to Norwich this morning very early with 10 Coomb of Wheat—and he returned by 4 in the Afternoon, time enough for Dinner—and brought back half a Chaldron of Coal from Locks. He brought me also the Mony for the Wheat at twenty six and sixpence Pr Coomb—in all—13. 5. 0.

Oct. 14. . . . Finding my new Maid (who came as Cook to us) to know nothing of her business, I therefore this Evening gave her notice that she must leave my Service and as soon as possible—I believe her to be a goodnatured Girl but very ignorant.

Oct. 15. . . . My new Maid Sally Dunnell left my Service this Morn'. Gave the Maid as she was going away for the Time she had been here at 6^d per Day 0. 3. 0. To Mr. Dade a Poor Rate for Land in hand at 10^d 1. 5. 2½. To Mr. Cary for things from Norwich &c. for last Week 16. 4¼. To my Niece Nancy for things p^d 0. 8. 6. Mr. Custance made us a long Morning Visit. Mr. Hall from Hampshire and a Mr. Fellowes of Haviland a Gentleman of great Fortune and Member for Andover called here on horseback whilst Mr. Custance was with us—I went to them and spoke with them, but they would not get of their Horses—having not time. My poor Maid Molly Dade, not so well to day as I could wish her, having somewhat of a Fever on her. She is one of the best Maids that ever we had and very much liked by us both and would wish to keep her but am very much afraid it will not be in our Power tho' we are both most willing to keep her. She is one of the neatest, most modest, pretty Girl[s] I ever had. She is very young, but tall, only in her 17th year. Ben went early this Morning beyond Dereham to buy me a Cow, now in her full profit, but could not. It was at a Sale of Colonel Dickens's near Dereham. Widow Greaves came to us again this Evening to be with us till we can get another Maid—I sent for her.

Oct. 16. . . . I sent for Molly's Sister this morning to Mattishall to do her Sister's business for a little time, as I intend that she should go home for a few Days. Molly's Father came here soon after I sent and he stayed and dined here with both his Daughters. Molly Peachman came to offer herself as a Servant this morning, but as she did not chuse to wash Dishes, I did not like to take her. Nancy had a Letter from her Brother Ralph this Even'. Molly's Sister and Widow Greaves dined, supp'd and slept here. Poor Molly's Sister fell of the Horse as she was coming to us, behind Jack, owing to the little Mares starting. She bruised herself something but not very materially.

Oct. 19. . . . I sent my Maid Molly Dade this morning behind Ben to Mattishall, to stay a few Days at home, to see if change of Air would do her Cough good. Her Sister Betty, continues in her Place. Poor Molly is as good a Girl as ever came into a House, I never had a Servant that I liked better—Nancy also likes her very much indeed—I wish to God she might get the better of her illness. Widow Greaves still with us and at present likely so to be.

Oct. 21. . . . Widow Greaves again here all day and Night. Cobbs Daughter of Mattishall whose name is Mary came here this Morning to offer herself as Cook for us—She seems a good, tidy, sharp Woman, very short, but she seems rather a pert one, however could not give her a positive answer—having had one recommended by Mrs. Davy to us this morning just before she came, Molly's Father brought over the Note from Mrs. Davy.

Oct. 28. . . . To John Pegg a Qrs Land Tax for Rec-

tory &c. pd. 3. o. o. To Ditto. ½ yrs. Window Tax
p^d 1. 2. 7. To Ditto ½ y^{rs} House Tax p^d o. 1. 9.
Widow Greaves here again all Day and night.

Oct. 29. . . . Sent Ben this morning to Reepham to
pay the Horse Tax for 2 Horses at 10^s 0^d each.
Mr. Peachman sent us a brace of Pheasants. Gave
Mr. Peachmans Man o. 1. o.

Oct. 30. . . . Rec^d a Letter this Evening from my
Brother Heighes sealed with a large black Seal, and in
which we received an Account of the Death of
Mr. Robert White Senr—who died on Tuesday the
19 Instant. His Death supposed to happen by falling
from his Horse in a Fit. The black Seal very much
alarmed self and Nancy. Pray God comfort my poor
Sister White and Family. Mr. White had made a
Will and left his Son James Executor.—His eldest
Son Robt ought to have been his Executor in my
Opinion. Nothing mentioned respecting his Circum-
stances. Nancy had a Letter also from her Brother
Sam in London—nothing of the above mentioned in
it or any thing else but an Account of his paintings.

Nov. 2. . . . Soon after breakfast I took my Men with
[me] a coursing. Set out about 11 and stayed till
after 4 in the Aft: we brought home a brace of Hares
and a Rabbit, both Courses with the Hares very fine
indeed. Whilst we were out, a Servant Maid came
to offer her Service here, who lately lived at Mr.
Eatons at Elsing and but a very little time indeed
only a Quarter of a Year—Nancy could not recollect
her Name or give any direct answer as I was out.
By the Account that Nancy gave me, don't think she
will do—she being rather high and her late Wages
8 Pounds per Annum—Her Friends live at Foxley
a place I by no means approve of—as it has [been]

proved that many from that Place have been guilty of many felonious Acts and but very few Years ago. She formerly lived at old Mr. Gurdons at Letton and for 9 years—She afterwards lived with his Son— N.B. Old Mr. Gurdon's House of Letton about 3 years ago was broke open and robbed of all his old family Plate, but was never discovered. The above Robbery was supposed to have hastened the death of poor old Mr. Gurdon a most worthy Man.

Nov. 3. . . . Sent Will: this morning to Mr. Smiths at Mattishall with a Hare—told him to call on Molly Dade, during the Time that he was gone Molly's Father called here—he gave us a very poor Account of our worthy Maid poor Molly Dade—that he believed she cannot recover. We were extremely sorry for her. He came after her Stays that were here, the others being too large for her—so much of late has she fallen away. Mr. Dade could not stay to dine with us to day. Will on his return also told us that Mr. Thorne had given poor Molly over and that he could do no more. Pray God Almighty comfort her— and with patience wait the Almighty's Will—As good a Girl as ever lived.

Nov. 7. . . . My Maid Betty Dade (in the room of her poor Sister Molly) went to see Molly this morning— My Man Ben carried her behind him. We sent her a Knuckle of Veal for Broth and a Jar of black Currant Jamm. Betty and Ben returned about 5 this Evening —she left her sister but very poorly and very weak. I read Prayers and Preached this Aft: at Weston. Mr. and Mrs. Micklethwaite at Church. Nobody from Weston House at Church to day.

Nov. 9. . . . After breakfast I rode down to Lenewade Bridge to attend Dr Bathursts Tythe Audit and

there dined and stayed till after 4 o'clock in the Aftr
and then returned home—All safe and snugg. I was
far from being well however to day. This Evening
I had a new Servant Maid come as Cook, Molly
Peachman, she is to have 5 Guineas Per Annum, Tea
included—Nancy prevailed on me to take her.

Nov. 10. . . . Widow Greaves left my House soon after
breakfast as I am now fitted with a Maid. I paid
her for the Time she was with me 0. 10. 6., being
three Weeks and 3 Days at 6ᵈ per Day. I paid her
also for some Eggs 0. 0. 9. I sent after Mrs. Davy
this morning and she came to us about 2 o'clock and
she dined, supped and slept here. I was very dull all
Day and very low, especially in the Aft: The Wind
was rather high this Evening and night which greatly
increased my heaviness.

Nov. 17. [He had gone to Norwich the previous day
to bank Dr. Bathurst's tithe at Kerrisons Bank.]
I breakfasted at the Kings Head—and stayed in
Norwich till 1 o'clock and then sat of for Weston.
Ben returned with my Mare to Norwich this Morn'.
To Studwell, China Man pᵈ a Bill of 0. 18. 6. To
Beale, Fishmonger pᵈ a Bill of 0. 7. 6. I went and
saw the Dwarf Man that is at Norwich by name
James Harris from Coventry—He is exactly 3 Feet
high, very well proportioned in every respect—But
with him, was a Girl which exceeded every Thing
I ever saw—she had no Hands or Arms, and yet
wonderfully cleaver with her Feet. She cut out
a Watch Paper for me whilst I was there with her
Toes she opened My Watch and put it in after done.
Her Name was Jane Hawtin, about 22 years old.
She talks very sensible and appears very happy in her
Situation—She uses her Toes as well as any their

Fingers. I gave her for cutting the Watch Paper 0. 1. 0. To the Dwarf gave 0. 0. 6. To Mr. Priest for Sal volatile &c. p^d 0. 3. 4. Called at Brownsmith's Silk Mercer, and there paid a Bill for Nancy for Silk, for a Gown &c. 6. 1. 0. I talked to them of their Behaviour to Nancy, in trusting her. At Bakers for a small Whip &c. p^d 0. 3. 0. To ½ P^d of netting Cord p^d 0. 1. 3. To a Pair of riding Gloves p^d 0. 2. 0. To my Barber, Mileham gave 0. 1. 0. To a very poor Weaver with a large Family and a Wife and can get no Work whatever gave last Night 0. 1. 0. At the Kings Head paid and gave 0. 7. 0. We got home safe and well (thank God) by 3 o'clock and escaped the Rain very well—but very cold it was. I found Nancy and Mrs. Davy brave and well. I dined, supped and slept again at home. Mrs. Davy, breakfasted, dined &c. &c. again here. Nancy breakfasted, dined &c. &c. again at home.

Nov. 25. ... I went to Church this morning and buried another Child of Horners Daughter Mann aged 7 Weeks. Am afraid they have been very amiss in care towards Children. Between 2 and 3 o'clock Mr. and Mrs. Custance came to us and they dined, spent the Afternoon and stayed till near 9 in the Evening with us, were highly pleased with their Entertainment and were very Merry. I gave them for Dinner, Some Skaite boiled with small Whitings fryed put round the Dish and Oyster Sauce, a Couple of boiled Fowls and a Tongue, a rost Leg of Mutton, and some Artichokes—2nd Course—a Rabbit fryed, a Duck rosted, the Charter for the first Time of ever making it and very good, Tarts, Rasberry Puffs, Blamange with black Caps in Custard. Fruit after Dinner— Almonds and Raisins, Golden Pippins, Nutts and

Grapes. After Coffee and Tea we got to Loo—lost at it—o. 5. o. Nancy won at Loo this Evening o. 9. o.

Nov. 26. . . . Mrs. Davy breakfasted and spent the best part of the Morning, and about noon, my Man Ben carried her home to Mattishall in a Market Cart that I borrowed of Mr. Buck in this Parish—Ben returned to dinner.

Nov. 27. . . . Mr. Peachman called on me just as I was going to dinner, and told me that he found a Hare sitting very near my House, I went out with him and coursed her and caught her very soon—I offered the Hare to him but he would not accept of her—I asked him to return with me home after, but he declined it.

Nov. 30. . . . Mr. Townshend of Honingham made us a morning Visit, stayed with us about half an Hour—Soon after Mr. and Mrs. Custance with Mr[s]. Townshend in their Coach called here and took Nancy home to Weston House to dine and sleep [t]here, as they promised, this Day being my Tithe Audit. They came from Dereham being at the Assembly last night and slept at Quebec at Mr. Charles Colliers. Mr. Townshend went to Weston House with them as he wanted to talk with Mr. Custance about a gang of Poachers, that infest his Woods. The following Parishioners paid me their respective composition for Tithes, and dined and stayed till near 10 at night at the Parsonage, Cary, Buck, Page, Andrews, Ringgar, Bask, Wm Bidewell, Mr. Mann's nephew J^n_o Rose for him, Js. Pegg, J^n_o Pegg, Case, Norton, Wm Leggatt, Baker, Burroughs, Peachman, Howlett, Girling, Selby, Thos. Leggatt for his Father, and Ross Beane for his Mistress Mrs. Pratt. Mr. Forster did not come to dinner but soon after. They were all highly pleased with their Entertainment but few dined in the Parlour. They that dined in the Kitchen had no Punch or Wine, but strong Beer and Table Beer, and would not come into Parlour to have Punch &c. I gave them for Dinner some Salt Fish, a Leg of Mutton boiled and Capers, a fine Loin of Beef rosted, and plenty of plumb and plain Puddings. They drank in Parlour 7. Bottles of Port Wine, and both my large Bowls of Rum Punch, each of which took 2 Bottles of Rum to make. Forster went away the most disguised of any. In the Kitchen they were all cheerfully merry but none much disguised— Howlett, J$\underline{n}\underline{o}$ Pegg and Will: Leggatt tho' Parlour Guests were rather pretty forward. Rec^d to day for Tithe &c. from above—234. 13. 0. Paid out of the above to Mr. Mann for Coal—0. 5. 0.

Dec. 1. . . . Nancy came home about Dinner time and she dined, supped and slept at home again and glad so to do. Nobody came in the Coach with Nancy home but she had 4 Horses in the Coach. I was quite dull all Day after the fatigue Yesterday. Mr. Girling and Forster had a Battle last Night after they left me at Mr. Peachmans—Forster much injured for the time.

Dec. 9. . . . To Mr. Palmer, Malster p^d a Bill for Malt &c. 28. 17. 0. Of Ditto, for 12 Coomb of Barley, bare measure at 12/9 per Coomb—rec^d 7. 5. 0. Widow Greaves breakfasted and dined here and in the Evening Will: carried her home. Bitter cold this Evening and very hard Frost.

Dec. 15. . . . Mr. Micklethwaite called on me this morning and paid me for Tithe for Land in Hand 1. 4. 0. Paid Henry Baker my Butcher this morning

his Bill for Meat for this last Year the Sum of 46. o. o.
Of Ditto for a Calf rec^d 1. 11. o. So that I paid him
the Calf ded: only 44. 9. o. Betty's Father Mr. Dade
was here this morning and told us that poor Molly gets
weaker and weaker.

Dec. 16. . . . To Mr. Cantrell of Lenewade Bridge p^d
a Bill of 6. 7. 6. To Mr. Forster, Miller of Lenewade
Bridge p^d 6. 8. 6. Sold to Mr. Forster 8 Coomb and
2 Bushl. of Wheat this morning at 1. 2. o. per Coomb
and sent it home to Lenewade Bridge in my cart this
Morning. N.B. He owes me for it 8. 16. o. He never
said any thing about paying for it either when here,
or when my Man Ben carried it there.

Dec. 17. . . . My Man Ben went [with] Betty this
morning early in a Cart of Bidewells to Mattishall to
see her Sister—they did not return till 5 o'clock this
Evening—Betty brought us but a very poor Account
of her Sister, as she gets worse and worse daily—
cannot live long. Pray God grant her a Speedy
relief from her present Situation—to Life if it be
thy good Pleasure, or happiness. Mr. Cary dined
with our Folks in Kitchen.

Dec. 23. . . . Paid Nancy this morning the Sum of
3. 19. o. which with 6. 1. o.—lately paid by me to
one Brownsmith Silk Mercer at Norwich makes
10. o. o. being her Annual Allowance from me to
her. To John Spaule, Blacksmith p^d a Bill of o. 19. o.
At Cribbage this Evening with Nancy won o. 1. o.
but lost it again at last by cutting for it at Cards.

Dec. 24. . . . Between 11 and 12 o'clock this morning
walked to Church and married one John Leggatt of
Elsing and Rebeccah Bowles of this Parish by Banns.
Rec^d for the same only o. 2. 6. having received before
the publication o. 2. 6. To Widow Horner for Hulver

[i.e. holly] which we did not want, having some before from Nortons, but which she knew nothing of I gave her o. 1. o. To my Chimney Sweepers Son Tom Holland for taking down a couple of Swallows Nests in the Chamber Chimnies gave o. o. 6. Gave him also for a Christmas Box o. 1. o. Sent Ben to Norwich this Morning early on foot after News-Papers &c. &c. from thence. At Cribbage this Evening lost o. 1. o.

Dec. 25. . . . I read Prayers and administered the H: Sacrament this Morning at Weston Church, being Christmas Day. Mrs. Custance at Church and at the Sacrament. Mr. Custance not there being ill at home. J^s Smith, my Clerk, Richd Buck, Thos Cushing, Thos Carr, Richd Bates, Thos Dicker, and Thos Cary, all dined at my House as usual on Christmas Day, I gave to each of them a Shilling to carry home to their Wives before they went away—in all— o. 7. o. I gave them for Dinner a Piece of rost Beef and plumb Puddings—and after dinner half a Pint of strong Beer apiece. N.B. All old Men.

Dec. 27. . . . To my Butchers Lad Billy Stonten a Xmas Gift o. 1. o. To my Blacksmiths Lad Charles Spaule Ditto. o. o. 6. To Mr. Cary for things from his Shop only p^d o. 5. o$\frac{1}{2}$. To Will: for things paid for me p^d o. 4. o. To Nancy for Butter &c. p^d o. 4. o. To Weston Ringers gave this Morning o. 2. 6. Mrs. Custance made us a long morning Visit tho' the Roads so bad with Frost and Snow. I wrote out a Song for her from the Poor Soldier. At Cribbage this Evening with Nancy won o. o. 6.

Dec. 31. . . . This being the last Day of the Year 1784 Nancy and self sat up this Night till after 12 o'clock. Then drank all our Friends Health wishing them all a happy new Year and then went to bed. My Maid

Betty Dade very bad in a head ache. Wrote a long Letter to my Sister Pounsett this Evening. Gave it to my Servant Man Ben to carry to Norwich to Morrow Morning, as Mr. Cary does not go, owing to the Weather which at present is very indifferent, as it sometimes snows, then hazy and at Night a Frost.

— 1785 —

Jan. 1. . . . Ben walked to Norwich this morning being a Frost. About Noon, Charles Roupe with Nunn Davy, came here on horseback, to stay one Night with us—was not so well pleased with their Intentions at first of staying here all night, being not so well provided as I could wish to make things convenient for them and Horses—and especially as my House Maid Betty was very indifferent in a bad head ache. However we did as well as we could. They slept in the Garrett over my bed Chamber, Charles Roupe is a very goodnatured Man, but very weak. They both dined, supped and slept here.

Jan. 2. . . . Mrs. Forster of Lenewade Mills sent Nancy some Bride Cake on Miss Le Neves being married on Thursday last to a Mr. Arnold, Apothecary at Loestoff, 48 Years of Age and she only 21 Years. Molly Peachman's Father and Mother and their youngest Daughter Deborah dined with our Folks to day.

Jan. 6. . . . Paid my Servants their Wages this morning that is to Willm Coleman a Y^{rs} Wages 5. 5. 0. To Ditto for dressing my Wiggs 0. 10. 0. To Ditto for 2 P^r of Shoes 0. 12. 0. To Ditto for Grains 4 Coomb 0. 4. 0. N.B. beside the above I give him his Cloaths. To Ben Leggatt a Y^{rs} Wages due now 10. 0. 0. To

Jack Warton a Y^{rs} Wages due now 1. 1. 0. To Betty Dade for half a Y^{rs} Wages due to her and her Sister Molly between them p^d 1. 6. 6. Mem: I then told Betty Dade that from this time I intended to give her 5 Guineas per Annum as I designed the same to her poor Sister, if her health would have permitted to stay with us—but now that is all over, she daily getting worse and worse, as her Father who came over here this Morn' told us, by whom Mr. Smith sent us some Medlars. At Cribbage this Evening and cutting the cards won 0. 2. 0.

Jan. 9. . . . I read Prayers and Preached this Afternoon at Weston. None from Weston House at Church being wet. Mr. Micklethwaite was at Church. I dreamt last Night that I went to Weston Church with a Corpse after me, and just as I came to the Church Yard Gate, saw another Corpse bringing from Morton Road way, and which had died of the small Pox. The corpse that I attended on seeing the other, I ordered to be carried into the Chancel, till the other was buried. When I returned to the Chancel, thought I saw a most elegant Dinner served up—particularly fish—whether I waked then or not I cannot tell, but could recollect nothing more of my dream besides. My Maid Betty Dade went to see her poor Sister Molly this morning behind Ben— they returned about 5 in the Afternoon. Poor Molly just alive and that all being in the last stage of a Consumption—she is very sensible of her approaching End and happily resigned to it. Pray God Almighty bless her and grant her an happy delivery from her present State and eternal happiness after it.

Jan. 12. . . . Between 2 and 3 o'clock this Afternoon, Mrs. Davy with Dr. Thorne came galloping up to

1785

our House and they stayed and took a Family Dinner with us and then returned home again. I paid Dr. Thorne this Afternoon a Bill of—7. 16. 6. We had nothing for Dinner but a Neck of Mutton rosted, cold boiled Beef and some Mince Pies. I buried poor Tom Dicker between 2 and 3 o'clock this Afternoon at Weston aged [not inserted]. At Cribbage this Evening with Nancy won 0. 0. 6.

Jan. 14. . . . About 12 Mrs. Davy came after Nancy in Mr. Thorne's one Horse Chaise to carry her to Mattishall to spend a few Days with her there— About 1 they set of from hence, not pleased with me for not going with them. But it was a very disagreeable, foggy Day and very cold, moreover very late in the Week. To Cantrell's Son for bringing me some Brandy gave 0. 0. 6.

Jan. 16. . . . Mr. Custance at Church but not Mrs. Custance. I was very dull and low this Evening, having no company at all, now Nancy is from home. And not used of late to be much by myself—better soon.

Jan. 18. . . . About noon mounted my Mare and went for Norwich. Will and Ben went with me—Ben to have my Mare back. Got to Norwich about 2 o'clock —supped and slept at the Kings Head as did my Man Will Coleman. As soon as I got to Norwich went to Kerrison's Bank got a Draught for £30 for Cash—put the said Note into a Letter—went to the Post Office— put the Letter into the same and sent it of to Dr. Bathurst at C[hrist] Church. Gave Watson at the Post Office his Xmas Box of 0. 2. 6. Then went to Mrs. Brewster and paid her a Bill of 9. 16. 6. Gave to her Maids in the Shop also 0. 3. 6. Then went to Locke's, Coal Merchant, and paid him a Bill for

Coal, the sum of 17. 19. 0. Paid Mr. Francis, Attorney, also a Bill of 9. 7. 4. for myself and Dr. Bathurst. Paid Beale's, Fishmonger his Bill of 0. 8. 2. Paid Studwell, China Man, also a Bill of 1. 4. 0. Paid Horth, Upholsterer also a Bill of 4. 16. 6. Paid also a Bill for Nancy to Mrs. Clarke lately Miss Bell, Mantua Maker of 2. 0. 0. Went to the Theatre in the Evening but it was so crowded did not chuse to stay, the Boxes being all full. It was so full on Account of Mr. Windham [1] bespeaking the Play. The Play was Grief A la Mode—Entertainment—Agreeable Surprise. Made no Dinner to day, but made an excellent Supper on Oysters &c. at the Kings Head, smoked a Pipe and went to bed. Quite lame this Evening walking so much on the Stones.

Jan. 19. I breakfasted, supped and slept again at the Kings Head. After Breakfast went to Priests and paid him a Bill for Wine &c. &c. of 17. 16. 0. From thence went to Forsters Attorney and paid him for the Miss Le Neves, a Years Rent for Coll: Land of 16. 0. 0. Paid also a Bill for Nancy to Miss Brownes, Milliners in Bedlam Street, the sum of 1. 15. 6. Then called at Lewis's Shop and paid him a Bill for Linen Drapery Goods of 4. 12. 0. Paid there also for 9 Yards and ½ of Cotton for a Gown and Coat for Nancy at 2/6^d per Yard, 1. 2. 6. Paid also for a Lining to the same of 0. 1. 0. At 2 o'clock went to Mr. Francis's by appointment and there dined and spent the Afternoon with him and Wife and Children—And a Mr. Stuart, Mr. Francis's Clerk. We had nothing for Dinner but an ordinary piece of boiled Beef and Norfolk Dumplins. Went to the Rampant Horse in the Evening to see Dr. Katerfelto's

Mr. Windham, the member for Norwich : see foot-note, p. 125.

Exhibitions, but meeting him on Top of the Stairs and his behaviour so exceedingly ungenteel, that I turned upon my Heel and went away.[1]

Jan 22. . . . About 1 o'clock Mrs. Davy with Nancy in Mr. Thorne's Chaise came here and Mr. Thornes Man with them. Mrs. Davy stayed here about half an Hour, would not dine here, and then set of back for Mattishall, leaving Nancy with me—Very glad she is come home. Nancy dined, supped and slept at home. Paid Nancy this Evening for some Patty Pans &c. o. 2. 6. and which she had paid for me to Mrs. Davy. Mrs. Davy did not by any means behave as she used to do towards me—was scarce civil to me.

Jan. 23. . . . Very fair and fine to day, quite a Summers Day. I read Prayers and Preached this Aft: at Weston. Mr. Dade of Mattishall came over here this morning to let his Daughter know, that her poor Sister Molly died last Night—poor Soul! I doubt not of her happiness in a future Life—She was long expected to die. Pray God bless her Spirit and comfort her Relations. Mr. Dade did not stay long here this morning. Mr. and Mrs. Custance both at Church this Aft. And they desired that we would dine with them on Friday next—and that they would send their Coach.

[1] Gustavus Katerfelto was a Prussian who successfully practised conjuring and quackery in England. He appeared in London in 1782, advertising himself under the title, 'Wonders, Wonders, Wonders!' He was occasionally less successful on tour in the provinces, being imprisoned at Shrewsbury as an impostor. Through one of his experiments he raised his daughter by means, apparently, of an immense magnet to the ceiling. This was at Whitby. No doubt Parson Woodforde missed some equally excellent tricks at Norwich, owing to his disgust at the conjurer's 'ungenteel' behaviour. He died on November 25, 1799, at Bedale in Yorkshire (see *D. N. B.*).

1785

Jan. 24. . . . Betty's Father came over here this morning from Mattishall after her to go home and be at the Funeral of her Sister to Morrow—and to return home Wednesday Morn'. Mrs. Greaves came here this morning by my desire to assist in the House during Betty's absence.

Jan. 25. . . . One Sucker from Mattishall a little Farmer came here this morning with his Son John about 13 Years of age to desire me to take his said Son at old Lady Day next in room of Jack Warton who then leaves me on Account of his now being too old for his Place—and which after some talk with the Father I agreed to take him then being well recommended before by Mr. and Mrs. Bodham and Mr. Smith. I gave the Boy, by way of earnest Mony o. 1. o. I am to give him per Annum for Wages 1. 1. o. A Coat and Waistcoat and Hat when wanted, to allow him something for being washed out and mended—And his Friends to find him in Stockings and Shoes &c. At Cribbage this Evening with Nancy lost o. 1. o.

Jan. 27. . . . About 12 took a ride to Mr. Custances and there spent an Hour with Mr. and Mrs. Custance and Lady Bacon. Mr. Custance then took a ride with me to Lenewade Bridge, there being a College Court held there this day. Mr. Francis and Forsters Son were there to do business. Mr. Custance stayed but a very little time—I stayed and dined there, with Mr. Francis, Forsters Son, Copland, Beeston, Stephen Andrews, Joh[n] Pegg and Forster the Miller —and Philip Page also of Weston. We had a good Dinner, a Leg of Mutton boiled and Capers, a Piece of rost Beef, a Couple of Rabbitts and Onions, a Couple of rost Fowls, Pudding and Tarts. N.B. the

College [1] paid the whole reckoning. Francis and Forster returned for Norwich about 4 o'clock. I stayed and smoked one Pipe after they went and then I went home and got home to Tea about 6 o'clock. Forster the Miller paid me for 8 Coomb of Wheat 8. 18. 6. this Afternoon, which I did not expect to receive this Day from him.

Jan. 29. . . . Nancy and self had a few words this morning but soon over, poor dear, I dont wish to make her at all uneasy. At Cribbage this Evening won with Nancy 0. 1. 0. Betty Dades Father came here this morning. Had a Letter this Evening from Dr. Bathurst.

Jan. 30. . . . I read Prayers and Preached this morning at Weston. None from Weston House at Church this morning. I read the Service for King Charles's Martyrdom. [2] Gave poor Joe Adcock who was at Church and lately had something of a paralytic Stroke 0. 1. 0.

Jan. 31. . . . At Cribbage this Evening with Nancy won 0. 1. 0. Gave Nancy after Play to shut up Card playing 0. 3. 0. Will and Ben went this Evening to Mr. Custances being invited (Hambletons Birth Day being kept to day) and they stayed all Night there by my leave.

Feb. 1. . . . About 1 o'clock Nancy and myself got into a Chaise from Lenewade Bridge and sat of for Norwich—Nancy's Maid Betty Dade went with us. Will Coleman also went on horseback with us. We got to Norwich about 3 o'clock dined, supped and

[1] i. e. New College, Oxford.

[2] This commemoration service was not removed from the Prayer Book till 1859 (*The Church of England in the Eighteenth Century*, by Alfred Plummer, D.D., p. 169).

slept at the Kings Head. We had the little dining Room and the two bed Chambers opposite to the same—quite snugg. Went to Buckles, Ironmonger, this Evening and paid him a Bill of 6. 5. 0. We feasted highly this Evening on some fine Oysters. To Newman Lenewade Bridge Driver gave 0. 1. 6.

Feb. 2. . . . Exchanging a bad Guinea at Bakers p^d 0. 1. 0. Called at Priests this morning but did not stay long. About 2 o'clock Nancy and myself took a Coach and went to Mr. Francis's where we dined and spent the Afternoon, and with Mr. and Mrs. Francis, Mr. Stuart, a Miss Darbin and a Miss Dodd. For the Coach to Mr. Francis's p^d 0. 1. 0. We had for Dinner a boiled Leg of Mutton and Capers, a Hare rosted (which I sent to Mr. Francis last Night) and some Mince Pies. After Tea, Mr. Francis, Nancy, Miss Darbin and Miss Dodd went in Coach to the Theatre—I walked there. Paid only for a Ticket for myself 0. 3. 0. Mr. Francis treated Nancy &c. The Theatre was very full. The Hon. Mr. Hobart[1] having bespoke the Play—which was, the Chapter of Accidents, and Shakespears Jubilee the Entertainment which was very entertaining. After the Play &c. Mr. Francis escorted Nancy with the young Ladies to the Kings Head—And there left her and then they went home. Sr Edmund Bacon walked with me from the Theatre to the Kings Head and supped and spent the Evening with us—Taswell of Aylsham also joined us at the Kings Head and supped &c. with us. For my Share of the reckoning this Evening I p^d 0. 4. 0.

Feb. 3. We breakfasted again at the Kings Head. Sr Edmund Bacon breakfasted with us and then he

[1] See foot-note, p. 310.

set of for Raveningham to his own House. To Mr. Clarke for 6 Quires of Fools Cap Paper p^d o. 5. 6. At Bakers for a walking Stick p^d o. o. 6. Called at Mr. Francis's this morning and saw the young Ladies. About 1 o'clock we went to Mr. Priests and from thence got into a Chaise and all set of for home— Took up a Hamper with Wine and Rum from Priests. The Chaise was well loaded with 3 of us and Baggage. We got home (I thank God) safe and well about 3 o'clock. The Driver stayed and dined at my House—gave him o. 2. o. He being Boot-Catch as well as Driver. Paid and gave at the Kings Head for Chaise and all other expenses there 1. 14. 8. We dined, supped and slept at Weston Parsonage. We were rather fatigued and tired this Evening. At the Post Office for a Letter for Mr. Custance p^d o. o. 4.

Feb. 4. . . . Finished reading Roderick Random this Evening.[1]

Feb. 9. . . . Nancy completely finished this Evening her new spot net Apron—and very pretty it looks.

Feb. 10. . . . Shaved to Day with Naples Soap which is very soft and which I bought at Mrs. Brewsters— p^d for it o. 4. 6. is in a small Galley Pot—and about Q^r of a P^d of it.

Feb. 14. . . . To 62 Valentines at 1^d each this morning gave o. 5. 2. About 4 o'clock this Afternoon Mr. and Mrs. Custance sent us word that they would drink Tea with us this Afternoon—which put us in a little hurry. In about half an Hour they came, drank Tea and Coffee played a Pool at Quadrille after and then went home again—they left us between eight and nine this Evening. At Quadrille this Evening lost o. 1. o.

[1] *Roderick Random* was Tobias Smollett's (1721–71) first novel: it appeared in 1748.

Feb. 15. . . . Mrs. Davy came here this morning before we were up and she breakfasted, dined and spent the Aft: here. About 11 o'clock this Morning the Rev^d Mr. Le Grisse came here to talk about Tithe—He did not stay long with me. He has the Living of Morton—He came to ask me what one of his Parishioners by name Reynolds who is lately come into Burroughs's Farm—pays me for some Land he has in the Parish of Weston. Bettys Father brought over Mrs. Davy on Horseback and he breakfasted, dined and spent the Aft: here. Mrs. Davy left us this Evening between 5 and 6 o'clock.

Feb. 20. . . . I privately baptized a Child of one Roberts's this morning by name—William—born also this Morn'. I read Prayers and Preached this Afternoon at Weston. None from Weston House at Church—being so very cold. Excessive cold indeed, colder than ever, if any thing. It froze exceeding sharp within Doors last night and continues to do the same in the day Time—tho' the Sun shone exceeding bright all the day long. The Thermometer down to 56, tho' in the Study and a fire constantly kept there—at 11 this Morning. The Barometer also down to 28—18—in the same Room. The Barometer has been falling ever since Sunday last tho' the Days have been very sun-shining and very hard Frosts. Rec^d this Afternoon for publishing Banns o. 2. 6. John Clarke dined with our Folks in Kitchen.

Feb. 22. . . . It being a tolerable Morning for tracing Hares, I went out with my Dogs, and had not been out half an Hour before we started a Hare and killed her after a tolerable good Course. No sport afterwards at all. Betty Dades Father came here this Morn and dined here.

Feb. 26. . . . I dreamt a good deal about Jenny Woodforde Frank Woodforde's Wife, of her being dressed
all in white, looked exceeding pale but very handsome.
I hope my Dream portends no ill to her.

Feb. 27. . . . Harder Frost than ever with high Wind
with some falling of very small kind of Snow—colder
than ever. I read Prayers and Preached this morning
at Weston. Very small Congregation indeed—not 20
Persons there and only two Women amongst them—
Palmers Wife of Morton and the Clerk's Wife Jenny
Smith. None from Weston House of any kind.
John Norton dined with our Folks in Kitchen.

Feb. 28. . . . The Frost severer than ever in the night
as it even froze the Chamber Pots under the Beds.
Wind very rough and tho' the Sun shone all the
morning very bright yet it continued freezing every
minute. Most bitter cold to day indeed, and likely
to continue. . . .

March 1. . . . I got up this morning before 8 o'clock,
about half an Hour after Mrs. Davy came here on
horseback behind my Maid's Father Mr. Dade, and
she stayed and breakfasted, dined and spent the
Afternoon with us by appointment—as did Betty's
Father in the Kitchen. We had for Dinner a boiled
Leg of Mutton and Capers a fine Hare rosted, Apple
Pudding and Tartlets. Mrs. Davy left us about
6 this Evening—after Tea. Mr. Du Quesne promised
to call on us this Day in a Note I rec^d from him on
Sunday last, as I then sent a Note by my Man Will
to him to enquire after him on his return from Ely,
where he has been for the last two Months to keep
his residence there. Du Quesne however never came
or sent, he intended to have called here on his Road
to Reepham to see his Friend Priest there. Mr.

Peachman called on me this morning about buying Turnips of me, I sent him to Ben to deal with him.

March 5. . . . Mr. Thorne sent Nancy over to day some Cod's Liver Oil about a Quarter of a Pint, for her to make use of about her stiff arm and lame Knee—She begun with it this Evening on her arm only—pray God ! send thy blessing upon it for her good.

March 7. . . . Read on the London Papers to day of the death of my Contemporary John Lucas Vicar of Milborne Port and Fellow of Winton College—found dead in bed. Pray God ! his change may be for a happier State.

March 8. . . . Of one Aldridge who called here this Morning with a Cart with things, for ½ Yard of Cambrick p^d 0. 5. 0. Of Ditto—for corded Muslin ½ Yrd for the Maids 0. 3. 6. and which I gave between them for Caps.

March 10. . . . Mr. Du Quesne made us a morning Visit on his road to Priests of Reepham—he looked mighty Well. Will: Coleman went early to Norwich this Morn' on my Mare, to Hylatts who was lately Gardener to Mr. Custance, after some Cucumber Plants which he promised him—He returned about 1 o'clock and Hylatt came with him and he dined here with our Folks. He did not come directly to my House as Mr. Custance's Coach was here with Mrs. Custance but put up his Horse at the White Hart and stayed till after. Mrs. Custance came here about Noon and staid with us till near 2 o'clock— She came very soon after Mr. Du Quesne left us— She came thro' the Kitchen to the Study, it being so very cold.

March 13. . . . I read Prayers, Preached and christened

a Child by Name, Tabitha Bithia, this morning at Weston Church. Mr. Custance and Mr. Micklethwaite were at Church. Mem: Bithia is a very uncommon Name, but it was the Name of Pharoah's Daughter—See 1 Chron. iv 18.[1] It was a Child of Reeves at the Hart and a pretty Girl. Bitter cold tho' fair all day—In the Evening it froze almost as sharp as any time this Year.

March 14. . . . Poor Neighbour Clarke's Wife and 4 Children are taken down in the small Pox—Their Neighbour Gooch, his Wife, nor any of a large Family of children belonging to them, have none of them had the Small Pox.

March 15. . . . Sent poor Clarkes Family a large Bushel Basket of Apples, to make Apple Dumplins for poor Souls. Sent another basket of same to Goochs Family. To Nortons and Downings Family sent each a Basket of Apples. . . .

March 16. . . . Dr. Thorne called here this morning— He has been inoculating John Gooch and whole Family. Nancy complained very much this morning of the Wind in her Stomach—I desired her to drink some strong Beer after Dinner instead of Wine, which she did and was better after it.—She was much oppressed by Hysteric wind before—She also by my desire had some Milk for breakfast and is to continue it. Neighbour Clarkes Wife and Family as well as can be expected.—It is a good kind of small Pox they have.

March 19. . . . I called last night at poor Neighbour Clarkes, but did not go in, found they were as well

---

[1] 'And his wife Jehudijah bare Jered the father of Gedor, and Heber the father of Socho, and Jekuthiel the father of Zanoah. And these are the sons of Bithiah the daughter of Pharaoh, which Mered took.'

as could be expected. I left with the Woman that nurses them, who is John's Mother, to buy some necessaries o. 2. o. Had a Note this morning from Mr. Custance to ask us to dinner on Monday next.

March 22. . . . Neighbour Clarkes Family continue tolerably well. Neighbour Gooch's Family begin to complain to day hope they will have the Small Pox favourably. Gave John Gooch to day to buy necessaries o. 2. o. Very fair in the morning and a hard Frost with bitter cold Winds—In the Evening Snow with Wind.

March 23. . . . Dr. Thorne called here this morning but did not stay long—He told us that his Patients our Neighbours in the Small Pox were all brave. The Weather still continues as cold as ever, Frost, Wind, Hail and Snow at different Times to day.

March 25. . . . I read Prayers this morning at Weston being Good Friday. Mr. Custance was at Church, complained of the Cold. To Widow Gaff and Widow Grant—gave each 1s/0d—o. 2. o. Very cold again to day, dark, cloudy and damp. Sent a long Letter to my Sister Pounsett by Cary. I eat no Meat all day being Good-Friday—neither did Nancy—and we did not dine till 5 o'clock. I dined on Fritters and toasted Cheese—Nancy had Eggs. Just as we were sat down to dinner Mr. Smith's Servant Boy with a Note from his Master came here. It was to desire me to serve Mattishall for him on Sunday next in the Afternoon —he being very ill. I sent an Answer back soon as I had dined that I wd.

March 26. . . . At the Assizes at Thetford in this County 8 Prisoners were condemned, three of the above were reprieved.—The other five left for execution—One Js Cliffen a most daring Fellow was hanged on Thursday. J͢ˢ Cliffen as mentioned on the last mentioned was hanged on Thursday last at Norwich on Castle-Hill and behaved most daringly audacious —His crime was robbing 2 old Men, Brothers, by names Seaman on the Yaxham Road, knocked them both down first, of which Blows one of them died soon after—the other recovered. Cliffen's Body was this Day carried to Badley Moor and there hung in Chains at one Corner of the said Moor.

March 27. . . . I read Prayers and administered the H: Sacrament this Morning at Weston Church being Easter day. Neither Mr. or Mrs. Custance or Micklethwaites at Church. It snowed all the morning and great part of the Afternoon. When I returned from Weston Church I dined directly then put on my Boots and a little before 2. mounted my Mare and rode to Mattishall and there read Prayers and Preached for Mr. Smith he being ill. My Man Ben went with me—put up my Horses at Mr. Smiths— found him much better than I expected. It snowed all the whole way going to Mattishall. After Service at Mattishall I smoked one Pipe at Mr. Smiths with Dr. Thorne—and then returned home. It froze exceedingly sharp on my return home. I got home between six and seven in the Evening. Heard at Mattishall by Mr. Smith that Mr. Bodham's Father of Swaffham died on Friday last there.

March 28. . . . Called this Morning at Goochs Stile and enquired how himself and Family were in the small Pox—and he told me that they were all finely— gave him 0. 2. 0. Called also at Clarkes and enquired how they were in the small Pox—they were also tolerable, gave them 0. 2. 0. Gave Gooch and Clarke another Bushell Basket of Apples apiece—the others being done. To my Clerk J^s Smith being Easter Monday gave o. 2. 6.

April 2. . . . Mr. Bodhams Father is supposed to have died worth £40,000. There are only 2 Children—our Mr. Bodham and his Sister. The latter has left her ten thousand Pounds.

April 4. . . . After breakfast, being fine Weather, I took a ride and Will with me, thro' Hockering, North-Tuddenham, to Baddeley Moor where Cliffen stands in Chains, most shocking road all around where he stands for some way thought we should have been mired—I then went thro' part of Yaxham on to Mattishall to see Mr. and Mrs. Bodham after the Death of their Father and there dined with Mr. and Mrs. Bodham and little Anne Donne. I got home between 7 and 8 in the Evening. Saw in my Road to day Mr. Shelford Senr, and Mr. and Mrs. Thorne. It turned out very fair and fine all the Day.

April 5. . . . Very fair and fine Day throughout—quite warm. My new Boy with his Father came here this Afternoon from Mattishall, by name Secker—The Father went back in the Evening leaving the Lad here—And soon after very much distressed on hearing that the Boy never had the Small-Pox—It being so near us. He must therefore return home to Morrow. He seems to be a very likely Boy—and therefore will get him inoculated by Mr. Thorne if I can.

April 7. . . . I took a ride to Mr. Du Quesnes this morning, stayed with him about an Hour and then returned home. Jack went with me—Will being brewing. Jack Warton left my Service this Evening and went home. He was to have went the 5 Instant —but the other Lad returning home the next Day—

Jack stayed a couple of Days longer with me—Jack has been a very good, sober Lad in my Service. And should have been glad to have continued him but he is very desirous of learning to plow &c. I paid him for his last Quarters Service 0. 5. 3. I paid and gave him besides 0. 5. 3.

April 9. . . . To a poor deaf Man from Mattishall gave 0. 0. 1. Mrs. Custance with her 2 Children William and Fanny came here this Afternoon about 5 o'clock without the lest notice and stayed with us about an Hour and then returned back to Weston House—did not drink Tea. I had not finished my Afternoon Pipe but put it away. I told Mrs. Custance that I had been smoking and hoped she did not dislike Tobacco —and she said she liked it. Nancy had a very long Letter from her Sister Juliana.

April 12. . . . I buried poor old Widow Pully this Aft: aged—80 y^{rs}. My Servant Willm Coleman was out all the Evening till just 11 o'clock—came home in Liquor behaved very rudely and most impudently to me indeed, I told him that I was determined never more to bear with such Behaviour, and that he sh^d certainly go to Morr'. Mr. Peachman called here about 7 o'clock and paid me for 4 Acres of Turnips at 30^s per Acre—6. 0. 0. He did not stay long with us— drank some fresh [?].

April 13. . . . I got up between 5 and 6 o'clock this morning had Will before me as soon as possible, paid him his Wages and dismissed him before 8 o'clock. For a Q^{rs} Wages at 5 Guineas p^d him 1. 6. 3. For a Q^{rs} dressing Wiggs at 10^s p^d him 0. 2. 6. For a Q^{rs} Allowance for Shoes at 12^s p^d him 0. 3. 0. For brewing-Grains 6 Coomb at 1^s 0^d p^d him 0. 6. 0. In all paid him 1. 17. 9. I threw him down a Couple of

Guineas for him to have the remaining, but he would not take one farthing more than the above 1. 17. 9. Being so much hurried last night and this morning made me quite ill all Day—vomited a good deal at Night after which took a Dose of Rhubarb and was much better.

April 14. . . . Had an exceeding good Night (thank God) and much better. Will had away his Chest early this morning and is now at work in the Garden at Mr. Cary's. I wish he might do well and better than he did here.

April 15. . . . Will: came to me to day to desire I would give him a Character if wanted, which I promised him. He seems to be rather cast down to day and at no work.

April 16. . . . Will: Coleman I hear went of early this morning for Norwich and in high Spirits. I had 2 yong Men offer themselves but neither w^d do as they never waited at Table in their lives.

April 18. . . . Saw the first Swallow this Season this Morning. Will: Coleman called here this morning very early to take his Leave of his late Partners—He was gone before I was below Stairs—He has got a Place at Catton—at 10^s/6^d per Week and no Board or 1^s/0. Per Day and board. Mr. Du Quesne came here about 2 o'clock in his Chaise and he dined and spent the Afternoon here and ab^t 4 o'clock we went with him in his Chaise to Norwich got to Kings Head about 6 o'clock—there met Mr. and Mrs. Custance, just going to the Play, we stayed after that and drank a Dish of Tea—and then we took a Coach and drove to the Theatre. Got there just as the first Act was over—We sat in the Mayors Box—The Mayor (Partridge) was there also. Lady Bacon and Mrs. Custance in the next Box to us. Sr William Jernegan came and spoke to us. The Play was the Duenna—and Farce the Divorce. Both bespoke by Sr Will and Lady Jernegan. After we came from the Theatre which was ab^t 10 we all supped at the Kings Head and there slept. Mr. and Mrs. Custance returned to Weston after the Play. The Kings Head was quite full of Company, Mr. Du Quesne and myself were obliged to sleep in one Room and down the Yard—Nancy just by us in a single Room and a very good one. We did not go to bed till after 12 o'clock.

April 19. We breakfasted at the Kings Head and stayed in Norwich till about 1 o'clock and then we returned as we went to Weston and there Mr. Du Quesne dined and spent the Afternoon with us—Mr. Priest of Reepham drank Tea with us this Afternoon and returned home with Mr. Du Quesne to Mr. Du Quesnes House at Tuddenham. Our Bill at the Kings Head &c., Tickets, Coach and Servants all included came to 1. 14. 6—p^d half—being 0. 17. 3. Mr. Du Quesne would insist on paying the other half. I gave his Man, Stephen England, to go to the Play 0. 1. 0. To a Dozen of sweet Oranges to carry home p^d 0. 1. 6. To my Fish Man Beale for Fish now and before p^d 0. 5. 6. At Bakers for 2 Wig Combs p^d 0. 1. 6. To the Boot-Catch for cleaning my Boots gave 0. 0. 6. We neither of us slept well at all last night—so disturbed by the Soldiers sleeping over us —and running up and down Stairs. I laid in a little Press Bed—the bed too short for me—close to a large Window and little or no Cloaths on the Bed. Called at Mr. Francis's this morning and likewise on Mrs. Micklethwaite who is at Lodgings in St. Stephens having very lately been brought to bed of a Daughter.

We called at Mr. Priests—saw him and Son John and Bekky Priest. Mrs. Priest did not make her Appearance at all.

April 22. . . . After breakfast Nancy went with me in Lenewade Chaise to Aylsham it being the Arch-Deacons Generals there to Day—We got to Aylsham at ¼ past 10 o'clock—Mr. Taswell being gone for London—Nancy was obliged to dine by herself at our Inn, the 3 black Boys. Ben went with us to open gates for the Chaise. Nancy went with us to Church at 11 o'clock, and heard Prayers read by one Mr. Bennett a Young Man, and who read very well— And heard a Sermon preached by a Mr. Leath another Young Man. The Arch-Deacon, Mr. Younge[1] attended but gave no charges. The Clergy present were Mr. Whitmell, Mr. Bryant, Mr. Priest, Mr. Carr, Mr. Candler, Mr. Baker, Mr. Bell, Mr. Bulwer, Mr. Leath, Mr. Bennett, Mr. Collier of Wroxham, Mr. Addison, and myself—for my Dinner &c. p^d 0. 3. 0. P^d for Nancy's Dinner and Wine 2^s 1½^d. P^d for Horses, Servant and Driver 4^s 6^d. Mr. Priest returned with us in our Chaise as far as Cawston and there we dropt him. We got home to Weston ab^t 6 in the Evening. Gave Lenewade Driver, Newman 2^s 0^d. Nancy liked her Jaunt very well. Rec^d of Mr. Buck (Churchwarden) this Morn' for a Copy of the Register 2. 6.

April 24. . . . Will: Coleman we heard to day was come again to Weston could not be easy at Norwich tho' he had employment.

April 25. . . . Will: Coleman came to us this morning as we were walking in the Garden, and said that he

[1] The Archdeacon was a nephew of the late Bishop of Norwich, Dr. Philip Yonge (see foot-note, p. 71, preceding).

could not be easy after his late bad behaviour, till he
had spoke to me and asked pardon for it—I then told
him that I would employ him as a Gardener and give
him a shilling a Day and his Board for 2 Days in
a Week—but that he must get a Lodging from my
House, and if he can somewhere in the Parish. He
appeared then quite happy and went directly about
his work in the Garden. To Mr. Cary for things
from Norwich &c. p^d o. 7. 6½. To Nancy for Butter
at 10^d p^d o. 2. 6.

April 26. . . . Bretingham Scurl a new Servant came
here whilst we were at Dinner, I ordered him into
Parlour directly and made him wait at Table and he
did pretty well. He appears to be a good-natured
willing young Fellow. Will: Coleman who is garden-
ing for me looked rather shy upon Scurl at first—
We call him Briton.

April 27. . . . My new Boy Jack Secker came back
from Mr. Thornes after inoculation this morning to
us. Clerk Hewits Son Will: brought him here behind
him, gave Will: o. 6. . . .

May 3. . . . To a poor infirm old Man by name Simonds
of Yaxham who lately had a paralytic Stroke gave
o. 1. o.

May 4. . . . Will: Coleman dined with our Folks to
day, he being here preparing the Vessels for brewing
to Morrow. . . .

May 6. . . . To John Pegg a Q^{rs} Land Tax p^d 3. o. o.
To Ditto old Window Tax ½ Year—N° 23—1. 2. 7.
To Ditto New Window Tax ½ Year—N° 19—1. 5. o.
To Ditto House Tax ½ Year at £7—o. 1. 9. To
Taylor Clarke making two Suits of Frocks and Waist-
coats, for my new Man and new Boy, Buttons,
Pockets, Thread &c. included p^d him 1. 1. o. Gave

him a Vomit to take in the Evening, as he complains of not being very well. To Cupper for a small Codlin and some Cockles p^d o. 1. 2.

May 8. . . . I read Prayers and Preached this morning at Weston C. Mr. and Mrs. Custance and their Son Hambleton at Church. Mrs. Micklethwaite's last Child a Girl died last Night. Mrs. Micklethwaite has also a younger Sister now laying dead, a Mrs. Towers who killed herself by raking. Willm Coleman dined with our Folks to day. I prayed for Rain this morning at Church—it being much wanted, especially the Lent crops of Barley &c.

May 17. . . . Smock-racing &c. at Morton white Horse to day. Most gracious and gentle Rain most part of the Day thanks to Almighty God for the same. Rain was greatly wanted in these parts. The Barley could not get out of Ground before, the late sown.

May 18. . . . At 11 o'clock this morning walked to Weston Church and publickly presented Mr. and Mrs. Custances little Girl Emily in the Church—The Sponsors, were Mr. Custance for a Mr. White-bread Junr, Mrs. Custance for Miss Schutdz, and my Niece Nancy for a Miss Rand. After the Ceremony Mr. Custance very genteely and handsomely pre-sented me with a Bank Bill value 5. 5. o. Nancy went from Church with Mrs. Custance to Weston House in their Coach with their five Children and Nurses. Mr. Custance returned home on horseback. I returned home on foot to spend the Remainder of the Morn. To Mr. Cary this morning for things from Norwich p^d o. 4. o. Of Ditto—for 2 Pints of Butter at 8^d rec^d o. 1. 4. Between 2 and 3 this After-noon Mr. Du Quesne came to my House on Horse-

back, he left his Horse here, and walked with me to
Weston House where we dined, and spent the
Afternoon with Mr. and Mrs. Custance, My Niece
and Mr. Smith—We stayed there till near 9 o'clock.
After Tea and Coffee we got to Loo at which I lost
o. 13. o. We all returned together in Mr. Custances
Coach to my House, where Mr. Du Quesne and
Mr. Smith mounted their Horses after staying a few
Minutes, for their own Houses.

May 20. . . . Who should come to my House this
Morning about 12 o'clock just as I was going out on
horseback, but my old Friend and brother Collegian
Dr. Bathurst—He came on horseback from the
Palace at Norwich, being there on a Visit to the
Bishop.—He looked very well but could not stay
long with me, as he was going on to his Curate
Mr. Wilson at Lyng—I rode with him to Lyng and
just by Wilsons I parted with him—I pressed him
much to dine with me but could not prevail. To
Will: Coleman this Evening for 2 Days Work p^d
o. 2. o. Nancy sent a long Letter to her Sister
Juliana. I was very angry with my Maid Molly this
Night for staying out after 11 o'clock, just as I was
going to bed.

May 22. . . . Mr. Peachman and Mr. Page called on
me this morning and desired me to draw up a Petition
for John Gooch who very lately lost a valuable Cow
by death, which I told them I would to Morrow
Morning. I read Prayers and Preached this Afternoon at Weston C[hurch]. Mr. and Mrs. Custance,
Mr. and Mrs. Micklethwaite, and my Niece at Church
—and a large Congregation. Will: Coleman dined
with our Folks to day.

May 23. . . . I drew up a Petition for John Gooch

this morning and gave it to him and with it gave for myself 5. o. Gave also for my Niece 2. 6. . . .

May 25. . . . Mr. Baker the Official and Mr. Morphew Junr came to my House this morning about 9 o'clock and they both breakfasted here on Coffee and Tea— After breakfast I walked with them to the Church to see it, they being come for that Purpose—The Arch-Deacon Mr. Yonge being indisposed—After that they went for Ringland &c. About 2 o'clock Mr. and Mrs. Custance called on us in their Coach, and took us with them to Mattishall and there we all dined and spent the Afternoon at Mr. Smiths with [him] and Mr. Du Quesne, and that was all the Company. After Coffee and Tea we got to Loo at which I lost o. o. 6. We returned home as we went about 9 o'clock.

May 26. . . . John Gooch has collected on his Petition about 2. 2. o.

May 29. . . . Betty Dade's Father, Clerk of Mattishall, walked over to my House early this morning to let me know that Mr. Smith did not come home last night, and that I would serve Mattishall Church for him in the Afternoon. He breakfasted with our Folks and then walked back. I read Prayers and Preached this morning at Weston. Mr. and Mrs. Custance, Mr. and Mrs. Micklethwaite and Nancy at Church this morning. About 2 o'clock took a ride to Mattishall and there read Prayers and Preached for Mr. Smith. Mrs. Bodham and Mrs. Davy at Mattishall Church. I then returned home to Weston and went to dinner. We did not dine to day till half past 5 o'clock. The Service this morning very long being the 29 of May.[1]

[1] Upon this day was held the thanksgiving service for the restoration of King Charles II, but when the day fell on a Sunday the rubric for the

June 1. . . . Mr. and Mrs. Custance called here about 11 o'clock and took Nancy with them in their Coach to go to Norwich. They would have taken me up also but I preferred going on horseback, about 12 therefore, I went to Norwich and took Briton with me, and we got there about 2 o'clock—but was wet getting thither. About 3 o'clock this Afternoon a violent Tempest arose at Norwich in the North East, very loud Thunder with strong white Lightening with heavy Rain—which lasted about an Hour— immediately after which Mr. Deckers Balloon with Decker himself in a boat annexed to it, ascended from Quantrells Gardens and very majestically.—It was out of Sight in about 10 Minutes, but appeared again on his Descent. It went in a South East Direction—I saw it from Brecondale Hill, and it went almost over my Head. Mr. and Mrs. Custance and Nancy were at Mackay's Gardens. They saw it also very plain from thence. A vast Concourse of People were assembled to see it. It was rather unfortunate that the Weather proved so unfavourable—but added greatly to the Courage of Decker that he ascended so very soon after the Tempest. It also bursted twice before he ascended in it, upon the filling it, if it had not, a Girl about 14 was to have went with him in it—but after so much Gas had been let out—it would not carry both. Mr. Du Quesne was there and in the Gardens. Mrs. Thorne, Mrs. Davy and Captain Thorne overtook me going to Norwich just by the Turnpike—I parted with them just by St. Giles's Gate and saw nothing more

service only required the Parson to read the special collects : it is not, therefore, quite clear why the service on this Sunday should have been so long.

of them afterwards—They were wet as well as we on the Road—I put up my Horses at the Wool-pack. The Tempest happened as I was on Brecondale Hill. I went directly to a red House adjoining, and was very kindly asked to walk in to a Parlour, which I accepted—Whilst I was there I found that I was got into Mrs. Thornes Brothers, Mr. Tho⁵ Agges. I saw a very pretty Quaker there, a young Woman. After I returned from seeing the Balloon—I went to a Perfumers Shop in the Haymarket by name Amyot and bought some Essence of Jessamine, Lavender, Bergamot for all which I paid o. 2. 3. I then called at Bakers and bought a Habit Brush for Nancy with a looking Glass at the back of it pᵈ o. 2. o. I then called at Priests, there saw Du Quesne, but neither eat or drank there—For some Amber Grease, Oil of Time, Lavender, and Spermaceti pᵈ o. 2. 3. After that I mounted my Mare and sat of for Weston —got home about 8 o'clock this Evening and then dined, supped and slept in the old House—Nancy was at home about an Hour before me—very much tired. We were very wet coming home this Even-ing. At Norwich for 1 half Pint of Porter and gave the Maid o. 3. Mr. and Mrs. Custance, Nancy, myself, and in short all that went to see the Baloon were highly pleased. We were all sorry that the Weather was so bad for it. Decker however has gained great Credit by it.[1]

June 2. . . . Very busy all the morning in making Pomatum.

June 3. . . . Mr. Du Quesne walked to my House about 3 o'clock with his measuring Wheel, and he dined and spent the Aft: here. We gave him for

[1] On the balloon craze at this time, see foot-note, p. 117.

Dinner Calfs Liver fryed and Bacon, Calfs Heart rosted, some Asparagus and cold rost Beef and cold Ham, with an Apple Tart. The road which he came was at the back of Mr. Micklethwaites, over part of Hungate Common, cross France Green to Mouse's House, which way measured two Miles, 6 Furlongs and 140 Yards. After Tea we walked part of the way with Du Quesne home, so far as Odnam Green, another way to his House. From my Garden Gate next the Yard to the first Gate at Odnam Green measured exactly one Mile.

June 5. . . . There was no Service at Weston Church to day, the Lead on the North Aile being part of it taken of, to be repaired. My Man Briton, whilst he was waiting at dinner, was taken in the Ague, and he went directly and plunged himself over Head and Ears in my great Pond in the Garden, after which I gave him a good Dram of Gin and then sent him to bed, where he laid and slept almost for 3 Hours—He then got up and was brave after.

June 8. . . . I dreamt very much last Night of Mr. Smith and Mrs. Davy and that connection entirely broke of—I told Nancy of it at breakfast.—Just as we were going to sit down to dinner, Mr. Matthews brought a Note to my Niece from Mrs. Davy—to let her know that she was in great distress, having rec[d] a Letter this morn' from Mr. Smith to break of any farther connection with her—his Friends being so very averse to the Match And that he was going to leave England directly. Mrs. Davy desires my Niece to come over to her directly—but she could not go.

June 10. . . . Nancy made part of a breakfast at home and at 8 o'clock this morning she sat of in Mr. Bucks Market Cart and Ben with her for Mattishal[l] Burgh to Mrs. Davys where she is to spend a few Days with her, as she is very low from what has lately happened by Mr. Smith. Sent a very long Letter to my Sister Pounsett by Cary. Sent also one for Nancy to her Brother Sam.

June 14. . . . About 12 o'clock I got into a single Horse Chaise from Lenewade Bridge with my little Mare by name Jenny in it and drove to Mattishall Burgh to Mrs. Davys, and there took up Mrs. Davy and my Niece in it with me, and drove to Mr. Bodhams where we dined and spent the Afternoon with him, Mrs. Bodham, Miss Bodham and Mr. Casters Donnes little girl by Name Anne—After Tea we got to Quadrille at which I won 2^s 0^d—As did Nancy the same—o. 2. o. At 8 o'clock I ordered the Chaise, and after taking Leave, Nancy and self sat of in it for Weston Parsonage and got home (thank God) safe and well ab^t 9.

June 16. . . . I got up this morning at 5 o'clock, The Wind being very high, which continued all the Morning and Evening and at Sun Setting rose much higher, and at Night rather higher with violent Storms of Rain at Times, and continued so all Night long till Sun rising and after—I did not go to bed till after 3 o'clock in the Morning, and there was but just got into bed, before the Wind alarmed me again, at which I dressed myself, and walked about my Room some little time, then laid down on the bed with my Cloaths on and slept till about 8 o'clock —then pulled of my Cloaths and went into bed and laid till 10 o'clock and then got up, the Wind then continuing very rough indeed. Nancy got up about 1 o'clock and stayed with me below Stairs in the Study till 3 o'clock and then she went to bed again.

I was very much jaded this day. Thank God, I had little or no damage done—Pray God protect all those that were dangerously exposed particularly on all poor Creatures at Sea and in it.

June 17. . . We did not get up till after 10 o'clock this morning. The Wind still continued rough all the morning. I had a few Tiles removed and some young Trees blowed down upon the ground in the night and my Chancel Window was a little damaged towards the East but not much. In the Afternoon the Wind abated much, Evening calm. Tho' we were so much deprived of Sleep last Night, we were quite brave all the day long and lively—and seemed rather better than the worse for it. To Tom Carr being rather ill gave 0. 1. 0. Mr. Custances Coachman, George, coming from Mattishall last Night had a fall from his Horse and broke his Collar Bone. We were very sorry for him as he was a very goodnatured Man.

June 20. . . . Molly Peachman went this morning, to spend a day or two with some Friends at some little distance. Widow Greaves came to supply her Place during her Absence. A Mr. Woodcocke from Norwich with Jⁿᵒ Pegg and Wᵐ Bidewell called here this morning to view my Windows—2 more charged. Mr. Du Quesne called here just before Dinner and he dined and spent the Afternoon with us—He was last Week in London at Handels Commemoration in the Abbey.[1]

[1] The poet Cowper, though he deeply venerated Handel's music, thought these commemorations a little overdone. In his poem *The Task*, published in this year, 1785, he speaks as follows:

> Man praises man. Desert in arts or arms
> Wins public honour ; and ten thousand sit
> Patiently present at a sacred song,
> Commemoration-mad ; content to hear

He returned by way of Ely, having business there. After Tea this Evening we got to Cribbage at wch I won 0. 1. 0. To Mr. Cary this Evening for things from Norwich &c. p^d 0. 2. 4. N.B. Dairy and Corn Chamber Windows charged, never charged before.

June 21. . . . Nancy breakfasted, and soon after breakfast she went in Cary's Cart for Mattishall to Mrs. Davys and Ben went with her—Nancy stays all night at Mattishall. About 12 I took a ride to Norwich and Briton with me. Briton returned home with the Horses in the Evening. I stayed and slept at Norwich—I dined supped and slept at the Kings Head. After Dinner I walked to Whitemans, Brazier in St Stephens and paid him a Bill for things 1. 5. 0. From thence went to Mr. Francis's to see Mrs. Francis. After that went to Quantrells Gardens and took a Ticket for to see the Balloon go from thence to Morrow. I paid Mr. Decker for the Ticket 0. 5. 0. I stayed at the Gardens some time with Decker. In the Evening called at my Sadlers, Allum and paid him a Bill of 1. 6. 0. This being Guild Day Allum was very drunk indeed. At 7 this Evening went to Bunns Gardens and stayed there till after 10 o'clock—p^d there 0. 1. 0. There was tolerable good Music, indifferent singing, some pretty transparencies and tolerable fire Works. To other expences this Evening p^d 0. 1. 0.

June 22. I breakfasted at the Kings Head—slept very

(O wonderful effect of music's power !)
Messiah's eulogy for Handel's sake.

.   .   .   .   .

Remember Handel ? Who, that was not born
Deaf as the dead to harmony, forgets,
Or can, the more than Homer of his age ?

The Task, Book VI.

well. After dressing myself I walked to Priests, there saw Du Quesne and Priest of Reepham—then went to my Fishmonger, Beale and paid a Bill of o. 5. 3. from thence went to Quantrells Gardens about 11 o'clock, and there stayed till 4 in the Afternoon saw the whole process of filling the Balloon, and its Ascension which was about a Q^r of an Hour after 3. Miss Weller, a very pretty Girl about 14 with Decker in the Balloon thrice attempted to ascend but could not therefore Miss Weller was obliged to be taken out, and then it ascended but not well at first setting of—It soon however afterwards ascended very well, and then went almost the same way as the last did, with Decker in it. Lord Orford,[1] S^r W^m and Lady Jernegan, Sr Edm^d Bacon, Sr Thos Beauchamp &c. present at the Ascension. Lord Orford appeared in the most shabby Dress. After it was over I met Betsy Davy, Mary Roupe, Mr. Castres Donne and Wife—Mr. Ashill and his Sister. Did not see Du Quesne or any of the Priests, they being in the half Crown Places. For Wine and Water at the Gardens p^d o. o. 6. For some Jellies for Betsy Davy, Mary Roupe &c. p^d o. o. 9. From the Gardens walked with Mary Roupe to Mr. Priests and there I dined with him, Mrs. Priest, Mr. Du Quesne, Mr. Priest of Reepham, John and Richd Priest and Mary Roupe. We had for Dinner, Soals, Veal Ham and Gooseberry

---

[1] Lord Orford (George Walpole, 1730–91) was the 3rd earl, and grandson of the Prime Minister, Sir Robert, whose wonderful collection of pictures at Houghton he sold in 1779 for £45,000 to the Empress of Russia. He was subject to temporary fits of insanity. His uncle, Horace Walpole, in a letter of July 25, 1785, refers to his sharing in the prevailing passion for balloons, even threatening to ascend himself. When he died in 1791 Horace succeeded him as 4th Earl of Oxford (see Walpole's *Letters* passim).

Tart. About 6 this Evening went to the Kings Head, paid my Bill, with which and Servants there p^d and gave o. 7. o. Ben came after me about Noon—and at 7 o'clock I mounted my Mare and returned home to Weston got there about 9 where I supped and slept. Nancy was just returned from Mattishall as I came home—Briton having been after her in Cary's Cart. Nancy supped and slept here, and not much fatigued.

June 24. . . . About 2 o'clock Mr. Du Quesne called on us, and he went with us in Mr. Custances Coach to Weston House where we dined and spent the Afternoon with Mr. and Mrs. Custance, and Mr. Eaton of Elsing. After Coffee and Tea got to Loo at wch I won o. 4. 6. About 9 o'clock Mr. Du Quesne came with us in Mr. Custances Coach to my House, where Mr. Du Q. mounted his Mare and went for Home. Mr. Custance came after us in his Coach and he returned back with us in it—His Coachman being not able to drive on Account of his very lately breaking his Collar Bone, the Postillon drove with only 2 Horses and they quite saucy, for upon going up the Hill by Weston House, the Postilon's Horse was rather restive and pranced about a little.

June 26. . . . No Service again at Church this Day, it being not done. Betty Dade and my Boy Jack Secker went to see their Friends at Mattishall to day —they walked there. Will: Coleman dined with our Folks to day.

June 28. . . . Billy Bidewell came to me this morning to desire me to lend him a few guineas—but I could not.

June 29. . . . Betting with Nancy this morning about Paper lost o. o. 6. Busy carrying my Hay all Day, after breakfast.

1785

June 30. . . . Mr. Du Quesne called here this morning
on his road to Reepham, but did not get of his
Horse—He told us that he buried poor Mrs. Howes
last night—she died on Sunday last—Her Disorder
was the Dropsy. Nancy and self very busy most of
the morning and evening in papering the Attic
Chamber over my Bedchamber. Finished carrying
my Hay this Afternoon all in very fine Order, and
a very good Quantity as well as Quality. I dare say
we have not less than 9 Ton from 6 Acres. Mr. Dade
of this Parish sent us a brace of Carp this Morn'
which we had stewed for Dinner and very well done.
Sent Mr. Dade in return a Couple of Cucumbers
and gave his Children that brought the fish o. o. 6.

July 6. . . . Mrs. Davy and Betsy came here this morning before we were down Stairs in Clerk Hewitts
Cart, and they breakfasted, dined, supped and slept
here. To Mr. Cary for things from Norwich &c. p^d
o. 7. 2. Gave Mr. Cary an old Wigg this morning.
After Tea, Mrs. Davy, Betsy, Nancy and self walked
to Weston House, stayed there about half an Hour
and returned home to Supper—Neither Mr. or Mrs.
Custance at home, they being at Sr Edm^d Bacons.

July 7. . . . Busy all Day, shewing Briton the method
of brewing. It made me rather cross—Ironing being
also about.

July 9. . . . Mr. Cary not going to Norwich to day
I sent Ben early thither after my News Papers &c.
By the Letter that Nancy rec^d from her Sister yesterday, poor old Alice Stacy (Will's Grandmother) is
dead, and that my Niece Anna Maria White is gone
to Bristol Wells to drink the Waters being it is much
feared in a Consumption.

July 13. . . . Mr. Thomas of Dereham called on us

this Morn' but did not stay. Sent Ben very early to Norwich this morning after Fish, he returned about 11 o'clock and brought with him eight pair of small Soals with two Couple of Chicken. Mr. and Mrs. Thorne and their Daughter Hannah and a Miss Pinching, and Mr. Thorne's Nephew Mr. Walker an Attorney about 18 Years of Age, Captain Thorne, Mrs. Davy, Betsy and Nunn, came to our House about 3 o'clock and they all dined, supped and spent the Evening, and stayed till 3 o'clock in the Morn with us. We had for Dinner some Pyke and fryed Soals a nice Piece of boiled Beef, Ham and a Couple of Fowls, Peas and Beans, a green Goose rosted, Gooseberry Pies, Currant Tarts, the Charter, hung Beef scraped &c. For Supper fryed Soals, a Couple of Chicken rosted, cold Ham &c. &c. Artichokes, Tarts &c. Fruit after Dinner and Supper—Strawberries, Cherries, Almonds—Raisins &c. &c. Miss Pinchings Brother came to us from Norwich about 10 o'clock this Evening just as we were going to sit down to Supper and he supped &c. with us. Just as the Ladies and Gentlemen were going to drink Coffee and Tea in the Garden, I was sent for to go to Weston House to name a Child of Mrs. Custances who was brought to bed this Afternoon about 2 o'clock —I therefore walked up directly to Weston House and named the Child by name Mary Anne, the smallest Infant I think I ever had in my Arms—The Child came 10 Weeks before its Time, therefore afraid that it would not live. I soon returned to my Company but lost my Coffee and Tea. After Tea the Ladies and Gentlemen got to dancing and danced and sang till Supper Time—About 12 o'clock this night we all got to dancing again—We had many droll Songs from Mr. Walker who sings with great good humour and very well—He is a mighty lively and agreeable young man indeed—They all stayed with us till 3 o'clock in the Morning and then they all returned to Mattishall but Betsy Davy who was left here to spend a few Days with us.—Upon the whole we spent a very agreeable, merry and cheerful Day, and every thing conducted and done extremely well by our Servants.

July 14. . . . We were all pretty much fatigued by Yesterdays raking and therefore went to bed this night in good Time.

July 17. . . . In the Afternoon walked to Church to do duty there but when I came thither, found the Church so extremely dirty, having been white-washed and not cleaned after, that I walked back to my House without performing duty—There was but very few People at Church, a very heavy Storm having just before happened. Will: Coleman dined with our Folks in Kitchen. Poor Newman, Post-Chaise Driver at Cantrells, was unfortunately drowned this morning at Lenewade Bridge by going out of his Depth in endeavouring to swim.

July 18. . . . Very sultry hot and in the Afternoon very heavy Storms with much Lightning and loud Thunder. A poor Man near Cawston was Yesterday terribly hurt by Lightning, getting under an Oaken Tree for Shelter, the Tree which he stood under was greatly damaged, and shivered the Mans arm in a terrible condition and tore his Cloathes and Hat—There are hopes however of his doing well, pray God he might —Lord make us thankful to have escaped. Briton came home this Evening from visiting his Friends.

July 22. . . . Sent a Letter to my Sister Pounsett to let

her know that I had turned Will: Coleman away and that he is soon going for the West to his Friends.

July 25. . . . About 11 this morning Mrs. Davy, Betsy and Nunn, Colin and George Roupe, all on horseback and single made us a morning Visit for about an Hour and half and then returned back to Mattishall. They eat some cold Meat and drank some Beer here. To Mr. Cary for things from Norwich &c. p^d o. 9. 7. Colin Roupe told us that the Baloon which Major Money went up in, went 7 Leagues on the Sea, and that Major Money was 5 Hours up to his Chin in the Sea before he was taken up, and then by chance, a Boat very providentially being returning by him. He was in the Sea till 11 o'clock Saturday Night.[1] Will: Coleman dined with our Folks in Kitchen, he intends setting of for the West to Morrow. Ben and Briton were up with Will, at the Hart, this Evening, stayed there till after 10 o'clock.

July 26. . . . Will: Coleman called on us this morning to take his Leave, I gave him to help pay his Expences. 1. 1. 0. Gave him also for a Deal Chest which I gave him to put his Cloaths in the Sum of o. 10. 6. Will: was very low on the Occasion as was Nancy. He left us about 1 o'clock to go with the Morton Carrier to Norwich—and there to take Coach at Night. I shall

[1] This was one John Money (1752–1817), who as a soldier served in the American war under General Burgoyne, participating in the disaster of September–October 1777 with which that versatile general's name is associated. He is described in the *D. N. B.* as ' one of the earliest English aeronauts '. The unfortunate event chronicled by the Diarist took place after an ascent from Norwich on July 22, 1785. In a book published in 1803 he advocated the use of balloons in war. His career in the British Army after he went on half pay in 1784 as a major was not exciting ; nevertheless he attained by steady promotion the rank of general in 1814. He died at Trowse Hall, Norwich, on March 26, 1817 (see *D. N. B.*).

be glad to hear that he is got safe into Somersett.
To Cuppers Wife for 10 Chicken gave 0. 5. 0.

July 27. . . . Mr. Custance called on us this morning,
stayed but a very short Time with us, being going to
Peachmans to meet Sr John Lombe [1] about putting
a path-road aside by Mr. Micklethwaites—from my
House to his. I buried one John Ward of the Parish
of Shipdam this Evening at Weston, aged 37 Years.
He was a Son in Law of old Mr. Carys. Old Mr. Cary
told me that he would pay me for burying him,
being a Stranger, to Morrow. It rained very hard
during the Time that I was burying the Corps and
most of the Afternoon—very heavy. Ben went after
a P^r of new Wheels for my Cart from Shorts of
Honingham this morning, and he did not return
with them till the Evening, and then was so much
in Liquor as to be obliged to go to bed directly.

July 29. . . . Very busy a brewing to day to teach
Briton the Way. Betsy Davy, dined, supped and
slept here.

July 31. . . . Poor Mr. Du Quesnes Spirits are at
present very low.

Aug. 1. . . . Coming from Mr. Custance's met with
a dumb Man almost naked—I gave him poor Creature
0. 0. 6. I sat and chatted with Mrs. Custance about
20 Minutes. Soon after we had dined, Mr. Du Quesne
came to us, smoked a Pipe with me and drank Tea
with us again.

[1] Sir John Lombe (1731–1817), of Great Melton, Norfolk, was created
a baronet on January 22, 1784. His father's name was Hase, but he
assumed the name of Lombe because of his maternal connexion with
the family of the famous brothers Lombe, who early in the eighteenth
century introduced the silk-throwing process into England. The baronetcy
has continued under the name of Jodrell (see Cokayne's *Complete Baronetage*, vol. v, pp. 240–1).

Aug. 4. [Mrs. Davy had turned up the day before] . . .
Mrs. Davy, Daughter and Son breakfasted, dined, &c.
&c. here again. Very busy again in brewing all day
to teach my new Man. There was a smart Tempest
about 4 o'clock this Afternoon with violent Thunder
and Lightning but did not last long. Thank God we
received no hurt whatever. I was tired pretty much
before I went to bed it being 12 o'clock, on Account
of tunning my Beer. Mrs. Davy also and Nancy
vexed me rather to night, being going to Morrow to
Norwich in Bucks Cart, and talking of buying such
a Number of things for the House &c. &c.

Aug. 5. . . . Mrs. Davy and Nunn breakfasted, dined
and spent the Afternoon here, but after Tea they
both went for their Home at Mattishall in Mr. Bucks
Cart and Briton with them. Mrs. Davy, Betsy and my
Niece were to have gone very early this morning, for
Norwich in Mr. Bucks Cart, but when I got up this
morning, which was at 5 o'clock, I thought it most
prudent for them not to go, very heavy Storms
appearing to be flying about—They were very angry
with me all day about it, but Betsy—And was partly
the reason for Mrs. Davys leaving us. To John Pegg
this morning a Q^{rs} Land Tax p^d 3. 0. 0.

Aug. 10. . . . Gave Betsy Davy a very pretty Cornelian
Seal of an Anchor to put on to a new Watch that her
Mama gave her on Monday last, and sent by Nunn
to her that day. For some Pinns for Nancy and Betsy
Davy at Cary's p^d 0. 1. 0.

Aug. 15. . . . Nancy, Betsy Davy and myself dined
and spent the Afternoon at Weston House with
Mr. and Mrs. Custance, and a Mr. Quarles of Foulsham an Attorney and Clerk to Mr. Custance. About
9 o'clock in the Evening we returned home. Mr.

Custance sent his Carriage after us going and coming.
We had for Dinner some fryed Dace, Leg of Mutton
rosted, a Couple of Fowls boiled and a Pigs Face—
Fricaseed Rabit, a rost Duck, Apricot Pudding,
collar'd Eel &c. &c. After Tea and Coffee we got
to Cards to Loo, neither won or lost. Betsy Davy
was highly pleased being at Weston House.

Aug. 18. . . . Betsy Davy and her Brother Nunn went
with me into a Close where we were shearing of Wheat
this morning and they wanted to give the Harvest
Men a Largess and I gave for them—to them—0. 1. 0.
Nunn Davy returned home about 7 this Evening.

Aug. 20. . . . This Week has been rather precarious
for Harvest having Rain almost every Day at one
time or another. Had a long Letter from my Sister
Pounsett and in it a bank Note for me of the Value
20. 0. 0. My Sister acquaints us that Will: has been
in Somersett upwards of a fortnight. I am glad Will:
Coleman is got safe into Somersett. Mr. Thorne
just called here this morning but did not stay.

Aug. 26. . . . Mrs. Davy, Betsy and Nunn breakfasted
here, and immediately after breakfast they all went
in Clarke Hewits Cart and my Horse Punch, for
Mattishall. I was sorry to part with my dear Girl
Betsy Davy. About 1 o'clock Mr. Du Quesne with
Mr. Hall called on us and they stayed and dined
with us—and after Tea Hall went for Norwich and
Du Quesne for home. Hall is come into Norfolk to
take Possession of another Living, the Rectory of
Ellingham near Bungay, given to him by Lord
Howard late Sr John Griffin Griffin. To my Servant
Man Ben for divers things p^d 1. 5. 4½.

Sep. 4. . . . I read Prayers and Preached this Afternoon
at Weston C. None from Weston House at Church.

Mr. and Mrs. Micklethwaite at Church in a new Carriage just come from London and very showy it is. Nancy went with me to Church. My Maids Father (Dade) dined here to day. He makes rather too free and comes too often to see his Daughter— but he is that Man as report goes.

Sep. 6. . . . I got up early this Morning to see about Britons brewing and to instruct him in the same. Was upon the Foot almost the whole Day wch tired me. The Wind was also very troublesome being remarkably high the whole Day through from the South West by W. Gave Nancy for doing a little Job to my Coat o. 1. o.

Sep. 8. . . . About 1 o'clock Nancy and self went to Reepham in Lenewade Bridge Post Chaise and there dined and spent the Afternoon at Mr. Priests with him, his Wife, their eldest Daughter, Mr. and Mrs. Priest of Norwich, and Mr. Du Quesne—After Tea we returned home and I thank God safe and well, the Driver a Boy was but a very fresh Driver, and drove sadly. We went thro' Morton, Attle-bridge, Alderford and Booton. We were very kindly received by all the Priests. We had for Dinner three fine Chicken boiled and a prodigious fine large old Ham, a Leg of Mutton rosted, pickle Salmon, Tarts and Custards. To the Driver Robt Stannard gave o. 1. 6.

Sep. 14. . . . Mrs. Davy and Betsy came here this morning ab^t 8 o'clock in Clarke Hewitts Cart drove by Billy Hewitt and they breakfasted, dined, supped and slept here. Finished Harvest this day before Dinner.

Sep. 15. . . . Mrs. Davy, Betsy, and my Niece, after Tea this Afternoon about 6 o'clock went from my

House in Clark Hewitts Cart (which was left here Yesterday) to Mattishall Parsonage where Mrs. Davy boards with a Mr. and Mrs. Matthews (which Mr. Matthews is an Exciseman and came from Lambourne in Berkshire) whose House Mrs. Davy and Betsy leaves at Michalemas next, on Account of the Affair being broke of between her and Mr. Smith, therefore Nancy went with them to spend a few Days there before they left Mattishall. They carried with them in the Cart some cold boiled Beef, stuffed with Parsley, some Turnips, Radishes, Colliflowers and 4 Cucumbers. My Boy Jack Secker drove them with my Horse in it.

Sep. 17. . . . To Neighbour Thacker for 7 Turkies p^d 0. 14. 0. I took them sooner this Year than usual, he living near Howlett and the Turkies getting into his Stubble threatened to shoot them.

Sep. 18. . . . I read Prayers, Preached, Churched a Woman and published the Banns of Marriage between J^s [Shipley] of Hockering and my Maid Molly Peachman, this Afternoon at Weston Church. Rec^d for publishing the Banns 0. 2. 6. Rec^d for Churching the Woman J^n Peggs Wife 0. 0. 6. Mr. and Mrs. Custance with their 3 eldest Children, and Mr. and Mrs. Micklethwaite at Church.

Sep. 22. . . . Mr. Custance sent us a brace of Partridges this Morn' which was very kind of him— Mr. Micklethwaite has not sent us any, tho' daily out with a Double-barrelled Gun and often in my Closes close to my House. To Largesses to day gave 0. 1. 0. J^n Pegg called on me this Morn' on account of the new Taxes on Male and Female Servants, Horses and Waggons &c. I entered one Male Servant Briton, and two Female, Betty Dade and Molly

Peachman—and two Horses.[1] I was to have went to Mattishall to day and dine at Mrs. Davy's, but the Weather proving so very wet, prevented me—I fully intended to have went.

Sep. 24. . . . Sent for Nancy this Morning in Mr. Bucks Cart and she returned to Dinner, got home very well and she dined, supped and slept at home.

---

[1] These were some of the taxes either first imposed, or increased, by Pitt in order to meet the burden left by the late war. The tax on men servants was first imposed by Lord North in 1777 (see foot-note, p. 234, vol. i). It was then a guinea. Pitt, in 1785, increased the tax to £1 5s. where only one servant was kept, with a progressive scale up to £3 where eleven or more were kept, and he doubled the tax for bachelors. Parson Woodforde only returns one servant—the faithful Briton, as Ben Leggatt was his farm servant, and therefore not assessable. The boy (who was really a personal servant) he tactfully did not return ! Rich Americans living in England to-day may reflect, with mixed feelings, when they gaze at their footmen, that they owe the tax they still have to pay for them to the ancestral rebellion of 1775–82.

The tax on female servants was the invention of Pitt in 1785, and ranged from 2s. 6d. for one servant, increasing progressively by 2s. 6d. up to 10s., according to the number kept. Bachelors again were charged double. The tax was repealed in 1791. As it was, Pitt was threatened with the fate of Orpheus for introducing it, and his coldness to the fair was said to be the explanation of it.

The tax on horses was also Pitt's invention in 1784–5, and survived till 1874, when it succumbed beneath a well-directed blow from Pitt's biographer, Lord Rosebery, whose House of Lords Committee condemned the tax as adverse to the breed of horses. The tax was 10s. for every saddle or carriage horse, progressively increased in 1789, according to the number kept, and extended to agricultural and trade horses in 1796.

The tax on wagons was a Coalition (1783) Tax, and was directed against smuggling. It was a development of the tax on coaches and carriages imposed in 1747 to meet the cost of the war of the Austrian succession. Pitt raised the tax on these latter. The tax on wagons and carts was repealed in 1792. In any case, Nancy's 'little cart' seems to have escaped. (This account is based on Stephen Dowell's *History of Taxation*, vol. iii, Bk. III, chaps. i, ii, and iii.)

Sep. 26. . . . Dr. Bathurst's Curate Mr. Wilson sent me a Letter this Afternoon to desire me to advance some Money to him by Dr. Bathursts desire—I sent him an Answer that it was not in my Power, but referr'd him to some of the Doctors Tenants. Mrs. Davy likewise desired Nancy to speak to me to lend her twenty Pounds—but it is not in my Power.

Sep. 27. . . . Took a ride this Morning to Weston House, did not see either Mr. or Mrs. Custance there —Mrs. Custance being much engaged with her Mantua-Maker, and Mr. Custance being gone out— After staying with the little Folks about half an Hour, mounted my Mare, and as I was just got out of the Yard saw Mr. Custance on his return home, he walked with me some little way and then he returned back. From Weston House went to Morton, called at Palmers and bespoke some Malt—from thence went to Lenewade Bridge, called at Cantrells and Forsters, then went to see the Poor House on Sparham Hill, and walked over the whole House and saw the People in it. They all appeared comfortable—and the House cleanly kept both above and below—Forster walked over the House with me. As I came away gave the Poor in it 0. 1. 0. My Man Ben and Boy Jack went after breakfast and assisted old Case in getting in his Barley &c.

Sep. 29. . . . We brewed again to day at which I assisted my Man Briton most part of the Day. To a poor distressed old Man of Mattishall by name Hudson for Oysters at 8^d per Score p^d him 0. 1. 6. He has bred up a large Family by the Blacksmiths business but since the Death of his Wife and being 60 Y^{rs} of Age and some of his Family not turning out well, obliged him to give up his business and broke, and become very poor.

1785

Oct. 1. . . . Mrs. Davy and Betsy with Mr. Ashill, in
a Dereham Post-Chaise called here this morning
about 8 o'clock, breakfasted here and then took
Nancy with them to a Place called Thurning about
10 Miles from Weston N.E.N. to look at a boarding
Place for Mrs. Davy and Betsy—I did not like that
Nancy should crowd into the Chaise with them and
for no Purpose whatever—It made me rather cross.
They all returned to dinner about 3 o'clock to my
House. I gave them for Dinner, a fine Rump of
Beef boiled and Dumplins, a rost Fowl and a rost
Duck and a large Damson Pye—Mrs. Davy, Betsy
and Mr. Ashull sat of for Mattishall about an hour
after Dinner. Mrs. Davy and Betsy have agreed to
board at Thurning at a Mr. Elwin's, very good, credit-
able People and genteel. They go there at the half
Quarter after Michaelmas. Mrs. Davy seemed displeased and uneasy all the Day. Nancy had a Letter
from her Brother Sam in London—who tells her
that he is going to Italy to finish his Studies in
Painting—Mr. Rich[d] Hoare made him the Offer
and with it £100 per Annum during the Time that
he is abroad.[1]

Oct. 7. . . . I married by Licence one Thomas Sisson
and Martha Neale both of this Parish, this morning
at Weston Church—received for the same—o. 10. 6.
It was a compulsory Marriage.

Oct. 9. . . . I read Prayers and administered the H:

[1] Richard Hoare (1758–1838) was the son of Richard Hoare (1735–
87) of the famous banking house who was created a baronet in 1786,
in which title our Mr. Richard succeeded him in 1787. He was grandson
—maternal—of the Mr. Henry Hoare mentioned earlier in the Diary
(vol. i), and succeeded to his property in Somerset in 1785. He was
eminent as an antiquary, and historian of Wiltshire (see Cokayne's
Complete Baronetage, vol. v, pp. 256–7, and *D. N. B.*).

Sacrament this morning at Weston Church. Mr. and Mrs. Custance and Mrs. Micklethwaite at Church and at the Sacrament. There were Alms collected at the Sacrament this Day for the first Time, since I have been Rector here, and there was collected in the whole o. 12. o. Out of which I gave, for an Offering o. 2. 6. Mr. Dades Daughter Betsy and Son Robert, spent half an Hour with us this Evening in my Study.

Oct. 10. . . . In the Afternoon my Maid Molly Peachman left my Service, being to be married to Morrow Morning. I paid her for 11 Months Wages at 5. 5. o. Pr Ann. 4. 16. 6. She paid me out of it, what I lent her being 1. 1. o.

Oct. 11. . . . I went to Church this morning and Married my late Maid, Molly Peachman to one Js Shipley by Banns. Received for marrying them only o. 2. 6. having had half a Crown before on publishing the Banns. Hambleton Custance, with his two Brothers George and William, with their Nurse Maid were present at the Marriage being a very fine morning.

Oct. 12. . . . I sent after my New Maid, Nanny Kaye, this Afternoon to Hockering, she returned home about 7 o'clock.

Oct. 20. . . . To 4 Score Oysters of poor Hudson of Mattishall pd o. 1. 6. Mr. Townshend by favour of Mr. Du Quesne sent me 20 brace and ½ of stock Carp —which I put into my large bason in my Garden— fine Stock they were. Mr. and Mrs. Custance, and a Mrs. Goodall who is with them on a Visit, drank Tea with us this Afternoon. After Tea we got to Quadrille at which I lost o. 1. o. They did not leave us till near 9 o'clock this Even'.

Oct. 22. . . . Had a Letter this Evening from my Sister Pounsett in which she mentions that Nancy's Brother Willm is coming into Norfolk to see us. My Man Briton had a new Suit of Livery brought home this Evening from Norwich, with a very good new great Coat of Brown Cloth and red Cape to it. I told Briton that I gave neither to him, but only to wear them during his Service with me.

Oct. 24. . . . The Tooth-Ach so very bad all night and the same this Morn' that I sent for John Reeves the Farrier who lives at the Hart and often draws Teeth for People, to draw one for me. He returned with my Man about 11 o'clock this Morning and he pulled it out for me the first Pull, but it was a monstrous Crash and more so, it being one of the Eye Teeth, it had but one Fang but that was very long. I gave Johnny Reeves for drawing it o. 2. 6. A great pain in the Jaw Bone continued all Day and Night but nothing so bad as the Tooth Ach. To Mr. Cary for things from Norwich &c. p^d o. 8. 8.

Oct. 25. . . . To Royal Ringgar this Morning ½ Years Poor Rate for Land in hand at £30. 5^s o. per Annum at 10^d p^d 1. 5. 2½. My Jaw bone still aches a good deal as yet. My Face much better and easier when I went to bed.

Oct. 26. . . . Had a very good Night of Sleep (thank God for it) and my face much better this Morning. To poor old Hudson for Oysters to day p^d o. 1. 0. Gave to him besides as a free Gift o. 1. 0. Was busy most part of the day in assisting Briton again in the brewing business to learn him.

Oct. 29. . . . We were in great expectation all this Evening of seeing Nancy's Brothers, Bill and Sam— But no Tidings of them neither Vell nor Mark.[1]

[1] See Addendum, p. 363.

Oct. 31. . . . Two strange suspicious Men about the Parish this Morn' one a blacksmith and the other a shoemaker as they say.

Nov. 5. . . . We were in great expectation again of seeing Nancy's Brothers, Will: and Sam[l] this Evening, but much disappointed in not hearing from one of them as they did not come this Evening.

Nov. 7. . . . To Nancy for 2 new yellow Ware Chamber Pots 1. 0. Bad news from Weston House this Afternoon, their youngest Daughter, Mary Anne Custance died to day. Was plagued again with a Letter from Wilson, Bathursts Curate about some more Money.

Nov. 8. . . . Went down to Lenewade Bridge this morning to attend at Dr. Bathursts Tithe Audit, dined there and stayed till near 6 o'clock this Evening —then returned home safe (thank God) with the Cash. All but one Person attended which was one Neale. Had not been home much more than an Hour before Nancy's Brother Will[m] came on horse-back to our House from the West—he supped and slept here. He came thro' London, called on his Brother Sam[l] who will also come to Weston in a few Days.

Nov. 10. . . . To John Pegg for Land Tax, &c., &c., pd. 5. 15. 0. About 11 o'clock this morning Mr. Press Custance called on me in a Post Chaise, and I went with him in it to Weston Church, clerically dressed, and there buried in the Church Mr. Custances youngest Daughter Mary Anne which was brought to Church in their Coach and four with Mrs. Alldis the Housekeeper and the Childs Nurse Hetty Yollop —only in it besides the Corpse. The Infant was only 16 Weeks old. After interring it—I rec[d] from Mr. Press Custance 5. 5. 0. wrapped up in a clean Piece of writing Paper. I had also a black Silk Hatband and a P^r of white Gloves.

Nov. 11. . . . After Breakfast the Captain [Will] and myself took a ride to Norwich, and dined at the Kings Head, which is now kept by one Raven—in the room of Probart. I went to Kerrison's Bank and got a Note for Cash for the Sum of 150 Pound which I immediately inclosed in a Letter to Dr. Bathurst at Langwith Lodge in Nottinghamshire, and put it into the Post myself. The Captain bought a P^r of new Boots of one Bear for which he paid directly for them 1. 2. 0. To a Pound of Powder for Nancy I p^d 0. 1. 0. To the Carriage of Boxes to Norwich for Bill p^d 0. 5. 0. For our Dinners &c. at the Kings Head I p^d 0. 7. 5. Gave the Waiter also besides 0. 1. 0. N.B. Neither Horses, or Servant included in the above. To one Number of Cyclopœdia at Chases p^d 0. 0. 6. We left Norwich between 4 and 5 this Afternoon and got home between 6 and 7 in the Evening. A very pleasant and cheerful Day we had indeed.

Nov. 12. . . . Mrs. Custance with 3 of her Children and Mrs. Collyer called here this morning and stayed some time. The Captain and self purposely took a walk out of the way, not being shaved or properly dressed. My Man, Ben, went very early this morning, with my Cart with 10 Coomb of Barley in it to sell to Mr. Locke—He returned about 4 o'clock with half a Ch[a]ldron of Coals. I rec^d for my Barley of him at 10^s 0^d—5. 0. 0. Ben also brought all my Nephews Boxes from Norwich.

Nov. 19. . . . As I was dressing for Dinner, Nancy's Brother Sam[1] from London came here in a Chaise, and he dined supped and slept here with his Brother —He sat out of London, last Night at 8 o'clock,

travelled all night in the Mail Coach—came here
about 3 this Afternoon.

Nov. 20. . . . Nancy and her two Brothers, Willm and
Saml, breakfasted, dined, supped and slept again at
Weston Parsonage. I read Prayers and Preached this
morning at Weston. Mr. Micklethwaite at Church
—none from Weston House. It gave me much
pleasure to see Nancy and her two Brothers appear
so happy here—and so in each other.

Nov. 21. . . . My Nephews breakfasted here, and soon
after breakfast they mounted their Horses to take
a little Tour to Ld Townshends[1] at Rainham, Mr.
Cokes at Holkham[2] &c. &c. They intend returning to
Weston to Morrow Evening. . . .

Nov. 22. . . . About 8 o'clock this Evening my Nephews
returned to Weston Parsonage, and they supped and
slept here. They were rather fatigued, but highly
pleased with their excursion, after seeing Ld Townshends and Mr. Cokes. They had very fine Weather
both Days and very pleasant.

Nov. 23. . . . My Nephews Willm and Saml breakfasted,
dined &c. here ag^n. After breakfast I took a ride
with my Nephews to Weston House, Mr. Townshend
and Mr. Du Quesne—Neither Mr. Custance, Mr.
Townshend or Mr. Du Quesne at home. Mr. Custance
was gone to my House, Mrs. Custance gone with
Mrs. Collyer to Mr. Greens—We saw their Houses
all over—Gave Mr. Townshends Servant o. 1. o.

[1] This Lord Townshend (1724–1807) was the grandson of the eminent
introducer of the turnip into English agriculture—Charles Townshend
(1674–1738). Lord Townshend had a varied career as soldier—he commanded at Quebec when Wolfe had fallen—and as politician—he was
Lord-Lieutenant for Ireland from 1767–72. He was created a marquis
in 1786 (see *D. N. B.*).

[2] For Mr. Coke of Holkham, see foot-note on p. 127.

We returned home to Dinner after a very pleasant ride and the Weather very pleasant indeed. To a Man for some Fish to day p^d 0. 4. 6.

Nov. 25. . . . My Nephews set of this morning very early and before breakfast, for Mr. Brigg Fountaines at Narford 5 Miles beyond Swaffham, to see some valuable Pictures there, they talked of returning to Night, but I think, it is too far for them to return the same Day. Mrs. Custance with Mrs. Collyer called here this morning, stayed with us full an Hour.

Nov. 26. . . . My Nephews returned here about 2 o'clock wet thro' and thro', obliged to change from top to toe—Neither carried his great Coat. They came from Swaffham this morning—Bills little grey Stallion by name Neptune or bye-debt was knocked up—fell down on the road. To my Maid Betty Dade for Butter &c. p^d 0. 9. 11.

Nov. 28. . . . Between 2 and 3 o'clock, Mr. Custance sent his Coach after us to go and dine at Weston House. Nancy my two Nephews, and self went in it, and dined and spent the Afternoon there with Mr. and Mrs. Custance, Mrs. Collyer Senr, and Mr. and Mrs. Collyer of Dereham.—After Tea and Coffee we got to Cards at Quadrille at which I lost 0. 4. 0. About 9 this Evening myself and Nephews put on our great Coats and walked home to Supper, as there was no Moon and too dark for a Carriage. Nancy was left behind where she supped and slept. Rec^d of Ben this Evening for 2 Piggs sold to his Father 1. 2. 0.

Dec. 1. . . . After breakfast my Nephews and self took a ride to Mattishall, called at Mr. Thornes, Mr. Smiths and Mr. Bodhams, neither of them at home —We saw Mrs. Bodham and Miss Bodham with whom we stayed about an Hour, drunk a glass of Wine apiece and eat some Cake and returned home to dinner after a pleasant ride. About 5 o'clock this Afternoon, Mrs. Davy and Betsy came here from Norwich in a Post Chaise, and they supped and slept here with my Niece. For Mrs. Davy to the Norwich Chaise Driver p^d o. 1. 6.

Dec. 3. . . . My Nephew Samuel drew my Picture to day in Crayon. He likewise drew his own Picture, his Brother's and Sister's, Mrs. Davy's and Betsy's.

Dec. 4. . . . I made my Nephew Saml a present this Evening of 5. 5. o.

Dec. 5. . . . Saml set of from my House for London by way of Norwich—His Brother Willm rode with him to Norwich. And Ben carried his Trunk &c. in Carys Cart to Norwich. My Nephew Sam: rode to Norwich on my little Mare Jenny. My Boy Jack went with Ben to have back Jenny. Mrs. Thorne of Mattishall with a Servant lad with her came here about 12 o'clock and she stayed and dined here and drank Tea and stayed till 8 o'clock this Evening. About 1 o'clock Mr. Du Quesne called here and stayed with us about an Hour—Soon after Mr. Du Quesne went Dr. Thorne came here and he dined and spent the Afternoon with us—About 6 o'clock this Even' my Nephew Willm returned to Weston after seeing his Brother Saml safely boarded in the Mail Coach for London at 4 o'clock—and he supped and slept here. To poor old Kitt Andrews of Witchingham losing a Cow gave him all the Silver in my Pocket which was o. 3. 6.

Dec. 6. . . . This being my Tithe Audit Day was engaged the whole Day in settling Accounts with my Tenants and being with them. Howlett, Girling,

Forster, Dade, Page, Mann, &c. &c. all dined and stayed till 10 at Night with me, but at that time they went away and pretty well. They had for Dinner, boiled Leg of Mutton, boiled and rost beef, Salt Fish and plenty of Puddings. Herring of Ringland brought me a Leash of Partridges. We did not get to bed till after 12 o'clock.

Dec. 9. . . . Mrs. Davy and Betsy breakfasted and spent the Morning here till near one o'clock and then they both went of in Lenewade Bridge Chaise for Thurning about 5 Miles beyond Reepham to one Mr. Elwins there to enter upon their new boarding Place. My Servant Man, Briton, went with them. Mrs. Davy was very low indeed on going away. Before they went, about half an Hour, came to my House Mrs. Bodham and her Cousin Frederick Donne of Norwich a young Gentleman, Son of Dr. Donne of Norwich in a new Post-Chariot of Mr. Bodhams and they stayed with us till 2 o'clock and then returned. I was very glad that Mrs. Bodham came here before Mrs. Davy and Betsy went away. Fred: Donne had a pair of very handsome pretty Buckles in his Shoes, small make, and in imitation of Pearls in small roses —they were of Silver I believe.

Dec. 10. . . . To my Maid Nancy for trouble at my Frolic gave 2. 6. To my Maid Betty for ditto gave 2. 6. To my Man, Briton for ditto gave 2. 6. To my Man, Ben for ditto gave 1. 0. To my Boy Jack for ditto gave 1. 0.

Dec. 12. . . . To Cobb the Rat-Catcher, his annual Stipend p^d 1. 1. 0. To my Butcher, Henry Baker, his Bill for the Year p^d 41. 5. 0. Paid him before my Nephew and Niece. Poor Tom Twaites of Honingham who was beat by the Poachers at Mr. Townshends the other day is lately dead of the Wounds he then rec^d from them. His Skull was fractured in 2 Places.

Dec. 14. . . . Myself and Nephew saw two very suspicious Fellows this morning walking very slowly and demurely across one of my Fields next to the Cover that was—dressed meanly but young People—I take them to be some of the Poachers that were at Mr. Townshends very lately, and by whom poor old Tom Twaites lost his Life. They parted at Car-Cross, one went towards the Heart and the other went by my House towards Cary's—the latter stopped at Charles Cary's Shop Window, and we saw him there as we went up to Carys at the Window. Nancy had a Letter from Mrs. Davy at Thurning this Aft.

Dec. 16. . . . Bill breakfasted early on Pork and Beer, and before I was down Stairs, was set of for Thurning to make Mrs. Davy and Betsy a Visit—He did not return till after 8 o'clock this Evening. He dined with Mrs. Davy &c. &c. To Mr. Palmer, my Malster, his Bill for the last Year for Malt, &c.—paid this Morn' 21. 18. 0. . . .

Dec. 18. . . . The Captain breakfasted, dined, &c. here again. I read Prayers and Preached this Morning at Weston. Mr. Custance was at Church this morning. Whilst I was at Dinner to Day, a Letter was brought me by my Butchers Lad, from the Bishop of Norwich to request me to preach the 19 of March next at St. Clements at Norwich, for the Benefit of the Charity Schools there. I did not relish it.

Dec. 19. . . . The Captain and myself took a ride to Norwich and the Servant with us—We got there

1785

between 1 and 2 o'clock, put up our Horses at the Kings Head and there dined at the Ordinary on a fine piece of boiled Beef and a Saddle of Mutton &c. After Dinner the Captain and myself, went and saw the learned Pigg at the rampant Horse in St. Stephens —there was but a small Company there but soon got larger—We stayed there about an Hour—It was wonderful to see the sagacity of the Animal—It was a Boar Pigg, very thin, quite black with a magic Collar on his Neck. He would spell any word or Number from the Letters and Figures that were placed before him paid for seeing the Pigg o. 1. o.[1] After that went with Bill to two or three Places and then returned to the Kings Head, soon afterwards my Nephew mounted his Poney and set of for Weston and my Servant with him. It was about 6 o'clock in the Evening that they went away, very dark and no Moon. After they went I walked about Town and paid several Bills and then walked to the Assembly-Rooms near Chapel Field and heard an excellent Lecture on Astronomy &c. spoken by one Walker, with a View of his Eidouranion of transparent Orrery —was highly pleased with it. A great deal of Company present I paid o. 2. 6. I then returned to the Kings Head and there supped, and slept. Supper

[1] This was the learned pig to which Cowper refers in a charming letter to the Rev. John Newton on April 22, 1785 : ' When I received your account of the great celebrity of *John Gilpin*, I felt myself both flattered and grieved. . . . Your letter was followed the next post by one from Mr. Unwin. You tell me that I am rivalled by Mrs. Bellamy ; and he, that I have a competitor for fame, not less formidable, in the Learned Pig. Alas ! what is an author's popularity worth, in a world that can suffer a prostitute on one side, and a pig on the other, to eclipse his brightest glories ? . . .' (Cowper's *Letters* in the World's Classics selection made by E. V. Lucas, pp. 198–9.)

being just going in for the Family I joined them, and there met with the best Supper I ever met with at an Inn.—Hashed Fowl, Veal Collopes, a fine Woodcock, a Couple of Whistling Plovers, a real Teal of the small kind and hot Apple Pye. For our Dinners and my Supper and Wine I pd. o. 6. o. Before I left Weston this Morn' I paid Robt. Buck of Honingham, Blacksmith, for new Tire to a Cart &c. 4. 4. o. To Mr. Francis, Lawyer pd. a Bill of 8. 14. 9. for self, Bathurst, and Quit Rents recd. for him. To Lewis and Hayward, Linen Drapers pd. a Bill of 6. 2. 7. To J. Horth, my Upholsterer pd. a Bill of 5. 4. o. To 2 Knives at Frears and Cairns pd. o. 5. 6. To a small book of the Taxes at Chases pd. o. o. 6. Nancy breakfasted &c. &c. again at home.

Dec. 20. I breakfasted at the Kings Head and afterwards walked about the City and paying Bills. At Beales, Fishmongers, paid a Bill of o. 4. o. At Bakers, Haberdasher's, paid ditto o. 5. 11. At Studwells, China Man—paid 1. 4. 6. At Mr. Priests, Wine Merchant pd. 4. 6. 6. At Mr. Forsters, Lawyer, 1 Y^{rs} Rent for College Land, late Mrs. Le Neves paid 16. o. o. At Mrs. Garlands, Taylor, paid 5. 14. 6. To her Head Man, Forster, &c. gave o. 2. 6. At Carbolds, Hatter, paid 2. 5. o. At Mrs. Brewsters, Tea Merchant paid 7. 10. 4. At Mr. Scotts, Breeches Maker, paid 1. 4. 6. At Mr. Smiths, Mercer, paid a Bill 11. 16. 6. About 11 o'clock this morning I walked down to the Bishops Palace and stayed there about an Hour with the Bishop—and I acquainted him that I had preached a Sermon at St. Stephens in the Year 1780 for the benefit of the Charity Schools. His Lordship said he did not know that I had and therefore told me that he would appoint another

1785

Clergyman to preach instead of me.[1] My Servant, Briton, came to Town about 11 o'clock and about half past 1 I sat of for Weston and got home to Dinner at half past 3 o'clock, and there supped and slept at the Parsonage House. My Nephew came to meet me at Easton on his little Poney, and then jogg'd home together. For my breakfast &c. at the Kings Head pd. 0. 1. 0. Gave the Chambermaid 1. 0. To Brown the Barber gave 1. 0. To the Hostler for my Horses I gave 3. 6. Nancy and her Brother breakfasted &c. at Weston.

Dec. 21. . . . This being St. Thomas's Day, had a great many poor People of the Parish to visit me, I gave to each of them that came, sixpence. Gave in all to day to the poor 1. 5. 6. About 12 o'clock Mr. Ashill of Norwich called here in his return home from Thurning, after visiting Mrs. Davy and Daughter there—The former sending for him on being taken exceeding ill about the late disagreeable Affair with Mr. Smith. Mr. Ashill says that it has almost made her distracted, she is very unhappy. Mr. Ashill eat some cold Mutton &c. and then at 2 o'clock sat of for Norwich again.

Dec. 24. . . . To Short, Wheelwright, pd. a Bill of 3. 7. 0. To Pyle, Carpenter pd. ditto of 2. 4. 0. To Ames, Cooper pd. ditto of 1. 12. 0. To Holland,

[1] In supplement to the foot-note on pp. 92–3 on Bishop Bagot, I find this pleasing tribute to the bishop in Cowper's *Tirocinium*, which was written in 1784 :

> For Providence, that seems concern'd t'exempt
> The hallow'd bench from absolute contempt,
> In spite of all the wrigglers into place,
> Still keeps a seat or two for worth and grace,
> And therefore 'tis, that though the sight be rare,
> We sometimes see a Lowth or Bagot there.

Chimney Sweeper for sweeping 6 Chimnies to day paid him o. 5. o. Gave to his Son, Frank against Xmas o. 1. o. The Weather this Afternoon is set in amazing sharp, very severe Frost this Evening with strong Wind from the East North East—and very cloudy also.

Dec. 25. . . . This being Christmas Day I read Prayers and administred the H. Sacrament at Weston Church. Mr. and Mrs. Custance, and Mrs. Micklethwaite at Church and at the Sacrament. Excessive cold with Snow and Frost also. The following old Men dined at the Parsonage to day, to each of them also I gave 1ˢ oᵈ in all o. 6. o,—Js. Smith my Clerk, Thos. Cushing, Thos. Cary, Thos. Carr, Rich'd Bates and Rich'd Buck. For an Offering at the Sacrament gave o. 2. 6. My large Wax Candle was lighted up this Evening for an Hour, being Christmas Day.

Dec. 26. . . . Yesterday I made my Nephew Willᵐ a Present of 3. 3. o. alias three Guineas—omitted Yesterday to be put down. . . . To Weston Ringgers this Morning gave o. 2. 6. . . .

Dec. 27. . . . My Nephew went out a coursing this Morn' in the Snow with my Greyhounds and killed a brace of Hares. Busy in assisting Briton in the brewing way.

Dec. 28. . . . To one Mason of Sparham, playing on 10 Bells of his own Construction, and Christmas Holidays gave o. 1. o. Nancy's Pigg was killed this morning and very fine Pigg it was, it weighed 16 Stone exactly.

Dec. 29. . . . Had a very long Letter from Mr. Smith this morning concerning Mrs. Davy and himself, wherein he lays the whole blame on her in a late affair accusing her for her too great familiarity to one

Clarkson. To my Butchers Man, Billy Stonton, Xmas Gift o. 1. o. To Neighbour Howes's Wife for 5 Chicken p^d o. 2. 6.

Decem. 31. . . To Mr. Hardy, for doing something to my brewing Furnace, being very foul, pd. him o. o. 6. Most bitter cold to day, froze sharp within doors all day long—tho' the Sun shone very bright. It being the last Day of the Year, we sat up to night, till after 12 o'clock, then drank a happy New Year to all our Friends and went to bed. Poor old Mr. Cary almost froze this Evening as he came from Norwich —so very severe was the Cold. He brought every-thing safe however. He brought me amongst other things a Hamper of Wine from Mr. Priests at Norwich —2 Dozen.

Anno Domini 1786.

Jan. 1. I breakfasted, dined, &c. &c. again at home. Nancy and her Brother breakfasted, dined, &c. here again. I read Prayers and Preached this Afternoon at Weston. None from Weston House or Hungate Lodge at Church. The Weather being so severe and Snow deep on the Ground—bitter cold to Day. It snowed very much this Evening and high Wind with it—Colder this Night I think than I ever felt it in my Life—froze sharp within Doors.

Jan. 3. . . . Mr. Custance made us a morning visit on foot tho' the Snow was so deep on the Ground. He stayed here about an Hour—Neither Nancy or Brother appeared. Mr. and Mrs. Custance sent us a brace of wild ducks.

Jan. 5. . . . Settled Accounts with Nancy this Morning for the last Year—and gave her on balance 7. 12. o. A fat Pigg of 16 Stone included also in the above.

Jan. 7. . . . I walked with my Nephew before Dinner up to our Church, but had great difficulty to get thither for the Snow, in the Lane by Billy Bidewells the Snow was full 4 foot deep in many Places—we were pretty near half an Hour getting there. In the Lane leading from Church Street to Car-Cross was quite full of Snow and up almost to the top of the Hedge.—We returned home rather a better way by Js. Smiths and down Blacker-Field. I sent Ben to Norwich this Morning as Cary did not go, but gave him orders not to run risk or danger if he met with difficulties from the Snow. He returned home safe about 4 o'clock this Aft.

Jan. 8. . . . No Divine Service at Church this Morning, owing to the Snow having rendered the roads almost impassable from most Parts of the Parish.

Jan. 9. . . . Dr. Thorne dined and spent the Afternoon here and did not leave us till near 9 o'clock—He was obliged he said to get over hedges into the Inclosures in some Places, the Lanes being impassable.

Jan. 17. . . . We brewed again today, at which I assisted and by making some close observations about it, found that in our last brewing, we lost six Pails of Liquor when standing to cool during dinner Time, at which Time Nortons Wife was carrying away from my house some Liquor that I gave them from the draining of the Grains after ours was finished—cannot positively say it was taken by her, but it is very suspicious, as I counted the Pails then that were taken out of the Copper and which were 30 Pails, and no more than 22 Pails put into the Barrells. This day I tried it again, but was present when Downings Wife carried her Liquor away—and I found that from 30 Pails and half taken out of the Furnace to drain we put 28 Pails and half into the Barrells. This plainly shows that there must be a defect somewhere. I rather strained my left arm to day in lifting so many Pails of Beer, being determined to examine particularly. It pained me very much all the Evening.

Jan. 18. . . . The Captain and myself with Ben went out a tracing of Hares this morning from 11 o'clock till after Three in the Afternoon and did not see a single Hare. I dare say we walked near 12 Miles in the Snow.

Jan. 23. . . . Captain Thorne called here this morning, stayed with us about an Hour, and returned home again—he was going on to Thurning to see Mrs. Davy and wanted my Nephew to go with him, but he was engaged to dine this Day at Weston House with me—they therefore concluded to go together thither to Morrow and that Capt. Thorne would breakfast here to Morrow. To Mr. Cary for things from his Shop only pd. o. 5. 3½. Browne the Barber from Norwich called here this morning and measured me for a Wig. At 2 o'clock my Nephew and self took a Walk to Weston House and there dined and spent the Afternoon with Mr. and Mrs. Custance, Lady Bacon, Captain Majendie and his Wife from Norwich. After Tea and Coffee we got to Cards, at Loo, at which my Nephew (tho' a Novice in the Game) won o. 14. 6. I believe my loss if anything was not more [than] o. 1. o. We did not leave Weston House till near 10 o'clock. Captain Majendie and Lady appeared very agreeable People.[1] We were obliged to have a Lantern being very dark.

[1] Presumably Captain Lewis Majendie, the son of the Dr. John Majendie who was sometime preceptor to the Prince of Wales and Prince

Jan. 25. . . . I sent after Betsy Davy this morning from
Thurning and about ½ past 2 o'clock she came here
with Captain Thorne and my Nephew, and they all
dined, spent the Aft:, supped and slept here. We
made it rather late to night by singing.

Jan. 27. . . . Betsy Davy and Capt. Thorne breakfasted, &c. &c. here again. Mrs. Custance with her
Sister Lady Bacon made us a Morning Visit, stayed
about half an Hour with us. At Cribbage this Evening, myself and Nephew against Capt. Thorne and
Nancy, after playing very late lost o. 2. o. To
Edwd Gooch, Gardner, pruning my Trees, having
been here 5 Days and ½ at 2^s o^d per Day not p^d o. 11. o.
No Allowance and no board being allowed by me.

Jan. 28. . . . Captain Thorne breakfasted, dined and
spent the Aft. here, and in the Evening he went
home to Mattishall. Mr. Elwin of Thurning (where
Mrs. Davy and Daughter board) breakfasted, dined
and spent the Afternoon with us. He is I think very
much like the late Mr. Baldwin and appears to be
a very agreeable Man. To Edwd. Gooch, Gardner,
as mentioned Yesterday, but not paid then, this
Evening pd. o. 11. o.

Feb. 4. . . . Sent my Servant Ben to Norwich to Day
after News &c. Had a Letter this Evening from my
Sister Pounsett, acquainting us with the Death of
poor Anna Maria White, my Sister Whites only
Daughter. Pray God comfort my poor distressed
Sister. Recd. also a Letter from Jeanes at New
College Oxon, informing me that he had accepted
the Witchinghams.

Frederick. Captain Majendie married in July 1783, Elizabeth, only
daughter of Sir Henry Hoghton, 6th baronet, of Hoghton Tower (Horace
Walpole's *Letters*, vol. xiii, p. 41, foot-note).

Feb. 10. . . . Mr. and Mrs. Custance dined and spent the Aft. here. After Coffee and Tea we got to Loo at wch. I won 0. 4. 0. Mr. and Mrs. Custance returned home about 9 o'clock. We gave them for Dinner, Ham and Fowls, a Leg of Mutton boiled and Caper Sauce, a fine rost Turkey, fryed Rabbit, Batter Pudding and Currant Jelly, Damson Tarts, Rasberry Puffs, Black-Caps in Custard and Blamange. Oranges, Almonds and Raisins, and Apples for Desert. Port and Mountain Wines to drink after.

Feb. 12. . . . I sent Nancy and Betsy Davy Yesterday Morn' to Coventry and have not as yet spoke to either of them.

Feb. 13. . . . Nancy and Betsy not sent for from Coventry as yet.

Feb. 14. . . . To 53. Valentines to Day gave 0. 4. 5. Nancy and Betsy Davy called home this Aft. from Coventry. The Captain after breakfast took a ride to Thurning to see Mrs. Davy and there stayed and dined and spent the Afternoon, but returned home to Supper.

Feb. 18. . . . Mr. Smith of Mattishall sent me a note this Morn' to desire me to meet him in Weston Churchyard privately, which I accordingly did, and there I stayed with him near an Hour, talking over the Affair between him and Mrs. Davy—by which he made out that Mrs. Davy was as artful and bad as any Woman could be. It surprised me astonishingly indeed. After breakfast the Captain took a ride to Mattishall and did not return till 12 at Night, just as I was going to bed after sitting up for him till that Time—I cannot say but I was rather displeased at it especially being Saturday Night. Had another Letter from Mr. Jeanes abt. Witchingham. Sent

my Man Ben with 10 Coomb of Barley to Norwich
to sell for me and he sold it at 9ˢ 0ᵈ per Coomb in all
recd. 4. 10. 0. He brought back ½ Chldrn of Coal
for which he paid Lock 0. 15. 2.

Feb. 24. . . . About Noon Mr. Thos. Elwin of Thurning called here and he stayed and dined here. He
brought a Letter from Pulham for Betsy Davy to
inform her that her Uncle John Roope was dead and
that Mrs. Davy was gone to his funeral and could
not be here to Morrow. We had for Dinner a boiled
Calfs Head, some Pork, Norfolk Dumplins and a rost
Leg of Mutton. Mr. Thomas Elwin appears to be
a very worthy Man, a married Man with 4 or 5
Children and a Wife. Every Person that knows him,
speaks well of him.

Feb. 25. . . . Sent Ben to Norwich this Morning after
Newspapers &c. Mr. Cary not going this week.
Nancy had a Letter from her Brother Sam[1] at London
—therein mentioning that he is going immediately to
Italy, and that Mr. Richd. Hoare had made him an
extra Present of 50. 0. 0.

Mar. 4. . . . My Maid Betty Dades Father came here,
just as we were going to dinner, and his too frequent
Visits here of late being far from agreeable to me,
I went out into the Kitchen and told him that he
had better have his Daughter home, as I did not like
for him to make too free here, and I also gave Betty
notice to leave my House at Lady Day next, on his
Account. Rec'd an oil Picture from my Nephew
Saml. from London, this Evening from Norwich.
The Picture was drawn from Nature from some
Forest near London—a small Picture.

Mar. 5. . . . Mr. Wilson of Lyng called here whilst
I was at dinner to day to enquire after the new

Rector of Witchingham and when he intends being in Norfolk. He stayed but a few Minutes with me. Sunday I hear is the only Day that he dares go out, being so much in debt and Bailiffs after him.

Mar. 6. . . . The Cold more severe and penetrating than any yet it freezes within doors in less than 10 Minutes. The Thermometer in my Study where a very good Fire was kept, was this Morn' at 10 o'clock down to 50—and the Room allowed to be a warm one.

Mar. 9. . . . Mrs. Custance made us a long morning Visit. My Nephew took a ride this Morn' to Mr. Du Quesnes caught him at home, but returned home to dinner Mr. Du Quesne having Company, that is, Mr. Smith of Mattishall and Mr. Carter of Ringland to dine with him.

Mar. 10. . . . My Nephew took a ride this morning to Elmham to see an ancient Roman Lamp lately dug up there and which he saw and returned home to dinner. The Captain seemed well pleased on seeing the above it was rather small but well preserved and is of Copper. He drew a Sketch of it on Paper with his Pencil.

Mar. 11. . . . Betsy Davy breakfasted, dined, &c. &c. here again. The Captain breakfasted, dined &c. &c. here again. Mr. Custance called on us this Morning, stayed with us about half an Hour, and desired our Company at dinner on Wednesday next with our Company. This Evening about 6 o'clock Mrs. Davy came here in a Post Chaise from Norwich in her way from Pulham having been there and in Suffolk on Account of the Death of a Brother of hers at Woodbridge. Mrs. Davy drank Tea this Aft. supped and slept here.

1786

Mar. 12. . . . I read Prayers and Preached this Morn'
at Weston Church. Mr. and Mrs. Custance at
Church. Neither any from my House at Church,
but self and 2 Servants. Mrs. Davy took on a good
deal to day, and soon after Tea this Evening she took
it in her head to go to bed. I had been persuading
her not to go to Mattishall.

Mar. 14. . . . A Sale this Day at Hockering Parsonage
House of all the Furniture &c. late Mr. Howes's.

Mar. 15. . . . We all dined and spent the Afternoon at
Weston House. Mrs. Davy, Betsy, Nancy, and the
Captain went in Mr. Custances Coach—I walked
there, tho' bitter cold. Captain Laton and Wife
dined and spent the afternoon at Weston House—
very agreeable People. After Tea and Coffee we got
to Cards, neither won or lost—I walked back from
Weston House, tho' it rained, snowed, wind high,
and very cold. Mrs. Custance proposed a Scheme
to Norwich to Morrow to see the Automaton—She
is to call here and take Mrs. Davy, Betsy and Nancy
with her in the Coach. The Captain and self to be
on horseback.

Mar. 16. . . . About 9 this Morning Mrs. Custance
called here with her 2 eldest Sons, and took Mrs. Davy,
Betsy, and my Niece with her, and sat of for Norwich.
The Captain and myself rode to Norwich, we all got
to the Kings Head about 11 o'clock, where we met
Sr. Edmd. Bacon and Mr. Taswell and they went
with us to see the Automaton in St. Stephens opposite
the rampant Horse, at which we were all highly
Astonished, it was a wax Doll, a female Figure,
dressed with a Trumpet in her Mouth, under a kind
of Canopy on Pillars. It answered distinctly every
Question proposed to it, and even proposed Questions

itself, the Deception indeed is wonderfully ingenious. We each paid 1 Shilling—I paid for 3. 0. 3. 0. After we had seen it we returned to the Kings Head, and from thence, The Captain and myself took a walk with the Ladies a shopping—then returned to the Kings Head and eat some cold Meat &c.—And at 2 o'clock Mrs. Custance with Mrs. Davy, Betsy and Nancy sat of for Weston—the Captain and me stayed about half an Hour after at Norwich—For Letters at the Post Office Pd. 0. 3. 9. in Number 4, one for me from Nancy's Brother Ralph requesting me to advance him some mony, another for the Captain from his Brother Saml. from Paris—another from Nancy's Sister Juliana and another from her Brother Ralph. Gave the Man at the Post Office his annual Gift which should have been given at Xmas 0. 2. 6. At Jaghire's Print Shop for 6 Picture Frames 1. 1. 0. At Chases for Books pd. 0. 9. 6. We returned home to Weston at ½ past 4 this Aft. Mrs. Custance after setting down Mrs. Davy &c. at my House returned to Weston House. I asked Mrs. Custance to dine with us—but she could not.

Mar. 17. . . . Mrs. Davy breakfasted, dined, supped and slept here again. Betsy Davy breakfasted here and about 12 she took leave of Weston Parsonage and went on horseback to Mr. Thorne's at Mattishall, and there she dined, supped and slept—poor dear soul— She was much hurried by her Mother on going away. Am much afraid it will be a very long time before she will be at Weston Parsonage again. The Captain took a ride to Mattishall with Betsy Davy and he dined with her there, and returned home to Supper. Dr. Thorne being from home at the assises at Thetford which begins this day.

Mar. 18. . . . Mrs. Davy breakfasted and spent part of the Morn' with us.—About 1 o'clock Mrs. Thorne of Mattishall came after Mrs. Davy to spend a few Days with her and they returned to Mattishall about 2 o'clock. Our Parting was rather cool than otherwise. Soon after they went, Bagshaw the Pedlar, called here, and I bought of him a Piece of Jennett, olive Colour for Breeches 2 yrds. and ½ at 4ˢ 6ᵈ pd. 0. 11. 0. For ½ a Pd. of 3 thread for netting pd. 0. 1. 6. For 6 Dozen of Wire Buttons for Shirts pd. 0. 1. 3. Sent Ben to Norwich this Morn' after News &c. Sent by Ben a Letter to my Sister Pounsett.

Mar. 19. . . . I read Prayers and Preached this afternoon at Weston. None of the Genteels from Weston House and Hungate Lodge. Mr. Micklethwaite of Hungate Lodge is said to be in a very dangerous way—in a decline.

Mar. 22. . . . After breakfast the Captain and I took a ride to Dereham, being very fine pleasant Weather and returned home to Dinner—We called on Mr. Thomas the Rector of Dereham and Brother to the Bishop of Rochester—We drank a Glass of Wine there. We put up our Horses at the Kings Arms pd. there 0. 6. Sent my Man Briton in Carys Cart early this morning to Dereham with all the Numbers of Chambers Cyclopædia 418 with Dr. Rees Supplement to the same to be bound by Barker the Bookbinder there.[1]

[1] Ephraim Chambers's *Cyclopaedia* first appeared in 1728, and was reprinted twice before Chambers died in 1740. Abraham Rees (1743–1825) re-edited the *Cyclopaedia* in 1778 and subsequent years at intervals, finally developing it into a forty-five volume work between 1802 and 1820. The original *Cyclopaedia* of Chambers is specially notable, as it gave rise to the monumental work of Diderot in France (see *D. N. B.*).

1786

Mar. 23. . . . Poor Mr. Micklethwaite is gone to Lynn, and it is thought will never return again as he declines very fast in a consumptive Complaint.

Mar. 25. . . . Nancy had another Letter from Ralph Woodforde to desire her to intercede with me to send him mony.

Mar. 28. . . . Nancy breakfasted and spent the Morning with us till after 1 o'clock, then Mrs. Bodham of Mattishall came after her in her Chaise, and she returned with her to Mattishall before Dinner and is to stay some Days with Mr. and Mrs. Bodham at South-Green.[1] Nancy's Brother breakfasted, dined &c,

[1] Mrs. Bodham requires notice, for she was the poet Cowper's ' my dearest Cousin ', or ' my dearest Rose ', of his delightful letters. She was his cousin because she was Anne Donne, the niece of Cowper's mother, also Anne Donne, who in turn was the daughter of Roger Donne (1673–1722), of Ludham, Norfolk, gentleman, descended from the great Dean of St. Paul's. Cowper considered that he himself was more of a Donne than a Cowper—see specially his letter to Mrs. Bodham of February 27, 1790. It was Mrs. Bodham who sent Cowper the picture of his mother, which drew from him the exquisite poem, ' O that those lips had language ! ' and it was ' to my cousin, Anne Bodham ', that in 1793 he wrote the lyric ' on receiving from her a Network Purse, made by herself '. Mrs. Bodham was born in 1748, and lived to be 98. She married the Rev. Thomas Bodham, M.A., Fellow of Gonville and Caius College, Cambridge, and sometime curate of Mattishall, and as they had no children they brought up their niece, Miss Anne Vertue Donne, who was the daughter of the Rev. Castres Donne. She is the diarist's ' Miss Anne Donne ', and at this time was about five years old. Mrs. Bodham was first cousin of Dr. William Donne (1735–1803), who was a well-known Norwich surgeon ; he is mentioned more than once by the diarist (see, for instance, vol. i, p. 337). One of her nephews was the Rev. John Johnson (1769–1833), rector of Yaxham, and Welborne, Norfolk, who has come down to fame as Cowper's ' Johnny of Norfolk '. It should be added that little Miss Anne Donne eventually married her cousin, Edward Charles Donne, and became the mother of William Bodham Donne (1809–82), the scholarly Librarian of the London Library (see *William Bodham Donne and his Friends*, edited by Catherine B. Johnson, published by

234

here again. I married this morning Harry Andrews, Widower and Mary Horner, Widow—rec^d for it o. 5. o.

Mar. 29. . . . Brewed some strong Beer to day, in wch assisted Briton.

Mar. 30. . . . Brewed again this morning some more strong Beer. Mr. Thorne and Nephew Walker, gave us a Call this Morning.

Mar. 31. . . . We were to have went to Mattishall to dinner to day at Mr. Bodham's, but my Nephew's little grey horse being taken very ill, and obliged to send for a Farrier, prevented our going according to promise. I sent a Note to my Niece who is there on a Visit and she sent me an Answer, that Mr. and Mrs. Bodham were very angry with us. Mr. Du Quesne was asked to meet us on purpose.

April 3. I breakfasted partly at home and then set of on an excursion. My Nephew breakfasted not at all at home, but sat of with me about 8 o'clock on a little Tour towards the South East Coast of Norfolk —Briton went with us. We went from home to Norwich but did not get of there but went on to a place called Porland about 5 Miles the other side of Norwich, and there we breakfasted at 11 o'clock on some cold hard boiled Leg of Pork and drank some strong beer at the Sign of the Dove paid there o. 2. 6. About 12 we went on for Bungay and there we dined at the three Tunns kept by one Utting, very civil People—paid and gave there o. 8. 6. Whilst at Bungay we went and saw the old Ruins of Bungay Castle—scarce worth seeing—gave there o. o. 6. From Bungay we went on to Beccles about 6 Miles

Methuen, 1905, specially the introduction, and the pedigree at the end of the book ; Cowper's *Letters* and *Poems*, passim).

from Bungay and there we supped and slept at a very good large Inn, the Kings Head kept by one Hindes, and there we eat some of the finest Colchester Oysters I ever saw—we travelled to day about 30 Miles.

April 4. We breakfasted at the Kings Head at Beccles on Oysters and Tea and bread and butter and a very hearty breakfast we made, we then mounted our Horses and went on for Southwold about 10 Miles from Beccles—paid and gave to Servants at Beccles this morning 0. 17. 0. We got to Southwold about 12 o'clock and there we supped, dined, and slept at an indifferent Inn, but very civil Landlord, the Old Swan kept by one Berry late Servant to Sr Thos. Gooch. Before Dinner we walked on the Beach which is close to the Town, for near three Hours, and after Dinner two Hours more, looking after curious Pebbles &c. but could find none very curious.

April 5. We got up this morning about 7 o'clock, paid our Bill, and mounted our Horses before breakfast, and went on for Lowestoff about 12 Miles from Southwold. Paid and gave at Southwold this Morn' 0. 17. 11. We got to Lowestoff about 10 o'clock and there we breakfasted at the Crown kept by one Casson. We had a very disagreeable ride being very hazy and cold. I heard a very remarkable Anecdote, of Mr. Casson the Landlord at Lowestoff, which was this, some few Years back, Mr. Casson being subject to violent Fits, during one of them, a Person put a Crown Piece of Willm the third, between his Teeth, which by some means or other got down his Throat and there remained for twenty Months in his Stomach and then was vomited up by him, I saw the Crown Piece, and what is remarkable he has been very well ever since and still remains so. As we came from

Southwold to Lowestoff we passed by a very noble House of Sr Thos Gooch's.[1] Southwold is but an indifferent Place, but the Situation being so near the Sea very pleasant. Lowestoff is a very good Town and large, and delightful Situation, close to the main Sea. There is a very handsome Light House there. Paid and gave at the Crown at Lowestoff o. 4. 6. Between 12 and 1 o'clock we sat of for Yarmouth about 10 Miles from Lowestoff, and got there ab^t 3 and there we dined, supped and slept at the Angel, kept by one Dark—a very good Inn. We walked on the Beach at Lowestoff near 2 Hours but could find nothing very curious. After Dinner at Yarmouth also we walked on the Beach there, but nothing curious to be found.

April 6. We breakfasted at Yarmouth and stayed there till 12 o'clock, then mounted our Horses and went on for Accle where we got about 2 o'clock being 11 Miles from Yarmouth and there we dined at Queens Head kept by one Birt. Paid and gave at Yarmouth 1. 1. 1½. To a Barber at Yarmouth gave o. 1. o. About 4 o'clock we sat of from Accle for Norwich and got to Norwich about 6 o'clock, and there we supped and slept at the Kings Head, kept by Raven. Paid and gave at Accle o. 6. 4. There being some remarkable good Cheese at the Inn at Accle, I desired the Landlord to spare me some, which he did accordingly 5 Pound and half for which I paid him at 6^d per

---

[1] Sir Thomas Gooch (1745–1826), of Benacre Hall, Suffolk, succeeded to the baronetcy (created in 1746) in 1781. He was Sheriff of Suffolk in 1785. He was grandson of the Sir Thomas Gooch who was Bishop of Norwich from 1738–48, and afterwards Bishop of Ely. It was the bishop who purchased the Benacre property in 1743 (see Cokayne's *Complete Baronetage*, vol. v, pp. 91–3).

Pound—o. 2. 9. It being Play Night we went to the Theatre after the third [Act] was begun and stayed there till after 10. The Play was the rival Queens or the Death of Alexander the great—The Farce a Pantomime called Harlequin Foundling, a droll thing. I paid at the Theatre for self and Nephew o. 3. o. We did not get to bed till 12 o'clock. Not a great deal of Company at the Theatre.

April 7. We breakfasted and dined at the Kings Head, and stayed at Norwich till near 6 in the Evening and then we sat of for Weston Parsonage, and there I thank God we got safe and well, where we supped and slept at the old House—Nancy not yet returned. Paid and gave at the Kings Head 1. 4. 4. At Norwich for a pair of neat Nippers p^d o. 2. o. For 3 Crucibles also p^d o. o. 9. To other little Matters for Fruit &c. p^d o. 2. 9. We saw the speaking Figure, a Boy, at Quantrells Garden, for which I paid for both o. 1. o. We went also and saw the new Iron Foundry, Mr. Ransom & Co, Proprietors—and very curious indeed. I gave to the Men at work between them o. 1. o. I rode home in a new Wig, made by Brown the Barber—gave his Boy, being customary o. 1. o. Called at Mr. Priests and bespoke some Wine, Rum and Gin. Went to Alderman Gay's and paid for Christenings, Burials and Marriages for Weston for a whole Year o. 4. 6.

April 8. I breakfasted, dined, supped and slept at home. My Nephew breakfasted, dined &c. here again. Sent Ben early to Norwich with my Cart this Morn' after Coal etc for me—He carried in the Cart to Norwich for J^n_o Norton 4 Coomb of Barley. Rec^d a Note from Dr. Thorne, to let me know that My Niece cannot come Home till Tuesday next and to ask us to dine there on Monday next. I sent him in answer that I was very sorry that my Niece could not return home this Day as settled on before, and that he must excuse me dining with him on Monday next—My Nephew might.

April 10. . . . Very hard Frost in the night and this morning early. Some Ice in one of our Tubs at the back door, full half an Inch thick at least. Paid John Spaul, blacksmith a bill of o. 5. o. To my Man, Ben for things p^d o. 8. 2. To my Man Briton for things p^d o. 5. 9½. The Captain went about 11 o'clock for Dereham and in his return to dine at Dr. Thornes—but where ever he went he stayed out all night. Mr. Priest of Reepham called here this morning in his way to Mr. Du Quesnes, he was on foot—did not stay but a little while with me.

April 11. . . . I took a ride this morning to Weston House and spent an hour with Mr. and Mrs. Custance —during my stay at Weston House, Nancy and her Brother returned home from Mattishall, Mrs. Thorne, Betsy Davy and one Walker came home with them, but they did not stay long.

April 14. . . . It being Good-Friday I went to Church at 11 o'clock this Morning and there read Prayers— no Sermon. Mr. and Mrs. Custance and their eldest Son at Church. Neither Nancy or Brother at Church—tho' fine Weather. We did not dine till after 4 o'clock this Afternoon.

April 15. . . . The Captain busy in making a small Sloop out of a Piece of Deal Balk or large Beam, which we got at Mr. Frosts when at Norwich and had it brought home in my Cart this Day Sennight from Norwich.

April 16. . . . This being Easter Day I went to Weston

Church this Morning and there read Prayers and administered the H: Sacrament to at least 30 Communicants. For an offering at the H: Sacrament gave 0. 2. 6. Mrs. Custance at Church and at the H: Sacrament, Mr. Custance not there being sent for unexpectedly to Norwich. Neither Nancy or Brother at Church. My Clerk, James Smith, dined with our Folks in Kitchen. My good tempered Cow Polly, had a Calf this Morning early.

April 18. . . . To Js. Smith my Clerk, his Easter Gift gave 0. 2. 6. Dr. Thorne and Wife and Daughter Mary Anne with Mr. Walker and Betsy Davy, dined and spent the Afternoon with us, and stayed here till after 7 in the Evening. Betsy Davy by much intreaty was permitted to stay one Night with my Niece, therefore she supped and slept here. We gave our Company for dinner some Fish (which I sent to Norwich after this Morning) a boiled Leg of Mutton and Capers, a rost Neck of Pork and a batter Pudding.

April 19. . . . Mr. Walker from Mattishall came here about 12 o'clock and he dined and spent the Afternoon with us—a very droll Young Man he is and an excellent Singer. About 1 o'clock who should come to my House but Mr. Jeanes the New Rector of the Witchinghams,[1] I mounted my Mare immediately and went with him to great Witchingham and inducted him into the Church &c. He then returned

---

[1] Jeanes or Jeans, Thomas (1759–1835), son of Thomas, of Christchurch, Hants, gentleman, Merton College, Oxford, 1767; Fellow of New College, B.A. 1773, M.A. 1776, D.D. 1816, rector of Witchingham, Norfolk, and vicar of St. Johns, Maddermarket, Norwich, 1785, until his death in 1835. (This is Foster's account in his *Alumni Oxonienses*, but I am doubtful of the accuracy of the statement that Mr. Jeanes was vicar of St. John's, Maddermarket, as early as 1785.)

with me and dined and spent the Afternoon with us
—In the Evening he returned to Norwich to his Wife
and another Lady who are at Lodgings in the City—
Jeanes was only married last Thursday in London,
she is very young it is said. We had some Fish and
a Surloin of Beef rosted &c. Betsy Davy returned
with Mr. Walker in the Evening to Mattishall to
Mr. Thornes. Nancy had a Letter from her Sister
this Evening.

April 24. . . . The Captain breakfasted here and then
went of for Norwich, to meet Dr. Thorne, Wife,
Betsy Davy and young Walker at Easton Dog—he
did not return to Weston this Day or Night—I also
took a ride to Norwich and Briton with me this
morning but returned home to dinner at $\frac{1}{2}$ past
3 o'clock. Called at Mr. Francis's but he was not at
home. Called also at Buckles and paid a Bill of
o. 19. o. For a pair of Buckles at Cairns p^d o. 3. 3.
For some plate Powder at Chases p^d o. 1. o. To
Gingerbread &c. p^d o. 1. o. As we were going into
Norwich we met Mr. Jeanes and his Wife and her
Aunt coming out of Norwich.

April 25. . . . After 3 o'clock, Mr. and Mrs. Jeanes, with
Mrs. Jeanes's Aunt, a Miss Short ab^t 30 Years of Age,
came here in a single horse Chaise and they dined
and spent the Afternoon with us and stayed with us
till near 8 in the Evening, and then they went down
to Lenewade Bridge and there they slept at the Inn.
Mr. and Mrs. Custance drank Tea with us in the
Afternoon with their eldest Son. After Tea we all
got to Loo at which I won o. 6. o. Nancy also won
at Loo this evening o. 6. o. The Captain did not
return till this Evening at near 9 o'clock—All the
Company were gone before. Captain Thorne of

Mattishall called here this Morning, I could not ask him to dine here. My Nephew since he has been out, has sold his little Horse, Saddle and Bridle—for the Sum of 10. 0. 0.

April 27. . . . To J$_{o}^{n}$ Pegg for $\frac{3}{4}$ of Years Servants Tax for Males and being a Batchelor, double p^d 1. 17. 6. To Ditto—for Female Servants Tax also for $\frac{3}{4}$ Year and being a Batchelor double p^d 0. 15. 0. To Ditto $\frac{1}{2}$ Years Horse Tax p^d 0. 10. 0. I pay for 1 Male Servant 2 Female Servants and for 2 Horses. For every Male Servant per Annum 2. 10. 0. For every Female Servant per Annum 0. 10. 0. For every Horse, for riding per Annum 0. 10. 0.[1]

May 1. . . . After Dinner I walked down with my Niece to Lenewade Bridge and drank Tea and Coffee with Mr. and Mrs. Jeanes and Miss Short, stayed there till near 8 o'clock this Evening and then walked back to Supper. Mr. and Mrs. Jeanes and Miss Short came part of the way back with us, over the little Common.

May 8. I breakfasted at home as did Nancy and her Brother, and immediately after breakfast we all went in a Norwich Chaise (which came this morning) to Norwich, and there we dined, supped and slept— We dined at Mr. Jeanes's Lodgings (Holtoway in St Andrews) with him, Mrs. Jeanes, Miss Short and Mr. Du Quesne—We had for Dinner, Cod and Oyster Sauce, a fore Quarter of Lamb rosted, Pudding &c. After Tea this Evening we all went to the Play together—I got 7 Box Tickets—p^d for them 1. 1. 0, a very full House—76 P^d taken this Night—for the Benefit of Mr. and Mrs. Charlton—The Play was All in the wrong, the Entertainment, the Jubilee

[1] See foot-note, p. 208, preceding.

VIEW OF THE RIVER WENSUM NEAR LENWADE BRIDGE

with the tedious Ode—All performed shockingly.
Mr. Du Quesne, myself and Nephew supped and
slept at the Kings Head—it was after 12 before we
got to bed. Nancy went from the Play with Mrs.
Jeanes and Miss Short to their Lodgings, and there
she supped and slept.

May 9. We breakfasted at the Kings Head, that is,
Mr. Du Quesne myself and nephew—About 11 this
Morning we called on Mr. and Mrs. Jeanes &c. at
their Lodgings but did not stay long—we then went
to different Places and in our Walk we lost Mr. Du
Quesne, but saw him soon after at the Kings Head—
About 12 o'clock Mr. and Mrs. Custance with their
2 eldest Sons came to the Kings Head, being on their
way to a Place near Scole where their eldest Son
Hamilton is going to School. Mrs. Jeanes, Miss
Short and my Niece paid their respects to Mr. Cus-
tance at the Kings Head this morning but Mrs.
Custance did not receive them with that openness
and Affability that I could wish, being rather hurried
and fluttered on her eldest Son going to School.
Mrs. Jeanes however could not help taking notice of
it. We left Mrs. Custance rather soon and then the
Captain and myself took a Walk with Mrs. Jeanes,
Miss Short and Nancy to divers Places in the City,
till Dinner Time. Mr. and Mrs. Custance &c. left
Norwich about 2 o'clock. Mr. Du Quesne also left
Norwich before Dinner. The Captain and myself
dined, supped and spent part of the Evening at Mr.
Jeanes's Lodgings with him, Mrs. Jeanes, Miss Short
and Nancy, who slept there again. To Cakes &c. at
Blacks Shop this Morning p^d o. 1. 8. To Beales
my Fishmonger for Fish &c. p^d o. 3. 6. At Chases
for Books p^d o. 2. 7. To a P^r of new Gloves at Scotts

1786

p^d o. 2. 4. To things at Bakers Shop p^d o. 1. 6. To 4 little Dutch Baskets at Studwells p^d o. 1. o. Rec^d of Mr. Snelgrove, Collector of Excise for Surplus Money paid by me for 1 Servants Tax o. 16. 3. My Nephew and [I] slept again at the Kings Head. [Next day they all returned to Weston.]

May 17. . . . Ben and Briton went very early this Morning with a Waggon Load of Wheat Straw for Norwich; to sell for me there and to bring back a Ch[a]ldron of Coal. Mr. Custance made us a Morning Visit. Ben and Briton returned home about 6 o'clock having sold my straw—rec^d of Ben for it 2. 10. o.

May 18. . . . Nancy went after breakfast in a Cart with Briton to Thurning to see Betsy Davy &c. at Mr. Elwin's there, and to carry some of Mrs. Davy's things left here by her, and to buy the little Cart of Mr. Elwin also. She dined &c. there and returned home in the Evening. About 1 o'clock Mr. Du Quesne called on us, and we went with him to Mr. Priests at Reepham, where we dined and spent the Afternoon with Mr. and Mrs. Priest and Miss Priest ; The Captain and myself returned home about 9 this Evening—Mr. Du Quesne slept at Reepham. We had for Dinner some Cod Fish, a Fillet of Veal rosted, a Tongue, and some Custards. After Tea we got to Quadrille at which I lost o. o. 6. Nancy got home this Evening about ½ Hour before us. Rec^d of Mr. Priest for two small Piggs o. 12. o.

May 20. . . . Ben sold my Wheat to the Marlingford Miller this Morning for 19 shillings per Coomb, to be carried thither next Week—My Miller, Forster would not give me more than 18 per Coomb tho' it was offered him first and which I would not take.

244

May 23. . . . Pile of Hockering, my Carpenter, applied to me this Morning for Cash, but it was not convenient to me. Dr. Thorne called here this morning, he wanted the Captain to go with him to Mattishall to day and dine with him this being Mattishall Gaunt, but he declined it, which I thought right for him so to do. Had a Note from Mr. Thomas of Dereham to desire us to dine with him, Friday next but we are engaged then. I sent him word in return, that we would dine with him, if agreeable, on Tuesday in the following Week. My Maid Betty and Boy, Jack, went to Mattishall Gaunt by my consent, their Friends living there. Sent Ben Yesterday—after breakfast with 13 Coomb of Wheat in Mr. Bucks Waggon to Marlingford Mills, received for it, a Note for Payment of the Money any Saturday at Norwich —forgot to be mentioned before.

May 25. . . . Nancy went with Briton in her new Cart to Mattishall this Morning to Mr. Bodhams and there spent the Day. About 1 o'clock the Captain and myself took a ride to Mr. Bodhams and there dined and spent the Afternoon. I called at Mr. Smiths going thither and stayed a few minutes. Mr. Smith dined with us at Mr. Bodhams. We returned home to Weston as we went about 9 o'clock.

May 26. . . . Mr. and Mrs. Priest and Miss Priest of Reepham, and Mr. Du Quesne dined and spent the Afternoon with us. After Tea and Coffee we got to Loo at which I lost o. 1. 6. We had for Dinner some very fine, fresh Maccarel, a large Piece of rost Beef, some Mutton stakes, Asparagus, and some green Apricot Tarts—Oranges after.

May 27. . . . Very fine Weather indeed for the Wheat &c. ' Lord make us more worthy thy Divine Favours.'

May 30. . . . We all went to Dereham this Morning
to Mr. Thomas's and there dined and spent the afternoon with him, Miss Thomas, Miss Betsy and Miss
Anne Thomas, and Mr. Du Quesne—It was very hot
to day. Nancy went with Briton in the little Cart,
and myself and Nephew went on horseback. We
returned home a little after 9 this Evening, we spent
a tolerable agreeable Day there—Miss Thomas is
very reserved and not handsome—Miss Betsy is very
agreeable and pretty—Miss Anne very still and coarse.
We had for Dinner a boiled Leg of Mutton and Caper
Sauce, a green Goose rosted and Gooseberries, Veal
Cutlets, Lobsters, pickled Salmon, Damson Tarts and
Syllabubs. Whilst at Dereham, I took a Walk by
myself to Barkers the Bookbinders and paid him a Bill
for binding my new Chambers Cyclopædia by Dr.
Rees—5 large Volumes Folio double lettered &c.
p^d 2. 5. 0.[1] To Ditto for binding Walpoles British
Traveller Folio and lettered only half-bound 1 Vol.
p^d 0. 4. 6.[2] To Do. for binding the Field of Mars
2 Vols Quarter and lettered, but only half bound
also p^d 0. 6. 0.[3] To Do. for 1 Doz. Mem: Books, half
Bound p^d 0. 8. 0. To Do. for 3 Quire Gilt Post

[1] See foot-note, p. 233, preceding.

[2] *The new British Traveller; or a complete modern universal Display
of Great Britain and Ireland, published under the immediate Inspection of
George Augustus Walpoole.* London, 1784, folio, 15s. With Plates. Published by Hogg. (See Lowndes' *The Bibliographer's Manual of English
Literature*, Part X, p. 2824.)

[3] *The Field of Mars : being an alphabetical digestion of the principal
naval and military engagements, in Europe, Asia, Africa, and America,
particularly of Great Britain and her Allies, from the ninth century to the
Peace of 1801.* This is the title of the 1801 edition, as given in the War
Office Library Catalogue, Pt. I, p. 386, but an earlier edition, 2 vols. in
quarto, had appeared in 1781.

Paper p^d 0. 3. 6. To Do. for a large Glass Inkstand p^d 0. 3. 0. To Do. for a new Court Calendar p^d 0. 2. 0. To Mr. Thomas's Servant Boy gave 0. 0. 6.

May 31. . . . To Norton's Wife for Washing my Boy's Shirts &c. for a whole Year, due at Lady Day or thereabout 0. 10. 6. As she grumbled about not being enough and rather discontented, I paid her up to this Day and told her I would get another to wash him, so I paid her for the Month extraordinary 0. 1. 0.

June 2. . . . About 1 o'clock we sat of for Mattishall to Mr. Smith's and there we dined and spent the Afternoon with him, Mr. Du Quesne, Mr. and Mrs. Bodham, Miss Anne Donne of Norwich, and a Mr. Lane a young Clergyman, whom Mr. Smith invited on my Account for me to speak to him to serve my Church during my absence from Weston, as I intend (Deo volente) spending a few Weeks with my Friends in Somersetshire soon. He seems a good kind of a young Man, and very willing to engage on it. He lives at Hingham, he is to enter on serving Weston the 25 of this Month, and to serve it from that Time for a Q^r of a Year for which I am to give him at the rate of 30 Pounds per Annum with all surplice Fees during that Time. We had for Dinner to Day some Maccarel, 3 spring Chicken and a Tongue, a Leg of Mutton rosted, Gooseberry Tarts and Custards. After Coffee and Tea we got to Quadrille lost 0. 0. 6. We returned home to Weston about ½ past 9 o'clock as we went—that is, Nancy went with Briton in the little Cart, The Captain and myself on horseback. We spent a very agreeable Day—Whilst we were at Cards we had a Syllabub carried round.

June 3. . . . Sent Ben to Norwich this Morning to receive some Money for me for the Wheat lately sold by me. By Ben sent a Letter to my Sister Pounsett to let her know that we should be with her the latter end of this Month, God willing. Ben did not return till near 8 o'clock this Evening owing to a Fair being on the Castle Hill to day—he brought me home the money for my Wheat 11. 15. 2.

June 5. . . . This being Whit Monday there was running for a Shift, plowing &c. &c. this Afternoon at the Heart.

June 8. . . . Had my Garden mowed again for the 2nd time. Got a pain in my right Ear to catching Cold I believe. Had a Tub of Gin brought me this Evening from Robt Buck of Honingham, blacksmith, by my Man Ben Leggatt. I am to pay for it to Ben 1. 3. 0.

June 9. . . . My Ear something better to day—took some Rhubarb last night. Bottled of my Gin this morning—19 Bottles. The Captain very busy about his Ship, as she is to be launched to Morrow, having Company to dine with us.

June 10. . . . My Ear pained me very much all the Morning. Mr. Custance sent us a nice Melon this Morning. The Captain very busy this Morning with his Ship. Sent Briton early this Morning to Norwich after Fish &c. he returned before 12 o'clock with Maccarel &c. He went in the little Cart and had the Horse Punch. Mr. and Mrs. Bodham with Miss Anne Donne from Norwich, Mr. Du Quesne, Mr. Smith, and Mr. Lane of Hingham who is to officiate for me at Weston during my Absence dined and spent the Afternoon with us. Just before Dinner the Captain launched his new Ship, before the Ladies and Gentlemen present but to his great Chagrin and the Company's disappointment it upset and went down to the starboard side almost immediately and took in Water and could not be righted. She was far too much over-masted. We were all exceedingly sorry on the Captains Account. We had for Dinner some Maccarel, a fore Q^r of Lamb, 3 boiled Chicken and a Pigs Face, Pigeons and Asparagus, Lobster, Apricot and Gooseberry Tarts and Custards. After Dinner by way of Desert—A Melon, Oranges, Almonds and Raisins. The Company left us about 8 o'clock this Evening.

June 12. . . . My Ear pained me much again this morning. To Mr. Cary for things from Norwich &c. p^d 0. 8. 6. To my Man Briton for things from Norwich &c. p^d 0. 14. 8. Took a good large Dose of Rhubarb last Night, as did also Nancy, made her get up at 4 o'clock this Morn'. The Captain got up early this morning and sat of for Mattishall to my Glaziers, Hubbard, after some Lead to put on at the bottom of the Ship by way of a false Keel and returned home with it 10 o'clock, with a long piece which weighed 25 Pound—After he had breakfasted he put on the Lead to the bottom of the Vessel and then she sailed as well as our most sanguine wishes could desire.

June 13. . . . My Ear pained me much again this Morning. Mrs. Davy and Daughter from Thurning came here early this Morning and they breakfasted, dined and spent the Afternoon here—An old Man came with them. Mrs. Davy and Daughter came in Mr. Elwins Cart, they returned back for Thurning about 7 o'clock this Even'. We had for Dinner some rost Beef, Lobsters and Tarts. Nancy paid Mrs. Davy for the Cart by my desire, and which we have had here some time from Thurning. She paid for the same to Mrs. Davy before me 1. 11. 6. and which I do not think by any means dear, as the Cart has an excellent Iron Axle and the Iron tire to the Wheels almost as good as new. I am to pay Nancy again for the Cart.

June 14. . . . Paid to Nancy this Afternoon for the little Market-Cart which she paid Mrs. Davy Yesterday and which Mrs. Davy had paid to Mrs. Elwin of Thurning for the Widow of the late Rev^d Mr. Headley of North Walsham 1. 11. 6.

June 18. . . . I read Prayers and Preached this Morning at Weston Ch[urch]. Mrs. Custance with her eldest Son at Church and my Niece. Mr. Custance at home on the late Death of Mr. Morris, a Relation. Nancys Brother not at Church also, not being dressed in time. Mrs. Custance with her three Sons drank Tea with us this Afternoon—Mr. Custance not at home—Mrs. Custance &c. came to see the Ship on the Water. She admired it very much indeed.

June 20. . . . I took a ride to Norwich this Morn to bespeak places in a Coach to London for us and to fix the Day. Briton went in my Cart to Norwich to Day also. We got to Norwich about Noon and got home by 8 at Night. Guild Day at Norwich to day —I did not look much after the Mayor's Shew— When I got to Norwich I went to Quantrell's Gardens which are to be illuminated this Evening, and there drank a Glass of Porter and ate 2 half Penny Cakes— p^d for it 0. 0. 2. From thence went to Bunns Gardens which are also to be illuminated this Evening and there had a Glass of Rum and Water for which paid 0. 0. 3. Walked after to Bakers in the Market Place and there took 3 Places in the London Coach from

the Angel to the Swan and 2 Necks Lad Lane London
for Friday Evening next. At Bakers Shop also for
a small Ship p^d o. 2. o. At Do. for a P^r of Nippers
for Lobsters p^d o. 2. o. Went then to the Kings
Head and bespoke a Chaise to be at my House on
Friday next in the Afternoon. For a Glass of Gin
and Water at the Kings Head p^d o. o. 3. Called at
Priests but they were all at the Guild. Paid and
gave at Courtman's &c. o. 2. 10. Sat out of Norwich
a little before 6 this Evening. My Nephew went
to Mattishall whilst I was from home, to take
his leave of Dr. Thorne &c. but the Dr. and Family
not being at home, he soon returned to Weston
again.

June 23. . . . Nancy and Brother breakfasted, and
dined here again. After dinner we all went to
Norwich in a Post Chaise which we had from thence,
and carried our Baggage with us, Briton went also in
my Cart with a Trunk for the Captain—We all got
to Norwich about 6 o'clock and drank Tea at the
Kings Head, and stayed there till half past 6 o'clock
and then went to the Angel Inn and at 7 o'clock
this Evening, myself, Nancy and Brother went in
the heavy Coach for London with three strange
Women in it also. Paid at the Kings Head at Norwich
for Chaise from Weston, Tea &c. about o. 15. o.
For 3 Peoples Fare to London I p^d 4. 10. o. For
extra Luggage—12 St. I p^d o. 15. o. It was very hot
this Evening, especially with a Coach full.

June 24. We had a very fine pleasant night of travelling
we went thro' Bury &c. we breakfasted very early but
where I know not—I paid for our breakfasts o. 3. o.
To the Coachman that drove us half way gave o. 3. o.
We all got to London (thank God) safe and well by

3 o'clock this Afternoon—to the Swan and 2 Necks in Lad Lane where we had some Rum and Water. To the last Coachman gave 0. 3. 0. After staying some little Time in Lad Lane we had a Coach and went with our Luggage to our old Inn the Bell Savage at Ludgate Hill where we supped and slept— and kept by the same People, Burton and his Wife. Nancy and her Brother walked out in the Evening by themselves, giving me the Slip, and did not return till Supper time, at which I was much displeased and gave it to them smartly, and to make it still worse soon as Supper was removed and having ordered a Bottle of Wine, they left me without drinking a drop and went to bed leaving me by myself—I sat up by myself very uneasy till about 12 and then I went.

June 25. We breakfasted, supped and slept again at the Bell Savage. Very much pestered and bit by the Buggs in the Night. After dressing ourselves, after breakfast we walked down to Charing Cross, and there took a Coach and went to Kensington Gardens and there we walked about till near 3 in the Afternoon—and then we walked back to the 13 Cantons near Charing Cross where we dined on Beef a la mode and which was very good. For the Coach and Turnpike to Kensington Gardens p^d 0. 3. 2. In our walk back we called at a House and refreshed ourselves with some Rum and Water and then walked on. We met the Prince of Wales's Carriage with him in it, as we walked back to Charing Cross. For our refreshment at the above house p^d 0. 1. 6. At the 13 Cantons paid and gave about 0. 2. 0. After we had dined we retired to an adjoining House to drink Cyder where I smoked a Pipe p^d there 0. 1. 6.

June 26. We breakfasted, supped and slept again at the Bell Savage. I was bit so terribly with Buggs again this Night that I got up at 4 o'clock this Morning and took a long Walk by myself about the City till breakfast time. After breakfast we walked to Osborn Place, Spital Fields to deliver a Letter for Mrs. Bodham to Miss Eliz: Donne at that Place, but she was from home, after leaving the Letter we immediately returned back—We went thro' a most black-guard Place going to the above House. We took Coach part of the way coming back and went to the 13 Cantons again at Charing Cross where we dined again on beef a la mode p^d there 0. 2. 0. For the Coach hire thither and back p^d 0. 3. 0. In the Evening we took Coach and went to the Circus in St Georges Fields and there saw wonderful Feats of Horsemanship &c. performed by Hughes and his Children. For Coach hire thither p^d 0. 1. 0. For 3 Pit Tickets at the Circus I p^d 0. 9. 0. For Oranges &c. to day p^d 0. 1. 0. For a little red Book of Prints p^d this Evening 0. 12. 0. I saw a vast number of strange Prints at the Shop. We were obliged to walk back this Evening from the Circus as we could get no Coach. Andrew Russ, Mr. Russ's son of Castle-Cary called on us this Morning, he lives as a Journeyman to one Gould an Hatter, near St Pauls Church Yard.

June 27. We breakfasted, dined and slept again at the Bell Savage. One George Pace, a young Man, and Mess Mate of my Nephews called on us this Morning and he dined supped and spent the Evening with us at the Bell Savage. Nancy and me walked about Town by ourselves this Morn'. The Captain and George Pace went with themselves. I shewed Nancy the Mews and the Kings Cream coloured Horses, also the Kings State Coach which she sat in. Gave to the Men that shewed us the same 0. 2. 0. For a Silver Fruit Knife for Jenny Pounsett p^d 0. 10. 6. At Charlesworths near Covent Garden for Gauze Gloves, Ribband &c. for Nancy I paid 1. 1. 0. For three Places in the Bath Coach for to Morrow Night, for part of the Fare thither p^d 3. 3. 0. In the Evening Nancy and Brother, George Pace, and myself went in a Coach to the Theatre in the Hay-Market late Mr. Footes [1]—and there saw a Play and Farce, both performed incomparably well—it begun about 7 o'clock and not over till after 10 or very near 11 o'clock. For 4 Tickets and Coach hire back and thither I p^d 0. 15. 0. To a Barber for shaving and dressing me p^d 0. 2. 0. George Pace did not leave us till near 12 this Evening. I did not pull of my Cloaths last Night but sat up in a great Chair all night with my Feet on the bed and slept very well considering and not pestered with buggs.

June 28. We breakfasted again at the Bell Savage. I did not pull of my Cloaths last Night again but did as the Night before, and slept tolerably well. After breakfast George Pace called on us and then went out with the Captain—Nancy walked with me to one Smiths in Surry Street, Strand, a Barber and there had her Hair full dressed—Smith was Sam Woodfordes Hair Dresser—I was shaved and had my Wig dressed there. I gave him for shaving and dressing 0. 1. 6. After that, the Captain and George Pace joined us and we walked about Town, shopping &c. till 3 this Aft: and then went to the 13 Cantons again and there dined again on Beef a la mode,

[1] i. e. Samuel Foote (1719–77), the eminent actor, wit, and dramatist.

I p^d for all o. 2. 6. The Captain and George Pace then left us and Nancy and myself walked back to our Inn, packed up all our things and were ready for our Journey by 6 o'clock. I paid at the Bell Savage, our Bill 3. 14. 0. To Servants at the Inn gave o. 10. 6. At a Q^r before 7 this Evening Nancy and self got into the Bath Coach, and were just setting out, after some time waiting for Bill, when he luckily arrived, but it was enough to make one very mad, he was at last obliged to leave some things behind him. We had four of us in the Coach and Guard on top. It carries but 4 inside, and is called the Baloon Coach on Account of its travelling so fast, making it a point to be before the Mail Coach. We trimmed it of indeed, tho' only a P^r of Horses.

June 29. About 4 o'clock this morning we all break-fasted but at what place I know not—p^d for the same o. 4. 0. To the first Coachman and Guard I gave o. 4. 0. For the other part of our Fare to Bath p^d 1. 7. 0. For extra Luggage—p^d also at breakfast o. 13. 0. We all got safe to Bath (thank God) this morning about 10 o'clock, to the Castle-Inn, where we made a second breakfast, and there also dined supped and slept. To the last Coachman gave o. 1. 0. After breakfasting at Bath we took a walk over the City till dinner time to shew Nancy the public Rooms &c. she being never at Bath before—gave for seeing them o. 1. 0. We had very good accommodation at our Inn.

June 30. We breakfasted and spent all the Morning at Bath, and about Noon we got into a Post Chaise and set forth with our Luggage for Shepton Mallet about 19 Miles from Bath, got there about 5 o'clock, had some Rum and Water at the George Inn, took

a fresh Chaise and sat of for Cole to Pounsetts—
thro' Ansford. At the Castle Inn at Bath for Chaise
to Shepton, our own eating, Lodging &c.—paid and
gave there 2. 7. 4½. For some Fish, Soals and a Crab
to carry to Cole p^d 0. 3. 2. To the Bath Driver and
for Rum and Water at Shepton p^d 0. 3. 0. We saw
my Nephew J^s White at Shepton Mallett. When
we got to Ansford Turnpike Gate we dropt the
Captain and his Trunk &c. there—who went to his
Fathers. Nancy and self went on to Cole, driving
pretty fast thro' Ansford, calling no where—and
thank God got to Cole to my Sister Pounsetts about
8 o'clock this Evening and found both my Sister and
Mr. Pounsett and Daughter brave. For the Shepton
Chaise and Driver—p^d and gave 0. 10. 6. To Turnpikes to day p^d about 0. 2. 0. We supped and slept
at Mr. Pounsetts, very little fatigued.

July 1. . . . My Brother John called on us this Afternoon, he looks but poorly—I wish to God he would
take more care of health.

July 3. . . . After breakfast I went out a fishing—
caught 3 fine Trout and 10 Eels this Morning—fine
Sport. Sister White, with her Son Robert and Wife
dined and spent the Afternoon with us—Sister White
slept here. Nancy's Sister Juliana dined and spent
the Afternoon here.

July 5. . . . After breakfast Nancy and self took a Walk
to Ansford called on Mr. J^s Clarke and Wife, Mrs.
Richd Clarke, my B[rother] John Woodforde and
Wife, Sister White, Robt White and Wife, my Brother
Heighes and Juliana and Sister Clarke. Nancy dined
and spent the Aft: at Mrs. Richd Clarke's. I dined
and spent part of the Aft: at my Sister Whites who
now lives in the House where Sister Pounsett did live.

Robert White and Wife dined and spent the Afternoon with us. We had for Dinner some nice Salmon
&c. In the Afternoon I walked down by myself to
Mrs. Richd Clarkes and there drank Tea with her,
my Brother John and Wife who lives with her,
Nancy and Juliana Woodforde. In the Evening
Nancy and self walked back to Cole.

July 12. [Constant interchange of visits and hospitality
fill the preceding days, but apart from the mere
record of names of relatives by now well known to
us, the entries are not notable : the following entry
is rather fuller.] . . . Nancy breakfasted and spent
the Morn' at Cole. About 2 o'clock Mr. J^s Clarke
came here in his Phaeton and took up my Sister
Pounsett and carried her to his House to dinner, as
did my Brother John in Mrs. R^d Clarkes Chaise take
up Nancy to go and dine at Dr. J^s Clarkes—I walked
thither by myself—Mr. P. could not go being
in the midst of his Hay-Harvest. I dined and
spent the Afternoon at James Clarkes with him, his
Wife, Jenny Ashford of Ditcheat, Mrs. R. Clarke,
my Brother John and Wife and Nancy. Miss Sophy
Dawe, Mrs. J^s Clarkes Sister and Nancy's Sister spent
the Afternoon with us at Dr. Clarkes, as did Painter
Clarke. We had for Dinner, some Whiting, boiled
Fowls and a Piggs Face, a fore Q^r of Lamb, a rost
Duck and Peas, a Codlin Tart and some indifferent
Syllabubs. Mr. James Clarke behaved exceedingly
kind to us. I walked back to Cole in the Evening
by myself. My Sister Pounsett returned home
behind Ellis on horseback. Nancy we left behind to
spend a few Days with Mrs. Richd Clarke and my
Brother John and Wife at Cary.

July 15. . . . After breakfast I walked out a fishing, had

not put my Line in Water more than five Minutes
before I caught a fine Trout of one Pound and a
Quarter with a Grasshopper. It measured in length
14 Inches and in the highest Season. Mrs. Pounsett
Sen[r] dined and spent the Aft: with us. After Tea
this Aft: walked out again with my Rod and Line
up the Bruton River and there caught another fine
Trout which weighed 1 Pound and ¼ and measured
14½ Inches. Mr. Sam: Pounsett supped and spent
the Evening with us.

July 16. . . . Walked in the Afternoon to Pitcomb
Church with Mr. Pounsett and heard John Goldsborough Preach and read Prayers. Captain Cour-
tenay and Wife, and Counsellor Hobhouse[1] at Church.
Sister Pounsett did not go to Church, it being very
hot. Brother Heighes dined and spent the Afternoon with us. To a poor Woman of Pitcomb gave
this Morn' o. o. 2. We did not dine to day till
4 o'clock in the Afternoon.

July 18. . . . I got up this Morning very ill indeed
with the Cholic, could eat no solids all day long, and
continued so all the Day long—in the Afternoon was
very bad indeed. Going to bed I took some Rhubarb
—Purging and vomiting almost the whole day—
I believe I made too free Yesterday with Currant
Tarts and Cream &c. A violent pain in my Bowels
and likewise in my stomach, very acute indeed.

July 19. . . . Very ill again to day, but not so bad as

---

[1] Henry Hobhouse, son of Henry Hobhouse of Bristol, arm., Brasenose
College, Oxford, matric. February 28, 1758, aged 15 ; B.A. 1761, M.A.
1764, of Hadspen House, Somerset, barrister-at-law, Middle Temple,
1766 ; died April 2, 1792. He was the father of Henry Hobhouse, Under-
Secretary of the Home Department, 1817-27, and ancestor of the Hadspen
Hobhouses (see Foster's *Alumni Oxonienses* and Burke's *Landed Gentry*).

Yesterday—kept close at home to day again—Eat some boiled Mutton.

July 20. . . . Something better to day, but still in pain, and of nights sleep but little—In the Aft: better—and in the Evening took some more Rhubarb. No Friends from Ansford or Cary this Day nor since last Sunday—or any Enquiry after any one here.

July 21. . . . I thank God, had a good Night of Sleep and rose up tolerably well this morning. My Brother John and Wife called here this Morning but could not stay to dine with us. Since Nancy has been to Cary, she has met with a misfortune, in straining her bad knee, getting up into J^s Clarkes Phaeton to go to Ditcheat Yesterday. So bad is it this Morning as to keep her bed. Nancy's Brother Willm dined supped and spent the Evening with us to day.

July 23. . . . Had a tolerable good night (thank God) but still a purging remains on me—I drank no Cyder Yesterday. Could not go to Church this morning being not well enough. Mrs. Pounsett Senr and Betsy Guppey dined with us to day. Robert White and Wife, and my Brother John spent the Afternoon with us—they all came on foot.

July 24. . . . I thank God am much better this morning owing I think to drinking of Port Wine last Night. To a Man of Bruton for Cakes, Gingerbread &c. p^d o. 1. 6. Brother Heighes dined and spent the Afternoon with us.

July 25. . . . The Water in the Mill Pond was drawn down this Morn' and we were very busy, all the Morning in catching Trout and Eels of which we caught a plenty. About 2 o'clock I walked to C. Cary and there dined and spent the Afternoon at Mrs. Rich. Clarkes, with her my Brother John and Wife, Nancy

Woodforde and Brother Willm, Robert White and Wife and Mr. Pounsett. Brother Heighes and Daughter Juliana spent the Aft: there. Mr. Pounsett rode to Cary and back again—I walked by myself. I was exceeding well all day blessed be God for it.

July 28. . . . My Brother John and Wife, Mrs. Richard Clarke and Nancy Woodforde dined and spent the Afternoon with us at Cole. Nancy was left behind and she supped and slept here. We had for Dinner some nice Salmon, but a most bad Leg of Mutton rosted which was obliged to be sent out. After Tea we got to Quadrille, My Brother John and Wife, Mrs. Richd Clark and myself, which at 1^d per Fish I won 0. 1. 6.

July 30. . . . Nancy's Brother Willm came over here this Morning and he dined and spent the Afternoon here. A Mrs. Forster (late Slade) came over here this Morning and she dined and spent the Afternoon here. Mr. and Mrs. Pounsett, Mrs. Forster, Sister White, Nancy and Brother, and Jenny Pounsett all went to Pitcomb Church this Afternoon. I stayed at home having a little Head-Ache and thinking also that they would be crowded at Church. Robert White and Wife, J^s White and Juliana Woodforde spent the Afternoon with us—a good house-full.

Aug. 2. . . . After breakfast, Mr. and Mrs. Pounsett and Daughter, Willm W. and myself went to Colonel Strangeways, Lady Ilchesters at Dishcoll, and to Ld Ilchester's Pheasantry this Morning and did not return till near 4 o'clock this Afternoon to Dinner.[1] My Sister Pounsett was carried to the above

[1] Lord Ilchester—Henry Thomas Fox-Strangways (1747–1802)—was the grandson of the rich, able, and vigorous Sir Stephen Fox (1627–1716), who by his second marriage in his 77th year with a lady of 25, had two

Places behind Ellis Coleman—We walked thither and back. Old John Fry at the Pheasantry behaved very civil to us.

Aug. 6. . . . Sister Pounsett and Daughter, Nancy and myself walked this Morning to Pitcomb Church where we heard Mr. J^n_o Goldsborough read Prayers, and instead of a Sermon he read an Act of Parliament lately passed concerning Donations &c. given to the Poor.[1] Brother Heighes dined and spent the Afternoon with us. Juliana Woodforde drank Tea here this Afternoon. Mrs. Pounsett Senr dined with us to day —she was in a very good humour—but have been very cross of late.

Aug. 7. . . . Robert Shoard who married Farmer Corps Daughter and since the Farmer died, has continued my Estate at Ansford, called on me this Morning and paid me a Years Rent due Lady Day last past the Sum of 35. 0. 0. I paid him out of it for Poor Rates and Church 1. 12. 2¼. I paid him also for a new Gate

---

sons who became peers, Stephen as 1st Earl of Ilchester, and Henry as the 1st Lord Holland. Stephen married Elizabeth, only daughter and heiress of Thomas Strangways Horner of Mells Park, Somerset, and eventually heiress of her brother, Thomas Strangways of Melbury Samford, Dorset —hence the relationship with the Strangways, and the addition of their name to that of Fox. It is curious, and indeed romantic, to reflect that Parson Woodforde was the contemporary of a man (for the *first* Lord Ilchester did not die till 1776) whose father was born two years after the death of James I, who had helped Charles II to escape after the battle of Worcester in 1651, and who had lived through the reigns of Charles I, Charles II, James II, William and Mary, and Queen Anne (see *D. N. B.* under Sir Stephen Fox, and Burke's *Peerage*).

[1] This Act (26 Geo. III, c. 58) was entitled : ' An Act for procuring, upon Oath, Returns of all charitable Donations, for the Benefit of Poor Persons, in the several Parishes and Places within that part of Great Britain called England.' Returns made by ministers and churchwardens were to be transmitted to the Clerk of the Parliaments.

o. 7. o. I gave Robert a Receipt on stampt Paper, and to let him with his Mother Law continue on the Estate. Poor Farmer Corp died just before we came down. He had over-heated himself it was said and was imprudent to drink cold Water after it. Brother John and Wife and J^s Clarke spent the Aft: with us. J^s Clarke supped and spent the Evening also with us.

Aug. 10. . . . Nancy and self very busy this morning in making the Charter having some Company to dine with us—But unfortunately the Cellar Door being left open whilst it was put in there to cool, one of the Greyhounds (by name Jigg) got in and eat the whole, with a Cold Tongue &c. Sister Pounsett and Nancy mortally vexed at it. J^s Clarke and Wife and Jenny Ashford dined and spent the Afternoon with us— We had for Dinner some Maccarel, boiled Beef, a Couple of Ducks rosted, a brace of Pigeons rosted and a Barberry Tart. Mrs. Pounsett Senr dined and spent the Afternoon with us.

Aug. 11. . . . J^s Lintern who keeps the Bear at Wincaunton and a Miss Wray from London called here in the Evening to let us know how Miss Tucker was now, but she was still very poorly tho' rather better than she has been.

Aug. 14. . . . Mr. and Mrs. Pounsett, Nancy and self dined and spent the Aft: at Mr. Sam: Pounsetts with him, a Mrs. Maynard and her Son, who live at Streat by Glastonbury. Nancy was taken very ill soon after breakfast, and quite ill at Mr. Sam: Pounsetts, she went to bed soon after she returned home, about 7 in the Evening. We had for Dinner to day some Peas and Bacon, a Leg of Mutton boiled but no Capers and a comical plumb Pudding. Nancy scarce eat any thing at all, being so ill, it is something of the Ague I believe.

Aug. 15. . . . Nancy breakfasted, dined, supped &c. again at Cole. She kept her bed all the Morning being very indifferent—She was to have dined at her Fathers to day to meet a large Party there, but could not go. Sister Pounsett stayed at home also with her—but neither of them could have went as it proved very stormy most part of the Day—Mr. Pounsett and self walked however to my Brother Heighes's at Ansford and there dined and spent the Afternoon with him, Sister Clarke, Sam Clarke, Sister White, Brother John and Wife, and Mrs. R. Clarke, Robert White and Wife, Juliana Woodforde and her Brother William—Painter Clarke spent the Aft: with us—We were very merry tho' a wet day—The design was to have dined under the Oaks had the Weather been fair.—We had for Dinner Peas and Beans, a fore Ham, a boiled Leg of Mutton and Capers, and some Cheesecakes, Roots &c. Beer and Cyder and Gin to drink. To Sam Dawe that waited at Table gave 0. 1. 0. To Jane Herod who was Cook gave 0. 1. 0. We returned home to Cole about 9 o'clock.

Aug. 16. . . . Nancy is something better but very little, did not get up the whole Morning. She took a mustard Vomit this Evening and Rhubarb after.

Aug. 17. . . . Nancy was a good deal better to day, but very weak. Nancy's Sister spent the Morning, dined &c. at Cole. Mr. and Mrs. Pounsett and self dined and spent the Afternoon at Mr. J^s Clarkes, with him, his Wife, Jenny Ashford and Mrs. Richd Clarke— My Brother John and Wife were invited, but could not come, the former being much indisposed owing to setting up late last Night. Mr. Pounsett and self walked it, Sister Pounsett rode. We had for Dinner some fryed Soals rather stale, a Loin of Pork rosted, a Couple of Ducks rosted and Apple Pye. Brother Heighes spent the Afternoon with us.

Aug. 18. . . . Nancy had a very bad night and very indifferent this Morning, we sent for Mr. J[s] Clarke to her who came about 2 o'clock but did not stay long here. In the Evening she took James's Powder which came from J[s] Clarkes and at the expiration of 12 Hours she is to take another, and for the Wind in the Stomach she is to take a Wine Glass of the Mixture of Pepper-mint &c. every six Hours. She was better after the Morning. Mr. J[s] Clarkes Wife came over with him.

Aug. 19. . . . Nancy better again to day till the Evening and then the Fever returned about 7 o'clock, and at 9 she went to bed quite ill—The Powder she took last night she brought up about an Hour after taking it, which J[s] Clarke said was a good Sympton—She took another at 10 this morning which kept down very well. She was well enough to day to play Cards after Tea this Afternoon—at which I won 0. 1. 0. J[s] Clarke and Wife called here this Morn but did not stay long—J[s] Clarke asked Nancy very few Questions indeed.

Aug. 21. . . . Nancy very weak this Morning and in the Afternoon still more so, in the Evening very bad, she took another Powder going to bed, which made her better, as it made her vomit a good deal of Phlegm. Mr. Pounsett got up very early this morning to go to the Assizes at Wells being summoned to attend as one of the grand Jury.—He returned however very late at Night, a sufficient Number being

present. Hotham[1] and Perryn,[2] Judges; Stephens,
High Sheriff. Nancy's Sister and Brother Willm and
Brother Heighes dined and spent the Afternoon here.
Mrs. Pounsett Senr dined and spent the Aft: with us.
To Robin Colley for a ball of large Twine p^d o. o. 6.
Brother John went with Mr. Pounsett to Wells and
returned with him to Castle Cary. Had good sport
a fishing this Morn' caught a brace of Trout and
5 Eels.

Aug. 23. . . . Nancy but indifferent this Morning, still
very weak. For Fish of Marshalls Son this Morn'
p^d o. 1. 9. Mrs. Forster of Cary and Seth Burge's
eldest Daughter came over here just at dinner time
and they dined and spent the Afternoon here as did
Mrs. Pounsett Senr. Nancy was most part of the
Day on the bed being worse did not come down to
dinner or Supper—I sent for Mr. Js. Clarke in the
Evening for her and he came about 9 o'clock and
ordered the Bark for her to Morrow. Mr. J^s supped
and spent an hour after with us. Nancy looked much
worse to day than she did, and is extremely weak
indeed—Vomited much this Evening.

Aug. 24. . . . Nancy still very indifferent, she began
taking of the Bark early this Morning, which I hope
will do her good—she is very weak and complains of

---

[1] Hotham, Beaumont, 2nd Baron Hotham (1737–1814). Baron of the
Exchequer, 1775; Commissioner for custody of the Great Seal, April
to December 1783; resigned his seat in the Exchequer Court in 1805;
succeeded his brother as Baron Hotham in 1813. His knowledge of the
law was so tenuous that he was accustomed, apparently, to refer cases of
any difficulty, and thus among lawyers was known as 'the Common
Friend'.

[2] Perryn, Sir Richard (1723–1803). Baron of the Exchequer and
Sergeant-at-Law, 1776. He made his name in Chancery work. He
retired from the Bench in 1799 (see *D. N. B.*).

a deafness and dizziness in her head and great itching of her Nose. Mrs. Donne of Westcomb and a Clergyman (by name Dr. Kent) with her, spent an Hour here this morning. Dr. Kent was of Magdalen College, Oxford, a very neat, sensible Man, about 50 Years of Age.[1] Nancy's Sister spent the Afternoon here and was very low on seeing her Sister so ill—cried a good deal. To Robin Colley for another Ball of Twine p^d o. o. 6.

Aug. 25. . . . Nancy worse if any thing than Yesterday, did not get up till after 12 at Noon—Her head very bad. Nancy's Sister and Brother Willm dined and spent the Aft: here—as did Mr. Saml. Pounsett. Brother John and Wife spent the Afternoon with us.

Aug. 26. . . . Nancy something better this morning and continued so most part of the Day—able to play Cards in the Even'. Nancy had a long Letter from Mrs. Bodham this Evening all well in Norfolk—Weston Parsonage &c. At Quadrille this Evening I won o. 1. 6.

Aug. 27. . . . Nancy still better to day, but will not take the Bark. Mrs. Pounsett Senr, Betsy Guppey, and one Jones a kind of Steward to Sr Richd Hoare[2] dined &c. with us to day. Brother Heighes and Daughter Juliana spent part of the Aft: and supped with us—went home soon after Supper. Did not go to Church this Afternoon as our Dinner Time interfered with the Time of Service.

Aug. 28. . . . Nancy still better this morning, got up pretty early and took the Bark twice to day—In the

[1] The Rev. Ambrose Kent (1727–93), Vice-President of Magdalen, 1769; D.D. 1768; Rector of Berkeley, Somerset, 1770; Vicar of Sanderton, Bucks, 1771 (Foster's *Alumni Oxonienses*).

[2] See foot-note, p. 210, preceding.

Evening brave. Brother Heighes dined and spent the Afternoon with us. After Tea this Evening we got to Quadrille lost o. 1. o.

Aug. 29. . . . J[s] Clarke and Wife made us a morning Visit. Nancy much better all day and eat very hearty—She rec[d] a Letter this Aft: from her Brother Sam[1] at Rome. He is very well—but complains of poor living there. The Letter was dated 9 of this Month—only 20 Days ago.[1] Brother John and Wife and Mrs. Rich[d] Clarke dined and spent the Afternoon with us—We had for Dinner Ham and Fowls, Tripe, green Peas, a fine Hare and Rasberry Tart. At Quadrille this Evening lost o. 1. o. Nancy borrowed of me last Night for Cards o. 2. o.

Aug. 31. . . . Nancy breakfasted at Cole but did not dine or sleep here—My Brother John coming after her about Noon to carry her to Castle-Cary to spend a few days with his Wife &c. Mr. Pounsett went out a coursing this Morn' and brought home a fine Hare very soon.

Sep. 1. . . . This being the first Day of Partridge Shooting, Mr. Pounsett went out about 6 o'clock this Morn' and returned home before 11 o'clock with four brace of Birds. S[r] Rich[d] Hoares deputy Game-keeper Rich[d] Barley went out with him—Mr. Pounsett killed the most Birds. . . .

Sep. 2. . . . About 11 o'clock my Brother John came after my Sister and Daughter in Mrs. Clarkes Chair to go and dine with them. About $\frac{1}{2}$ past 11 I walked by myself to my Brother Johns at Cary and after staying some little Time there, myself and Brother took a Walk all over Castle-Cary—called at Mrs.

[1] To-day, perhaps, three days from Rome to Cole, Somerset : how long will it take in another 140 years' time ?

Melliars and she walked over her Garden with us called also on Mr. Thomas, Mr. Willm Ashfords, the Miss Russ's, Dr. Dewlings, Miss Lucas's, Mr. Francis's, old Mrs. Maby &c.—and at 2 returned to Mrs. R. Clarke's and there dined and spent the Afternoon with her, my Brother John and Wife, Nancy W, Mr. and Mrs. Pounsett and Daughter, and Mr. J^s Clarke and Wife. Brother Heighes and Daughter Juliana, and Mr. Thomas spent the Afternoon with us at Mrs. R. Clarkes. We spent a very agreeable Day at C. Cary—and had a very genteel as well as substantial Dinner, namely Ham and Fowls, a fine Piece of Salmon, Beef Stakes, 3 Partridges rosted and a large Apple Pye and Cream. Sister Pounsett returned to Cole on horseback and myself, Mr. Pounsett and little Jane walked it back and got home about 9 o'clock in the Evening. A Man called here this morning with Salmon, of whom I bought 6 Pound at 7^d per Pound p^d o. 3. 6.

Sep. 3. . . . Did not go to Church this morning at Pitcomb. My Sister Pounsett and Daughter went, but were both very wet returning from Church—it began to rain about 11 o'clock this Morn' and continued all day. To Jenny Pounsett and Betsy Guppy for learning the Collect for the day gave 1^s o^d.

Sep. 5. . . . I walked to Ansford this morning by myself, and made several Visits—viz., Sister Clarkes, Sister Whites, Brother Heighes, Robert Whites, Dr. Clarkes and my Brother Johns—I dined at Sister Whites with only her and her son Robert—In the Afternoon I walked down to the half Moon with my two Brothers, J^s Clarke, and Mr. Pounsett and there smoked a Pipe and stayed till after 8 this Evening—and then Mr. P. and self walked back to Cole. We had for Dinner at Sister Whites some Peas and Bacon, a Leg of Lamb rosted, and part of a cold Apple Pye. To Willm Coleman at Sister Whites gave 0. 1. 0. Paid at the half Moon for Brother H. and self 0. 2. 0. Sister Pounsett stayed at home being washing Week.

Sep. 10. . . . We did not go to Pitcomb Church this Afternoon—I read a Sermon to them at home of one Fishers. Mr. Robert White and Wife dined and spent the Aft: here.

Sep. 12. . . . After breakfast my Sister Pounsett, Daughter and self took a walk up to Sally Poyntings who had a Mother 87 Years of Age, but we did not see her, I left with her Daughter for her, to buy Tobacco for her 0. 1. 0. Sister White walked over from Ansford to Cole this Morning and she dined, supped and slept here. Nancy's Brother Willm spent the Aft: supped and spent the Evening with us. Sam: Pounsett supped &c. with us. At Quadrille this Evening with Sister White, and Mr. and Mrs. Pounsett—at 1^d per fish won 0. 0. 6.

Sep. 15. . . . A Miss Nancy Chiddock of Batcomb drank Tea with us this Afternoon at Mrs. Donnes— an agreeable well looking middle Aged Maid.

Sep. 19. . . . Gave Brother Heighes this morning a Pair of Spectacles with a very handsome Tortoise-shell Case and Silver mounted—they were formerly the Treasurers [1] I believe. Brother Heighes with his Son Willm and Daughter Juliana dined and spent the Afternoon with us. Robert White dined and spent the Afternoon here. At Quadrille this Evening lost 0. 2. 6.

Sep. 20. . . . After breakfast Nancy, myself, and little

---

[1] See vol. i, p. 20.

Jane Pounsett walked into Bruton and being Prayer
Day we went to Church and heard Prayers read by
one Roberts—We sat in a noble old Seat of the late
Lord Berkeley's. After Prayers we went to Hoddinots
Shop, there I left the Females and walked by myself
to Mr. Harry Martins and paid him for a Years
Interest of 650 Pound the Sum of 29. 10. 0. After
that I joined them again and went to another Shop,
Princes, and there bought a P^r of Gloves p^d 0. 1. 3.
For some Gingerbread also at another Place p^d 0. 0. 3.
In our Walk we met Mrs. Donne, Dr. Penny, Dr.
Paget, Capt: Goldsborough, Capt: Courtenays Wife
or Sister, a Miss Mogg a very pretty Girl—A Phaeton
with a Gentleman and 2 Ladies in it—returned home
to dinner. . . .

Sep. 21. . . . Nancy, Sister Pounsett and self went to
Ansford this Morn' on foot with Nancy's Brother Willm
who came over to breakfast and we all dined at Castle
Cary at R: Clarkes with her, my Brother John and
Wife and Juliana Woodforde and her Father—We
had for Dinner, a Neck of Mutton boiled and Capers
and a rost Shoulder of Pork alias mock Goose and
a nice plumb Pudding. J^s Clarke spent part of
the Afternoon with us. My Brother John indifferent
to day being merry last Night and very near being
killed last Night going home from Ansford Inn to
his own House on horseback and falling of—His face
is cut but little however. We all drank Tea this
Afternoon at Mr. John Burges with him, his Wife
and her Mother Mrs. Millward. Nancy and self
walked back to Cole in the Evening, Jenny rode.
Mr. Pounsett went of early this Morning a hunting
and he dined &c. at Mrs. Donnes at Westcomb.

Sep. 23. . . . Went out a coursing this morning with

Mr. Pounsett towards Godminster, killed a brace of Hares and a Rabbit. I parted with Mr. Pounsett before we returned, and walked by myself into Bruton and went to Mr. Harry Martins by appointment and borrowed of him 50. 0. 0. for which I gave him my Bond—so that I owe Mr. Martin now on Mortgage and Bond 700. 0. 0. For drawing the Bond &c. p^d him 0. 12. 6. I was very uneasy all the Morning long. Patty Davidge a Tenant of mine at Ansford called here this Afternoon and paid me only 1. 1. 0. out of 4. 4. 0.—I gave her out of that also 0. 2. 6. At Quadrille this Evening neither won or lost.

Sep. 26. . . . Walked out a coursing this morning with Mr. Pounsett. Had no Sport and came home wet thro' and thro'. Brother Heighes and Daughter Jully dined and spent the Afternoon with us—Nancy not well again and very low. Poor honest Jas: Perham dined and spent the Aft: here. Nancy's Sister talked so much to her this Evening about her parting with her soon—made her exceeding low. At Quadrille this Evening lost ab^t 0. 0. 6.

Sep. 27. . . . Nancy very ill all day and kept her bed till near 7 o'clock this Evening—eat nothing all day —vomited frequently when she was up—took some Rhubarb, but that did not stay on her Stomach any time—She after took a Powder which was left of James Clarkes and that settled very well and she went to bed directly after it. For Fish this Morning of a Man—I paid 0. 1. 11. To poor old John Tally the Fidler gave 0. 1. 0. Sister Clarke, Sister White and Wm Woodforde with Robert White dined and spent the Afternoon here. They all came very unexpectedly. Sister White with Nancy's Brother came from

Shepton Mallet in a Post-Chaise—and they took up my Sister Clarke.

Sep. 30. . . . Nancy a good deal better to day thank God for it. A Hare was found sitting near Lisbury and Mr. Pounsett and self went and saw her coursed —soon killed. To the Man that found her (Will Curtis) gave 0. 0. 6. After that Mr. Pounsett and self went out a coursing till Dinner time, coursed a brace and killed one. At Quadrille this Evening won 0. 2. 6. Out of which Nancy owes 0. 0. 6.

Oct. 1. . . . Nancy brave again this morning and all Day also. Did not go to Pitcomb Church this Morn' but read our Books at home—Mr. Pounsett went to Church. Brother Heighes and Daughter Juliana dined and spent the Afternoon with us—Brother John and Mrs. Robert White and Daughter Sophy spent the Aft: here. Mr. Willm Webb from London and his Sister a Mrs. Hussey of Wincaunton also spent the Afternoon here.

Oct. 3. . . . Brother Heighes spent the Morning here but went home before Dinner without any of us knowing it. We all drank Tea this Afternoon with old Mrs. Pounsett. Very busy in packing up things for our Journey to Morr'.

Oct. 4. I breakfasted and spent part of the Morning at Cole. Nancy breakfasted, and spent part of the Morn' at Cole. After taking Leave of our Cole Friends, Nancy and self set forth in a Chaise from Bruton for Weston. Gave to my God-Daughter Jenny Pounsett 0. 2. 6. To poor little Betsy Guppey, an Orphan gave 0. 2. 6. To Mr. Pounsett's three Servants gave 1. 1. 0. Mrs. Pounsett's Senr Maids Sybil and Sally gave 0. 5. 6. We called at Wincaunton to see Miss Tucker, but she was gone. From Win-

caunton we went on to Meer and there changed
Chaises and went on to Hindon—there we were
obliged to bait the Horses as we could get no Chaise
and then went on in the same Chaise for Sarum.
N.B. At the same Inn at Hindon was Mr. Pitt the
prime Minister, in the same Dilemma as we were
all the Horses being engaged—He was going to
Burton Pynsent.[1] We got to Salisbury to the White
Hart about 6 in the Evening and there we supped
and slept, a good Inn, kept by one Weeks—The Inn
almost full being the Salisbury Musick Meeting this
Week. For the Chaise to Meer and Driver p^d o. 14. 6.
For the Chaise to Salisbury and Driver p^d 1. 5. 6. To
Turnpikes and some refreshment for ourselves o. 3. 6.

Oct. 5. We breakfasted, dined, supped and slept again
in Sarum. We walked about Salisbury a great deal
to day, saw the Bishops Garden—and the Cathedral—
and also the Company returning from another Church
after the grand Musick.—All the Ladies highly dressed.
To the Girl that shewed us the Cathedral gave o. 1. o.
For a pair of Scissars and a Penknife to day p^d o. 5. o.
For 2 Places in the London Coach for to Morrow
Morn early—paid half price on taking the same
o. 18. o. Paid our Bill this Evening—which with
Serv^ts came 1. 15. o. Nancy also bought a neat p^r
of Scissars for o. 4. 6.

Oct. 6. We got up about 4 this morning and at 5 got
into the London Coach and set forth for London.

[1] Burton Pynsent was the estate in Somerset which had been left,
together with nearly £3,000 a year, to Pitt's father, Chatham, in 1765
by Sir William Pynsent, Bt., a country gentleman quite unknown to the
great Minister, but an admirer of him. It was here that Lady Chatham
died in 1803. William Pitt the younger, when the diarist and Nancy
saw him in this travelling dilemma, was in the third year of his seventeen
years' unbroken period of premiership, and was only just twenty-seven.

We had one Passenger from Salisbury with us an Officer in the Guards, an handsome young Man. At Stockbridge where we breakfasted we took up an other Gentleman, a sensible old Man. For our breakfast at Stockbridge p^d 0. 2. 0. We all dined together at Staines Bridge and there I paid for Nancy and self 0. 5. 0. For the other part of the Fare and extra Luggage 1. 4. 0. We got to London (I thank God safe and tolerably well) about 6 o'clock in the Evening, there parted with our Company, and we stayed at the Inn where the Salisbury Coach, Inns, at the Angel at the back of St. Clements in the Strand—a very good Inn, and there we supped and slept and had good beds. To the Coachmen to day gave 0. 4. 0.

Oct. 7. We breakfasted, supped and slept again at the Angel. We dined at Bettys Chop-House on beef Stakes p^d 0. 3. 6. In the Morning we walked down to St. James's Palace and saw the Guards relieved and heard the German Band. Nancy was much frightened, being hurried at the Soldiers marching quick, and we being in their way. They however soon passed us on our standing still. After Dinner we [went] in a Coach and called on Miss Pope in Newgate Street at a Mr. Whites—who is a Hatter—there stayed till near 9 in the Evening, and it being very wet, before I could get a Coach to go back to our Inn, after walking Miles, I was wet thro' and thro'— at last did get one and got back to our Inn between 9 and 10 o'clock. For the first Coach to Miss Popes p^d 0. 1. 6. For the last Coach being very wet gave 0. 2. 6. I was pretty much fatigued this Evening being wet &c. Nancy I thank God pretty well, but very sorry for me.

Oct. 8. We breakfasted, dined supped and slept again at the Angel. A Miss Stevenson, No. 33 Greek-Street-Soho, Nancy's London Millener breakfasted with us this Morning. I went by myself and saw the Guard relieved again this Morning at St. James's Palace. Miss Pope drank Tea with us in the Afternoon at the Angel—and after Tea we took Coach and went to Magdalen Chapel in St Georges Fields being Sunday and heard Prayers read and a Sermon. Very excellent singing at Magdalen Chapel.[1] The Women had a thin green Curtain before them all the Time, one of them played the Organ. Dr. Milne[2] preached from these Words ' And Nathan said unto David thou art the Man.'—Another Clergyman read

[1] The Magdalen House or Hospital, for the reformation and relief of penitent prostitutes, was founded in 1758, among the founders being Sir John Fielding, half-brother of the novelist. The hospital was at first in Prescot Street, Goodman's Fields, but was moved in 1772 to St. George's Fields—the south end of Blackfriars Road—a part which was regarded then as relatively rural. In 1863 it was again removed to Streatham, where accommodation was subsequently provided for 190 inmates (see Wheatley and Cunningham's *London Past and Present*, vol. ii, p. 454).

[2] Doubtless this was the Rev. Colin Milne, LL.D. (1743 ?–1815), an Aberdonian who began his career as a tutor in the Duke of Northumberland's family, took orders, and became a notable preacher. He was evening preacher to the City of London Lying-in Hospital, and became Rector of North Chapel, near Petworth, Sussex. He resided, however, at Deptford, where he was a lecturer to the Old and New Church. There, in 1783, he founded the Kent Dispensary, now the Miller Hospital, Greenwich. He was also a botanist, and published several botanical works (see *D. N. B.*).

The famous, though unfortunate Dr. Dodd (see foot-note, vol. i, p. 199) was at one time chaplain to Magdalen House, and caused fashionable congregations to weep through his eloquence. Dr. Milne's text (2 Sam. xii. 7) on this particular occasion was also certainly sufficiently striking in the circumstances.

Prayers—We had a first Seat. Gave towards the Charity at going in o. 3. o. We kept the Hackney Coach all the time in waiting for us, and after Divine Service we returned in it to the Angel, and Miss Pope supped and spent the Evening with us—For the Coach to the Magdalen Chapel and back again p^d o. 4. 6. Andrew Russ spent the Evening with us. I hired a Coach and carried Miss Pope home in it and went with her—For the Coach p^d o. 2. o.

Oct. 9. We breakfasted, dined, supped and slept again at the Angel. Nancy very ill all day, and vomited much and often. Pray God send her better—and safe to Weston. I went and saw the Guards relieved again this Morn' at St James's Palace—Horse and Foot. After that returned home to Nancy stayed a little Time with her, then walked into Bishopsgate Street, to the black Bull, and there took 2 Places in the Norwich Expedition Coach which carries 4 Passengers, and sets of from London at 9 to Mor: Night. Paid there, for our half Fare or rather part 1. 1. o. To Books &c. this morning p^d o. 2. o. Andrew Russ supped and spent the Evening with us.

Oct. 10. We breakfasted dined and spent the Afternoon at the Angel—After breakfast we took a Coach and went to Charlesworths, Haberdasher in great Russel Street, Covent Garden, and there Nancy bought divers things—I lent her the same 1. 1. o. For the Coach to Russel Street paid o. 1. o. From thence we walked to Southampton Street very near the last Place, and there at a very good Linen-Drapers Shop, kept by a Mr. Jeremy, a very civil Man, bought some Table Linnen, Muslin, a piece of Holland, Cravats &c. paid there 13. 6. o. At the Angel this Afternoon paid my Bill 3. 4. 5. To the

Servants at the Inn very civil People gave o. 12. 6. In the Evening about 6 o'clock we took a Coach and our Baggage with us to the Bull in Bishopsgate Street —a very good Inn—and there we drank Tea—For the Coach to the Bull p^d o. 1. 6. For Tea &c. at the Bull p^d o. 1. 9. About 9 we got into the Expedition Coach and sat of for Norwich—To the Porter gave o. o. 6. We had 2 very civil Men with us, Passengers. It was a very pleasant warm Moon light Night.

Oct. 11. After travelling all Night (thank God safe and well) We got to Newmarket to breakfast, and there stayed half an Hour—paid for our breakfasts o. 2. o. To the Coachman and Guard gave o. 3. o. Whilst we were at Newmarket and changing Coaches and Luggage, found that a small red Trunk of my Nieces was left behind in London, in which were all her principal Matters—It vexed her at first very much—but on my assuring her that I saw it safely lodged in the Warehouse, she was more composed. I would not pay the remaining part of our fare or for our Luggage till the Trunk was forthcoming. We changed Horses at Thetford and there parted with our 2 Men Passengers that came with us from London. They were very civil obliging People—We then went on to Norwich by ourselves in the Coach. Got to Norwich about 2 o'clock to the Maids Head and there dined and spent the Afternoon. To the Coachmen from Newmarket gave o. 2. o. For our Dinner &c. at the Maids Head p^d &c. o. 4. o. In the Evening went in a Hackney Coach both of us and our Luggage to the Kings Head our old Inn, and there drank Tea supped and slept. For the Coach to the Kings Head p^d o. 1. o. Nancy quite ill after she got to the Kings Head.

Oct. 12. We breakfasted, dined and slept again at the Kings Head. Mr. Priest called on us this Morning at the Kings Head. We drank Tea, supped and spent the Evening at Mr. Priests, with him, his Wife and their Son John. Mr. Barker and his Wife (a very pretty and agreeable Woman) drank Tea with us this Afternoon at Mr. Priests. After Tea we played a Pool at Quadrille won 0. 2. 6. We got back to our Inn soon after 10 this Evening. Made all the enquiry I could and sent the same to London. Nancy but indifferent and thinking too much on her Trunk, as no Trunk was brought by either of the Mail Coaches.

Oct. 13. We breakfasted at the Kings Head at Norwich and about 12 set of for Weston Parsonage in a Post-Chaise of Ravens at the Kings Head and (I thank God) about 2 o'clock we got safe and tolerably well to the old Parsonage House at Weston, found all my Servants tolerably well and things tidily—Paid and gave at the Kings Head for Chaise &c. 1. 7. 6. To my Barber and his Boy at Norwich gave 0. 1. 6. Paid at Beales for Fish now and time back 0. 5. 0. At Bakers for 2 small powder Machines 0. 1. 0. Lent to Nancy to buy some Flannel 1. 1. 0. To the Norwich Driver besides a Dinner gave 0. 1. 6. We dined, supped and slept at our old House again. My Niece seemed something better on being at home.

Oct. 14. We breakfasted, dined, supped and slept again at home. Mr. and Mrs. Custance very kindly called on us this Morn' as did Mr. and Mrs. Jeanes from Lenewade Bridge, they all stayed with us about an Hour, and then Mr. and Mrs. Jeanes went with Mr. and Mrs. Custance in their Coach to Lenewade Bridge—Mr. and Mrs. Jeanes walked to my House. Mr. Thorne (being sent for to see Nancy) came here

this Morn'. I sent my Man Ben early after Mr.
Thorne, and likewise to go round to Mr. Bodhams,
Mr. Smiths, Mr. Du Quesnes, Mr. Lanes (my Curate
in my Absence) who lives at Hingham, and at Mrs.
Micklethwaites, to enquire after them all. Nancy
something better to day, but far from well.

Oct. 15. . . . Mr. and Mrs. Townshend, and Mrs.
Micklethwaite sent to enquire after us this Morning
with Compts. I read Prayers, Preached, and christened 2 Children this Afternoon at Weston Church
by Name, Howard and John. Mr. and Mrs. Custance
both at Church this Afternoon. Gave Mr. Dades
Man — my Greyhounds having killed a Lamb belonging to him o. 2. 6.

Oct. 16. . . . After breakfast I took a ride to Weston
House, spent an Hour there with Mrs. Custance and
her Children—then went to Lenewade Bridge and
paid my respects to Mr. and Mrs. Jeanes, they were
very glad to see me. Returned home to dinner, in
my return met Mrs. Custance in her Coach and
Nancy with her going to Mrs. Micklethwaites to
make a morning Visit—they returned soon after to
my House, Mrs. Custance got out of her Carriage
and stayed a little time with us. Mr. Du Quesne
called on us about 2 o'clock, during the time that
Mrs. Custance was with us and he stayed, and dined,
and spent the Afternoon with us.

Oct. 17. . . . Mr. Matthew Lane of Hingham (my
Curate at Weston during my Absence) came here
about 2 o'clock by appointment, and he dined and
spent the Afternoon with us—a very good natured
Man. I paid him for serving my Church 16 Weeks
9. 4. 6. He owes me out of a ten Note I gave o. 15. 6.
Mr. Custance sent us a Note this Aft: to meet

Mr. and Mrs. Jeanes at Weston House on Friday next.

Oct. 19. . . . Mr. Priest of Reepham called on us this Morning in his Way to Mr. Du Quesnes, and stayed with us half an Hour. Soon after Mr. Priest left us the Honble Charles Townshend made us a morning Visit of about an Hour. About 3 o'clock Mr. Jeanes returned from Norwich to my House and dined and spent the Afternoon with us. We had for Dinner Ham and Fowls, a rost Pigg, and some Rasbery Puffs. Mr. and Mrs. Jeanes returned to Lenewade Bridge before Tea this Aft:—Mrs. Jeanes went in my little Cart. N.B. Mr. Townshend wanted us to fix a Day for our dining with him, but there being no Moon, we could not.

Oct. 23. . . . Mrs. Custance spent most of the Morning with us. Mr. Smith of Mattishall made us a Morning Visit—he brought us a brace of Partridges. Dr. Thorne called to see Nancy but did not stay long. He came whilst Mr. Smith was here, but did not come into the same Room, there being rather a Coolness between Mr. Smith and Mr. Thorne.

Oct. 24. . . . Sent Mr. Custance this Morn' a Coomb of Apples, fine Beefans, 3 Bushels, a present from me. Very busy all the Morning in gathering our Apples. Nancy very busy in making a black Silk Hat for Mrs. Custance, all this Day and best part of Yesterday. Nancy was not quite so well again to day.

Oct. 25. . . . I christened a Child this Morning at my House of Willm Large's by name—Mary. Mr. Thorne and his eldest Daughter called here this Morn'. Just as they were gone Mrs. Custance came to us and took Nancy out an Airing with her, returned about 2 o'clock, and Mrs. Custance stayed and dined

with us. Whilst Mrs. Custance and Nancy were out
an Airing Mr. and Mrs. Bodham of Mattishall called
here and spent an Hour at Weston Parsonage—
Mrs. Custance and my Niece returned soon after
Mr. and Mrs. Bodham came here, Mr. and Mrs.
Bodham never in Company with Mrs. Custance
before—They seemed to like each other. Mr. Jeanes
called whilst the above Company were with us—but
he could not unlight. We had for Dinner to day
some fryed Herrings, a boiled Leg of Mutton and
Capers, a rost Duck, Apple Pudding and some Rasberry Puffs. To 2 Piggs that Ben sold for me rec^d
1. 14. 0. Of Briton for 2 smaller Piggs rec^d 0. 10. 0.
Oct. 28. . . . Rec^d a Letter this Evening from an old
School-Fellow no less than Mr. Thos Elbridge Rooke
who is at present at a Mr. Haymans Sadler-Street
Wells, Somersett—under great distress, having lost
both Feet, all his Family Friends dead, and humbly
hoping that I would contribute something to his
relief—What Changes have happened to that Family
—Whilst his Father Mr. Rooke of Somerton was
alive things had every appearance of success, but his
untoward Son the Writer of the above Letter to me
who spent every thing he had and what his Father
left him after he died, which was almost of a broken
heart on seeing his Son going on so very badly. In
my next Letter to my Sister Pounsett shall desire
her to make enquiry after him, and to send him
something for me—tho' little is in my Power to do,
having many very near Relations that are in want.
Nov. 2. . . . To a poor dumb Man of Drayton who carries
about the Country some odd things to sell—for same
p^d 0. 0. 6. Mr. Du Quesne called here this Morning,
whilst he was here, Mrs. Custance came to us, and

took Nancy out an airing with her in the Coach for an Hour. After the above were gone, Mr. Thorne called to see Nancy. Nancy's Mantua Maker of Reepham by name Batchelor called also here about 2 o'clock, brought her 2 new Gowns. Sent Ben with my Cart to Tuddenham after 500 Bricks.

Nov. 3. . . . To J_o^n Pegg $\frac{1}{2}$ Years Land Tax, ditto Servants Tax—ditto House Tax—ditto Window Tax —ditto Horse Tax in all paid him 11. 0. 0.[1] Sent Mr. and Mrs. Jeanes this Morning a large Sack of Apples (Beefans) a Couple of Pigeons and a very fine fat Duck ready for the Spit—to them at their Parsonage at Witchingham, they being very lately got in there with almost every inconvenience, they were highly pleased with the above. Had my brewing Copper new set by Mr. Hardy.

Nov. 7. . . . Lent Nancy for Card Mony this Morn'

---

[1] The reader should note that Parson Woodforde's taxes have gone up 20 per cent. since 1779 (see vol. i, p. 270, entry for November 30, 1779). This was, of course, due to the American War and the drastic increase in taxation which Pitt was compelled to impose in 1784 and 1785 to meet the burden (see foot-note on p. 208, preceding, for some of these taxes). Horace Walpole, writing to Sir Horace Mann on July 8, 1784, expressed himself on this subject as follows: ' There is much noise about a variety of new taxes, yet only a few have a right to complain of them. The majority of the nation persisted in approving and calling for the American War, and ought to swallow the heavy consequences in silence. Instead of our colonies and trade, we have a debt of two hundred and fourscore millions ! Half of that enormous burthen our *wise* country-gentlemen have acquired, instead of an alleviation of the land-tax, which they were such boobies as to expect from the prosecution of the war ! Posterity will perhaps discover what his own age would not see, that my father's motto, *Quieta non movere*, was a golden sentence. . . .' (Walpole's *Letters*, vol. xiii, pp. 166–7.) But, alas, posterity, internationally, had, as late as 1914, made no such discovery ; on the contrary the European catastrophe, 1914–18, has increased our own debt alone to £7,646,000,000.

o. 10. 6. We dined and spent the Afternoon at Honingham Hall at the Honble Charles Townshends Esq. with him, his Wife, Mrs. Cornwallis, Widow of the late Abp: of Canterbury being Sister to Mr. Custance, [a mistake, he means sister to Mr. Townshend] Mr. Du Quesne, Mr. and Mrs. Custance, Mrs. Collier Senr and my Niece. Nancy went in Mr. Custances Coach, myself on horseback. We did not dine till after 4 o'clock, and then had for Dinner, some fine Soals, Soup, a Saddle of Mutton rosted, Tongue and boiled Turkey, some Patties and some Stakes—2nd Course a Pheasant, Apple Pye, a fine Hare, amulet, Blamange, Maccaroni, and some Eggs on Something. No Desert whatever after Dinner— Wines Port, Cherry, Madeira, and Champaigne. After Tea and Coffee we got to Cards at Cribbage 2 Tables—at which I won at 3^d—o. 2. o. We returned home as we went about 9 o'clock. We had a pleasanter and warmer ride back than as we went, Briton went with me on horseback. Mr. and Mrs. Townshend very chatty and agreeable.

Nov. 9. . . . Rec^d a Note from Mr. Custance &c. this morning, that they would drink Tea with us in the Afternoon. Mr. and Mrs. Custance with Mrs. Collyer drank Coffee and Tea with us this Afternoon and stayed till about 9 o'clock. At Cards this Evening lost o. 5. o. Nancy also lost at Loo confined to 15 pence o. 2. o. Poor Mrs. Collyer coming in at my Kitchen Door an old Nail caught hold of her Apron, a very fine Muslin one with a deal of work on it, and rent it in a most shocking manner indeed. We were all very much concerned about it.

Nov. 10. . . . Went out a Coursing this morning for an Hour or so, but saw no Hare. We dined and spent the Afternoon and part of the Evening at Weston House till after 9 o'clock with Mr. and Mrs. Custance, Mrs. Collyer Senr and a Mr. Chamberlain who is a Roman Catholick Priest and lives with Sr Wm Jernegan and Family and what is most remarkable in him is, that he was bred up a Protestant, was at the University of Cambridge, had Preferment in the Church of England to the Value of £800 per Annum all of which he has lately given up, renounced the Protestant Religion, and has been made a Monk. A very good kind of Man he appears to be and very sensible—has been in France &c. He is now Chaplain to Sr Wm Jernegan, that Family being of the Romish Persuasion. After Coffee and Tea, Mrs. Custance, Mrs. Collyer, Nancy and myself got to Cribbage at wch won 0. 2. 0. Nancy lost all that was lost being 0. 5. 0. Mr. Custance and Mr. Chamberlain did not play. It being Friday Mr. Chamberlain eat no Meat only some Fish and some Rice Pudding. Mr. Chamberlain slept at Weston House, the Evening being wet and dark—We returned as we went in Mr. Custances Coach. It made it rather late with us before we got home as we waited some time for Moonlight. It was near 12 before we got up stairs to night.

Nov. 18. . . . Sent Briton this morning early in my little Cart after News, Books &c. from Norwich— and he returned home about 2 o'clock this Aft: with the same. Nancy sent a Letter by him to her Aunt John Woodforde. Received a Letter by Briton from my Sister Pounsett who informs us that Mrs. Sam: Burge was brought to bed and died the Day after—and the Child soon after. And that Mrs. J^s Clarke has got a Daughter and that the Doctor was not a little proud of it.

Nov. 22. . . . Nancy very well when she came down Stairs this Morning, but very soon after taken very ill in an Ague, vomited very much, was laid on the bed most of the Morn', could not get up to dinner— but rather better about 5 o'clock this Afternoon and came down Stairs and was much better after Tea. I buried this Afternoon about 4 o'clock, John Plummer an Infant aged only 5 Weeks. I knew nothing of burying the above Infant till 3 o'clock this Afternoon, then on hearing the Church Bell, I sent to Church to enquire the reason, and word was brought me, that there was a Child then at the Church Gate for Interment—It being my Dinner Time, I went as soon as ever I had finished my Dinner—Some Mistake of my old Clerk or the Father of the Child —in not acquainting me.

Nov. 23. . . . Went out a coursing this Morning till dinner time, found no Hare—but had good Sport with a Squirrel which my Dogs killed after some time. Nancy brave to day to what she was Yesterday.

Nov. 29. . . . Nancy very well again to day thank God for it. Rec^d an Answer this morning early to my Note to Mr. and Mrs. Custance, informing us that they would with great pleasure wait on us Saturday next. Soon after breakfast, being a fine Morning, I took a ride to Mr. Du Quesnes found him at home hearty and well, stayed with him about half an Hour, then went on to Mattishall to Mr. Bodham's stayed with Mr. Bodham about an Hour, found him hearty and well, did not see Mrs. Bodham, as she was gone to see my Niece and Miss Johnson with her.[1] Then

[1] Miss Johnson was Catherine Johnson (1767–1820), sister of Cowper's correspondent, cousin and devoted friend, ' Johnny of Norfolk' (see foot-note, p. 234, preceding).

called at Mr. Smiths but he was gone out with his Dogs—I left a Note for him. From thence returned to Dinner and on my return met Mrs. Bodham and her Niece Miss Johnson in their Carriage, had a little Chat with them and but a little, as some Rain fell. I returned home before 3 o'clock, found Nancy quite pleased, having had Mrs. Bodham and Miss Johnson with her for 2 Hours this Morn'. Mr. Thorne spent an Hour also at my House this Morning, during the time that Mrs. Bodham was there. Sent another Note this evening to Mr. Custance to acquaint him (by Mr. Du Quesnes desire) that he could not wait on them Friday next—as Mr. and Mrs. Chamber from Norwich were to be at Honingham Hall at Mr. Townshend's on that Day.

Dec. 3. . . . Mr. Smith breakfasted with us and soon after he mounted his Horse and went home for Mattishall. Mr. Smith had nothing but a bason of Milk for breakfast. I read Prayers and Preached this Morning at Weston C[hurch]. Mr. and Mrs. Custance with Mrs. Collyer at Church. I churched a Woman this Morn for which rec^d 0. 0. 6.

Dec. 5. . . . This being my Day for the Tithe Audit the following Farmers dined and spent the Afternoon and Evening till after 10 o'clock at Night at my House —namely, Peachman, Howlett, Girling, Andrews, Bidewell, Ringgar, J^n_o Pegg, J^s Pegg, Mann's Nephew J^n_o Rose, Cary, Norton, Baker, Forster, Dade, Silvey, Reynolds, J^n_o Heavers, Willm Leggatt Senr (and Willm Leggatt Junr) and Widow Pratts Man Ross Beane, and Robt Rising. They were all pleased and went away in good Spirits.[1] J^n_o Buck paid me his Tithe but did not

[1] The Essex farmers in Cowper's excellently amusing poem, *The Yearly Distress*, written a little before this date for the shy Rev. William

dine with us. Mr. Heming came in the Afternoon and spent the Afternoon and Evening with us. Nancy dined in the Study to day by herself. We had for Dinner, Salt Fish, a Leg of Mutton boiled and Capers, boiled and rost Beef and plenty of plumb and plain Puddings—Punch, Wine and Strong Beer after Dinner. There was six Bottles of Rum made into Punch, 3 Bowls, 2 Bottles of Rum in each. There was seven Bottles of Wine—great Quantities of strong Beer—9 Lemons —1 P^d and $\frac{1}{2}$ of Sugar and half a Pound of ·Tobacco made use of. Rec^d in all to day about 260. 0. 0. Mr. Dade paid me almost all that was due to me for last Year and this present Year. It was after 1 o'clock before we got to bed to night. Rec^d of Ben for a Pigg that he sold for me to one Lane about 3 Quarters old 0. 11. 6.

Unwin—who found these tithing time dinners very trying—were apparently less jovial than Parson Woodforde's Norfolk neighbours ·

. . .

The punch goes round, and they are dull
  And lumpish still as ever ;
Like barrels with their bellies full,
  They only weigh the heavier.

At length the busy time begins,
  ' Come, neighbours, we must wag.'—
The money chinks, down drop their chins,
  Each lugging out his bag.

One talks of mildew and of frost,
  And one of storms of hail,
And one of pigs that he has lost ﹍
  By maggots at the tail.

Quoth one, ' A rarer man than you
  In pulpit none shall hear ;
But yet methinks, to tell you true,
  You sell it plaguy dear.'

. . . .

Dec. 7. . . . Not at all well all this Day—worse at Night. Took some Camphire and Nitre going to bed. Nancy's Pigg was killed this Morning and a nice, fine, fat White Pigg it is. It is to be weighed to Morrow Morning. We are to make some Somersett black Puddings to Morrow, if we can by our Receipt from thence.

Dec. 8. . . . John Page, Mr. Pages Son, came to me this morning and settled his Fathers Tithe Account with me for last Year—and paid me for the same 15. 12. 0. He still stands indebted to me for Turnips his Father had last Year of me 2. 5. 0. which I doubt much of getting the whole—His Son offered me half, but I would not take it. Nancy very busy indeed in making black Pudding all the whole Morning, and very good indeed it turned out when done—we had some for Dinner. Sent Briton this Morning with a Basket of Potatoes which would hold a Bushell, with several fine Savoy Cabbages, to Mr. Jeanes of Witchingham. Briton did not return so soon as intended. Nancy's Pigg weighed in the whole 14 Stone but 3 P^d which at 3/6 Pr Stone which I am to give her (after my fatting the same with Peas at 15/0 Per Coomb which I paid Mr. Dade for, and which Pigg had eat near two Coomb) amounts to 2. 9. 0. Nancy finished a long Letter to night to her Sister which Ben is to carry to Norwich to Morrow early. Betty Dades Father called here in the Morning but did not stay long—I asked him to drink and told Betty to draw some but he would not let her draw him any after my back was turned. Bettys Father I believe behaved rather unkind to her, as she cried soon after his leaving her.

Dec. 10. . . . I read Prayers and Preached this Afternoon at Weston C[hurch], Mr. and Mrs. Custance at Church and a large Congregation besides at Church being fine, cheerful Weather. Nancy had two Letters from Mrs. Davy this Afternoon done up in a parcel, and with the same a little Lump of something, but what, I know not—as Nancy never mentioned a word of what it was, nor of a single word in either of the Letters—I care not for it, but shall take care to be as private myself in matters.

Dec. 11. . . . Nancy quite bluff and rather pert this morning. I privately named a spurious Child of one Mary Parker's this morning by name John. The Fathers Name I could not get intelligence of. The Wind was very high most part of last Night. Sent Mrs. Custance this Morning a large Baskett of my Potatoes, fresh dug, as she praised them so much. To Ben this Evening for things from Norwich &c. p^d 10. 7. Gave him besides for my Tithe Frolick 1. 0. To Briton for divers things p^d 6. 0. Gave him besides for my Tithe Frolick 2. 6. To Betty for divers things p^d 6. 9. Gave her besides for my Tithe Frolick 2. 6. Gave to Nanny my Cook, for my Tithe Frolick 2. 6. Gave to my Boy, Jack, for my Tithe Frolick, 1. 0.

Dec. 13. . . . After breakfast, shaved and dressed, and mounted my Mare and went to Mr. Jeanes at Witchingham found both him and Wife at home—spent a full Hour with them and returned home to Dinner. In my Way to Witchingham near Mr. Jeanes we met a large Hare, and the Hounds not very far behind her of Mr. Branthwaites—I pushed on my Mare and by good Luck avoided them tho' within sound of them—Soon after I was at Mr. Jeanes's, Mr. Custance called there and stayed there as long as I stayed and

then we went together from Mr. Jeanes for Weston—
Mr. Custance asked Me to dine at Weston House
—but I declined. Called at my Millers Mr. Forsters
and paid him a Bill for flour the last Year of 4. 14. 6.
Called also at Cantrells and paid him a Bill for Wine,
Porter &c. for the last Year of 9. 14. 0.

Dec. 14. . . . Mr. Du Quesne gave us a Call this morning in his Way to Mr. Priests of Reepham. Very
high Wind almost all last Night—it alarmed most of
us—a Brick was blown down from the Kitchen
Chimney into Britons Chamber—also some Tiles
moved from the old part of the House but (I thank
God) no other Damage done. Mr. Du Quesnes
Man, James, called here in the Evening in his return
from Reepham, with compts from his Master, with
a present of a brace of Fish, called Eel-Pouts, a small
Fish the Size of a very small Whiting, and which he
had sent to him from Ely.

Dec. 18. . . . Busy all the Morning in assisting Briton
in brewing.

Dec. 19. . . . Henry Baker, my Butcher, called here
this Morning by my desire, and I paid him a Bill for
Meat for the last Year, the sum of 33. 2. 6. for which
I took a stamp Receipt in full. Mr. Custance made
us a morning Visit on foot and stayed with us a full
Hour—during his being with us, Mr. and Mrs.
Jeanes came to our House and they dined, supped
and slept here by appointment. Mrs. Jeanes does
not look by far so well as she did. Has been much
hurried by change of Servants &c. We gave them
for Dinner some Soup, a boiled Neck of Pork, a fine
rost Turkey, Apple Pye and Puffs. After Coffee and
Tea we got to Cribbage lost 0. 1. 0. We did not get
to bed to Night till 12 o'clock. Mr. and Mrs. Jeanes

slept in Nancys Room and Nancy slept over my Bed Chamber. Mr. Jeanes's Servant Lad George England about 15 Years of Age dined supped and slept here. Mr. Jeanes's one Horse Chaise was put into my Barn. Two of Mr. Jeanes's Horses also were with my Horses all Night. Mr. Jeanes's Servant Lad G. England seems fonder of Kitchen Fire than any Work.

Dec. 21. . . . This being St Thomas Day, I gave to the poor of my Parish that came to my House at 6^d each 1. 7. 0.

Dec. 23. . . . Walked out a coursing this morning till Dinner time, had Ben and Jack with me, we had two fine Courses indeed, lost one of the Hares but the Dogs caught the other which we brought home. There being a good deal of Snow on the Ground we had fine sport in tracing after the Hares. I was rather tired when I got home being out 4 Hours. . . .

Dec. 25. . . . I read Prayers and administered the H: Sacrament this morning at Weston Church—Mr. and Mrs. Custance at Church and at the Holy Sacrament. There were 30 Communicants at the Altar. I gave for an Offering at the Altar 0. 2. 6. Mr. and Mrs. Custance gave the same as I did. It being Christmas Day, I had the following old Men dine at my House on rost Beef and plumb Pudding, and after Dinner half a Pint of strong Beer to each and a shilling to each to carry home to their Wives,—Richd Buck, Thos Cushing, Thos Cary, Thos Carr, Nathaniel Heavers, John Buckman, and my Clerk J^s Smith. Just as I returned from Church this Morning, my fingers almost froze with cold, had a Note to answer from one of Mr. Smiths to me, with an invitation to his house at Mattishall on Thursday next, but I sent him in answer back, that the Weather being so severe at present, that we could not accept the same. Nancy also had a Note from Mrs. Bodham on the same to South-Green, but she also excused herself.

Dec. 26. We breakfasted, dined, &c. &c. again at home. To the Weston Ringgers, their annual Gift of 0. 2. 6. To my Malsters Man a Christmas Gift gave 0. 1. 0. To my Blacksmiths Son a Christmas Gift 0. 0. 6. Mr. Girling, Mr. Custances Steward, called here this Afternoon and paid me Mr. Custances Composition for Land in hand, for Tithe the Sum of 13. 12. 6. Very sharp Frost indeed last Night and this Morning it froze the Water in my Bason this Morning that I wash in, quite over, in half an Hour after it had been brought up Stairs.

Dec. 29. . . . Had another Tub of Gin and another of the best Coniac Brandy brought me this Evening ab^t 9. We heard a thump at the front Door about that time, but did not know what it was, till I went out and found the 2 Tubs—but nobody there.[1]

Dec. 30. We breakfasted, dined, &c. &c. again at home. Sent Briton with my little Cart to Norwich after News &c. Sent Ben to Mattishall with a Note from

---

[1] Where are the swains, who, daily labour done,
With rural games play'd down the setting sun ;

. . .

Where now are these ?—Beneath yon cliff they stand,
To show the freighted pinnace where to land ;
To load the ready steed with guilty haste,
To fly in terror o'er the pathless waste,
Or, when detected, in their straggling course,
To foil their foes by cunning or by force ;
Or yielding part (which equal knaves demand),
To gain a lawless passport through the land.

So Crabbe describes the country smuggler in his early poem *The Village*, published three years before this date, in 1783.

Nancy to Mrs. Bodham, to let them know that we would spend a few Days with them next Week, if agreeable—the Weather being now much more mild than before. They both returned by Dinner time. Mr. and Mrs. Bodham will be glad to see us. Had a Letter from Dr. Bathurst this Evening.

Dec. 31. We breakfasted, dined &c. &c. again at home. I read Prayers and Preached this Morn' at Weston C[hurch]. Neither Mr. or Mrs. Custance at Church this Morn'. They sent us a wild Duck this Morning. This being the last Day of the Year, we sat up this Night till after 12 o'clock—then drank Health and happy New Year to all our Somersett Friends &c. and then went for Bedfordshire alias to bed.

— Anno Domini 1787 —

Jan. 1. We breakfasted, and spent part of the Morn' at home. To Charles Cary, Shoemaker, pd. a Bill of 0. 10. 0. About Noon set of for Norwich and Briton with me. Left my Niece at home, but Mrs. Bodham is to come after her this Day to spend some Days with her at Mattishall. I promised to meet her at Mr. Bodhams on Wednesday. We got to Norwich about 2 o'clock—On the road Mr. Du Quesne overtook me—We both dined and spent the Afternoon at Mr. Priests with him, his Wife and 2 Sons and Mr. Priest of Reepham.—I also drank Tea there this Evening with the above and young Wilkins. Mr. Du Quesne and Mr. Priest of Reepham supped and slept there. I went to the Theatre this Evening by myself, went in at the 3rd Act for which paid half price 0. 1. 6. Gave Briton to go to the Play 0. 1. 0. The Play was Richd. the 3rd and Harle-

1787

quin Nabob, Farce. Did not come from the Theatre
till after 10 o'clock, supped and slept at the Kings Head.
Jan. 2. Breakfasted, dined, supped and slept at the
Kings Head. Spent most of this Day in walking
about Town and paying my Annual Bills. To Rum
and Water at the Swan and other things pd. 0. 1. 3.
Sent a Letter this Morning to Dr. Bathhurst at
Oxon in answer to his last and in it I inclosed two
bank Notes of Norwich of the Value of 15. 5. 0.
Jan. 3. I breakfasted and spent most the Morn' at
Norwich. At one o'clock after paying my Bill at the
Inn set forth for Mr. Bodhams at Mattishall, got
there about 3 o'clock and there dined, supped and
slept. Briton and my Horses also at Mattishall.
Mr. and Mrs. Bodham, Miss Kitty Johnson, my
Niece and Mr. Smith at Dinner, and Supper to Day.
At Quadrille this Evening won 0. 0. 6. Paid the
following Bills whilst at Norwich. Qualification for
killing Game, 2. 3. 0. Pension to College, 1. 12. 0.
Incurations and Pascals for 2 Years, 0. 19. 3. Sub-
scription to Clergymens Widows, 1. 1. 0. Mr. Smith
Mercer, 7. 16. 6. Mrs. Garland, Taylor, 5. 14. 0.
Mr. Whistler, Painter, 6. 0. 0. Mr. Lock, Coal
Merchant, 12. 18. 6. Mr. Forster, for College Land,
16. 0. 0. Mr. Browne, Barber, 2. 2. 0. Mr. Priest,
Wine Merchant, 6. 12. 0. Mrs. Brewster, for Tea,
&c., 3. 10. 6. Ditto for Miss Woodforde, 3. 6. Mr.
Jagger, for a Picture Frame, 0. 15. 6. Mr. Scott,
Breeches Maker, 1. 17. 0. Mr. Buckle, Ironmonger,
2. 12. 0. Mr. Willmott, Hatter, 0. 19. 0. Mr.
Manning, Brazier, 1. 1. 0. Mr. Rump, Grocer,
0. 18. 6. At the Kings Head, paid and gave, 1. 0. 0.
At Mrs. Brewster[s] Shop, gave 0. 3. 6. At Mr.
Lockes, Clerk gave 0. 1. 0. To my Barbers Boy,

Tranch—gave 0. 2. 0. To Mr. Studwell, China Man pd. 0. 5. 0.

Jan. 6. I breakfasted, dined, supped and slept again at home. As soon as I had breakfasted I went out with my Greyhounds to try to kill a Hare for Mr. Bodham whose Carriage would be here by 1 o'clock. Two were coursed and luckily we killed the last just before the Carriage came—had not been home 10 minutes before Mrs. Bodham, Miss Johnson, and my Niece came to my House—they left Nancy with me, stayed about a Quarter of Hour and then they went back, carrying the Hare with them. Nancy dined, supped and slept at home—she is much lamer than when she went to Mattishall.

Jan. 9. . . . Bad day for drying Linnen, N.B. washing Week. At Cribbage this Evening with Nancy lost 0. 0. 6. Nancy very indifferent with her lameness.

Jan. 10. . . . Nancy a very small matter better in her left Knee. To Ben, this Morning for things pd. 3. 4. 3. To Ben, also for a Years Wages—pd. him 10. 0. 0. To Betty, for things pd. 0. 5. 8½. To Betty, also for a Years Wages—pd. her 5. 5. 0. To Briton, for things pd. 0. 18. 1. To Briton, also for a Years Wages—pd. him 8. 0. 0. Briton made me uneasy being discontented. To Nanny, for a Years Wages—pd. her 5. 5. 0. Of Nanny, having lent her, recd. 1. 1. 0. To Jack, for a Years Wages pd. him 1. 1. 0. At Cribbage this Evening with Nancy neither won or lost.

Jan. 16. . . . Paid to Nancy this Morn' her Annual pay 10. 0. 0. To ditto also for a fat Pigg 2. 9. 0. Recd. of ditto for divers things pd. for her 8. 9. 6. To a Man for some Cod Fish and Oysters pd. 0. 5. 1. At Cribbage this Evening with Nancy—won 0. 0. 6.

Jan. 18. . . . Nancy very indifferent indeed all day—worse. Sent Briton to Reepham on foot this Morning with my Watch to be mended, the main Spring being broke, owing to my putting it forward by the Key. Briton did not return till 4 this Afternoon and then very wet and dirty, owing to the very sudden Thaw. It was quite a hard Frost when he set out, and I thought it more safe for him on foot than horseback but poor Fellow he had a terrible bad walk back being both very dirty and very wet. I gave him a glass of Gin on his return. Betty being gone to her Friends at Mattishall and Briton also out at dinner Time, I was with pleasure under the necessity of assisting at Dinner. Nancy complained a good deal in the Evening. We diverted ourselves at Cribbage this Evening at which neither won or lost.

Jan. 21. . . . Nancy very indifferent again this morning, had her breakfast in bed, did not get up till after One o'clock. I read Prayers and Preached this Afternoon at Weston C[hurch]. Neither Mr. or Mrs. Custance at Church this Afternoon. Nancy was down Stairs on my return from Church and seemed pretty cheerful till about 10 Minutes before Dinner and then had several Symptoms of her late Fever, could not eat but very little indeed for Dinner and that little she brought up soon after, and then was something better, and better still after Tea. She had little or no sleep all last Night.

Jan. 24. . . . Nancy had rather a better Night than last Night but breakfasted in her Chamber, came down about Noon, and stayed down all day afterwards. At 11 o'clock this Morn' I went a coursing and did not return till just 4 o'clock this Afternoon, had prodigious fine Sport with 2 Hares, especially the

last on France Green, but killed neither. Another
Hare also stole away from us near Hockering Heath
which none of the Dogs saw. I was rather tired
when I came home but very little. Mr. and Mrs.
Jeanes called on my Niece during my being out as
did also her Doctor Mr. Thorne. Ben and Jack went
out with me this Morning. Nancy could not prevail
on Mr. and Mrs. Jeanes to stay and dine with us,
they had been at Weston House this morning—
Mrs. Jeanes looked pale Nancy told me, but as she is
far advanced with Child, hope 'tis nothing more than
a consequence. Mrs. Custance sent word by Mrs.
Jeanes that she would come any Morn' and sit with
my Niece, when again able.

Jan. 25. . . . Nancy had a very indifferent Night and
rather worse today, being still weaker. She did not
come down Stairs till 2 o'clock this afternoon. However she made a good Dinner on a boiled Leg of
Mutton and Caper Sauce and was better after. Rode
to Ringland this Morning and married one Robert
Astick and Elizabeth Howlett by Licence, Mr. Carter
being from home, and the Man being in Custody,
the Woman being with Child by him. The Man was
a long time before he could be prevailed on to marry
her when in the Church Yard ; and at the Altar
behaved very unbecoming. It is a cruel thing that
any Person should be compelled by Law to marry.
I recd. of the Officers for marrying them 0. 10. 6.
It is very disagreeable to me to marry such Persons.[1]

[1] These so-called compulsory marriages, though not compulsory by
law, were an inevitable effect of the law as it stood, specially of the
Bastardy Act of 1733 (6 George II, c. 31). For under that Act a woman
had only, upon oath before a justice, to charge any person with having
gotten her with child to enable the said justice, on application of the

I took a ride from Ringland to Weston House and
there sat and chatted with Mrs. Custance about half

overseers of the poor, to apprehend and imprison the man charged,
unless he gave security to indemnify the parish. By another clause of
the Act the marriage of the woman caused the release of the man from
penalty. Hence, in numerous cases, if the man could not indemnify
the parish, he preferred wedlock to imprisonment. The Poor Law
Commission of Inquiry of 1834 (see specially pp. 92–9) bears terrible
testimony to the evil effects of the law as it was put into practice, and
the great Poor Law Amendment Act of 1834 (4 and 5 William IV, c. 76),
following the report, repealed the Acts imposing penalties on the putative
father. At the same time a maintenance order on application of the
overseers could only be made by the Court of Quarter Sessions if the
evidence of the mother was corroborated, and the child had become
chargeable. The law was further improved by the Act of 1844 (7 and 8
Victoria, c. 101), by which bastardy and poor relief law and administration were separated, the mother was made responsible for seeking redress
from the putative father, and the parish officers were strictly prohibited
under penalty from endeavouring ' to induce any person to contract
a marriage by threat or promise ' (see *A History of the English Poor Law*,
by Sir George Nicholls, K.C.B., vol. ii, pp. 23, 149–50, 274, 295, 383–4,
and the report, referred to above).

The same scene which Parson Woodforde here describes so graphically
in prose was described by the poet Crabbe with incomparable power in
verse, twenty years later, in 1807, in *The Parish Register* :

> Next at our altar stood a luckless pair,
> Brought by strong passions and a warrant there ;
> By long rent cloak, hung loosely, strove the bride,
> From ev'ry eye, what all perceived, to hide.
> While the boy-bridegroom, shuffling in his pace,
> Now hid awhile and then exposed his face ;
> As shame alternately with anger strove,
> The brain confused with muddy ale to move :
> In haste and stammering he perform'd his part,
> And look'd the rage that rankled in his heart ;
> (So will each lover inly curse his fate,
> Too soon made happy and made wise too late.)
> I saw his features take a savage gloom,
> And deeply threaten for the days to come.

an Hour—Mr. Custance not returned from going with his eldest Son to Palgrave School. I asked Mrs. Custance to dine with us to day, but she could not as Mr. C. was expected home at Dinner, and their Carriage is with Mr. Custance. From Weston House rode on to Witchingham and spent an Hour with Mrs. Jeanes, Mr. Jeanes was rode out, but I saw him on my return home he having been to my House to see Nancy. I got back to Weston before 3 o'clock. My Man Briton went with me this Morning. At Cribbage this Evening with Nancy won 0. 2. 0. So that she owes me now at Cards 0. 13. 0. Nancy was a good deal better this Evening.

Jan. 26. . . . Nancy had a good Night and was much better this Morning, but breakfasted in her Room. She came down Stairs about Noon and seemed in good Spirits. Mr. Thorne came here about 1 o'clock to see his Patient, and was glad to find her better, left more things for her and among the rest a mercurial Bolus to be taken going to bed to Night, and a black Dose of Physick to be taken to Morrow Morn'. I hope the above will have their desired Effect. Pray God they might. I privately named a Child this morning of Paul Bowdens by name William. Nancy continued pretty well all the Day. At Cribbage this Evening with Nancy won 0. 1. 0.

Jan. 28. . . . Nancy pretty well this morning and is certainly better, but breakfasted a bed, and after

Low spake the lass, and lisp'd and minced the while,
Look'd on the lad, and faintly tried to smile ;
With soften'd speech and humbled tone she strove
To stir the embers of departed love.

.   .   .   .   .   .

The Parish Register, Part II.

breakfast about 11 o'clock got up and came below Stairs, where I found her on my return from Church. I read Prayers and Preached this morning at Weston Church neither Mr. or Mrs. Custance at Church, nor above 20 People in all at Church—The Weather being extremely cold and severe with much Snow on the ground and still more falling with cutting Winds. After Service I buried a Daughter of Harrisons an Infant aged only 5 Weeks—I think that I never felt the cold more severe than when I was burying the above Infant. The Wind blowed very Strong and Snow falling all the time and the Wind almost directly in my Face, that it almost stopped my breath in reading the funeral Service at the Grave, tho' I had an Umbrella [1] held over my Head during the Time. Nancy brave all day but still very lame, she did not go to bed till after 10 o'clock this Evening. Mr. Thorne called again on his Patient this After: about 3 o'clock—soon after we had dined.

Jan. 31. . . . Nancy near the same as Yesterday rather better than worse, breakfasted, dined, and supped below. Directly after breakfast went out a coursing on foot with Ben and Jack and stayed out till after

---

[1] This is the first mention of an umbrella by Parson Woodforde. It may be thought that there is no great significance in that fact. Nevertheless there is, for umbrellas did not come into general use in England before the 1780's, and the man who first appeared with one in 1778 in London was jeered by the mob. They were regarded as effeminate, probably for three reasons : firstly, they had hitherto only been used by women since the early eighteenth century, secondly—as male equipment —they emanated from France, thirdly they supplanted or succeeded swords, which up to 1780 or so were carried by gentlemen on fashionable occasions. It is significant that in 1787 Parson Woodforde only succumbed to having one held over his head during a frightful blizzard at a funeral (see Lecky's *England in the Eighteenth Century*, vol. vii, pp. 187–9).

3 o'clock and never saw a single Hare—but after sitting down to dinner a few Minutes, notice was given me that Ben had found an Hare sitting in Carys Turnips about an Acre and half and next the College Pieces. I got up from Dinner and went thither but we had no kind of Course, the Greyhounds Chopping her up immediately—I then returned and finished my Dinner. Gave Ben for finding her o. 1. o. Mr. Thorne came to see Nancy whilst I was out. Mr. Custance also sent us a large Cottenham Cheese whilst I was out and a very nice one. I sent the Hare this Evening to Mr. Custance as they were much in want in one and had tried many People—Lady Bacon being there and a good deal of Company expected to Morr.

Feb. 1. . . . Nancy near the same as Yesterday, breakfasted, dined, and supped below Stairs. I privately named a Child of Dinah Bushells this morning at my House by name Robert. The Mother brought the Child herself, though the Infant was only born the 18 of January and the Mother quite hearty and strong. Yesterday and today were so warm and lively that it had more appearance of Summer than Winter. May they not be succeeded with uncommonly severe and rough Weather—Or, as the Norfolk People commonly call such fine Days in Winter Weatherbreeders—producing bad Weather.

Feb. 3. . . . Nancy had but an indifferent night and after taking her Physick this Morning was very sick and brought up some of it, her breakfast would not stay on her Stomach also, nor anything else but a little Water Gruel, and that but a little Time, was extremely ill all the Day long till about 8 in the Evening and then was a small matter easier. The

Mercury she took last Night was much too strong for her weak frame at this present. The Physic she took this morning had little or no effect, as she brought it up almost the whole, therefore she had violent griping pains in her Bowels the whole Morning without much coming from her as the Mercury only operated without the Aid of Physick to carry it of, therefore there must be a great deal of Mercury left behind—however when she went to bed, she was somewhat easier. Mr. Thorne called here this Morning accidentally having been to bleed Mrs. Custance at Weston House. He was not pleased on hearing that Nancy was so bad as not to be seen by him being above Stairs. I am afraid she caught cold, as her pain within her was so bad that she could not get from the close-Stool for near 2 Hours together. I went up to see her in the Evening, and she was very low and cried a good deal—but seemed rather easier—after she had her Tea and Toast she seemed something better and soon after came down Stairs and stayed the rest of the Evening. When she went to bed she was tolerably easy. I was very uneasy indeed the whole Day on my dear Nieces Account. 'Pray God give her more ease.' I sent Briton to Norwich this Morning after News, &c. in my little Cart,—he returned by dinner time. No letters from the West, or elsewhere, as there were none from the West, I wonder much at it ; as Nancy has long expected one from her Aunt and one from her Sister Juliana.

Feb. 4. . . . I slept very indifferent indeed last night as Nancy was so bad all Day Yesterday. Nancy had a tolerable good Night considering, but complained much of pains about her, especially a great soarness in her Throat, Teeth and Mouth. I sent early after Mr. Thorne this Morning to see her. He did not come till 2 o'clock this afternoon and was sorry that the Mercury should have so strong Effect on her Constitution, as it was no more in Quantity than what she had taken before, only 5 grains. However he said that he would send some Powders that should effectually remove the Mercury from the Constitution. I therefore sent Briton (as Ben went in the Morning) after Dinner for the above Powders and he returned about 7 o'clock, and Nancy took one of them immediately and another going to bed. I hope they will soon remove the bad Effects. Nancy dined, supped and spent the Evening below. She appeared tolerably easy going to bed. I read Prayers, Preached and christned a Child of one Bowles's this Afternoon at Weston Church by name Anne. Mr. Custance and Capt. Beauchamp at Church.

Feb. 5. . . . Nancy (I thank God) is something better to day, but complains much of her Mouth and Glands. She breakfasted above Stairs, but came down about Noon and dined, supped &c. below. She slept very well last Night and was in good Spirits all day, but complained of Lassitude. She took 4 Powders to day and eat some hash Mutton for Dinner and Supper very well. . . . My Mare Phyllis had a Foal this afternoon whilst she was out in the Cover to day with the rest of the Horses—It is a Horse Foal. Mrs. Crossley called here this morning with her Son Charles, desiring me to take him in place of my present Boy Jack, who is going away at Lady Day and we soon agreed—gave him 0. 1. 0.

Feb. 9. . . . Nancy breakfasted, dined, &c. below Stairs and seemed much better to day. I took a ride to

Witchingham this morning with my Greyhounds to see for a Hare, but there had no sport whatever, tho' out till after 2 o'clock. I sent a Note to Mr. Jeanes this morning by Briton that I would dine with them to-day if agreeable therefore after coursing at Witchingham I went to his House and there dined and spent the Afternoon with him and his Wife—We had for Dinner some Salt Fish with Eggs in their Shells, Potatoes and Turnips, a Hare spoiled in roasting, some Parts much over done, others scarce hot thro', with the Head taken off, split in two and laid on each side of the Dish also a Pudding made of Cranberries and in a large white Bason. The Paste very ordinary I think. After Coffee about 5 o'clock I took my Leave and returned home to my Niece. I cannot say that I made a very good Dinner but met with a very friendly and warm reception.

Feb. 10. . . . Nancy tolerable this morning but did not come down to breakfast, nor was below Stairs till Noon', just as she was coming down stairs Mrs. Custance came to us and stayed till near 3 o'clock. She seemed far from well, having a low nervous Fever hanging about her, and very far gone with Child. I tried to divert her as much as I could, showed her some Medals of mine &c. I was quite sorry to see her so very low and weak. Nancy dined, supped &c. below Stairs and was tolerably well and cheerful all Day.

Feb. 12. . . . Nancy breakfasted, dined, &c. below Stairs again and was better than she was Yesterday, her Spirits very good with a good Appetite, but her lameness still continues, tho' I think, not quite so bad. Mrs. Bodham sent Nancy a Note this Morning, to excuse her not coming over to see her, being ill with a cold—Nancy returned an answer to it. Mr. Thorne also called here about Noon to see his Patient, stayed here about an Hour, during that time Mrs. Custance made us a visit and stayed with us till 3 o'clock, learning of Nancy to make the Diamond-edge-netting. I wrote it out for her. Mrs. Custance much better than on Saturday last. Sent Ben this Morning with my great Cart to Mr. Du Quesnes after a large Walnut Tree to transplant into my Garden—which we did directly; it was planted well and supported with 3 Stakes. I wish it might live, but have some doubt of it, as it is so large and the Roots injured much. Mr. Thorne left no Medicine whatever for Nancy.

Feb. 13. . . . Nancy breakfasted, dined, &c. &c. again at home, was very well and in good Spirits till about an Hour before Dinner, but was then ill by being much troubled with Wind in her Stomach, after she had dined, was much better and continued so. Had a note from Mr. Jeanes this Morning with a present of a small Salt Fish and some Oysters and in his Note mentions that himself and Wife being obliged to set of for London very soon on some important Family Matters where he is to meet his Wifes Mother and will be absent 2 or 3 Sundays, desires me to officiate for him in his absence at Great Witchingham on Sunday Sennight and the following Sundays in his absence, and which I engaged to do for him and sent him a Note. Mr. Thorne called at the Garden Gate this Morning but did not get from his Horse. To Mr. Jeanes's Servant that brought the Fish gave 0. 1. 0.

Feb. 16. . . . Nancy very well this Morning and eat very heartily of boiled Leg of Mutton and Capers for Dinner, but about Tea Time this Afternoon she was taken with very violent Pains in her Bowels, vomited very much indeed, obliged to go to bed at 9 o'clock. She eat some Mutton Broth for Supper which I hope will do her some good. To see her in the Pains made one's heart ache again. Mr. Custance sent us this Even' a wild Mallard. I did not get to bed till near 1 in the Morn.

Feb. 17. . . . I sent early this Morn' after Dr. Thorne for Nancy. Poor Nancy had a dreadful Night of it, in violent Pain all the Night, about 3 o'clock this Morn' somewhat easier and afterwards had some rest. She breakfasted above Stairs and in bed, but about Noon she came down being rather easier, and to see Mr. Thorne who came here about that time and saw her and talked a great deal to her. Nancy in the Night had occasion to make use of the Stoole once or twice, which I was very glad to hear of, as it would have been perhaps of very alarming nature, had she not, as an inflammation of the Bowels might have perhaps taken place, thank God, that the Complaint had that effect, and that she was something easier after, but a good deal of Pain still remained all the Day. I sent Ben again this Afternoon to Dr. Thorne's after Medicine, and he returned about 6 o'clock with the same—As soon as he returned she took 2 large Table-spoonfuls of a Potion wch. he sent to her, and after taking it not more than a Quarter of an Hour, it made her vomit very much indeed, and brought on the Cholicky Pains again, and was obliged to go to bed before Tea was over this Evening. She drank very little Tea indeed, all of that little soon came up again. I sent Briton early this Morning to Norwich in my little Cart, after News, Letters &c. &c. he returned about 4 o'clock this afternoon. The vomiting continued on Nancy till after 11 o'clock this Night, and being rendered very weak and nature quite tired, she went to sleep.

Feb. 19. . . . Nancy I thank God a good deal better today but did not get up till 1 this Afternoon. Mrs. Custance called here this Morning with her eldest Daughter and stayed with us an Hour. Nancy was not below when she came, but was soon after. Mr. Thorne and Betsy Davy called here just as Mrs. Custance was going away and they stayed with us an Hour, I would have had them dine here but they were ordered to the contrary I suppose. Betsy Davy was grown much taller, but very shy to me, and rather affected in her way. I sold 2 acres and ½ of Turnips today to be fed of to Gould of Attlebridge for 2 guineas and half. Turnips now are very Cheap indeed in Weston as there are many to sell and Weather so very fine. Had a Note from Mr. Smith of Mattishall this Morning by Dade, to desire me to serve his Church on Sunday next, but was obliged to return for answer that it was not in my Power as I was pre-engaged to serve Witchingham for Mr. Jeanes who is gone to London with his Wife. Nancy continued brave all the Day and sat up till after 10 at Night—then took a Rhubarb Bolus and went to bed quite cheerry.

Feb. 21. . . . Nancy still better, thank God, but did not get up till after breakfast, and dined, supped, &c. below Stairs, and continued very well all day. Ben went early this Morning to Norwich with 10 Coomb of Barley in My great Cart, and he returned home about 5 o'clock this afternoon with half a Ch[a]ldr[o]n of Coal and 2 Hampers of Wine from Mr. Priests— 2 Doz: of Port and 2 Doz: of Mountain. Mr. Thorne was here again this Morn' to see Nancy. Recd. of Ben for my Barley at 11ˢ 0ᵈ per Coomb—5. 10. 0.

Feb. 25. . . . Nancy (thank God) still grows better and better. I read Prayers and Preached this Morn' at Weston C[hurch]. Neither Mr. or Mrs. Custance at Church this Morn'. A strange Gentleman and his Son were at Weston C[hurch] this Morning, the Gentleman being dressed like a Clergyman and addressing himself to me before Service began, I shewed him and Son into my Seat in the Chancel. After Divine Service he came to me again in the Chancel and after some talk found that he was a Clergyman and that he served Morton and Attlebridge and lives at Norwich, but could not find out his Name. I asked him and his Son to dine with me but they could not. When I returned from Weston Church I mounted my Mare, and Briton with me and went to G[reat] Witchingham and there read Prayers and Preached, and christned a Child this afternoon for Mr. Jeanes—Did not get home to Dinner till near 5 o'clock this Afternoon—a cold, damp, wet disagreeable Day.

Feb. 27. . . . Nancy now daily improves, thank God for it. Sent a Note to inquire after Mr. Du Quesne who is very lately returned from Ely, and likewise to ask him to dine with us to day and meet Mr. and Mrs. Custance at my House in the Afternoon, but he could not do either having no Horse fit. Mr. and Mrs. Custance with their Son George drank Coffee and Tea with us this afternoon and stayed with us till near 9 o'clock this Evening. After Tea we had no Cards, but I shewed them all my Pictures and Prints, with which they were well pleased, especially Mr. Custance.

Mar. 2. . . . Nancy still continues mending (thank God for it), and breakfasted, dined, &c. &c. again at home. I had very little rest all Night, the Wind being very high the whole Night, got out of bed 3 or 4 times to look out of the Window, it was very clear and very light, the Moon being almost full, and mild. I got up about 9 o'clock and the Wind then was rather higher than it had been all Night and so continued till dinner time 3 o'clock, then some Rain fell for a little time, and the Wind rather abated a little. To a Fisherman of Norwich with a Cart, by name Mansel, for Skaite at 3^d per Pound pd. o. 2. 1½.

Mar. 3. . . . Nancy had a long Letter from her Sister this Aft: All our friends well but Mr. Pounsett who is confined almost to his bed in the gout.

Mar. 4. . . . I rode to G[reat] Witchingham this Morning and there read Prayers, Preached, and Christned 2 Children for Mr. Jeanes by name John and Charlotte. My Man Briton went with me, and a wet ride we had, as it rained all the Way there and rough Wind, directly in our Faces—better back. Very cold and uncomfortable at Mr. Jeanes's House nothing but a cold Kitchen to set in and little Fire—The Stable where my Horses stood unroofed, and as the Wind was high, was afraid that the high ends of it would be blown down on the Horses. Mr. Jeanes's Servant (Jeremiah Allden) had a Letter from his Master in the middle of the week, which I saw and read. Not a word said of his returning or enquiry or Compts. after anyone. I read Prayers and Preached this Afternoon at Weston. Neither Mr. or Mrs. Custance at Church. Weather bad.

Mar. 5. . . . I had 2 Stoves put up in my Kitchen to

day by Hardy. About 3 o'clock took a walk to Weston House and there dined and spent the Afternoon with Mr. and Mrs. Custance and Major Loyd of Belaugh. I returned about 9 o'clock this Evening as I went. Had a very disagreeable Walk to Weston House and rather worse returning from it, as it was very cold with sleet and wind.

Mar. 10. . . . Sent Briton on Horseback to Norwich after News &c. He returned about 4 this Afternoon, and told us that News was just arrived at Norwich from London that the last City Election for Norwich was declared void by the House of Commons, and that there would be a fresh Election for that City very soon. The City when Briton came from it was all in a Hurly Burly, full of People and in large parties. Mr. Hobart was returned for the late Election, and is supposed to succeed in the new Election. Sr. Thos. Beevor was his opponent in the late Election and a Petition preferred against Mr. Hobart by him.[1] It is supposed that Sr. Thomas Beevor will stand again.

[1] There had been a by-election at Norwich in September 1786, consequent upon the peerage bestowed on Sir Harbord Harbord (see footnote on p. 125), and Mr. Henry Hobart had been returned. This election was eventually declared void, and he had to stand again, as described by the Diarist, being returned victorious on March 28, 1787. Mr. Henry Hobart, who was a son of the 1st Earl of Buckinghamshire, was born in 1738 and died in 1799. He was for many years Member for Norwich, and was for some time Chairman of the Committee of Ways and Means in the House. He married Anne Margaret, daughter of John Bristow, of Quiddenham Hall, Norfolk (see the *Return of Members of Parliament, Part II : Parliaments of Great Britain, 1705-1796*, p. 179, and Burke's *Peerage*, under Buckinghamshire).

Sir Thomas Beevor (1726-1814), of Hethel, Norfolk, was created a baronet on January 22, 1784 : according to Cokayne he was ' a great agriculturalist '. He married July 7, 1750, Elizabeth, daughter and heiress

Mar. 11. . . . I read Prayers, Preached and Churched a Woman this Morning at Weston Church—gave the Woman her 6ᵈ. Mr. Custance at Church—very few besides there. Very soon after I returned from Weston Church I mounted my Horse and went to Witchingham, and there read Prayers, Churched one Woman, and christned 3 Children, by names Susannah, Anne and Henry, this Afternoon. Did not return from Witchingham till near 5 o'clock this Afternoon. We did not dine to day till 5 o'clock this Aft: Recd. for Churching the Woman at Witchingham o. o. 6. No Tidings whatever of Mr. Jeanes or his Wife.

Mar. 13. . . . Whilst we were at breakfast, Mrs. Davy from Thurning with a Servant with her, called here and drank a Dish of Tea with us, stayed about half an Hour afterwards and then went on to Mr. Thornes at Mattishall. I did not ask her to stay and dine with us. She talked of returning back to Thurning Thursday or Friday next—I did not ask her to call on her return. Nancy was highly pleased to see her. Mrs. Davy behaved as free as if nothing had been said respecting her Character by Mr. Smith. She is grown much fatter than she was. I never knew a Woman of much greater Effrontery. The Election for the City of Norwich comes on Thursday next, a strong Contest is expected.

Mar. 14. . . . Read to my Niece to day a great many Letters of Mr. Fenns[1] new Publication of antient

of Miles Branthwaite, of Hethel (see Cokayne's *Complete Baronetage*, vol. v, pp. 246–7).

[1] This was Sir John Fenn (1739–94), a Norfolk antiquary of note, who was the purchaser of the original manuscript and first editor of the famous *Paston Letters*. These he published in four volumes, between 1787 and 1789. A fifth volume was published by his nephew after his death. George III knighted him for his work on May 23, 1787. The

Letters, lately published, in the reigns of Henry the sixth, Edward the fourth, and Richd. the third.

Mar. 15. . . . This Day the Election for Members for the City of Norwich commences, for one Member only as the late Election was declared void. The Honourable Henry Hobart and Sr. Thos. Beevor, Candidates, I hope that Mr. Hobart will gain the Election. Mr. Windham is the other Member that has long sat for Norwich. Busy in brewing Beer this Morning.

Mar. 16. . . . This Morning heard from Weston House that the Election for Norwich was ended last Night abt. 8 o'clock and that Mr. Hobart had a Majority of 118—above Beevor—am very glad for it. Mrs. Davy and Betsy called here this morning in their road from Mattishall to Thurning and stayed with my Niece near an Hour. I was gone out with my Greyhounds—but I think I saw them at a great distance from me going to Lenewade Bridge from Greensgate. I returned home soon after but no Hare with me. Mrs. Custance called on us at 1 o'clock and spent an Hour with us. All the talk now is abt. the Election ; The meanest actions the Beevor Party were guilty of on the above Occasion and very much

letters were published under the title, *Original Letters written during the reigns of Henry VI, Edward IV, Richard III, and Henry VII, by various persons of rank and consequence, and by members of the Paston family* (see *D. N. B.*). Horace Walpole, writing on February 1, 1787, to the Countess of Upper Ossory, refers to these letters : 'The Letters of Henry VI's reign, etc., are come out, and *to me* make all other letters not worth reading. I have gone through above one volume, and cannot bear to be writing when I am so eager to be reading. . . . What antiquary would be answering a letter from a living countess, when he may read one from Eleanor Mowbray, Duchess of Norfolk ! ' (Horace Walpole's *Letters*, vol. xiii, p. 443).

nettled on losing the Election—Branthwaite, Ives, &c. &c. some of the principal People against Mr. Hobart. Mr. Du Quesne called here about dinner time and he dined and spent the Afternoon with us.

Mar. 17. . . . Sent Briton on horseback to Norwich after News &c. He returned about 4 o'clock with the same. No Letter or any Tidings whatever of Mr. and Mrs. Jeanes. Mr. Hobart had only 80 Majority of Sr. Thos. Beevor. The Election at Norwich conducted with great credit to the City. No appearance of a Riot or any disturbance whatever, but all things were carried on in the greatest Order and Peace. No Stavesman whatever on the Occasion. Sr. Thos. Beevor is said to have demanded a Scrutiny at first, but has since dropped it, is said. For Churching a Woman at Witchingham recd. o. o. 6. Briton returned home from Norwich with a Hobart Favour in his Hat, and highly pleased.

Mar. 18. . . . I read Prayers, Preached and churched a Woman at Witchingham this Morn', for Mr Jeanes. Mr. Jeanes Man is gone to London to his Master with Mr. Jeanes Stallion, being sent for by him. Mr. Jeanes is expected in the ensuing Week. I read Prayers and Preached this Afternoon at Weston C[hurch]. Also churched 2 poor Women at Weston Church. Mr. and Mrs. Custance at Church this Afternoon and a very full Congregation at Church this Aft: I gave the two poor Women the Churching Fee. I met Mr. Custance on my return from Witchingham this Morning on the little Common, and he very genteelly desired me for the future to go thro' his inclosures by his House whenever I wanted to go to Witchingham or Lenewade Bridge, &c. as that way is somewhat nearer than the other. Nancy told me this Evening that Mrs. Davy had had an offer of marriage made her, but not said whom—also that her Daughter Betsy has had an offer also from young Walker who was lately at Mr. Thornes. The above are very great Secrets.

Mar. 21. . . . Very pleasant, cheerful Day, thank God for it.

Mar. 22. . . . Mrs. Bodham with her Niece Miss Kitty Johnson, made us a morning Visit and stayed with us more than an Hour, eat part of a Lobster here and drank some Porter, could not prevail on them to dine with us, as they promised to return home to Mattishall to dinner. Mr. Custance sent us this Evening 3 fine Snipes by his Servant John who also brought a Letter for me from Mr. Jeanes at London, Mr. Custance's Servant having been lately at Norwich. In Mr. Jeanes's Letter, he mentions it rather dubious whether he can be home till next week.

Mar. 24. . . . Sent Ben to Norwich this Morning with my little Cart after News &c. and also some Reed abt. 2 Fathom. He returned home about 4 o'clock, and he brought me a Letter from my Sister Pounsett —all Friends well. She likewise informed us that Mr. Sam. Burge intends to make an Offer of Marriage to Mrs. R. Clarke. Also that there was a bad Fever at Castle-Cary wch. proves fatal to some. Cary Russ and Wife both died of it leaving behind them 8 small Children. Pray God befriend the poor Orphans, and that they might find Friends. . . .

Mar. 26. . . . Polly my Poll-Cow had a Bull Calf this Morning.

Mar. 27. . . . Mrs. Custance made us a morning Visit and stayed with us an Hour—She is quite hurried and uneasy on Account of her little Boy, William, having got the Measles, and herself never having them, and also that she is very near her Time of being brought to bed, having scarce a Month to go with Child. Am exceeding sorry for poor Mrs. Custance indeed and likewise for Mr. Custance who must be very much concerned. Busy brewing some strong Beer to day.

Mar. 29. . . . Mr. Du Quesne called here about 2 o'clock on horseback and I went with him to Weston House and there we dined and spent the Afternoon with Mr. and Mrs. Custance and Mr. Press Custance. After Coffee and Tea we got to Cribbage (being the most fashionable Game of Cards at present) Mr. and Mrs. Custance against Du Quesne and self at which we each lost o. 1. 6. We went to Weston House in Mr. Custance's Coach and returned in the same to my House—Mr. Du Quesne returned home from my House on horseback. Nancy was invited but cannot as yet get into a Carriage, being still very lame and helpless tho' better.

Mar. 30. . . . Mr. Custances Coach damaged my great Gates last Night. About Noon, Mr. and Mrs. Jeanes from London came here in their road home to Witchingham, and stayed an Hour with us, and refreshed themselves with some cold rost Beef and Porter &c. and then went for home. Mrs. Jeanes looks much better. Mr. Jeanes whilst in Town bought a close Carriage and a pair of black Horses to go in the same. Mrs. Jeanes came down in it. It looks smart. Mr. Jeanes came down on his fine Stallion as he could not dispose of him for so much as he asked. For a fine Eel 2 pd. weight pd. o. o. 6.

Mar. 31. . . . About Noon took a ride to Mr. Du Quesnes, and there dined and spent the Afternoon

with him, Mr. and Mrs. Bodham, Miss Kitty Johnson Mrs. Bodhams Niece, and Mr. Smith of Mattishall. Rotation Day and the first Rotation this year.
We had for Dinner some Cod-Fish and Oyster Sauce,
2 Fowls boiled and Piggs Face, a Leg of Mutton
rosted, some Damson Tarts and the Charter. We all
left Mr. Du Quesnes before 7 this Evening. No
playing at Cards after Tea this Afternoon. Nancy
had a Letter this Evening (brought by my Man Ben
whom I sent to Norwich this Morning after News &c.)
from her Brother Samuel from Rome, he is very well
and very happy where he is. Sam. mentions in his
Letter that he has been introduced to the following
English People of Fashion and Rank now resident at
Rome—the Duke and Dutchess of Buccleaugh, Lord
and Lady Clive, Lord and Lady Gower, Sir Cecil
Bishop &c.[1]

[1] (1) This Duke of Buccleuch (1746–1812) was the 3rd Duke, and
perhaps his best title to remembrance is the fact that he was the patron,
kinsman, and friend of Sir Walter Scott. He married in 1767 Lady
Elizabeth Montagu, only daughter of the Duke of Montagu, and thereby
obtained immense wealth in land, personalty, and jewels.

(2) Lord Clive (1754–1839) was the eldest son of the great Clive (who
died in 1774), and was himself a person of distinction : he was a very
efficient Governor of Madras (1798–1803), in which office he co-operated
with Wellesley in his brilliant Indian exploits. He married in 1784
Lady Henrietta Herbert, daughter of the last Herbert Earl of Powis,
that title being afterwards conferred on Clive in 1804.

(3) Lord Gower (1758–1833) was George Granville Leveson Gower,
son of the 2nd Earl Gower afterwards 1st Marquis of Stafford. Lord
Gower was a good scholar, a much travelled person, and a patron of art.
In public life his most important post was as Ambassador in Paris in the
terrible years 1790–2. He married in 1785 Elizabeth Sutherland, Countess
of Sutherland in her own right, and thus it was that, in 1833 when he was
made a duke, he chose the Sutherland title. Through his wife, through
his father, and through his maternal uncle the last Duke of Bridgewater,
he attained to wealth beyond the dreams of avarice. Stafford House

1787

April 3. . . . Recd. a printed Letter Yesterday by our Apparitor from our Bishop, Dr. Bagot, to inform me that he intends having a Confirmation at Foulsham on Wednesday the sixth of June next ensuing. Sent Mr. Jeanes this morning four Coomb of Oats for which he is to give me at 10/6 per Coomb—2. 2. 0. I sent him also a large Basket of Potatoes for Seed. Mr. and Mrs. Custance drank Coffee and Tea with us this Afternoon and stayed till 9 o'clock. After Tea we got to Quadrille at which I lost 0. 2. 0.

April 4. . . . Nancy paid Mrs. Jeanes for a Shawl she bought for her in London—11ˢ 6ᵈ—also for a whole piece of narrow white Ribband—36 Yards—4ˢ 0ᵈ also for 6 Yards of Crape Gauze white 6ˢ 0ᵈ. I enter the above here as I think them very cheap.

April 5. . . . My Boy, Jack Secker, left my Service this Day and went home with his Father who came after him about Noon. I paid him for Wages due 5. 6. My new Boy, Charles Crossley, of this Parish came to my House this Evening about 5 o'clock. Mr. Custance sent us a fine Cucumber this Morn'.

April 6. . . . This being Good Friday I read Prayers this Morning at Weston Church—no Sermon. Mr. Custance at Church this Morning. My Niece and me eat no animal Food this Day. Our Dinner was fritters and bread and Cheese.

April 10. . . . About 1 o'clock took a ride to Mattishall to Mr. Smiths (this being his Rotation day) and there

owes its name to him : he purchased it in 1827 for £72,000 from the Duke of York—of the column—who had begun to build it.

(4) Sir Cecil Bishopp, Bt. (1753–1828), was the 8th Bt., of Parham, Sussex. He was M.P. for New Shoreham from 1780 to 1790, and 1796 to 1806. He was a F.R.S.

(For the Buccleuchs, Clives, and Gowers, see *D.N.B.*; for Bishopp, Cokayne's *Complete Baronetage*, vol. i, p. 157.)

dined and spent the Afternoon with him, Mr. Du
Quesne, Mr. and Mrs. Bodham, Miss Kitty Johnson
and her Brother John Johnson,[1] and Mr. Ashill of
Norwich—a Mr. Ray of Suffolk, a Clergyman and
acquaintance of Mr. Smith's spent the Afternoon
with us and is to sleep ar Mr. Smiths tonight. Soon
after Coffee and Tea, myself and Mr. Du Quesne
mounted our Horses and returned to our Homes.
I got home by 8 o'clock this Evening. We had for
Dinner, Cod Fish and Shrimp Sauce, a nice piece of
boiled Beef, a Couple of rost Fowls and a Piggs Face,
a baked plumb Pudding, some Plovers Eggs, Custard
Iced over, Tarts, &c.

April 12. . . . A Gentleman by name, Shute, Rector of
Brancaster in this County, a young Man and of
Gloucestershire and acquainted with Dr. Penny,
called here this morning about 9 o'clock and breakfasted with us, he came from Norwich here in his
road to Brancaster. I asked him to dine with us but
he could not. I took a ride with him after breakfast
to Mr. Custance's Gate, he went on for home and
I went up to Weston House and there spent an Hour
or more with Mr. and Mrs. C[ustance]. From
Mr. Custances went to Witchingham and spent half
an Hour with Mr. and Mrs. Jeanes—I went to ask
them to meet the Rotation Company at my House
on Tuesday next. I returned home to dinner by
3 o'clock. Nancy liked Mr. Shute very well—he is
very easy. Mr. Custance sent us some fine Eels this
Evening.

April 16. . . . Sent Briton early this Morning to
Norwich to get some Fish for Dinner to Morrow,
having Company. He returned about 1 o'clock with

[1] See foot-note, p. 234, preceding.

some Skaite. Paid to Mr. Howlett an half Years poor Rate 1. 2. 8½. at 9ᵈ in the Pound—30. 5. 0. I also privately baptized a Child this Afternoon of Clegbourne's by name Mary. Mr. and Mrs. Custance sent us some fine Bunches of Asparagus and 2 Cucumbers both very great Rarities at this time.

April 17. . . . This being my Rotation Day Mr. and Mrs. Bodham with them Miss Kitty Johnson, Mr. Du Quesne, Mr. Smith and Mr. and Mrs. Jeanes, all dined, and spent the Afternoon with us—We had for Dinner, some Skaite and Oyster Sauce, Knuckle of Veal and a Tongue, a fine Fore Quarter of Lamb and plumb Pudding. 2nd. Course, Asparagus, Lobster, Rasberry Tartlets, black Caps set into Custard &c. We had also Cucumbers and Radishes. There were three Carriages, 5 Servants and 8 Horses. Soon after Coffee and Tea, they all left us.

April 18. . . . Received this afternoon of Mr. Gould of Attlebridge for 2 Acres and half of Turnips sold to him 2. 12. 6. Paid to him a Bill for Farriery 0. 6. 0. viz: 5ˢ 0ᵈ for my Nephew Willms. Horse last Year and coming to see my Mare Phyllis being ill—1ˢ 0ᵈ. Very cold, dry, cutting Winds from the N.E.N.

April 21. . . . Mrs. Custance made us a morning visit, soon after she had been here, Mrs. N. Micklethwaite with her Sister Miss Branthwaite, called on us, and they all stayed with us about an Hour, and then went in their Carriages for their respective homes— Mrs. Micklethwaite and her Sister were full dressed in the highest Mode of Fashion. Had a Letter this Evening from Norwich from Ben Jeffries of New College but dated from Brecon in Wales, about some Norfolk Turnip Seed, Quality and Price. Mr. Cary brought my News, &c. from Norwich.

1787

April 26. . . . Nancy was advised Yesterday by Mr. Thorne to pour cold Water on her weak Knee every Morning, and she begun this morning to try its effects.

April 27. . . . Nancy says that the Cold Water makes her knee look very red afterwards—that I hope is a good sign. To Forster for a Church Rate at 1½ pd. o. 2. o. I took a ride by myself to Mr. Jeanes, there spent an Hour with Mr. and Mrs. Jeanes—from thence went to Weston House and there spent half an Hour with Mr. and Mrs. Custance and then home again. The Arch Deacons Visitation this Day at Foulsham, but did not go as it was so far and bad roads.

May 2. . . . Mrs. Custance not brought to bed yet, tho' much expected the latter end of April.

May 6. . . . I read Prayers, Preached, and churched a Woman this morning at Weston Church. Mrs. N. Micklethwaite and Miss Branthwaite at Church. None from Weston House at Church. For churching a Woman this morning recd. o. o. 6. Soon after my return from Church, one of Mr. Custances Servants called here to let us know that Mrs. Custance was brought to bed of a Boy about 11 o'clock this Morn'. She with the little stranger as well as can be expected. I buried this Evening one Willm. Hill aged 65 yrs. He was ill but a very little Time—was well respected and a great many People at his burial.

May 8. . . . I rode to Weston House again this morning and spent half an Hour with Mr. Custance. Mrs. Custance and her new born Son, as well as can be expected. Mr. Custance has not as yet fixed on a Name for his new Son, having sent to Sr. Thos. Beauchamp &c. about it. From Weston House went

on to Mattishall to Mr. Smiths Rotation, and there
dined and spent the Afternoon with Mr. Smith.
Mr. and Mrs. Bodham, Miss Johnson and Mr. Du
Quesne. After Tea we got to Quadrille at which
lost 0. 1. 0. We had for Dinner some Skaite, a Fillett
of Veal rosted, a hind Quarter of Lamb Leg boiled
Loin fryed, a very fine Tongue and a small plumb
Pudding and Asparagus, Tarts, Trifle, Cheese-cakes,
&c. I returned home about half past 8 o'clock.
Mr. and Mrs. Thorne made my Niece a long Morning
Visit from 12 till near 2 o'clock, in my absence.

May 10. ... To J_o^n Pegg, a Qrs. Land Tax pd. 3. 0. 0.
To Do Window Tax ½ Year 22 pd. 2. 13. 3. To Do
House Tax ½ Year pd. 0. 1. 9. To John Pegg also for
Male Servants Tax for ½ Year, being a Batchelor pd.
1. 5. 0. To Do. Female Servants Tax ½ Year
pd. 0. 10. 0. To Do. Horse Tax for one Year pd.
1. 0. 0. Paid him in all this Morning for Taxes
8. 10. 0.

May 11. ... I took a ride to Weston House this Morning to enquire after Mrs. Custance &c. Mr. Custance
was rode out, but I stayed till he returned which was
after 2 o'clock, soon after his return I walked up
with him into the Nursery and there privately
baptised his new-born Son—by name John. Mr.
Custance told me that he had been at Mr. Du
Quesne's, Mrs. Micklethwaites, and to my House.

May 12. ... Sent Briton early this morning to Norwich
in my little Cart, for News &c. &c. he returned home
about 2 o'clock and brought home some Maccarel
which we had for Dinner—The first Time of our
seeing any Maccarel this Year—$4\frac{1}{2}^d$ a piece. The
Honble. Henry Hobart is declared by the Committee
of the House of Commons, duly elected which we

were very glad of, having been so very unjustly persecuted by a violent factious Party.

May 19. . . . I bottled of this morning a Tub of Moonshine. Mr. Du Quesne called here on Horseback but did not get of.

May 20. . . . I read Prayers, Preached, gave notice of a Sacrament next Sunday, being Whitsunday, and likewise gave notice of the Bishops holding a Confirmation for this Deanery on Wednesday the 6 of June at Foulsham, this morning at Weston Church.[1] Mr. Custance with his two Sons George and William and likewise Mrs. N. Micklethwaite and her Sister Miss Branthwaite, all at Church this Morning. Mr. Custance's Coach and four and Mrs. Micklethwaites Chariot and a pair of Horses made a good appearance.

May 21. . . . Mr. Jeanes made us a short morning Visit. Of John Gooch for Turnips for his Cow almost all the Winter recd. of him 1. 1. 0. but I returned it to

---

[1] The rite of Confirmation, as the reader has doubtless already surmised from Parson Woodforde's silence on the subject, was not much observed in the eighteenth-century Church of England. 'Confirmation', said Whiston in 1747, 'is, I doubt, much oftener omitted than performed. And it is usually done in the Church of England in such a hurry and disorder, that it hardly deserves the name of a sacred ordinance of Christianity.' Fifty years later the position does not seem to have greatly altered (see on this subject Abbey and Overton's *The English Church in the Eighteenth Century*, pp. 470–1, revised edition, 1896). It appears to me that the explanation is not far to seek. It was not so much eighteenth-century Church slackness that was responsible, but the eighteenth-century state of the roads and inconvenient means of travel, which made it utterly impossible for bishops to get frequently to remote parishes, or for children to get to some central parish. As the reader will see, under the entry for June 1st, Foulsham was 10 miles from Weston, and doubtless this was the reason why no mention is made of Weston children at the Confirmation on June 6th.

him again immediately. Very busy all the morning in cutting the Weeds in my Bason and cleaning the same, and likewise in launching the Ship Anna in the same.

May 22. . . . I sent Ben very early this morning after Fish &c. to Norwich, my Rotation being to day and he returned by Noon with some fine, fresh Maccarel. Mr. Priest of Norwich with Mr. Forster of Lenewade Bridge made us a morning visit. Mr. Custance soon after also made us a long Visit. Mr. Du Quesne, Mr. and Mrs. Bodham with Miss Johnson, Mr. Smith, Mr. and Mrs. Jeanes and with them Miss Short all dined and spent the Afternoon with us. They all left us soon after Coffee and Tea. We had for Dinner some Maccarel, a Chine of Mutton rosted, Ham and 3 Chickens, 3 Pigeons rosted, and Asparagus, The Charter, Apricot and Gooseberry Tarts, Rasberry Jam Tartelets, Cucumber &c. Port and Mountain Wine, Porter, and Beer. Oranges, Almonds and Raisins, Nuts and Apples.

May 23. . . . A most gracious Rain about Noon and continued so all the Evening—very gentle and soft warm Rain. Thank God the Rain came without a Tempest.

May 25. . . . I took a ride this morning to Weston House and spent near an Hour with Mr. and Mrs. Custance. Mrs. Custance very finely thank God after Childbed. From Weston House went on to Mr. Jeanes's at Witchingham and there took a Family Dinner with him, his Wife and Miss Short. After Coffee and Tea I returned home to Weston. My Servant Man Briton went with me. We had for Dinner at Mr. Jeanes's some Salt Fish heated up with chopped Eggs and Potatoes, fryed Beef and Cabbage, Eggs and

Spinnage, a fryed Rabbit very small one, hot and cold Mince Pye, Gooseberry and Cranberry Tarts.

May 28. . . . Mr. and Mrs. Jeanes with Miss Short dined and spent the Afternoon with us. We had for Dinner a nice boiled Leg of Lamb, a very nice small rosting Pigg, Apricot and Gooseberry Tarts Oranges and Nutts by way of desert. Soon after Coffee and Tea, They returned for Witchingham and took my Niece with them in their Carriage to spend a few Days with them.

May 29. . . . It seemed a little strange to be quite alone not being used to be so—In the Evening rather dull. Willm. Bidewell (who has taken Collisons Estate that John Pegg had from Michaelmas next, and to which Estate is annexed a publick House where Bens Father at present lives but is going out at the above Time) called on me this morning and another man with him, to ask my consent for the above public House to be continued on, and one Page (lately a Farmer and lived in this Parish, last Year and broke here) to live in it, but I said that I would never consent to it by any Means. The above Phillip Page is an old Man, had a Bastard about 3 Years [ago] by Charlotte Dunnell.

May 30. . . . In the Evening about 5 I took a ride to Norwich and Briton went with me, we got to the Kings Head about 7 o'clock and there supped and slept. Almost the first thing I heard when at Norwich was the sudden death of Mr. Lock my Coal Merchant who shot himself this Afternoon, he had been in a very low way some time it is reported. Poor Man, I am very sorry for him indeed. Went to the Theatre this Evening after the 3rd Act, sat in the Boxes—

paid for the same o. 1. 6. The Theatre pretty full—- Mr. Revett's Benefit.

June 1. I breakfasted and dined and spent the Afternoon at the Kings Head at Norwich. To Mr. Hughes for Coach and Luggage 1. 19. 6. due in October last from Nancy and self. After breakfast I dressed myself and went down to the Cathedral and there heard divine Service and sat in the stalls next to Archdeacon Gooch. After Service I waited on the Bishop at his Palace and spent half an Hour with him, talking with him about Confirmation at Foulsham on Wednesday next, being near 10 Miles from Weston. From the Palace walked about the City and in my Walk saw at a Print Shop, 2 Pictures of my Nephew Saml. Woodforde's—bought them both —one was a Wood Nymph the other a Shepherdess. I paid for them both o. 7. o. To Mr. Frost, Master Builder, for Deals pd. 2. 13. o. To 9 Yards of plaid Ribband for Nancy o. 7. o. To 1 Pair of Soals to carry home pd. o. 1. o. Whom should I meet in my Walk this morning but the bold Roger Hall and he dined with us at the Kings Head at the ordinary there at 1ˢ oᵈ Head And we had for that Shilling, some very fine fryed Soals, a piece of boiled Beef, a Pudding, and a fore Quarter of Lamb with Cucumber, Lettuce, &c. Mr. Du Quesne being as I heard at Priests I went to him before Dinner, and we agreed to go home together in the Evening—He came and drank Coffee and Tea with Hall and me at the Kings Head this Afternoon—and soon after that about 7 o'clock I mounted my Mare and rode with Mr. Du Quesne to the Dog at Easton—and there we parted, Mr. D. went for Tuddenham and I for Weston. Roger Hall marched of also for Bungay.

I paid and gave in the whole at the Kings Head for Horses and self 2 Nights and 2 Days 1. 4. 7½. To Rum and Water and Orange &c. pd also 0. 1. 0. We got home thank God safe and well to Weston Parsonage about 9 o'clock this Evening; had the Soals dressed for Supper, smoaked a Pipe and went to bed.

June 2. . . . About Noon took a ride to Weston House and spent an Hour with Mrs. Custance and her Children. From thence went on to Mr. Jeanes's and there dined and spent the Afternoon with him, his Wife, Miss Short and my Niece A. M. Woodforde. We had for Dinner some Fish, Knuckle of Veal and Bacon, a small piece of rost Pork and Tarts. After Coffee and Tea, Mrs. Jeanes and Miss Short and Nancy got into Mrs. Jeanes's Carriage and sat of for Weston Parsonage and myself with them on horseback. Got there about 8 o'clock. Mrs. Jeanes and Miss Short, did not stay with us above 10 Minutes before they returned back, leaving Nancy behind with me.

June 5. . . . Mr. Thorne made us a long morning Visit. Nancy is making use of the Imperial Oil to her Knee.

June 7. . . . Walked to Bens Fathers this Afternoon and read Prayers to his Wife, she being dangerously ill.

June 9. . . . I went and read Prayers again this morning to Mrs. Leggatt and administred also the H. Sacrament to her—she was very weak indeed and but just alive. She was sensible and showed marks of great satisfaction after receiving the H. Sacrament. She never received it before. Pray God bless her. Sent Briton early to Norwich this morning with my little Cart after things from thence.

June 10. . . . I prayed for Bens poor Mother this Morning at Weston Church—She is but just alive.

1787

June 11. . . . I cut my 4th Finger of my right hand this Morning very much with the Garden Sheers. However I took a ride to Mattishall about Noon to Mr. Bodhams, it being his Rotation, and there dined and spent the Afternoon with Mr. and Mrs. Bodham, Mr. Du Quesne and Mr. Smith—very flat. We had for Dinner a piece of boiled Beef rather course, and a fore Qr. of indifferent Lamb with some plain Gooseberry Tarts, &c. After Coffee and Tea we played one Pool at Quadrille and then returned home to Weston. At Quadrille, only 1.5 Shilling Pool lost 0. 3. 0. Bens poor Mother died this Morning— hope she is happy.

June 12. . . . Our Archdeacon Mr. Younge and Morphew Junr. breakfasted with us this Morning at 9 o'clock. After breakfast I walked with them to our Church to see the same—As the Archdeacon is going round to survey the Churches of this Deanery. And there I took my leave of them for the present. We had Tea and Coffee for breakfast. Nancy likes the Archdeacon much, he is a very cheerful merry little Man and sensible, and came out of Devonshire some few Years ago. The late Bishop of Norwich was his Uncle. About 3 o'clock this Afternoon took a ride to Mr. Jeanes's and there dined and spent the rest of the Afternoon with Mr. and Mrs. Jeanes, the above Archdeacon and Mr. Morphew Junior. We did not dine till near 5 o'clock this Aft. We had for Dinner 3 Chicken boiled and a Tongue, a piece of rost Beef, Asparagus, a baked plumb Pudding of the Custard Kind &c. We had Coffee and Tea about 7 in the Evening and at 8. I mounted my Mare and returned home to Weston. The Archdeacon and Morphew sleep at Lenewade Bridge.

1787

June 13. . . . To an old Man for 8 Crabbs paid o. 1. o.

June 15. . . . I took a ride this morning to Weston House and there spent an Hour with Mrs. Custance, and old Mrs. Collyer of Wroxham. I asked them to drink Coffee and Tea with us this Aft. which they promised. Mr. Custance was gone after Hambleton at School and does not return till to Morrow afternoon. About 6 o'clock Mrs. Custance with Mrs. Collyer, with George and Willm. Custance, came to us and they drank Coffee and Tea with us and stayed with us till after 8 o'clock—we spent a very agreeable Afternoon. Nancy had a Letter from her Sister this Evening, it was brought by Mr. Custance's Servant from Norwich. All our friends in the West tolerably well. Mrs. Richd. Clarke is going to be married to Sam. Burge.

June 16. . . . Ben went with my Mare Phyllis this Evening to Mr. Jeanes of Witchingham and she took his fine Grey Horse Godolphin—She goes again Monday. Mr. Du Quesne's Maid Betty England called here this Evening in her Cart and drank a Dish of Tea with Nancy.

June 17. . . . I read Prayers and Preached this Afternoon at Weston C[hurch]. Mr. and Mrs. Custance with Mrs. Collyer Senr. Mrs. Nat. Micklethwaite with her Mother and Miss Branthwaite at Weston Church this Afternoon—likewise some smart young Ladies in Peachmans Seat, and a great Congregation of Common People at Church.

June 19. . . . To one Lancaster at Mouse-House for six very fine large, white Chicken pd o. 3. o. After breakfast I took a ride to Norwich and Briton went with me and we returned at Night. It was Guild-Day at Norwich—a great Feast. To a Pound of the

328

mixed Pinns for Nancy pd. 2. 4. To other trifles at Bakers pd. 0. 5. To a Qr. of a Pd. of Globar Salts at Priests for Nancy to take for a giddiness in her Head—pd. 0. 3. I had it divided into proper Doses— 1 oz. each Dose. I did not see any of the Priests Family being engaged at the Guild—Harvey the new Mayor. To Rum and Water and other trifles pd. 0. 0. 11. To 2 nice Cucumbers pd. 0. 0. 5. Mr. Du Quesne was at Norwich in the Morning but I did not see him, as he returned home to dinner. I dont think there was a Great deal of Company at Guild. I was glad to get home this Even' having tired myself a good deal walking about the hard Stones in Norwich Streets.

June 21. . . . About 3 o'clock this Afternoon I walked up to Weston House and there dined and spent the Afternoon with Mr. and Mrs. Custance, Mrs. Laton of Drayton and with her the two Miss Randalls of Norwich her Nieces, Mrs. Micklethwaite and her Sister Miss Branthwaite. After Coffee and Tea, Mr. Custance, Mrs. Laton, Mrs. Micklethwaite and self played a Rubber of Whist. Mrs. Laton and self Partners at which I won 0. 3. 0. Then Mrs. Custance and self played another Rubber with Mrs. Laton and Mrs. Micklethwaite and then we won a full Rubber which gained me more 0. 5. 0. Then Mrs. Laton and self played another Rubber with Mrs. Custance and Micklethwaite won then 0. 3. 0. So that I won in the whole this Evening 0. 11. 0. N.B. Mrs. Micklethwaite gave me a light half Guinea. We had for Dinner some Maccarel, a Saddle of Mutton rosted, Ham and Chicken, some young Beans, and Couple of young Ducks rosted and green Peas, Rabbit fryed, Blamange, Custards, Lemon Cream, Asparagus, Tarts,

&c. I did not get home till near 10 o'clock this Even'. The two Miss Priests from Mr. Du Quesnes walked over to my House this morning about 11 o'clock and spent the whole Day with my Niece and in the Evening returned as they came, and Nancy walked with them as far as Odnam Green.

June 23. . . . To my Boy's Mother, Mrs. Crossley, for a Calf's Pluck, viz. Heart, Liver, and Lights—a large one—pd. o. 1. 6. Mr. and Mrs. Jeanes dined and spent the Afternoon with us. It was Mrs. Jeanes's Birth-Day to-day, who only enters into her one and twentieth Year. We gave them for Dinner some boiled Beef, Calf's Liver fryed, Hassh-Mutton, a fat young Goose, and Peas, and Gooseberry Tarts. Lent my Horse Punch to Mr. Cary to go to Norwich. My old Mare, Peggy took Mr. Jeanes's Horse to day.

June 24. . . . I read Prayers, Preached and Christned a Child by name John, this Morning at Weston Church. Mr. and Mrs. Custance, Mrs. Micklethwaite and her Sister Miss Branthwaite at Church. Nancy was at Church this morning and walked there and back. My Niece has not been able to go to Church since she returned from Somersett in October last.

June 28. . . . We brewed some small Beer to-day. We had Peas for the first time out of our Garden.

June 29. . . . Sr. Willm. Jernegan sent me by Mr. Custance a Treatise on the Plant called Scarcity Root.[1]

---

[1] The Scarcity Root was the mangel-wurzel, and was so called owing to confusion of the German word Mangel, meaning *want*, with the German word Mangold, meaning *beet*. Wurzel managed to retain its identity as *root*. Peter Pindar in 1788, however, got the meaning right in his *Peter's Prophecy*! He is satirising some contemporary scientists unwisely, but nevertheless wittily:

> Great Duckweed Thompson, all my soul reveres!
> And Mulgrave charms me with his arctic bears.

1787

July 1. . . . I read Prayers, Preached, read a Proclamation for the better observing the Lord's Day, and Christened a Child of Barkers this Afternoon at Weston C[hurch]. Mr. and Mrs. Custance and Children, Hambleton, George and William at Church this Afternoon. Nancy also walked to Church this Afternoon. There was a large Congregation at Church this Aft.

July 2. . . . Mrs. Davy and her Daughter called here this Morn' in their road from Mattishall to Thurning, and stayed with us about an Hour. Poor Betsy Davy looked shocking bad indeed, pale as a Ghost. When they were gone I mounted my Mare and went to Witchingham to Mr. Jeanes's—Nancy also set of on foot at the same time for Weston House. Our Maid Betty walked with her to help her. I dined and spent the Afternoon at Mr. Jeanes's with him and Mrs. Jeanes. Nancy dined and spent the Afternoon with Mr. and Mrs. Custance. I returned home between 8 and 9 this Evening as did Nancy also near the same time. Mr. and Mrs. Custance were so kind as to return with Nancy in their Coach—but did not

> My eyes with shells, lo ! limpet Davies greets !
> And Doctor Lettsome with his rare horse-beets !
> Beets, that with shame our parsnips shall o'erwhelm,
> And fairly drive potatoes from the realm !
> Beets ! in whose just applauses we are hoarse all ;
> Such are the wond'rous pow'rs of *Mangel-Worsal*.

(see Wolcot's *Peter Pindar's Works*, vol. ii, pp. 131–2, and the N.E.D.). It should be added that the mangel-wurzel was first brought into notice in England in 1786 by Sir Richard Jebb, a distinguished doctor and scientist, while another doctor, John Coakley Lettsom (1744–1815) —to whom Pindar refers above—translated in 1787 a pamphlet from the French of the Abbé de Commerell entitled, ' An Account of the Mangel-Wurzel or Root of Scarcity '. This was probably the treatise to which Parson Woodforde refers (see *D.N.B.* on Dr. Lettsom).

walk into our House, it being rather late. They behaved extremely kind indeed to Nancy the whole Day at Weston House. We had for Dinner at Mr. Jeanes's some Peas and Pork, Goose-Giblets stewed, cold beef and cold Lamb, &c. Mr. Jeanes rode part of the way with me back to Weston.

July 3. . . . Mr. and Mrs. Custance, with their Sons, Hambleton, George and William, drank Coffee and Tea with us this Afternoon and stayed till 8 o'clock. They all walked about my Garden and were well pleased, particularly the young Gentlemen with the Ship. Glorious Time now (thank God) for the Haysell.

July 5. . . . All my Hay up in Cock and very finely made thank God.

July 9. . . . Mr. Jeanes made us a short morning Visit, and he acquainted us that his Wife was brought to bed of a Daughter this morning about 7 o'clock, and as well as he could wish her to be in her state. She was not more than 10 hours in labour. Mrs. Jeanes's Mother, Mrs. Springer, was to have been with them at the time, but is expected to Morrow. Mrs. Custance 2 Daughters Fanny and Emily came to our House this Evening on a Walk, and they drank some Milk and Water and eat some Cakes. I walked with them and the Maid Sally good part of the way back, as far as John Bakers, and there the Rain overtook us but not much, and there another Maid Sukey, met us, and there I left them. I was wet thro' on my return back to my House. The little Folks, I hope, got home without being wet. I gave to each of the little Ladies a Medal apiece in imitation of an half Guinea in kind of brass. My Folks busy in bringing our Hay home and stacking it all Day long. The Major Part of it stacked to day.

July 11. . . . I was very busy all the Morning long in helping them in the Field, as we were busy carrying our Hay. We finished about 8 this Evening and then came Rain.

July 13. . . . Mr. Custance called here this Morning and he desired me to dine with him to day to meet Mr. Taswell of Aylsham—and likewise to desire my Niece and self to dine at Weston House to Morrow to partake of a fine Haunch of Venison. I rode up to Weston House between 2 and 3 o'clock this Afternoon and there dined and spent the Afternoon with Mr. and Mrs. Custance and Family. In the Evening after Tea and Coffee Mr. Taswell with his Nephew Master Taswell came to Weston House and they stayed, supped and slept there. I returned home to Supper between 8 and 9.

July 14. . . . About 11 this morning, Mrs. Custance and Mr. Taswell with Hambleton Custance in Mr. Taswell's Whiskey, and Master Edmund Bacon (eldest Son of Sr. Edm. Bacon's) on a little Hobby, came to our House and spent an Hour with us—The little Folks were highly pleased with the Ship in my Bason. Paid my Blacksmith, Spaule, a Bill of 0. 13. 6. About Noon I mounted my Mare, and took a ride to Weston House, and from thence, Mr. Taswell with his Nephew, George Custance, and Master Bacon, and self, took a ride to Witchingham and made a morning Visit to Mr. Jeanes, and after staying there about an Hour, we returned to Weston House, and there dined and spent the Afternoon. Whilst we were at Mr. Jeanes's my Mare took Mr. Jeanes's Horse Godolphin. Mr. Custance sent his Coach after my Niece to dine at Weston House. Mr. Du Quesne and Mr. Press Custance also dined and spent the Afternoon with us. We had for Dinner at Weston House, some fryed Soals, green Peas Soup, a very fine fat Haunch of Venison (given to Mr. Custance by Sr. J̄n̄ō̄ Woodhouse) Tarts, Blamange, Jelly, &c. &c. Mr. Taswell with his Nephew and Master Bacon went for Aylsham between 7 and 8 this Evening. About 8 Nancy and self, and Mr. Du Quesne with us in Mr. Custances Coach, returned home—and then Mr. Du Quesne mounted his Horse and went for his Home. We spent a very agreeable Day at Weston House, &c. We did not see Mrs. Jeanes at Witchingham (she being in the Straw) or her Mother—only Mr. Jeanes. Ben went to Norwich after Coal for me to day, and he returned about 5 o'clock this Afternoon. Ben informed me that fine Soals were sold at three pence per Pound to day at Norwich.

July 18. . . . I took a ride to Mr. Jeanes's this morning, saw him, Mrs. Jeanes, Child, and Mrs. Jeanes Mother, a Mrs. Springger, who has been a fine Woman. I returned home to Dinner.

July 21. . . . Nancy very busy this morning in making some Rasberry Jam and red Currant Jelly. She made to day about 8 Pd. of Currant Jelly and about 9 Pound of Rasberry Jamm. This Evening as we were going to Supper, a covered Cart drove into my Yard with 3 Men with it, and one of them, the principal, was a black with a french Horn, blowing it all the way up the Yard to the Kitchen Door, to know if we would [like to see] a little Woman only 33 Inches high and 31 Years of Age. As we did not give our Dissent, she was taken out of the Cart and brought into our Kitchen, where we saw her and heard her sing two Songs. I dont think she was any taller than represented, but rather deformed, seemed in good Spirits, sang exceeding high with very little Judgment and was very talkative. She was called by the black Polly Coleshill of Glocester. The Black told me that he formerly lived with the Earl ot Albermarle I gave him o. 1. o.[1] Ben returned from Norwich about 4 this afternoon.

July 26. . . . Had but an indifferent night of Sleep, very Nervous. Took some Camphire and Nitre going to bed last Night as I found myself rather low —and took some this Morn'. Nancy complained a good deal this Morn' of Wind. About Noon took a ride to Mattishall to Mr. Bodhams being his Rotation Day, and there dined and spent the Afternoon with him, his Wife, old Mrs. Donne, Mr. Smith and Mr. Du Quesne—Mr. Donne of Brome and Mr. Francis Attorney at Norwich. We had for Dinner some fryed Soals, hash'd Calfs Head, a large Round of Beef—Beans and Kidney Beans, a Couple of Ducks rosted and Peas, Lemon Cream and Tarts. After Coffee and Tea we got to Quadrille

---

[1] As a natural consequence and offshoot of the slave trade, numerous negroes were brought to England in the eighteenth century, and until the great decision of Lord Mansfield in 1772 in the case of the slave ' Somerset ', were treated as slaves. By Lord Mansfield's judgement every slave, by the mere fact of landing on English soil, became free. It was presumably as a consequence of that judgement that Parson Woodforde's black friend had been able to leave Lord Albemarle's service and earn a free and cheerful living with his French horn and his little dwarf show. Doubtless in many cases the negro slaves continued happily as free servants—the little negro boy, for instance, who was given to Lady Shelburne in 1768, and who was possibly the same person as Lord Shelburne's famous negro servant nicknamed ' Junius ', a nickname which involved the poor negro after his death in the Junius mystery (see Lecky's *England in the Eighteenth Century*, vol. vii, pp. 359–60, and Lord Fitzmaurice's *Shelburne*, vol. i, p. 396, and vol. ii, pp. 329–30).

lost o. o. 6. Returned home about 9 o'clock this Evening. Mr. and Mrs. Custance with some of their Children drank Tea this Afternoon with my Niece.

July 29. . . . Nancy begun making Use of Goulards Pomatun this Morning 'Pray God it may do her good.' I read Prayers and Preached this Aft. at Weston C[hurch] Mrs. Custance at Church but not Mr. C.

July 30. . . . Lent to Nancy this Morning to pay for a Gown she bought of Robt. Buck of Honingham 1. 5. o. To Robt. Buck for an East India Hankker-chief 6. o.

July 31. . . . About 9 o'clock this Morning Mrs. Davy with her Daughter came to my House in a one Horse-Chaise and they dined and spent the After-noon with us—In the Evening Mrs. Davy returned home to Thurning but left her Daughter to spend a few Days with Nancy, Betsy being far from well, having a violent palpitation of the heart—she is now however much better than she has been of late. We had for Dinner some Veal, Beans and Ham, a piece of boiled Beef, a Green Goose and some tarts. Betsy Davy supped and slept here.

Aug. 2. . . . To John Piper of Mattishall, Gardner and his Man for 2 Days work in my Garden in nailing up the branches of the Apricots &c. at 1^s 0^d per Day—o. 4. o. N.B. I boarded them both for the time. Mr. Custance spent about an Hour with us this Morn'.

Aug. 4. . . . Mrs. Lombe of Attlebridge and a Niece of hers by name Anne Greaver of Stibbard a Girl of about 10 Years old, were going in a one Horse Chaise from Attlebridge to Mr. Peachmans, the

Horse in the Chaise took fright in the Craft by my House and ran away with the Chaise and they in it, the little Girl shrieking and crying out all the time. I was walking in the Garden and saw it, it frightened me very much, but thank God the Horse stopped just at my great Gates, and they received no hurt whatever by God's Providence, but were very much frightened, I went out to them and they came into my House and stayed near an Hour with us, drank some Wine and Water, took a turn round my Garden, and when perfectly recovered, they got into the Chaise and drove home quietly the Servant Man riding gently before them. The Horse went very quietly on his return back. One of the main Springs behind was broke, but not so as to prevent their making use of the Chaise. Sent Briton on horseback early this Morn' to Norwich after News &c. he returned about 1 o'clock.

Aug. 6. . . . My Study Chimney begun to be raised higher with Brick-work in the outside and to be contracted, Bean of Norwich, the Mason, has undertaken it. My Parlour Chimney is to be done after the same. Pray God ! No Accident may happen in the doing it.

Aug. 7. About 1 o'clock took a ride to Mr. Du Quesnes being his Rotation Day and there I dined and spent the Afternoon with him, Mr. Priest of Reepham and his Daughter Rebeccah, Mr. and Mrs. Bodham. Mr. Smith not there owing, I think, to Betsy Davy being at my House and his imagining that she might be at Mr. Du Quesnes. After Tea at Quadrille lost — 0. 3. 0. We broke up early, was at home by 8 o'clock.

Aug. 9. . . . Mr. Pringle of Reepham an Apothecary came here this morning to see Betsy Davy, she being under him. To a Man this Morn' for Earthen Ware pd. o. 1. 1. Very hot and sultry this Evening and some Lightning.

Aug. 10. . . . About 1 o'clock this Morning there was a most violent Tempest—very much Lightning and the most vivid, strong and quick I think I ever saw before—Not so much Thunder but very loud what there was—The Rain was some time before it came but then it was very heavy, the Rain did not last long. We were much alarmed, the Maids came downstairs crying and shrieking at 1 o'clock. I got up immediately and thinking when I went up Stairs to bed last Night that there was likelihood of a Tempest being so hot, I had lighted my little Lamp, and only laid down on my Bed with most of my Cloathes on and was just dozing when I heard the Maids all of a sudden shrieking at my Door. We lighted some Candles. Nancy had one in her Room, they were much frightned. It continued incessantly lightning from before 1 till 4 this Morning—then it abated and then I went to bed and slept comfortably till 9 o'clock. Thank God Almighty, for preserving us all safe from so violent a Tempest. May all others escape as well. It was most dreadful to behold the Lightning. Mr. Massingham, Dr. Thornes Apprentice, just called here in the Evening to enquire after Betsy Davy &c.

Aug. 11. . . . My Parlour and Study Chimnies finished this Day and I thank God safe and well. I gave the Men to drink on the Occasion o. 1. o. A great deal mentioned on the Papers concerning the dreadful Tempest on Friday Morn' last, but thanks be to the Lord, but very little damage done or any Lives lost. May all other Parts escape as well.

Aug. 12. . . . I read Prayers and Preached this Aft. at

Weston C. Mr. and Mrs. Custance at Church this Afternoon they returned from Yarmouth last Friday. The Cossey Singers at Weston Church this Afternoon. I likewise christned two Children this Aft: at Church.

Aug. 17. . . . Mr. and Mrs. Townshend and one of their Daughters made us a Morning Visit of about half an Hour. Yesterday about 5 o'clock in the Afternoon (forgot to be inserted Yesterday) I buried poor Sarah Lawrence aged 30—late Servt. to Mr. Custance. Very indifferent this Evening with a sore throat. I took some Rhubarb this Evening going to bed.

Aug. 18. . . . Had a very bad night of it very little sleep indeed my throat very sore and Stomach very bilious. Tho' so very indifferent, being engaged at Weston House, about half past 2 o'clock, Mr. Custance sent his Coach after us, and self, Nancy and Betsy Davy got into it and went to Weston House and there dined and spent the Afternoon with Mr. and Mrs. Custance, Mrs. Micklethwaite, and Mr. and Mrs. Jeanes. A Thunder Storm with some lightning and Rain, was but just over when we went to Weston House. We returned as we went about 8 in the Evening. After Coffee and Tea, Mr. and Mrs. Jeanes returned home. We stayed and played one Rubber at Whist, myself and Mrs. Micklethwaite against Mr. and Mrs. Custance at which we won—at 1^s 0^d Whist I won 0. 2. 0. I could eat but little my Throat being sore. We had a prodigious large and fine Melon after Dinner.

Aug. 20. . . . Mrs. Davy from Thurning came here this morning on horseback and a Servant with her, by half past 8 o'clock, before Nancy or Betsy were down Stairs, and she breakfasted, dined and spent the Aft: with us. Mrs. Davy left us about 5 o'clock this Evening. Had a very indifferent Night again last night. Somewhat better (thank God) this Afternoon.

Aug. 22. I breakfasted, supped and slept again at home. Nancy breakfasted, dined &c. &c. again at home. Betsy Davy breakfasted, dined &c. here again. Soon after breakfast I walked to Church and there buried Mary Cushing Wife of poor Tom Cushing who was ill but very few Days aged 63 Years. On my return home from Church, found Mrs. Micklethwaite at my House, who came to inform us that having been disappointed of some part of the Company that we were to meet at her house to Morrow, begged to put of the Engagement to Tuesday next. As she walked to my House by herself, I walked back with her and stayed half an Hour with her, during that Time Captain Laton and Lady called there. On my return home from Mrs. Micklethwaites, whom should I find at my House but Roger Hall who dined and spent the Afternoon with Nancy and Betsy. My being engaged to Mr. Townshends could not dine with him, but shall to Morrow (deo volente) as he has engaged himself to dine with me to Morrow. Between 2 and 3 o'clock I took a ride to Honingham Hall and there dined and spent the Afternoon with Mr. and Mrs. Townshend, Mrs. Cornwallis, Mr. Du Quesne, Mr. Priest of Reepham and Mr. and Mrs. Jeanes. Mr. Jeanes was in a very frenchyfied Dress, black silk Coat, Waistcoat and Breeches with a Chappeau de brache under his left Arm.[1] After Coffee

---

[1] Parson Woodforde's contempt for the French extended to their language. By a *chappeau de brache* he evidently means a *chapeau-bras*

and Tea, Mrs. Cornwallis, Mr. Priest, Mr. Du Quesne
and self got to Cribbage won 0. 1. 0. Returned home
to Weston about 8 o'clock. Nancy and Betsy Davy
were heartily tired of Halls Company, he was gone
to sleep at Lenewade Bridge before I returned. To
Cupper of my Parish gave 0. 0. 6.

Aug. 23. . . . Mr. Custance sent me a Note this
Morning to desire that I would dine with him on
Saturday next to meet the Bishop at Weston House.
I privately named a Child of Richmonds this Morning
at my House—by name—John. To 5 fine white
Chicken pd. 0. 2. 6. To 2 full grown Guinea Fowls
pd. 0. 2. 0. Mr. Hall dined and spent the Afternoon
here again. In the Evening he rode to Mr. Du
Quesnes to sleep.

Aug. 25. . . . Mr. Du Quesne called here about 2
o'clock in his Chaise and I went with him in it to
Weston House where we dined and spent the Afternoon with Mr. and Mrs. Custance, the Bishop of
Norwich, Dr. Baggott and Lady, Mr. Archdeacon
Gooch, a Miss Chester, and a Mr. Hay, the two
latter Relations, to Mrs. Baggott. The Bishop left
us above 7 o'clock. Mr. Du Quesne and self returned
home about 8 o'clock. Remarkable high Wind about
10 o'clock this Even'.

Aug. 28. . . . My Greyhounds being both very full of
fleas and almost raw on their backs, I put some Oil
of Turpentine on them, which soon made many of
them retire and also killed many more. We all
dined, spent the Aft: and supped at Mrs. Mickle-

which is defined in Fairholt's *Costume in England* (vol. ii, p. 119) as
' a hat made to fold, and carry beneath the arm, by beaux who feared to
derange their wigs'. From Planché one learns that the hat was made of
silk, was flat, and three-cornered (*Cyclopaedia of Costume*, vol. i, p. 89).

thwaites, with her, Mr. and Mrs. Branthwaite of Taverham, a Mrs. Hawkins Sister to Mrs. Branthwaite, Mr. and Mrs. Day of Horsforth and Jonathan Micklethwaite. One of Mrs. Micklethwaites Coach Horses being lame Mr. Days Carriage was sent after Nancy and Betsy. We all returned in Mr. Branthwaites Coach soon after Supper but then after 10 o'clock. After Tea and Coffee we got to Cards the Game Vingt' one or one and twenty at which I lost abt. 1. 0. 0. Very good Dinner and Supper, but I eat very little at either. I was quite ill all day with pains within me of Wind, like Stiches in the Side and Bowels. I walked thither but returned in the Coach and four. Nancy nor Betsy played at Cards at all this Evening.

Aug. 30. . . . About Noon took a ride to Norwich, got there about 2 o'clock and Briton went with me till about a mile from Norwich and then I dismounted and sent Briton back with the Horses. I walked from thence to Norwich went to Priests where I was engaged to dine and there found Du Quesne. As I was setting out from home to Norwich, Mr. Jeanes called on us, and wished us to accept of an Haunch of New Forest Venison to be dressed to Morrow and to invite Mr. and Mrs. Custance and them &c. to it, but as I was engaged and uncertain of returning at the above Time I begged to decline accepting &c. Mr. Jeanes was much uneasy on the Occasion. I dined, spent the Afternoon, supped and spent the Evening at Mr. Priests in St. Giles's with him, his Wife, Son John, Mr. and Mrs. Priest of Reepham their two Daughters, Rebeccah and Mary, Mr. Du Quesne and a Mr. Wilkins a young Man Son of the Grocers. A Mrs. Cooper drank Tea, supped and spent the

Even' with us. After Coffee and Tea we got to Cards at which won o. 2. 6. I slept at my old Inn the Kings Head.

Aug. 31. I breakfasted, and dined at the Kings Head. After breakfast I went to Mr. Priests and from thence went with Mr. and Mrs. Priest of Norwich and their Son, Mr. Du Quesne, Mr. and Mrs. Priest of Reepham, and Daughters, Mrs. Cooper, to see the Bridewell, St. Andrews Hall, the Iron Foundry and the public Gardens at Bunns, and then walked back again, they to Mr. Priests and I to the Inn. The Gentlemen each paid for seeing the above 1. 6. I dined at the Ordinary at the Kings Head but soon after dinner walked to Mr. Priests and spent the remaining part of the Afternoon there. Paid at the Kings Head for my Dinner &c. o. 3. 3. To Chambermaid &c. at the Kings Head gave o. 1. 6. To trifling little things at Norwich pd. o. 3. o. Mr. Du Quesne going home in his Carriage this Afternoon about 6 o'clock, he offered me a place in the same, which I accepted (tho' I had ordered my Horses to be at Norwich to Morrow) and I went with him in it as far as France Green at the end of Mr. Townshends Paling and there I got out and walked home, being but a little more than a Mile from my House and was at home before 8 this Evening, very much unexpected. I supped and slept at home ; found Nancy and Betsy at work and rather surprised at my coming home. They both breakfasted, dined, &c. again at home. Mr. Du Quesnes Coachman by name William, quite ill on his return from Norwich. Something of the Gravel. He appeared to me to make too much of his Complaint by groaning violently whilst on the Coach Box and very loud.

Sep. 1. . . . Mr. Custance called here this morning
and desired us to dine at Weston House on an Haunch
of Venison which Mr. Jeanes gave him, and to
Meet them also, which we could not refuse—therefore
between 2 and 3 Mr. Custance sent his Coach after
us and we dined and spent the Aft. at Weston House,
with Mr. and Mrs. Custance, and Mr. and Mrs.
Jeanes. We returned home as we went about 8
o'clock. Mr. Jeanes (I think) might have had his
Venison at home and invited a few Friends. It was
a very small Haunch, but very good. The Weather
rather precarious and damp for the Harvest and has
been so some Days though the Barometer has been
and is still quite high. To Cantrells Son this Morn'
for bringing Porter gave 0. 6.

Sep. 3. . . . To a Lad of Downings that was shearing
Wheat for me, of his own accord this Even'. gave
0. 1. 0.

Sep. 4. . . . About 11 o'clock this Morning walked to
Weston Church to christen Mr. Custance's last little
Boy, but the Company not being arrived Mr. Custance
sent his Coach after me to go to Weston House
which I did and there stayed about half an Hour
with Mr. and Mrs. Custance, Sr. Thomas and Lady
Durrant, the latter is Mr. Custances own Sister and
a very fine Woman, there was a Daughter with them
about 11 Years old, her Name as her Mothers
Susannah. Mr. and Mrs. Collyer of Wroxham then
sent word that they were waiting at Church, we all
then went in two Coaches and four to Weston
Church where I publickly presented (being privately
named by me before by name John) the young
Gentleman. Sr. Thomas Durant and Mr. Collyer,
God Fathers, and Lady Durant the only Godmother.

Two Coaches and four and a Post Chariot at Church.
After the Christning we walked about Weston Church
about 20 Minutes, then the Company went for
Weston House—and I walked home to the Par-
sonage. About 2 o'clock I dressed and walked up to
Weston House and there dined and spent the Aft.
with Mr. and Mrs. Custance, Sr. Thomas and Lady
Durrant and Daughter, Mr. and Mrs. Collyer, and
Mr. Press Custance—After Coffee and Tea Sr. Thos.
and Lady and Daughter set of home to a place called
Scottow—Sr. Thos. invited me to his House.[1] After
they were gone, Mrs. Custance, Mrs. Collyer, Mr.
Press Custance and self sat down to Cribbage at
Shillings, at which I won 0. 3. 0. Mrs. Collyer and
Self against Mrs. Custance and Mr. Press. About
8 this Evening I walked home. N.B. Mr. Custance
very genteelly made me a present for christning the
Child, wrapped in White Paper of the Sum of 5. 5. 0.
In the Morn' I sent a Dozen of very fine Anson
Apricots to Weston House which were on the table
after Dinner and all eat, but not a word mentioned
from whence they came, therefore suppose that
neither Mr. or Mrs. Custance knew anything of the
Matter.

Sep. 7. . . . Poor old Thomas Cushing of this Parish
died this Morning.

Sep. 9. . . . I buried poor old Thos. Cushing this Even'.
aged 82.

Sep. 10. . . . Very fine Weather (thank God) for the

[1] Sir Thomas Durrant (1722–90), of Scottow, Norfolk, was created
a baronet on January 22, 1784. He married, *circa* 1773, Susanna, first
daughter of Hambleton Custance, of Weston, Norfolk, by Susanna,
daughter and heiress of John Press (hence Mr. Press Custance), Alderman
of Norwich. He was Sheriff of Norfolk in 1784–5. His wife survived him
till 1833 (see Cokayne's *Complete Baronetage*, vol. v, pp. 241–2).

Harvest now. Mr. and Mrs. Jeanes and Daughter, their Nurse Maid and 2 Men Servants dined and spent the Aft. here.

Sep. 11. . . . Betsy Davy breakfasted and spent part of the Morn' here. About 11 o'clock this morning Nancy and Betsy Davy went in my little Cart and Ben with them, to Thurning about 10 Miles of, and I went with them on horseback and Briton with me. We got to Thurning about 1 o'clock and there dined and spent the Afternoon at Mr. Thos. Elwins with him, his Wife, Mrs. Davy and Mr. Charles Roope, Mrs. Davy's Brother—They were surprised to see us. We had for Dinner some beef Stakes, a neck of Mutton boiled and a Couple of rost Chicken. As we went thro' Witchingham we just called at Mr. Jeanes's—saw him and Mrs. Jeanes. Soon after Dinner Nancy and Betsy Davy returned with Ben as they came to Witchingham to Mr. Jeanes's to spend a few days with Mrs. Jeanes, Mr. Jeanes being going to Norwich for 2 or 3 Days. Gave to Mr. Elwin's Servant Maid 0. 1. 0. After Tea at Mr. Elwins, Mr. Charles Roope and self took a ride to Holt about 5 Miles from Thurning, and there we supped and slept at the Feathers Inn, kept by a Mrs. Shepherd. Holt stands well and a good decent Town.

Sep. 12. I breakfasted at the Feathers Inn, and soon after set forth for Wells—leaving Charles Roope behind at Holt. Paid and gave at Holt abt. 0. 11. 0. We got to Wells about Noon, there eat some bread and Cheese and Butter and drank some Porter at the Standard Inn on the Quay pd. at Wells 0. 1. 6. About 1 o'clock mounted my Mare and went on for Burnham Market where we dined, supped and slept

346

at Pitts Arms kept by one Ballard. Burnham Market is a very pretty Country Town. Lord Camelford[1] has a good Estate there and almost a new built House large and very good—but it is all going to be sold— Also lives in the Town Sr. Mordaunt Martin[2] a married Man with 5 daughters and one Son—the Eldest a girl of about 22. Very pleasant ride from Wells to Burnham all by the Sea and by Holkham House, Mr. Cokes—a rider supped and spent the Evening with me.

Sep. 13. Got up about 6 o'clock this morning and set of before breakfast for Brancaster about 5 Miles from Burnham, got there about 8 o'clock, called there on Mr. Shute the Rector, found him a bed but he soon

---

[1] Thomas Pitt, 1st Baron Camelford of Boconnoc, Cornwall (1737–93), a nephew of Lord Chatham. He entered the House of Commons in 1761 and continued a member till 1784, when he was made a Peer. He was a lord of the Admiralty in the Grenville ministry, 1763. It was he who helped to bring about Chatham's reconciliation with Lord Temple in 1774. He violently opposed the North Ministry and the Coalition Ministry. He owed his peerage in January 1784 to his cousin, the Prime Minister, the younger Pitt. He was a person of very considerable talent, very artistic, a good speaker, and with parts enough as a young man at Cambridge to attract the attention of the fastidious Gray. He married a fortune in 1771, namely Anne, daughter and co-heiress of Pinckney Wilkinson, merchant of Hanover Square, and of Burnham, Norfolk. Thomas Pitt's name was one of those suggested as a possibility for an alternative administration to the Coalition in March 1783. George III was turning in every direction in order to avoid the Coalition, and when Lord Gower mentioned Thomas Pitt, the distracted king desired him ' to apply to Mr. Thomas Pitt or Mr. Thomas anybody '. But it all came to nothing (see Fitzmaurice's *Shelburne*, vol. ii, p. 256, for the ' Thomas anybody ' story, and the *D.N.B.* for other dates and facts).

[2] Sir Mordaunt Martin, Bt. (creation of 1667), of Burnham Westgate Hall, Norfolk, and of Long Melford, Suffolk, was born in 1740 and died in 1815. He was some time Marshal of the Vice-Admiralty Court in Jamaica. The baronetcy became extinct in 1854 (Cokayne's *Complete Baronetage*, vol. iv, p. 42).

came down, and I breakfasted, dined supped and slept at the Farm House where Mr. Shute boards, one Farmer Chadwick—A large Farmer. Paid and gave at Burnham Market about o. 12. 9. After we had breakfasted Mr. Shute took me a very pleasant ride to Hunstanton Light House about 5 Miles from Brancaster all by the Sea Side, we did not return till near 4 o'clock to dinner, as we walked a long time on the Sea Shore. The Rev. Mr. Weatherhead (who has the Living of Easton near me) and who lives at Brancaster and near Mr. Shute, dined, supped and spent the Evening with us. My Horses were in Mr. Shute's Stables at the Parsonage and Briton had a bed procured for him at the Inn. Mr. Shute is building a new Parsonage House of Brick. We had for Dinner a Piece of rost Beef, some hashed Mutton and a plumb Pudding. We spent a very agreeable Day together. Gave to the Farmers Harvest Men a largess o. 1. o. The Sea comes up very near Mr. Shutes House. Mr. Weatherhead is a Married Man and has 8 or 9 Children.

Sep. 14. I breakfasted at Brancaster with Mr. Shute and soon after mounted my Mare to return back to Weston. To Mr. Shute's Man John, gave o. 1. o. To the Farmers Maid Servant gave o. 1. o. We got to Fakenham about 12 o'clock 14 Miles from Brancaster, and there we dined and spent the aft. at the red Lion, kept by one Dade, a Somersett Man. Paid and gave at Fakenham abt. o. 5. o. Paid my Servant, Briton, for things o. 3. 6. About 2 o'clock we set of from Fakenham for Weston about 14 Miles and thank God got safe and Well to Weston between 6 and 7 this Evening, found only my Maid Nanny, Ben and Charles at home. My other Maid Betty being with her Mistress at Wi[t]chingham where she has been all the Time in my absence. I was rather tired this Evening, therefore supped soon and went to bed about 10 o'clock. Mr. Custance [sent] us a brace of Partridges this Morn' which I had this Evening for Supper.

Sep. 15. . . . Soon after breakfast I sent my little Cart after Nancy and her Maid from Witchingham, and they returned home about 1 o'clock and glad they were home. Nancy dined, supped and slept at home. Mrs. Jeanes sent by Briton unknown to Nancy a brace of Partridges—Nancy very well and hearty. I was rather ill this Evening with a pain in my Bowels—took some Rhubarb going to bed. To Largesses to day gave 0. 2. 0. Mr. Du Quesnes Maid (Betty England) drank Tea here this Afternoon—she came in a Cart. I thought myself very ill indeed this Evening as I was going to bed—my Pulse very uncommon which made me rather low and frightned me.

Sep. 16. . . . Had but an indifferent Night of rest, but (thank God) Got up better than I expected, but very weak. I read Prayers and Preached this Morn' at Weston C[hurch] it was very wet this morning, but nevertheless Mrs. Custance, her Sister Lady Bacon, a Miss Gore about 22 Years of Age and Captain Beauchamp, Mrs. Custances Brother were all at Church. Something better this Evening but still not well.

Sep. 24. . . . Carried all my second Crop of Clover to day. Have now finished every part of my Harvest both Corn and Hay—and (thank God) very well.

Sep. 26. . . . Nancy went in her little Cart and Briton with her to Mr. Du Quesnes this Morning, and [I] went with them on Horseback and there we dined and

spent the Afternoon with Mr. Du Quesne, Mr. and
Mrs. Priest of Reepham and their two Daughters,
Miss Priest and Miss Mary, and Mr. and Mrs. Priest
of Norwich. We had for Dinner, some Herrings,
Ham and Chicken, Pigeon Pye, rost Beef, a rost
Duck, Tarts, Cheese Cakes, Charter, &c. As we were
at Tea this Afternoon about 5 o'clock, a Tempest of
Thunder, Lightning and Rain happened which
frightned my Niece much, as she was to go home
soon after Tea in her Cart, however than[k] God, it
did not continue long, and after a fine Evening with
almost a full Moon, and about 6 o'clock we returned
home as we went and the rest of the Evening quite
fine. We Got home (thank God) very Safe and well.
All the Priests sleep at Mr. Du Quesnes. It was so
very hot and fair when we came from home this
morning, that I had No great Coat. To a Fisherman
at Mr. Du Quesnes for some Soals to carry home at
4^d per Pound pd. o. 1. o.

Sep. 28. ... I spent a good part of the Morning at the
Church and in the Church Yard, my People being
busy in laying some Gravel upon the Walks there
and making the Church Yard more decent.

Oct. 2. ... Nancy went in her little Cart with Briton,
and I on my Mare to Witchingham about 1 o'clock
and there we dined and spent the Afternoon at
Mr. Jeanes's with him, his Wife, Mr. Du Quesne,
Mr. and Mrs. Priest of Reepham with their two
Daughters, Rebeccah and Mary. We had for Dinner
a Couple of small Chicken boiled, and a Tongue,
one stewed Duck, a fine Haunch of Venison and
a baked Pudding. Mr. Du Quesne fell backward
from his Chair in the Afternoon and bruised himself
much. The Ladies were not in the Room at the time.

We returned as we went directly after Coffee. Mr. Du Quesne went with me, he complained a good deal of his Fall when on horseback in giving him much Pain. Mr. Du Quesne should have went in his Carriage especially as Mr. Jeanes desired him, and to take up my Niece with him in the same, and which he might have done. We spent a very agreeable Day and did due justice to the Venison which came out of the New Forest from Mr. Jeanes's Father.

Oct. 7. . . . I read Prayers, Preached, churched 2 Women, christned three Children gave Notice of a Sacrament next Sunday and read a long Proclamation against profaneness &c. this Afternoon at Weston Church—a large Congregation. Mrs. Micklethwaite, and my Niece at Church. None from Weston House, their Coach being mending. A very fine fair and warm Day.

Oct. 8. . . . I took a walk about 11 this morning to a Sale by Auction at Mr. Dades, who is obliged to give up his Farm and retire elsewhere. Both Mr. and Mrs. were very unhappy about it. I saw Mr. Jeanes there who bought two Cows. There was not a great deal of Company there.

Oct. 11. . . . Nancy breakfasted at home, and soon after the Weather being fine, she went in the little Cart and Betty with her to Weston House, where she dined, spent the Aft. supped and slept, and Betty stayed with her—they return Saturday. About 2 I walked up to Weston House, and there dined and spent the Aft. and part of the Evening with Mr. and Mrs. Custance and Nancy. I returned as I went about 9 o'clock. After Tea we got to Quadrille at wch. lost 0. 2. 0. the only money that was lost at all. Spent a very agreeable day at Weston House.

Oct. 13. . . . Soon after breakfast I sent Briton with my little Cart after Nancy from Weston House and she returned about two o'clock after taking a ride to Attlebridge and calling at Miss Lombe's, but she was not at home therefore she did not see her. Nancy had a long Letter from her Sister this Evening. Sent Ben early this Morning to Norwich after News, &c. and also to carry a sample of Wheat to sell and which he did sell but only at 1. o. o. per Coomb to Forster of Lenewade Bridge—10 Coomb—it is to be carried to him the ensuing Week. Northern Lights remarkably strong and very red this Night about 10 o'clock —very light indeed. By Nancy's Sisters Letter all our Friends in the West are I thank God tolerably— Mrs. R. Clarke not married yet to Sam Burge, but supposed to take place very soon.

Oct. 15. . . . Very fine and fair and a Frost early in the Morn'. I was very busy this morning in my Garden making some new Strawberry Beds.

Oct. 17. . . . St. Faiths Fair to day. I would not let any of my Servants go to it, on Account of a very bad Fever of the putrid kind, raging there and of which many have died there already. To 2 Dozen fresh Herrings paid o. 1. o.

Oct. 18. . . . Nancy took an Airing in her little Cart this Morning being very fair and fine—Briton with her. Went out a Coursing this Morn with my Dogs, ran one Hare and killed it—a very fine one.

Oct. 20. . . . By the Papers this Evening, Amsterdam has surrendered to the Prussian Troops, and matters in a fair way of re-instating the Statholder.[1]

[1] Parson Woodforde's references to foreign affairs are so infrequent that at first sight it would appear odd that he should mention this affair. The explanation almost certainly is that he was pleased: firstly that the

1787

Oct. 27. . . . Sent Briton with my little Cart early this Morn' to Norwich after News &c. he returned by dinner. Sent Ben also to Norwich this Morning to receive Mony for my Wheat sold last Week to Forster he returned by dinner and brought me a bank Bill of Norwich for the same of 10. 0. 0. being 20^s 0^d per Coomb for ten Coomb.

Oct. 31. . . . Mr. Priest of Reepham called here this Morn' in his road home from Mr. Du Quesne's, on foot. He drank some Rum and Water and then walked on. Very fair and fine Weather with a good deal of Sun, tho' the Barometer is much sunk to day.

Dutch were being bullied by England's Prussian allies ; and, secondly, that this blow indirectly injured the ancestral enemy, France. As regards the first, despite the Revolution, the reign of William III, and the Dutch alliance up to 1780, Englishmen still retained their jealousy of the Dutch as a very powerful naval and commercial power. This jealousy, which was mutual, caused the Dutch to act with the enemies of England in the war of American Independence. As regards the second, Dutch internal politics from the seventeenth century were dominated by the intestine feud between the Orange (Stadtholder) and Republican parties. The first, for dynastic and other reasons, was friendly to England ; the second to France. At this particular time the Republicans were dominant, and had concluded a close Treaty with France at Fontainebleau on November 8, 1785. In the following year the Republicans deprived the Stadtholder, the Prince of Orange, of his ancestral military powers, and in June 1787 they arrested the Princess of Orange who was on her way to the Hague. Now the Princess was sister to Frederick William II, King of Prussia. By a secret treaty England and Prussia decided to intervene, and to restore the Prince of Orange to his ancient power. In September the Prussians invaded Holland, and on October 10 Amsterdam—the centre of the Republican party—surrendered. In April 1788 England, Prussia, and the Netherlands made a triple alliance, and the policy of France was thus decisively frustrated (see Lecky's *England in the Eighteenth Century*, vol. v, pp. 355–61 ; some account of earlier Orange and Republican rivalries will be found in my biography of *Sir George Downing*, 1623–84).

Mr. Custances Gardner brought us this Morning a Basket of Winter Peaches by order of Mr. Custance. The Aurora borealis very strong and red to Night.

Nov. 1. . . . Left of drinking Tea for breakfast in a Morning and took to Milk and Water. Very low all the day, having the bleeding Piles.

Nov. 3. . . . Sent Ben very early this Morning to Norwich with 10 Coomb of Barley full measure, that is, 10 Coomb and two Bushels. He is to sell it for me. Ben returned about 5 this Aft. with half a Ch[a]ldr[o]n of Coal—He sold my Barley to Mr. Bloome who has taken the business late Mr. Locke's —He offered 10ˢ 0ᵈ per Coomb, but Ben would not take that, but however left it with him, and therefore I shall expect half Guineas for the same. He recd. for me for the Wheat last Week from the Marlingford Miller at 18ˢ 9ᵈ—9. 7. 6. which he paid to me on his return home. Ben also brought me home a new Screen for Corn, for which I owe him 0. 18. 0.

Nov. 6. . . . Recd. a Letter this Evening (by Mr. Custance's Servant who had been to Norwich to day) from my Sister Pounsett with a Sussex Note in it of 10. 0. 0. All Friends (thank God) well in Somersett.

Nov. 9. . . . Mrs. Custance with her Children, Fanny, Emily, and Willm. made us a long Morning Visit. To a Man this Aft. for Lobsters &c. pd. 0. 2. 0. Mrs. Custance showed us a very pretty Doll cut out in Paper with several Dresses to it about 6 Inches long—quite flat.

Nov. 12. . . . Soon after breakfast I walked out a Coursing and took Ben and the Boy with me, did not return till near three, afternoon, we had tolerable Sport, coursed one Hare and a Couple of Rabbitts,

all of whom we killed, it was a very large Hare.
I think I never knew so pleasant a day so far in
November, it was more like Summer than Autumn.
I was very indifferent the whole Day, could eat but
very little for Dinner being over fatigued and like-
wise my Spirits but very bad.

Nov. 14. . . . To a poor Man of Easton having lost
a Horse, 0. 1. 0. Poor Neighbour Downings Wife
bad in a Fever.

Nov. 15. . . . Recd. this Morning of one Platt of
Hockering a Pigg Jobber, for 6 small Piggs at 13ˢ 6ᵈ
each—4. 1. 0.

Nov. 21. . . . Mrs. Bodham with her Brother and Sister
Donne and their two Children Anne and Castres,
came over from Mattishall and made us a long
Morning Visit—Eat some cold Pigg &c. and at 1
returned as they came, back to Mr. Bodhams. We
dined and spent the Afternoon at Weston House
with Mr. and Mrs. Custance, and Mr. and Mrs.
Jeanes. We went thither and back in Mr. Custances
Coach. Mr. Du Quesne and Mr. Carter were
invited, but did not go.

Nov. 22. . . . I privately baptized 2 Children this
Morning at my House—one of John Reaves by
name Mary, and the other of Harrisons by name—
Judith. My Greyhound, Hector, had a long Course
this Morning by himself with a fine Hare and killed
it in the Croft before my House. It was by chance
put up in one of the College Closes.

Nov. 24. . . . Mr. and Mrs. Thorne and Betsy Davy
made us a long Morning Visit—all on Horseback.
I sent Ben to Norwich after breakfast for News &c.
I also sent a Hare by him to Mr. Francis. Ben
returned about 4 this afternoon. Recd. of James

Pegg this Afternoon 10. 16. 0. being his Brother John's Composition for Tithe for this last Year, due at Michaelmas last.

Nov. 29. . . . I took a Walk this Morning to Weston House, spent an Hour with Mrs. Custance and son William, and returned home to dinner, did not see Mr. Custance. To Gould of Attlebridge for a Cow (that he has been looking out for me some time) now in her full Profit, having a Calf by the side of her, but is sold to a Butcher at Causton and goes away next Thursday paid Gould for the Cow only 6. 6. 0.

Dec. 4. . . . Mrs. Custance made us a Visit this Morning, but did not stay any time, as this was my Tithe Day. This being my Tithe Audit, the following People waited on me, and dined and stayed till after 12 at Night. Peachman, Girling, Howlett, Forster, Herring, Buck, Mann's Son, Js. Pegg, Step. Andrews, Bidewell, John Page, John Baker, Reynolds, Ben's Father, Norton, Silvey, Ross Bean, Thos. Cary, John Heavers, Willm. Case, Charles Hardy of Ringland, and my Clerk Js. Smith. Received to day for Tithe about 250. 0. 0. I gave them for Dinner, some boiled Beef, a Leg of Mutton boiled and Capers, a couple of Rabbitts boiled and Onion Sauce, a large Surloin of Beef rosted, with vast Quantity of plumb Pudding, and plain Pudding. There were 6 Bottles of Rum made into Punch, 8 Bottles of Port Wine also drank, besides a great Quantity of strong Beer. Everything passed of as agreeable as one might expect from such a Meeting, &c. Reynolds and Bens Father did not dine with them.

Dec. 5. . . . Barnard Dunnell called on me this Morn' and paid me for Tithe 2. 2. 0. Dull and heavy today being kept up so late last Night and drinking more than usual.

Dec. 6. . . . To Henry Baker, my Butcher, for Meat for the last Year to the 1st December pd. 40. 15. 0. Balance included for a Calf &c. To my Maid, Betty, for things pd. 0. 7. 10½. To my Man, Ben, for things pd. 0. 14. 2. To my Man, Briton, for things pd. 0. 17. 2. I gave this Evening to my Servants on my late Tithe Audit Account—as follows. To my Maid, Betty Dade gave 0. 2. 6. To my Maid, Nanny Haye gave 0. 2. 6. To my Man, Briton Scurl gave 0. 2. 6. To my Man, Ben Leggatt gave 0. 1. 0. To my Boy, Charles Crossley gave 0. 1. 0.

Dec. 7. . . . Paid Mr. Palmer of Morton my Malster for Malt and Hopps &c. for a whole Year 19. 8. 10. Paid Mr. Cantrell at Lenewade Bridge also this Morning for Porter, Wine, &c. 6. 10. 0. Sent Briton this Morning with a Note to Mr. and Mrs. Bodham of Mattishall with an invitation to Weston Parsonage for a few Days next Week and if Miss Mary Donne of Norwich was with them to bring her also when they came. About 3 o'clock Briton returned with a Note that they Could not at present fix any time.

Dec. 10. . . . To Cobb—Rat-Catcher 1 yr due Dec. 1st pd. 1. 1. 0. Mr. and Mrs. Bodham sent us a Note that they would wait on us to Morrow to Dinner and bring Miss Mary Donne of Norwich with them. They cannot stay longer than Thursday Morning. Mrs. Davy from Mattishall made us a long Morning Visit, eat some cold Chicken &c. drank some Porter, and at 2 o'clock returned back to Matt[ishall]. She came on horseback behind Mr. Thorne's Boy Robt. To my Maid, Betty, for things pd this Even' 0. 5. 0½. To my Man, Briton, for Do. pd. ditto 0. 15. 9.

Nancy's Pigg was killed this Morning—weight 11 Stone.

Dec. 11. . . . I took a ride this Morning to Weston House and spent half an Hour with Mrs. Custance— Mr. Custance being walked out—I went to ask them to dine with us to Morrow to meet Mr. and Mrs. Bodham. Mrs. Custance seemed much pleased with it, but could not promise till she had seen Mr. Custance. Mrs. Custance having ordered her Coach to go to my House, I desired her not to counter-order it, therefore she with 3 Children went and spent half an Hour with my Niece and then returned back again. About ½ past 2 o'clock Mr. and Mrs. Bodham with Miss Mary Donne of Norwich came to my House to spend a day or two with us. Mr. and Mrs. Bodham with Miss Mary Donne, dined, supped and slept at my House—Miss Donne slept with my Niece in the Attic Story over me. Miss Mary Donne is a very genteel, pretty young Lady and very agreeable with a most pleasing Voice abt. 21 Yrs. very tasty and very fashionable in dress. Mr. Bodhams Coachman Js. returned home to Mattishall with his pair of Horses before Dinner and is to come again on Thursday Morning after them. Mr. Bodhams Footman Thos. dined and slept here. We had for Dinner to day a boiled Leg of Mutton with Capers, a Couple of Chicken rosted and a Tongue, a Norfolk plain batter Pudding, Tripe, Tarts and some blamange with 4 Sorts of Cheese. For Supper some Oysters, a wild Duck rosted, Potatoes rosted, and some cold Chicken &c. After Coffee and Tea we got to Quadrille, viz: Mr. and Mrs. Bodham, Miss Donne and self. I won 0. 3. 0. I did not get to bed to Night till after 12 o'clock.

Dec. 12. . . . Mr. and Mrs. Bodham, and Miss Donne breakfasted, dined, supped and slept again at Weston Parsonage. Mrs. Custance sent a Note to my Niece this Morning and is very sorry they cannot wait on us to dinner this Day, there being no Moon and Nurse Maid very ill. After breakfast Mr. Bodham and self went out a coursing till near dinner time— We had an excellent Course with one Hare indeed, but she escaped, and which I was not sorry for. Mrs. Custance sent us a brace of Snipes this Morn'. We had for Dinner to day some Skaite, Ham and Chicken, a fine Turkey rosted, batter Pudding with Currant Jelly &c. 2nd Course a Duck rosted, Bulley Tarts, Blamange &c. For Supper, a brace of Snipes rosted, &c. &c. After Tea and Coffee we got to Quadrille lost o. o. 6.

Dec. 13. . . . Mr. and Mrs. Bodham breakfasted here as did Miss Donne and About 12 they left Weston Parsonage and went home to Mattishall to their own House. They went away well pleased with their reception here.

Dec. 15. . . . Sent Ben to Norwich this Morning after breakfast for Letters &c.—He returned home to Dinner. Sent by him to be put in the Post Office a long Letter to my Sister Pounsett in Answer to her last. Mr. Custance's second Son George (who came home from School Yesterday in the Afternoon) took a walk to my House this Morning to make us a Visit. He is grown a good deal and looks very well. He promises to be a steady, sensible young Man.

Dec. 17. . . . About Noon I took a ride to Norwich, and my Servant, Briton, went with me, got to Norwich about 2 and there dined, supped, and slept at the Kings Head. As soon as I got to Norwich I walked to the following Houses and paid my Bills there. To Mr. Scott Breeches Maker pd. 2. 1. 0. To Mr. Forster, Attorney, for Coll. Land—pd. 16.0.0. To Willm. Dowe for Coal pd. 5. 9. 4. To Mr. Bacon, Bookseller pd. 0. 8. 3. To Mr. Manning, Brazier pd. 0. 11. 0. To Mrs. Locke, for Coal pd. 1. 9. 4. To Mr. Willmot, Hatter pd. 0. 7. 6. To Mr. Horth, Upholsterer pd. 1. 9. 0. To Rum and Water and gave away 0. 2. 6.

Dec. 18. I breakfasted, supped and slept again at the K[ings] Head at Norwich, soon after Breakfast, I walked about the City and paid the following Bills. To Mrs. Brewster for Tea, &c. pd. 5. 19. 0. To Mr. Jagger, Picture Shop pd. 0. 7. 0. To Mrs. Garland, Taylor pd. 3. 15. 0. To Mr. Buckle, Ironmonger pd. 1. 16. 6. To Mr. Francis, Attorney pd. 5. 5. 7. To Mr. Smith, Mercer pd. 6. 15. 0. To Mr. Studwell, China Man pd. 1. 10. 0. To Mr. Priest, Wine Merchant pd. 15. 13. 0. To Mr. Beale, Fishmonger pd. 0. 1. 4½. Sent Briton Home this Morning before Dinner. Sent home by Briton to my Niece a present of some Yards of different kind of Ribbon of the most fashionable pd. for the same abt. 10. 0. I went to Goss's Sale at Elm Hill this Morning but did not buy any thing at all. I dined and spent the Afternoon at Mr. Priest's with him, his Wife, Son John and Southtern. I drank Tea by myself this Aft. at my Inn. Saw Roger Hall at Norwich but did not have much talk with him, he looked mean and shabby. After Tea this Aft. I walked into London Lane to Royal and Kents Shop, Linen Drapers and there paid for divers things 8. 0. 0. At Buckles for Pig Tail Tobacco ¼ Pd. 0. 0. 9. To a Cloathes Brush for the

1787

Kitchen pd. o. 1. 6. To divers small Articles to day pd. o. 1. o.

Dec. 19. I breakfasted and spent the Morning at Norwich. About 1 o'clock, I mounted my Mare and made my best way to Weston Parsonage. My Servant, Briton, came to Norwich this Morn' about 10 o'clock, and he returned home with me. To Mark Bean, Mason, for altering my Chimnies in the Summer time pd. 1. 2. o. At the Kings Head paid and gave abt. o. 17. o. To extraordinaries this Morn' gave o. 2. 6. We got home, I thank God, safe and well abt. 3 o'clock this Afternoon and there dined supped and slept—but very much fatigued. I called this Morning at Mrs. Micklethwaites Lodgings in Sarry Street, but she was not at home. Nancy was well pleased with the Ribbons.

Dec. 21. . . . To poor People of my Parish against Christmas being St. Thomas's Day—6ᵈ each gave 1. 7. o. To my Miller, Mr. Wade and Forster, paid him a Bill this Morn' for Flour of 5. 9. o. Mr. and Mrs. Custance with their 2 eldest Sons drank Tea and Coffee with us this Afternoon. After Tea we all played at Cards, at Commerce 1 Pool at 6ᵈ per Head, and Hambleton Custance, Mr. Custances eldest Son won the Pool o. 3. o. They went away about 8 o'clock to Weston House. We brewed also to day—all Hurry to day. Mr. Wade in partnership with Forster my Miller called on me this Morning—paid him a Bill of 5. 9. o.

Dec. 23. . . . I read Prayers, Preached, and read the Proclamation against profaneness and Immorality this Morn' at Weston C[hurch]. None from Weston House at Church this Morning. Paid Nancy, Mony borrowed of her for the Poor, o. 5. o.

1787

Dec. 24. . . . We were invited to Weston House to dinner to meet Mr. and Mrs. Branthwaite, Mr. and Mrs. Layton, Mrs. N. Micklethwaite, and Mr. and Mrs. Jeanes, but we begged to be excused, Nancy being so lame, and rather more so as the Weather is so cold.

Dec. 25. . . . This being Christmas Day I read Prayers and administred the H: Sacrament this Morning at Weston Church—For an Offering gave o. 2. 6. Mr. Custance at Church and at the H: Sacrament. Mrs. Custance not there the Weather being very bad. The following old poor Men dined at my House to Day being Christmas Day, and after Dinner I gave each of them 1^s 0^d—in all o. 6. o,—Richd Buck, Thos. Cary, Thos. Carr, John Peachman, Nath: Heavers, and Js. Smith my Clerk. We had for Dinner a Surloin of Beef, plumb Puddings and mince Pies.

Dec. 27. . . . To a Lad for 3 Score of Oysters pd. o. 1. o. Mr. Jeanes made us a Morning Visit. To a poor old singing Man gave—o. o. 6. At Cribbage this Evening with Nancy won o. 1. 6.

Dec. 28. I breakfasted, dined, &c. again at home. Nancy breakfasted, dined, &c. again at home. To a poor Sailor with one Arm gave o. o. 6. Dr. Thorne made us a morning Visit. At Cribbage this Evening with Nancy lost o. o. 6. My Maid Betty was carried home in my little Cart with Ben to spend a Couple of Days at her Fathers at Mattishall being Christmas Holidays.

ANOTHER VIEW OF THE RIVER WENSUM

ADDENDUM

October 29, 1785. . . . 'But no tidings of them, neither Vell nor Mark.'

The phrase, *Vell nor Mark*, is of Dorset dialect origin, and means no trace or sign of a thing: thus, ' I cān't zee vell nar mark o't.' *Mark* seems to be a shepherd's word, applied to the marking of sheep, and *Vell* is apparently the same word as *Fell*, a skin, or hide, and applied to lost cattle (see the English *Dialect Dictionary*, edited by Joseph Wright, under *Vell*, *Fell*, and *Mark*).

INDEX

PART I. GENERAL

(For Persons, see Part II (*a*), and for Places, Part II (*b*). For principal authorities cited, see Part III.)

Roman numerals refer to the parts of the Index ; ed. refers to editorial matter.

Abstinence (Catholic), 284 ; *and v.* Good Friday.

Accidents, 4, 53, 104, 148, 195, 198, 201, 202, 236, 270, 327, 337, 350.
(to chaise), 67.
(to decanter), 46.

Aged marriage, 137.

Air balloon : *v.* Baloon.

Alms, 6, 9, 55, 63, 64, 79, 80, 82, 91, 101, 112, 119, 162, 173, 180, 181, 183, 187, 195, 203, 209, 212, 258, 276, 341, 361.
(at offertory), 211, 241, 291, 362.

Amber grease [ambergris], 192.

American war, ed. 10, 11, 12, 13.

Anna (model ship), 323, 332, 333.

Anthem, 118.

Archbishop : *v.* II (*a*). Cornwallis.

Armless girl, 161.

Art patron, 37, 210, 229 ; *and v.* II (*a*). Hoare.

Assizes, 180, 232, 264.
(sermon), 146.

Astrea, frigate, 50.

Astronomy lecture, 220.

Auction sale, 80, 231, 351, 360.

Aurora borealis vel Northern Lights, 352, 354.

Automaton, 231.

Bad money, 80, 174, 329.

Baloon *vel* Air balloon, 117 *and* ed., 128, 191, 192, 196, 197, 202.
(coach), 255.
(hat), 142.

Bands, 65, 129, 274.

Banknotes, Norwich, 18, 353.
Sussex, 354.

Banns, 24, 137, 156, 176, 207.

Baptisms, 21, 61, 79, 80, 81, 94, 97, 98, 114, 123, 176, 188, 200, 279, 289, 301, 303, 308, 309, 311, 317, 319, 321, 330, 331, 339, 341, 344 *et seq.*, 351, 355.

Barber's fee, 100.

Bargains, 250, 317.

Bark (red), 133 ; *and v.* Medicaments.

Barometric pressure, 16, 61, 62, 176, 344, 353.

Base [bass] viol, 54, 106.

Beasts (wild) at Tower, **28** *and* ed.

' Bedfordshire ' *alias* bed, 293.

Beer-money, 78.

Bellringers, 52, 166, 223, 292.

Beverages, 6, 15, 19, 22, 32, 46, 287, 326.
e. g. :
beer (strong), 119, 166.
brandy, coniac, 292.
champaigne, 283.
cherry wine, 283.
coffee, 89, 93.
cyder, 252.
Geneva, 61.
gin, 21.
(smuggled), 39 *et alibi.*
Madeira, 92.
mountain (wine), 6, 22, 228, 307, 323.
port, 76, 96, 259.
punch, 108.
rum and water, 96.
tea, dish of, 23.
sage, 3.
Souchong, 19.
tent (wine) for sick, 152.
white wine, 149.
and v. Vol. I, Index (General).

365

367

PART II

(*a*) NAMES OF PERSONS. (*b*) NAMES OF PLACES

Note.—In sub-headings, for clearness, *alphabetical* sometimes cedes to *logical* sequence.

(*a*) NAMES OF PERSONS

382

388

PART III

PRINCIPAL AUTHORITIES CITED BY EDITOR

Abbey and Overton, *English Church in the Eighteenth Century*, 322.
Annual Register, 16, 145.

Blomefield, *History of Norfolk*, 68.
Burke, 125, 258, 261, 310.

Cokayne, 49, 85, 125, 127, 203, 210, 237, 310, 311, 317, 345, 347.
Cowper, 195, 196, 222, 234, 235, 286, 287; *and 'Letters'* (*in* 'The World's Classics'), ed. E. V. Lucas, 220.
Crabbe, 292, 298, 299.
Cunningham, *English Industry and Commerce*, 102.

D. N. B., 93, 100, 125, 127, 147, 171, 202, 210, 215, 233, 261, 265, 275, 317, 331, 347.
Dowell, Stephen, *History of Taxation in England*, 97, 208.

Edes, Ella B., *Bishop Blaise* (*Dublin Review*), 68.

Fairholt, *Costume in England*, 341.
Fitzmaurice, Lord, *Shelburne*
   in re Lord North, 11.
      Peace of Versailles, 57.
      Coalition of 1783, 63, 64.
      slave and 'Junius' mystery, 335.
      Thos. Pitt or 'Thos. anybody', 347.
Foster, *Alumni Oxon.*, 240, 258, 266.

Holy Bible, 81, 179.

Kitson, *Captain James Cook*, 145.

Lecky, *England in the Eighteenth Century*, 13, 26, 28, 57, 64, 87, 112, 147, 300, 335, 353.
Lowndes, *Bibliographer's Manual*, 246.

Mundy, *Life of Rodney*, 26.

N. E. D., 331.
Nicholls, Sir George, K.C.B., *History of English Poor-Law*, 298.

Return of Members of Parliament, 310.

The Parliamentary History, 11.
The Poor Law Commission of Inquiry, 1834, 298.

Venn, *Alumni Cantab.*, 70.

Walpole, *Letters*, ed. Paget Toynbee (Clarendon Press), 13, 26, 40, 57, 90, 117, 145, 197, 227, 282, 312.
War Office Library Catalogue, 246.
Wheatley and Cunningham, *London*, 275.
Winstanley, *The University of Cambridge in the Eighteenth Century*, 71.
Wolcot, *Peter Pindar's Works*, 331.

Young, *Life of Captain James Cook*, 145.

also

Editor's *Godfather of Downing Street*
   in re Lee descent, 49.
      Dutch affairs, 353.